Violence and Civil Disorder
in Italian Cities, 1200-1500

Published under the auspices of the
CENTER FOR MEDIEVAL AND RENAISSANCE STUDIES
University of California, Los Angeles

Contributions of the
UCLA CENTER FOR MEDIEVAL AND RENAISSANCE STUDIES

1: Medieval Secular Literature: Four Essays. Ed. William Matthews.

2: Galileo Reappraised. Ed. Carlo L. Golino.

3: The Transformation of the Roman World. Ed. Lynn White, jr.

4: Scientific Methods in Medieval Archaeology. Ed. Rainer Berger.

5: Violence and Civil Disorder in Italian Cities, 1200–1500. Ed. Lauro Martines.

UCLA CENTER FOR
MEDIEVAL AND RENAISSANCE STUDIES
CONTRIBUTIONS: V

Violence and
Civil Disorder in Italian Cities
1200-1500

Edited by

LAURO MARTINES

UNIVERSITY OF CALIFORNIA PRESS
BERKELEY • LOS ANGELES • LONDON, 1972

University of California Press
Berkeley and Los Angeles, California
University of California Press, Ltd.
London, England

ISBN: 0–520–01906–7
Library of Congress Catalog Card Number: 71–145791
Copyright © 1972 by The Regents of the University of California
Printed in the United States of America

ACKNOWLEDGMENTS

In May 1969 the Center for Medieval and Renaissance Studies of the University of California, Los Angeles, held a symposium on "Violence and Civil Disorder in Italian Cities, 1200–1500." The papers offered here were first presented and publicly discussed on that occasion.

The symposium was made possible by the University of California, Los Angeles, and its Center for Medieval and Renaissance Studies. Professor Lynn White, jr., the first director of the Center, originated the suggestion that we conduct a symposium on medieval and Renaissance Italian cities; the administrative details were handled by Professor Richard H. Rouse; and I wish to record thanks to them here, speaking both for myself and for the other participants in the symposium.

Lauro Martines

CONTENTS

I.

INTRODUCTION: THE HISTORICAL APPROACH TO VIOLENCE
LAURO MARTINES,   3
University of California, Los Angeles

II.

VIOLENCE IN THE LATE MIDDLE AGES: A BACKGROUND
J. R. HALE,   19
University College, London

III.

ORDER AND DISORDER IN ROMAGNA, 1450–1500
JOHN LARNER,   38
University of Glasgow

IV.

THE ASSASSINATION OF GALEAZZO MARIA SFORZA
AND THE REACTION OF ITALIAN DIPLOMACY
VINCENT ILARDI,   72
University of Massachusetts

V.

CRIME AND PUNISHMENT IN FERRARA, 1440–1500
WERNER L. GUNDERSHEIMER,   104
University of Pennsylvania

VI.

SOME PSYCHOLOGICAL AND SOCIAL ROOTS OF VIOLENCE
IN THE TUSCAN CITIES
DAVID HERLIHY,   129
University of Wisconsin

VII.

THE FLORENTINE *POPOLO MINUTO* AND ITS POLITICAL
ROLE, 1340–1450
GENE A. BRUCKER,   155
University of California, Berkeley

VIII.
CRIME, PUNISHMENT, AND THE TRECENTO VENETIAN STATE
        STANLEY CHOJNACKI,   184
        Michigan State University

IX.
THE ANATOMY OF REBELLION IN FOURTEENTH-CENTURY
SIENA: FROM COMMUNE TO SIGNORY?
        WILLIAM M. BOWSKY,   229
        University of California, Davis

X.
CONTEMPORARY VIEWS ON FACTION AND CIVIL STRIFE IN
THIRTEENTH- AND FOURTEENTH-CENTURY ITALY
        J. K. HYDE,   273
        Manchester University

XI.
VIOLENCE, DISORDER, AND ORDER IN THIRTEENTH-CENTURY
ROME
        ROBERT BRENTANO,   308
        University of California, Berkeley

XII.
POLITICAL VIOLENCE IN THE THIRTEENTH CENTURY
        LAURO MARTINES   331

Violence and Civil Disorder
in Italian Cities, 1200-1500

I

INTRODUCTION:
THE HISTORICAL APPROACH
TO VIOLENCE

Lauro Martines

The Historian of Violence

*T*HE NOTION of violence does not itself provide a direction of study. It is too general and elusive. A fifteenth-century merchant, moving things around in his *palazzo*, accidentally drops a small iron gate and hurts himself. In pain and rage he hurls it through an open window, unwittingly killing a passerby. Here is an act of violence. Is it the sort to attract the interest of the historian? If not, why not? Can we as historians dismiss the act by pointing to its random character? And if so, why should chance put the act beyond our purview?

The primary concern of the historian of violence is of course violence but not any kind of violence, or, at any rate, not violence approached or studied in indiscriminate fashion. Violence may include a vast multiplicity of acts and even specific attitudes. Heresy can be a state of mind, an attitude, but yet a crime in certain places and periods. Random cases of individual violence, like the one involving the grate, belong to one side of a spectrum. The action is unplanned, unpredictable, fits no necessary historical configuration, and goes beyond the psyche of the individual only by chance. On the other side of the spectrum is the type of violence which batters governments, starts civil and international wars, or perpetrates genocide: namely, organized violence committed on a large scale, by groups, by rebellious armies, or by governments proper.

3

Historians are more likely to be attracted by the institutional
or group violence on one side of the spectrum, but not because
it has more color or narrative interest. The details of any *crime
passionel* may provide more effective intrigue or more compelling psychological interest. In most cases, however, individual acts of stray violence—the sort which can occur at any
time and place—offer very little in themselves to the historian,
little to engage his distinctive methods of analysis, although
they may supply the novelist or psychoanalyst with a suggestive body of material. If we can distinguish the main features
belonging to each side of the spectrum, we shall have a clearer
idea of what the historian of violence seeks. Comparison with
the novelist may help us to see the distinctions.

Confronted with the details of a crime of passion or a political
conspiracy in fifteenth-century Venice, the novelist is more
apt to be drawn to the former, the historian to the latter. But if
the novelist chooses the conspiracy, his artistic passion will converge upon the individual conspirators, fixing upon their personal psychologies, their appearance, dress, and movements,
their intimate family relations, the cut of the eye and ring of
the voice, the glint of the dagger and sound of the boot striking
the cobblestone. So doing, he furnishes only as much of the
institutional context or historical "atmosphere" as enables him
to catch and hold his reader. He makes context and atmosphere
subservient, subject to the novel's two or three leading characters. His overriding preoccupation centers upon the conspirators or antagonists, on their actions and on their moral and
psychological dilemmas. His vision continually focuses ever
more sharply and narrowly; it takes in fewer and fewer people;
it moves away from the public world of the conspiracy, from
all its larger issues and rich social cushioning, to the internal
world of the conspirators and their personal dramas. The novelist pursues an arrangement of timeless moral and psychological
coordinates.

Not so the historian, whose vision increasingly opens out to the whole setting, political and social, of the conspiracy. He is not interested—not seriously interested—in the glint of the knife or click of the boot, and he can afford to disregard the eccentricities of the conspirators, even when these promise to add seasoning to his narrative. Instead, he must examine the public policies and political conditions, seek to throw light on the pertinent institutions, and explore the political and social relations of the conspirators. He dare not conduct his analysis without having a firm grasp of the workings of Venetian government. While the novelist swiftly abandons the public tide of things in order to step back into the internal moral and psychological universe of the plotters, the historian of violence moves in a contrary direction—out toward politics, controversial debate, society, and institutions: but, in short, to the center of the historical mainstream, rather than toward the random personal eddies at the edges. The objectives of the psychohistorian seem to raise difficulties here and I shall touch upon them in due course.

Let us suppose what is perfectly imaginable but unlikely: that the historian of violence undertakes to do a study in depth of an obscure *crime passionel* of the fifteenth century. And incredibly, to help him in his task, he comes upon a full transcript of the trial in the state archives of Venice, on two or three highly pertinent diaries, and on a secret cache of incriminating letters—the stuff of novelists and dramatists. We can easily imagine him producing a brilliant historical monograph. But the question of his approach remains. Will he represent the case in the manner of a journalist, with an eye to satisfying prurience and easy human interest, or of a novelist with a penchant for fast action and romance, or will he do an analysis entirely different in scope and method, going far beyond the crime itself? Whatever the journalist or novelist does with the case, the historian of violence will "use" it differently. He may dwell upon many details of the crime, but he will do so, paradoxically, only so as to get away from it. For he will constantly be looking beyond the criminal action itself to the whole world of the crime. His main concern will be to "fit" the crime into the surrounding moral, institutional, or social context, which means that he will have to understand the context fully as much as the crime itself. Indeed, the context will nearly always present more complexities and a greater challenge, for many crimes turn upon simple actions and relatively simple motives, but a larger social setting can scarcely ever fail to circumscribe numerous variables. Looking beyond the individual act of violence, the historian will strive to make analytical statements about a variety of matters, while concentrating more on some than on others, depending upon his preparation and inclinations. He may fix upon the administration of penal justice or upon the nature of popular and official attitudes toward the human passions; or, again, he may choose to study the sociology of the particular crime, the tacit values governing criminal law, or another kindred theme touching directly upon the public mind and upon conditions and environments. If he should venture into the psychodynamics of violence, his enabling act there will be to work his grasp of the appropriate psychic mechanisms into the flux of a specific place and time. Hence we are back to the larger sweep of things, back to the historical mainstream. And by the historical mainstream I mean the stream of ideas and attitudes prevailing in any age; I also mean the concomitant institutions and their course of change—the economy, the social system, the state, forms of worship, and codes of law.

The analysis of violence in the context of the mainstream is what distinctly marks the work of the historian of violence, whether he treat individual crimes or entire trends and patterns. This may be obvious but it is not perhaps rightly understood, for the observation also implies that the more conscious the effort to distinguish the reciprocities between violence and the central currents of the mainstream the more effective and important the analysis. By taking this approach, the historian is compelled to study his theme in terms of change and fluctuation; he is driven to seek explanations for the rising and falling curves in the charting of historical violence. This is the most demanding kind of historical analysis and in one way or another most of the papers in this collection try to provide it, some more and some less so, with or without statistical data.

But the emphasis properly falls upon the affiliation with the mainstream, which alone enables us to understand why historians of violence may proceed along very different routes, grapple with general problems or with specific cases, and yet somehow always converge upon a kind of *voie royale*. The same emphasis reveals why the historian may correctly single out a particular crime, a single act of violence, and train all his intellectual resources upon it. In his paper on the assassination of the lord of Milan (1476), Vincent Ilardi straightway puts his hands, so to speak, into the historical mainstream because the daggers of the tyrannicides were directly pointed in some respects at the state itself, a fact that greatly affected the course of Italian diplomacy. The government's reaction to the assassination instantly highlighted the high degree of malfeasance and corruption in Milanese public life. But if Ilardi had chosen, instead, to study the murder of a Milanese shopkeeper or hawker of goods, he would have confronted the whole problem of trying to "find" the mainstream and trying to establish its relation to the crime: that is, the problem of looking for a way to take hold of the crime in its concrete historical context, which might include the courts, the laws, the outlook of magistrates, the incidence of homicide, the social values of murderer and victim, the applicable economic strains and social barriers, or, more likely, some select combination of these. Unlike the novelist or psychoanalyst, as a historian he would have been drawn to the crime by aims other than that of a concern for the petty retailer himself.

We see those aims with exemplary clarity in Gene Brucker's treatment of the poor in Florence (the *popolo minuto*). The case of the novice prostitute, Monna Riguardata, lured away from her husband by a clever procurer, holds Brucker's attention only long enough to help him put the problem of prostitution into the context of poverty. It is one of the details he uses to sketch a profile of the Florentine poor. His guiding purpose, however, is to seek out the provisional connections between poverty and the propensity for political violence.

Of the eleven contributors to this collection, Ilardi alone examines the particulars and ramifications of one crime, but his procedure, as we have indicated, is wholly in keeping with our general line: the victim, Galeazzo Maria Sforza, was the head of state and his assassination, therefore, automatically provided the affiliation with the mainstream. Most of the other contributors to this volume cite individual crimes but they do so only to illustrate a pattern, a trend, a process—aspects or manifestations of the mainstream. In this fashion Werner Gundersheimer studies the incidence of capital punishment at Ferrara in the second half of the fifteenth century. His evidence shows that the death penalty was more often imposed upon foreigners than upon natives (a finding with precise social and legal implications); it also reveals a close social link between the crime of treason and members of the highest nobility, and this brings into focus the thrust of political instability in that city. In his paper on the Romagna, John Larner adduces a variety of individual crimes mainly for the purpose of outlining the pressures and tensions that encouraged the penchant for violence in the Romagnol towns. He underscores the blood-feud tradition and the provincial cult of honor, the prevalence of weak and corrupt government, the poverty of the Romagnol countryside, and the ensuing economic hardships that exasperated the nobility and ground down the poor.

As a rule then, the historian who studies violence will treat individual crimes or acts of violence as details in a larger picture, a picture that aims to represent a view of the mainstream, however fragmentarily. The assassination of princes or presidents, or the study of individual conspiracies, presents no exception to this rule: in these cases the historian has selected samples of violence from the manifest middle of the mainstream. The obvious reciprocity, crime-mainstream, satisfies the critical requirement. The trouble arises, as I have already suggested, when the historian decides to linger over a more ordinary crime involving obscure men, be they artisans, lovers, noblemen, business partners, or peasants. How is the connection with the mainstream then to be made?

The easiest and most common method (and the most deceptive), employed by every paper in this collection, is that of relying upon examples and types. In his essay on how contemporaries explained political violence, J. K. Hyde refers to a rich assortment of texts but takes the testimony of their recurring, identical judgments as the expression of their typical or representative character. This is standard historical procedure. Whether or not he make an explicit acknowledgment, the historian is greatly inclined to select events or incidents or cases that he supposes to be representative, or which seem to exemplify a trend. In this sense he assumes them to have typicality. Despite appearances, accordingly, when lingering over such a case, the historian is no longer in fact considering the individual case but a whole class of cases, a whole class of men, or a type of man: lord, merchant, or peasant, poor, rich, noble or common. He is examining the case or the particular event in the light of historical processes and trends: in other words, he is dependent upon the purported nature and direction of the mainstream. Stanley Chojnacki relies heavily upon this approach. His view of Venetian political stability and his admiration for the Republic's justice and equity are based upon researches that seem to indicate that criminal courts in fourteenth-century Venice treated all men alike, rich and poor, native and foreigner, nobleman and commoner; and he cites no criminal case if not to help him build up a picture of the fairness of Venetian penal justice.

This is not the place to consider the question of how depressingly easy it is to slip into circular argument when adducing institutional or social types as a way either of gaining methodological support from the mainstream or of throwing corrective light upon it. Does the historian sample a large number of cases first, before he is able to recognize what is typical and before he can refer things back to the mainstream? Or does he somehow acquire a sense of the mainstream first and then come to recognize typical cases as if by intuition? More likely he does both simultaneously, which may cause some degree of circular reasoning to be unavoidable. This raises a grave and perhaps insoluble problem. I mention it here only because it seems to me that the historian of violence should be no less mindful of it than other historians, possibly more so. For the requirements of the argument regarding the mainstream will constantly drive him to the practice of looking for samples and types. And he will rarely if ever be granted the luxury to explore an act of violence in and for itself.

Let us take stock of what has been said so far. The distinctive aim of the historian of violence is to consider the problems of violence in strict relation to the mainstream, that is, in their vital contact with the major institutions and flow of prevailing ideas and attitudes. But as these are things in flux, changing and having a direction of change, the analysis of violence is best and most challenging when done with an eye to the processes of change. The student of the subject, accordingly, will not be seriously interested in random or personal violence, unless it falls into patterns that reveal trends and disclose the play of impersonal currents, or when there are other demonstrable relations between the mainstream and acts of random personal violence. This being so, the historian of violence will be most attracted to the analysis of certain classes of violence: political disorder and upheaval, group crime, institutionalized violence (e.g., war, poverty, police repression), and personal or private violence of the kind that promises a view of the mainstream.

These observations in part make for standard historical fare and in part not, but the soundness of the more unusual part— emphasis on relations between private violence and the main- stream—is fully borne out by the papers in this collection. Even the most general and widesweeping of them, John Hale's, ranging in interest from woodcuts and individual role- playing to public executions and war, is in search of the age's nervous tension as a gauge for estimating "the potential violence within society at large." Here is a readiness to use any means in order to get at an aspect of the mainstream. William Bowsky's title, "The Anatomy of Rebellion in Fourteenth-Century Siena," speaks for itself: his theme is organized political violence and the commune's methods of dealing with it. He can there- fore analyze relations between the butchers' guild and the gov- ernment of Siena or, focusing much more narrowly, discuss the behavior of *individual* butchers, yet always keep to his main concern: organized conspiracy and governmental response. The essay by Robert Brentano on thirteenth-century Rome is a montage of snapshots that offer fleeting views of the major public motifs: the lawlessness of the prominent Roman families (though individual features appear), the unstable quality of municipal government, the impact and pull of the papacy (more individual faces), the streaming streets of a medieval city, and the anonymity of swarming pilgrims. There may be individual faces in this montage but they are faces in a crowd.

Still, what of the individual face? Is it true that the historian of violence may not seriously study individuals as such? He may of course devote detailed study to individuals but he must get beyond them, too. Even the psychohistorian cannot pre- tend that his preoccupation is individuals per se, as he is usually bound to a finely articulated clinical theory, with the result that he is unable to approach the individual unless it be through the gridwork of an elaborate system. Moreover, he seems fatally attracted to the psychobiography of outstanding individuals, above all of *public* men with a sure place in history: Hitler, Woodrow Wilson, Luther. The historical grounding, or the affiliation with the mainstream (as I have preferred to say), is thus instantly established, leaving only the particulars to be worked out, and the substantive part of these may be conveniently supplied by psychoanalytic theory. In electing to study important historical personalities the psychohistorian chooses men marked by their profound public involvements and this, not the theory, is what provides such study with an easy access to the mainstream.

Any critical conjunction between the mainstream and the psychodynamics of violence is bound to have enormous importance for the historian of violence. When the psychohistorian works for the establishment of such a bridge, he puts historical responsibilities foremost. But when, in the course of an analysis, he forgets time and place and affects to be getting at the real individual, the personality essence, then he has drifted away from the mainstream and his subject of study may just as well have lived anywhere at any time—under Caesar, Charlemagne, Cromwell, or Stalin. Such an exercise is antihistorical, good clinical practice but bad history. Violence can have little meaning for the historian outside the context of place and time, and this obvious but fundamental point has the effect of eliminating programmatic emphases on alleged timeless motives.

In his paper on Tuscan cities, David Herlihy raises one of the questions that most exercise psychohistorians—the question of the historical consequences of sexual repression. He cleaves to the historical mainstream by basing his findings upon the evidence of new demographic data and the copious observations of contemporaries. So doing, he is able to draw some important distinctions between the fourteenth and fifteenth centuries, linking critical changes in the Italian economy with changing patterns of marriage and with fluctuations in the level of urban violence. It remains to be seen whether or not further study will continue to make good his claim that young men were more given to violence than their elders.

The Two Faces of Violence

Few historians are likely to applaud violence, historians of the academic sort. Like most people, they see it as bad in itself. But also, like most people, they tend to see only the more obvious forms of violence: crime, civil disorder, and war. Often they take no notice of the grayer or more devious and concealed forms of violence, such as abject poverty, moral and psychological coercion, or institutional duress. This astigmatism of the historian and his readiness to strike spontaneous moral attitudes, as in his abhorrence of violent men, should give him pause when he takes up the study of violence. Of all topics this is the one most likely to make him careless with the rigorous demands of historical analysis. Consequently, when treating problems of violence, the historian should continually reexamine and challenge his hidden or unconscious presuppositions. To fear or loathe the violence of the present gives him no license to mourn unthinkingly or to condemn out of hand all past violence, no right to refuse to come to terms with it as a historian.

Violence is defined by government and its laws. The relationship is dialectical: you do not get one without the other. Where government and law have no existence there can be no violence, save in that anarchy, the state of perfect violence, "the state of nature"—which is a lucubration. Apparently, therefore, in some respects the historian of violence must also be a student of the history of law. He can have no functional grasp of violence apart from the way it is defined by the government and laws of the community he happens to be studying. Nor do his responsibilities end there, for the nature of violence changes: the laws change and men alter or even transform their definitions of violence. Abortion, adultery, blasphemy, bankruptcy, witchcraft, and political dissent may or may not be crimes, may or may not be considered expressions of violence. It follows that when the historian undertakes to study violence, knowing that he is dealing with changing and changeable values, he should also strive to discern the basic assumptions that underlie the laws that define violence. I mean the prevailing views regarding the state, the individual, the group, and the nature of the human community. The history of violence is also a history of the values and institutions that define it.

Not surprisingly, therefore, in the collection before us, the image of powerful family groups is almost obsessive. The rich urban families, the oligarchical families, tended to monopolize the public forums of the cities of late medieval and Renaissance Italy. Generally speaking, they controlled the institutions of government, and their spokesmen best expressed the politico-social values that we have come to associate with those cities. Whether at Florence or Venice, Padua or Genoa, the affairs and direction of government were bound up with the practical interests of the political families. Indeed, it is not wholly metaphorical to say that government and the principal families were indivisible; and when they were not, then political violence was profound, men overturned governments and the streets were delivered to lawlessness.

To speak thus of families is to have recourse to the idea of social class: it is to identify a large social category in terms of its unique position and functions and to make conceptual use of it. I see no way of getting round this. Three or four of the papers in this volume, by statement or clever formulation, seek to de-emphasize the effects of class. Curiously, we continue to respond favorably to the exaggerated reaction set off by the alleged Marxist note in Gaetano Salvemini's *Magnati e popolani* (1899), a reaction first strongly articulated by Nicola Ottokar (1926) and sustained down to our own day by the historians Enrico Fiumi, Emilio Cristiani, and others. Every so often philosophers try to suppress the category of substance but somehow it always reappears. So also with the idea of social class: historians have sometimes resolved to do without it but it keeps filtering back into their analyses. And Marx is or should be completely beside the point here. The perception of class, its conceptual use in historical analysis, is found centuries before Marx, in the works of Botero, Guicciardini, and Machiavelli, as well as in some of the leading chroniclers of the fourteenth century. They had no sophisticated view of class, no refined grasp of it; but their formulations have meaning and utility. The differences that rend a class or a social group may undermine its unity of action, may weaken and disperse its energies; they do not eliminate it as an identifiable whole. One or many noblemen may join a popular political movement, but neither one nor a dozen swallows makes a summer. In the deferential world of the Italian cities, haunted by snobberies and riven by privilege, the imprint of class and group, even on the varieties of violence, was ineradicable.

Up to about the end of the fourteenth century urban government in Italy was unstable, often dramatically so. It is not true to say that the ascent of the signory (government under one-man rule) ushered in the peace and stability denied to the cities when under the governance of republican communes. After the emergence and triumph of the so-called despots (*signori*), political instability persisted for a century or more, even in cities where the ardor of civil strife was cooled.

The present collection of papers indicates that the historian of violence is inclined to tell his story from the viewpoint of government. Subtly he makes himself counsel for the prosecution. This posture is regrettable but not easily avoidable. The surrender to partisanship results in part from the historian's inability to keep his heart and vision open (a failure in imagination), once he has taken the state to be the source of civil order and legal definitions. In part the surrender also results from his conditioned abhorrence of violence, which surely affects his perception and analysis of it. Human limitations thus seem to raise a methodological barrier, but not perhaps an insurmountable one. The historian, as we shall see, is not compelled to assume that violence originates on one side only of a given line.

Other difficulties also arise. How will the historian be sure of his viewpoint, of the steadfast nature of his definitions, when called upon to examine violence in the infelicitous context of unstable government? Furthermore, if there be irresponsible or even criminal government, as there sometimes was in thirteenth- and fourteenth-century Italian cities, and the historian of violence persists in telling his story from the government's point of view, then either he has shut his eyes or he has risen in intellect to an ideal plane, where the patterns are pure and the state has perfection. Not even then, however, will he free himself and manage to be impartial, unless he call attention to the coercive or brutal features of shifty government, as well as to the more obvious violence of the streets and marketplaces. To emphasize one at the expense of the other is to succumb to bias. Wherever there is large-scale or persistent violence, the historian should look for it on both sides, so to speak, of the barricades. After all, rampant political and social violence seem to be the mark of communities undergoing a profound *malaise*, at times affecting the whole body politic; and organized rampant crime is unlikely to occur without the connivance of parts of the police establishment.

During the thirteenth and fourteenth centuries, the legitimacy of political authority in the cities of central and upper Italy was often on very shaky ground. Jacob Burckhardt rightly observed that usurpations and illegitimacy abounded. And if, looking back now, there is something to be said for the government of despots and callous oligarchs, there are also things to be said for their would-be assassins and for the unhappy legions of scheming political exiles. The preservation of "law and order" under illegal despotisms or under unresponsive or usurping oligarchs is not superior per se to tyrannicide or civil insurrection.

Violence may be defined by the state and its laws but it has two sources, two faces: individual or group violence and that which is somehow the state's. No institution is capable of greater, more durable violence than the state in its moments of alarm: the presumed will of the community poised in its punitive or coercive positions. Though obvious, this observation is usefully kept in mind. We may assume that governments exist, on the whole, for "the public good." The assumption is true a priori, so long as they maintain (however corrupt) a system of courts, a police force, and a defense establishment. But in looking round the world today, or in studying the Italian city-states, we need no gift of imagination to see that governments, strong or unstable, may fail to serve the public good, may indeed undermine it. Governments not infrequently make tragic mistakes. They can also wage campaigns of destruction against given parts of their own communities. At least the possibility of this is always present. Which is why it is absolutely essential for the historian of violence to give some prominence to the category of legal or legitimate or institutional violence: that is, the varieties of coercion which are naturally and automatically available to governments, be they legal or illegal. In this connection it strikes me as impractical and even dangerous for the historian, in the course of a specific analysis, to try to draw distinctions between the state and government, lest he introduce refinements that can serve only to aggravate or mask ideological prejudice.

The following papers appear in reverse chronological order. Beginning with the period around 1500, we move back from a time when governments are more stable—the state somewhat more fully evolved—to a world in which the texture of urban political institutions is looser and more porous. Civil strife and political instability are basic to the condition of the thirteenth-century Italian city: not so in the fifteenth and sixteenth centuries. The usual progression is thus reversed: we pass from the perception of greater to lesser order. This seems to make for a more effective starting point. The end of any period serves to give an alignment to the preceding phases.

John Hale's paper, the first in the series, is more general than any of the others and more optimistic. As we proceed through the collection the optimism fades (the paper on Venice excepted), which is fitting, for the context of analysis plunges ever more deeply into a world of instability and disorder. Finally, by reversing the expected order of things, we hope to provide, in Kenneth Burke's phrase, "perspective by incongruity." [1]

We decided to omit discussion of the cities of southern Italy, the reason being that their nature and history posed the whole problem of violence in so different an institutional environment [2] that it seemed wise to avoid them altogether for the sake of achieving a semblance of unity.

The absence of a paper on Genoa will be noted—the collection's major lacuna. We were unable to find an expert prepared to write an essay on the subject. For the rest, we deal with a variety of more or less representative cities, while at the same time including Florence and Venice, which were unique in some respects.

[1] *Permanence and Change: An Anatomy of Purpose* (New York, 1935), p. 118.
[2] Cf. especially G. Galasso, *Dal comune medievale al unità: Linee di storia meridionale* (Bari, 1969).

VIOLENCE IN THE LATE MIDDLE AGES:
A BACKGROUND*

J. R. Hale

$\mathcal{B}$Y WAY OF preface to the detailed studies of Italian cities which are to follow, I would like to think in very general terms about Western Europe as a whole, and to cling to the terminal date of this conference, 1500, where I feel most at home. Perhaps in overreaction to the present atmosphere in this state, in much of the world, indeed, my instinct is to play down the role of violence at that time. Living amidst violence it is tempting to look for violence in the past. And if history is to remain a living subject, crucial (as I believe it is) to people's emotional and intellectual well-being, we have a duty to give those who are preoccupied by a particular phenomenon in the present an objective picture of its operation in the past. Certainly, we have the right to specialize, to concentrate on one aspect; if the past were recoverable in its totality it would, after all, overwhelm the present. But before we move in close to observe moments of violence in specific Italian cities I should like to ask two questions; if we stop the clock and look out over the whole landscape of Western Europe, how much violence do we see? and when we do see it, how far are we qualified to make sense of it?

In a moment I shall suggest that when we stop the clock around 1500 we shall not see enough to justify our con-

* Since delivering this paper, some of the arguments have been elaborated in parts of my *Renaissance Europe, 1480–1520* (London, 1971).

centrating on it unduly—were it not for the circumstances of our own times. But first I would like to consider methodology, the problem of making sense of the violence we do see.

Historians are trained to be alert to the dangers of personal subjectivity; we are surrounded by violence, so we study violence, but we know why we are doing it (though we may not consider how far we are conniving with a psychological displacement of our own aggressive urges). But we are also trained to be alert to the preoccupations of our colleagues in the social and behavioral sciences. Aiming at an understanding of conflict from the French Revolution to Maoist China, from machine breaking in early industrial England to the ripping up of railroads in modern India, from the Paris commune to the Chicago Convention, from the mechanism of bared throat and exposed belly among animals to the similar function of kinship recognition symbols among packs of men, from the child's smashed rattle to global war, records have been ransacked, computers fed, survivors interviewed, laboratories programmed in the interest of spotting analogies and providing explanations.

It is no sneer to say that, either between them or alone, the students of animal behavior, the social psychologists and anthropologists, the economists, political scientists, and demographers have not come up with a generally accepted explanation of violence. But they have come up with models that purport to explain it or, at least, to guide its study. And it is when confronted with a social scientific model, coupled to a particularly intriguing current phenomenon, that serious historians tend to bow so deep to fashion and demand that they can only see the ground beneath their feet. Subjectively, the subject of violence will attract the historian for more or less the same reasons that it attracts the social scientist. But the latter's models are seductive because the historian has little so apparently promising to replace them with. The danger confronting him is that he will emphasize violence then not only for its own sake, or in response to a justifiable call for relevance, but also because there is an impressive body of opinion on the nature of violence in the literature of neighbor disciplines he has learned to admire and, in extreme cases, defer to.

Let us take a familiar model. Postulate an abrupt and general change in living conditions, be it the plugging-in of a subsistence economy to a market-based one or a political take-over by a group large enough to affect the styles of life of a significant number of the community concerned. Individual disorientation follows the challenge to traditional role playing, it seeks leadership, parties are formed, they challenge the representatives of the old way of life, are overthrown or victorious. That is, latent violence, the product of our animal or psychological makeup, is released by social and economic changes with which the individual cannot cope, perturbations crystallize about class interests and political ideologies, and violence follows, programmed by leaders who envisage and can convince others of a permanent change for the better.

Such a model has considerable color when applied to the situations which have been studied most closely by social scientists, that is, nineteenth- and twentieth-century ones. Leaving aside the question of evidence, which decreases with giant strides as one travels backward, there are formidable problems to our using this sort of methodology.

Where are the abrupt and general changes in living conditions around 1500? Local booms and slumps, yes; a quietly burgeoning Antwerp, a Venice momentarily nonplussed by the withdrawal of one of its chief trade commodities, eastern spices, but nothing lastingly traumatic on the economic front. Conquests through war, yes, and some of them enduring, as was to be the domination of the Milanese and of Naples by Spain. But broadly speaking the wars of the late fifteenth and early sixteenth centuries did not lead to lasting or significant changes of government or frontier and, when they did, the consequences to the vast majority of those affected were small —and the same is true of those larger areas that changed hands through escheat, inheritance, or marriage. Class interests? I shall try to suggest that in meaningful Marxist, that is, self-consciously activist, terms, these interests could lead to no more than intermittent conflict. Political ideologies? They were all on the side of conservatism. The west European communities were overwhelmingly princely in their form of government. There was little thought of changing this system. Where there was dissent, it took the form (among a tiny minority) of deciding who was the right prince or how he should perform his traditional function. In the few republics, the appeal was almost always to the past: let us reproduce the splendid days of yore when liberty, prosperity, and expansion went hand in hand! The future, as the homeland of "progressive" malcontents, did not exist. For the materialist, the future was when later generations would still read the inscription on his monument. For the intellectual it was the time when increasing numbers of men would become wise. For the millenarian it was a time when God would judge on earth the fruits of his creation. For most it was the timeless void the church had sliced into hell, purgatory, and heaven. Lacking the technological-secularist, humanitarian view of progress, there could be no political ideology that could fling the imagination forward and enlist support for an ongoing program of change.

There were, of course, scattered outbursts of violence, a Xenophobic Evil May Day in England, factious mobs in Florence, food riots in French towns, miners' strikes in Bohemia, a peasant-backed Swiss war against the Emperor. But outside the area of the Upper Rhine and Alpine Germany, where the Bundschuh movement had caused alarm well before the explosion of 1517, there is little evidence at the turn of the fifteenth and sixteenth centuries that contemporaries were especially disturbed about the incidence of violence, let alone that they were under the impression that it was increasing. The myth of the Golden Age, the notion of an Earthly Paradise did express nostalgia for a peaceable kingdom,[1] but at least in part, this was a yearning for a state of innocence, for an escape less from worldly than from spiritual conflict. Manuals for confessors [2] urged the clergy to dissuade parishioners from provoking others to quarrel, but from this source and from sermons it seems clear that the church was far less concerned about violence than about other fallings away from Christian behavior, for example extramarital and unconventional sex and social pretension. The closing of town gates at dusk, curfews, and provision for the chaining off of streets, the need to travel through much of Europe in convoy or with an armed guard—precautions of this sort were routine and remained unchanged. There was no move to improve police forces during the period. Criminal justice was, indeed, showing in its processes signs of becoming more merciful in its sentences and fairer to the accused. The horror of torture and of dismemberment was reserved in the main for crimes against the state and against public order. Treachery, conspiracy, brigandage: these forms of violence met the full violence of the law. Person-to-person violence was more likely to be dealt with by fine and compensation, even in cases of homicide.[3]

A high degree of emotional volatility that could lead an individual to commit an act of violence was taken for granted. Laws against gambling recognized that the commonest forms of assault arose from games of chance; governments forbade it in taverns, captains on shipboard, guild statutes to apprentices. One motive behind sumptuary legislation was to damp down the *kermesse* that so frequently led to broken heads. The speed with which an insult or grievance could lead to violence was

[1] Henri Baudet, *Paradise on Earth* (New Haven, Conn., 1965).
[2] E.g., C. Brunel, *Opuscules provençaux du XVᵉ siècle sur la confession* (Toulouse, 1917).
[3] J. S. C. Bridge, *A History of France from the Death of Louis XI* (Oxford, 1921–1936), V. 82, and Yvonne Bézard, *La vie rurale dans le sud de la région Parisienne de 1450 à 1560* (Paris, 1929), pp. 266 ff.

reflected, too, in the laws forbidding the carrying of arms. There was, of course, a strong element of class distinction in this legislation. Gentlemen could gamble; although included in the sumptuary laws, they were not prosecuted under them; they were entitled to carry arms. But then the old and still meaningful theory of social classification by function actually required one of the three estates to be violent for the protection of others, and the growing number of gentlemen who turned to the law or to court service led moralists to remind them of their divinely appointed militant role.[4] The point to be made here, however, is that these regulations were not new and that there was little attempt to put new teeth into them.

That men relished the spectacle of violence is clear. Many of the pastimes of both rich and poor were violent and were expected to produce casualties; diaries and chronicles show that bourgeois spectators shared this relish.[5] Executions and, on some occasions, tortures were public and drew large and appreciative crowds.[6] The stage managers of morality and mystery plays showed an inventive gusto in the skill with which they substituted a dummy for a live actor the moment before the red-hot pincers sizzled into a martyr or a recent arrival in hell.[7] Monstrous births and scenes of carnage figured largely in popular woodcuts. Animal combats made deliberate the general indifference to the suffering of animals. Yet unless some local panic started a search for scapegoats it was an age kindly to cretins, not ungenerous in providing hospitals, sympathetic even to voluntary indigence.

[4] E.g., W. J. B. Crotch, *The Prologues and Epilogues of William Caxton* (London, 1928), pp. 82–84.

[5] E.g., Antonio de Beatis, *Voyage du cardinal d'Aragon*, trans. Madeleine Harvard de la Montagne (Paris, 1913), p. 293; Robert Mandrou, *Introduction à la France Moderne: Essai de psychologie historique 1500–1640* (Paris, 1961), p. 79.

[6] E.g., J. Huizinga, *The Waning of the Middle Ages* (London, 1924), p. 15.

[7] G. Cohen, *Histoire de la mise en scène dans le théatre religieux francais du moyen âge* (Paris, 1926), pp. 148–149.

There was, indeed, what was possibly a novel self-consciousness about the nature of cruelty. "Why," Ficino asked Tommaso Minerbetti, are boys crueler than old men? Insane men crueler than intelligent men? Dull men crueler than the ingenious? Therefore the cruel men are called inhumane and brutal." [8] A quasi-evolutionary strain came with Piero di Cosimo's inspired pictorial musing on man's inheritance from the time when he was little better than the beasts whose lives he shared. An older, chivalrous note sounds in Juan Aguero's comment on the treatment of women by Trisao da Cunha's men during a raid on the Somali coast. "Good men would never do such a thing, if only because women are 'vessels of generation' and of tender, delicate flesh and gentle condition. ... Worthy of reprimand are such cruel deeds, but you may be sure that the ones who did such foul things were not the ordinary nor the best of men." [9] Outside the more-or-less shared values of their continent, Europeans, affected by isolation, fear, greed, religious zeal and the fact that the law was in their own hands, could burn up a cargo of peaceful men, women and children, as Vasco de Gama did, or exterminate a whole people —the Spaniards reduced the Arawaks of the West Indies from about three hundred thousand to sixty thousand by 1508, forty-six thousand by 1510, sixteen thousand by 1520. [10] But within Europe, apart from the law and the routine admonitions of the church, there were fairly complex moral restraints that inhibited the infliction of deliberate cruelty.

The scenarios of morality plays show that men could be

[8] P. O. Kristeller, "The Philosophy of Man in the Italian Renaissance," in *Intellectual Movements in Modern European History*, ed. Franklin L. Baumer (New York, 1965), p. 23.

[9] James B. McKenna, ed., *A Spaniard in the Portuguese Indies: The Narrative of Martín Fernández de Figueroa* (Cambridge, Mass., 1967), p. 75.

[10] Figures (to be treated with hesitation) from S. E. Morison, *Admiral of the Ocean Sea: A Life of Christopher Columbus* (Boston, 1942), p. 493, and R. Mousnier, *Les XVIe et XVIIe siècles* (3d ed.; Paris, 1961), p. 429.

moved quickly from tears to jeers. It has been suggested that the waning of the Middle Ages was accompanied by an increase in emotional volatility which increased the potential violence within society. The popularity of the Dance of Death has been called to witness, as have the minutely contemplated pre-Loyolaesque devotion of the Passion, the preoccupation in art with the process of physical dissolution and in homilectic literature with the last pangs or the Art of Dying.[11] But popular devotion also led to the promotion of milder cults, of Saint Anne, the Rosary, the Immaculate Conception, and preachers bent on terrifying their audience out of their sins could criticize the artists for portraying the Last Judgment in too optimistic terms.[12]

In any case, the connection between imagining violence and being violent is, as we know all too well, very uncertain. The implications of evidence brought forward to suggest an enhanced and excitable preoccupation with the macabre should be treated with caution. Moreover its novelty (as opposed to the increased circulation brought about by the press and the increased graphicness made possible by shifts in literary form and artistic style) is in the main unproved. Nor, I think, is the perturbation that is perceptible as the mystic year 1500 approached much more than a footnote to the pathology of millenarianism in general. At a time when the vast majority of men did not know their own ages (though governments acted as if they did) and the knowledge of what a year date was was restricted to a small number, it is unlikely that "1500" meant much to many. And those to whom it did have a meaning, or who heard about its meaning, continued to make wills, to plan

[11] On this theme see, apart from Huizinga, A. Tenenti, *La vie et la mort à travers l'art du XVᵉ siècle* (Paris, 1952), and E. Mâle, *L'art religieux de la fin du moyen âge en France* (Paris, 1925) and T. S. R. Boase, "King Death," in *The Flowering of the Middle Ages*, ed. Joan Evans (London, 1966).

[12] A. Renaudet, *Préréforme et humanisme à Paris pendant les premières guerres d'Italie (1494–1517)* (Paris, 1916), pp. 243–244.

business deals that took a future for granted; there was no extra rush of pious benefactions to catch Saint Peter's eye, no unusual demand for the Jubilee indulgence of that year, no particularly dense cluster of visions and portents.[13]

Nor will our impression change much if we shift our ground and try to estimate the effect of attitudes to life expectations, affective relationships, and economic and social pressures. First, what of the notion that living conditions that produced a holocaust of stillbirths and infant deaths and a short life expectancy for the survivors led to an indifference to suffering which licensed violence? Simply, I think, that there is no evidence that satisfactorily sustains it. There was fatalism but not indifference to the deaths of babies in references in memoirs, to deaths at sea in the logs of the early voyages of discovery; though childhood was not yet conceived as a separate, privileged state, all the evidence—and it is, of course, socially selective—points to a parent's anxious and loving concern for their children. And though statistics may suggest that a boy of twelve had a life expectancy of perhaps another twenty-five or thirty years,[14] contemporaries did not see themselves in terms of statistics; they were less concerned with the possibility of a premature death than with time's violence to the aging body, with the rapid loss of beauty, strength, and, above all, virility. The popu-

[13] For portents see Franco Simone, *Il Rinascimento francese* (Turin, 1961), p. 120; L. von Pastor, *The History of the Popes*, Eng. trans., Vol. V. (London, 1898), pp. 77–80; O. Benesch, *The Art of the Renaissance in Northern Europe* (rev. ed.; London, 1965), p. 6. Not all visions and portents can be tied to Chiliastic hopes and fears, nor can opinions that the world was so old that it was about to come to an end for natural causes. "An expectation of Doomsday was perhaps a trait of temperament" (Gerald Strauss, *Sixteenth-Century Germany, Its Topography and Topographers* [Madison, Wis., 1959], p. 4).

[14] See R. Mousnier, *Etudes sur la France de 1494 à 1559* (Cours de Sorbonne, n.d.), p. 22; Creighton Gilbert, "When Did Renaissance Man Grow Old?" *Studies in the Renaissance, XIV* (1967), 12; Karl F. Helleiner, "The Population of Europe from the Black Death to the Eve of the Vital Revolution," in *The Cambridge Economic History of Europe*, Vol. iv, ed. E. E. Rich and C. H. Wilson (Cambridge, 1967).

larity of such legends as the fountain of life reflects not an assumption of premature death but of the humiliations of old age, and although attempts have been made to suggest that there were so few oldsters about that they were held in special veneration,[15] this seems to conflict both with the evidence of age given by witnesses in law courts and with the urging of preachers that the young should treat their seniors with deeper respect. In spite of puerperal and malnutrition diseases and of plague, men were not callous, life was not held cheap. Suicide, the sociologist's indicator of personal disequilibrium within society, was apparently rare.

If a feeling of alienation from family and from community is a potential cause of personal violence, as is frequently urged in terms of modern society, then we should look at this aspect of the emotional life as well. It can certainly be argued that affective contacts were in fact stronger than ever in the late fifteenth century. Far more significant than the dawning notion of individualism was the enduring need of men to identify themselves with groups and the effectiveness with which this need was catered to.

The solidarity of the family was still enhanced by its being the center of, not a retreat from, production. Respect for the familial *pietas* of ancient Rome, coupled with a distrust of monastic morals and a growing belief that the fully Christian life could be lived within the context of the home, produced an idealization of family life. There are, of course, intimations that the atmosphere within the family was not without its strains. Woodcuts portrayed husbands and wives literally struggling over who was to wear the trousers; that the family did not always care for its oldest members is suggested by the contracts whereby parents made over their property to their children in return for a guarantee of support; parents were scolded from the pulpit for allowing their children to become delinquent. And it is clear, too, that sexual strain was induced

[15] E.g., Mandrou, *op. cit.*, p. 66.

not only by late marriage, enforced continence and recourse to unreproductive sexual practices condemned by the church, but by a fear of women's sexuality produced in part by economic worries, buttressed by medical and clerical opinion, and reinforced by a castration anxiety.[16] But when these qualifications have been made, alienation from the structure or the values of the family cannot be seen as a theme of much importance. The family was still a tightly knit community of mutual services and accepted roles. Within it servants could minister to masters with little if any conscious sense of social divisiveness. The sense of satisfaction with the family as a social unit led to the multiplication of household scenes in illumination, painting and woodcut, sometimes as backgrounds for, say, the birth of Saint Anne, but also as genre scenes, and in these interiors the servants are treated as equal to their masters in physical dignity.

Nor were the men of this clubbable, conversable, nonprivacy-seeking age less satisfied when they turned to associations larger than the family. In the countryside, except for those areas where sharecropping, or reclamation patterns, or migrant husbandry made the nucleated village unworkable, the parish met the need for a purposefully organized gregariousness. In the town, with its craft- or trade-oriented streets, its village-like administrative units, its associations that catered to economic, religious, recreational, and cultural interests, the opportunities for identification with groups larger than those

[16] For an example from the pulpit, Joseph Nève, *Sermons choisis de Michel Menot* (Paris, 1924), p. 81; from medicine, J. B. Wadsworth, *Lyons 1473–1503: The Beginning of Cosmopolitanism* (Cambridge, Mass., 1962), p. 145. Mandeville's story (*The Travels of Sir John Mandeville* [New York, 1964], p. 188) that "of old time men had been dead for deflowering of maidens, that had serpents in their bodies that stung men upon their yards" sounds like a European folk superstition transplanted to Africa. It recurs in writings of travelers, e.g., *The Travels of Lodovico di Varthema*, trans. J. W. Jones, ed. G. P. Badger (London, 1863), pp. 109–110, chiefly in an Indian context, and is an element in the plot of Machiavelli's *Mandragola*.

of kin were manifold. The secular confraternity, as has been pointed out recently, could conform strictly to its etymology, settling quarrels fraternally among "those who are not on speaking terms," preventing causes of resentment such as bribing of servants and workmen from one master to another, and trying to preserve economic fair play among members.[17]

Another popular thesis today is that an atmosphere of social and economic competitiveness can produce feelings of frustration, inadequacy, and resentment which may lead to violence because men are led to expect what they cannot obtain. But this age, I would suggest, was not notably competitive in either respect. In both town and country, incomes—and the manner of living that went with them—varied so enormously that class consciousness can have been but a most tenuous concept. In Hamburg a merchant earning 5,000 marks was at the bottom of the class of the really rich (40,000 was the largest income),[18] but this salary was thirty-three times that of a tradesman; in Valladolid a lowish patrician income—2,000 ducats—was twenty-nine times that of a laborer.[19] It was the same in the parallel hierarchy of the church; the translation fees paid by a bishop of Lincoln would have paid the annual stipend of a curate in his diocese three hundred times over.[20] The ideal of filling a place in society by serving a superior in return for his protection retained its emotional appeal even though the feudal structure that had nurtured it was changing. Society required a number of roles to be played and while there was much literary comment on how best to play them there was little suggestion

[17] Bartolome Bennassar, *Vallodolid au siècle d'or: Une ville de Castille et sa campagne au xvi⁰ siècle* (Paris and The Hague, 1967), p. 423.

[18] Heinrich Reincke, quoted by P. Dollinger, *La Hanse* (Paris, 1964), p. 165.

[19] Benassar, *op. cit.*, pp. 426–427.

[20] Margaret Bowker, *The Secular Clergy in the Diocese of Lincoln 1495–1520* (Cambridge, 1968), pp. 8, 144.

that one could be exchanged for another. The merchant, for example, was urged to live up to the skills and virtues expected of him by society, not to turn himself into a gentleman. The humanistic celebration of man rebutted not the social but the moral hierarchy of medieval thought; humanism may have enriched the vocabulary through which the individual could think about his despairs and his hopes, but it took for granted the traditional social limits of his actions. Costume still distinguished the various occupations. This visual cataloguing, with its emphasis on preordained role-playing, was formalized in processions and in public entertainments like the Nuremberg Schembart festival [21] and by associating occupations with the fixed influence of the planets as on the Tarot playing cards. As far as prints, print, and pulpit were concerned, the overwhelming assumption was that a man would remain in the station to which he was born.

There was, it is true, a fair body of criticism, in sermons and satire, directed against those who aped the manners of their superiors, against peasants who tried to imitate the fashions of the burgess, against the bourgeois who tried to live like an aristocrat.[22] The bulk of these criticisms were, however, directed against women; they also suggest that social climbing with the intention of improving status and acclaim within a class was far more prevalent than the expectation of climbing from one class to another. The first analysis of society having a true sociological ring about it, that of Claude de Seyssel early in the sixteenth century, does accept a degree of mobility from the "commoner" to the "merchant and bureaucrat" class, and

[21] Samuel L. Sumberg, *The Nuremberg Schembart Carnival* (New York, 1941), *passim*.

[22] Out of a long literature see the recent work by Jean V. Alter, *Les origines de la satire anti-bourgeoise en France. Moyen âge—xvi⁰ siècle* (Geneva, 1966).

from the latter, by way of royal reward for service, to the aristocracy, and he justifies this as providing safety valves without
which "those whose ambition is irrepressible would conspire
with other members of their estate against those above them."[23]
As a piece of observation, however, this analysis is weakened
when we remember that some 90 percent of the population
lived outside the towns, where alone there was some chance of
rising socially within a generation, and that even there such
mobility was seriously hampered by the difficulty of accumu-
lating capital. Given the weight of assumptions about society as
static, the very rare examples of rags-to-riches careers, and the
infrequency with which even moderately notable examples of
social mobility could actually have been witnessed in any single
community, it is difficult to feel that social competitiveness was
more than a minor irritant, and that only to a few. And it is
especially likely to be true at a time when economic rivalry was
sharper between towns and governments than within a particular community, where the tone was set by guild self-protec-
tiveness and by the price-fixing of essential commodities, and
where pulpit and municipal ordinance still stressed the just
price. Neither from what they saw, heard, nor—were they liter-
ate—read were the majority of men given the impression that
social and economic competitiveness were challenges set by
society to the individual. The cost of bread, the imposition of
a new tax: these could lead to revolt, but this was unpro-
grammed desperation, an attempt to survive, not—save among
the Bundschuh leaders—to dispossess.

The uncertainty felt by the mass of the population as to
whether the harvest would tide them over into the next year
has always to be borne in mind. The effect of a predominantly
farinaceous diet for all but the reasonably well-to-do (because
of the price of meat, fish, eggs, and butter, few had access to
the reasonably balanced 3,500-odd calories a day planned for

[23] Jacques Poujol, ed., *La monarchie de France* (Paris, 1961), p. 125.

da Gama's crew)[24] is unclear, but it is at least possible that it could lead under stress to irrational terrors.[25] To recurrent outbursts of plague and sweating sickness was added a new horror, the extraordinarily swift extension throughout Western Europe of a new strain of syphilis. It was a period that witnessed an ugly surge forward in the persecution of those sexual scapegoats and social misfits, the witches (the *Malleus Maleficarum* was published in 1486), and the expulsion of the Jews from Spain and from parts of France and Germany. Yet even with these factors in mind, it is possible, I think, to see this as a time that was—apart from actual warfare—basically so adjusted that (again excepting southern Germany), potential violence was kept within bounds, when administrative and moral bounds were more effective than they had been previously or were to be by the middle of the sixteenth century. The drastic effects of price rises and sectarian fury lay in the future, and other seeds of violence were only now pressing the soil. National self-consciousness was already clearly defined, though it was not yet nationalism itself. Governments still lacked the standing armies that could help unpopular measures to be forced through, though the centralizing wedges tapped into feudal and municipal enclaves were forcing out men who would not or (for economic reasons) could not conform and helped staff the swelling numbers of outlaws, smugglers, and the do-anything, go-anywhere mercenary bands.[26] Increasing immigration from the countryside to the towns, particularly north of the Pyrenees and the Alps, was producing an insecurely employed proletariat and the beginning of what was to be a well-defined criminal class.

[24] Rations given in H. H. Hart, *Sea Road to the Indies* (New York, 1950), p. 89, compared with calories estimated for a comparable diet of 1600 in Frederic Mauro, *L'expansion européenne 1600–1870* (Paris, 1964), p. 116.

[25] Mandrou, *op. cit.*, 34–35.

[26] See e.g., Jean-François Bergier, *Genéve et l'économie européenne de la Renaissance* (Paris, 1964), p. 189.

Of war itself, the most drastic and obvious form of violence, there is space to make only a few blunt points. From the beginning of the Italian wars in 1494 armies became larger (thirty to forty thousand being a not uncommon figure), campaigns involving the same troops longer, and the difficulty civil society found in reabsorbing discharged men greater. Changes in the rules of war, which meant that the common soldier had less chance of getting rich through ransoming a rich prisoner or plundering a city taken by storm, led to shorter shrift being meted out to prisoners and less mercy being shown to civilians. The Florentine diarist Luca Landucci, commenting on the storming of Ponte di Sacco in 1495, adopts the same tone of shocked apology that Aguero used; "our men, behaving like barbarians instead of Italians, having learned from the French and hating them for many reasons, took pleasure in slaughtering and butchering them all without pity, because you can find Italians who are wicked and cruel." [27] There was, of course, nothing new about "rapacious and licentious soldiery." It was, however, new for a nation as a whole to become deeply infected with militarism, as did the Swiss. Zwingli's verse comment was based on his knowledge of how deeply cantonal politics were subordinated to war fever and his experience with the troops themselves as chaplain.

> Our honor stands on blood and war,
> Nature's rights are drowned in gore,
> Now all the furies loose from hell.
> How could anybody tell
> That we are Christians save by name,
> Without patience, love, and shame?
> If God grant not that wars have ceased
> We shall have turned from man to beast.[28]

[27] *A Florentine Diary from 1450 to 1516*, trans. Alice de Rosen Jervis (London, 1927), p. 22.

[28] Quoted and trans. Roland H. Bainton, *Christian Attitudes Towards War and Peace* (London, 1961), p. 143.

The comment comes from the second decade of the sixteenth century. But the phenomenon itself had begun at least in 1477 when a horde of unemployed young soldiers sacked its way from Lucerne to Geneva in a spirit ruefully dubbed "the mad life." [29] And this connection between delinquency and war was to be made with increasing frequency—as was the connection of both with brigandage and revolt—as the sixteenth century wore on.

So we return to methodology. This rapid and superficial tour of western Europe around 1500 has itself, of course, been methodologically motivated; I have been asking what sort of violence we might expect to find as well as what we do find. We do, for instance, find ideologically motivated individuals (like the would-be tyrannocide Pierpaolo Boscoli), we do not find ideologically motivated political movements, and we do not expect to find them. They were the product of cheap books, enhanced literacy, reasonably effective communications, the recognition of an impersonal "state," lastingly conscious class antagonism and an idea of secular, humanitarian progress. Between the *libertà* of the Renaissance and the "freedom" of, say, Rousseau, there is an enormous gulf, broadly speaking the gulf between looking back or across (as Florentines in 1494–1495 looked back past the Medici or across to Venice) and looking forward.

Without limbering up in the gymnasium of social scientific theory, the historian runs the risk of being an antiquarian; not asking enough questions of his sources, not creating a resonance in his reader's mind. But most social scientific inquiry into violence has been applied to the post-Renaissance era, so how dare we use its fruits?

Violence can be divided into four categories: personal violence (assault, rape, murder); group violence (men conspiring to common action to achieve economic or political goals); or-

[29] W. E. Rappard, *Collective Security in Swiss Experience, 1291–1948* (London, 1948), p. 12.

ganized illegitimate violence, as in brigandage or sea piracy; organized legitimized violence (legitimized, that is, by the laws as well as the values of both church and state) in the form of armies and navies, and possibly of the mass exilings and other punishments that can follow a successful coup d'etat.[30] All these categories were recognized, and seen to be interconnected, in the Renaissance.[31] Evidence for actions within all of them has of course long been used by legal, social, and political historians of medieval and early modern Europe. But an overall concept of violence has not been used, I think, as a common denominator that can link them or (more practicably) widen the treatment of a particular category. The concept—and it is not too far from the social scientific model I cited—assumes that in any age there is a predisposition to violence, more or less mensurable, which determines the crime rate, affects possibly the timing and certainly the conduct of group protest, conditions the composition of robber or outlaw bands and public attitudes to them, and, finally, influences voluntary recruitment to armies, and thus their behavior both on and off the battlefield. It assumes, that is, the existence of a pool of latent personal violence which can add to the dimensions and change the mood of violence in the other categories. Unemployment, the price of bread, the desire of crafts guilds to be represented in civic government, cooperation with the aims of another occupation group or faction: these are among the conscious factors that can start a rising. The insurrectionary core is then inflated by those in whom it triggers off the release of violence without a specific, let alone a reasoned motive, and it is with the inflated core that the final settlement has to be made.

It is surely a timely concept; our own experience can sharpen our vision. It connects the state of mind of the individual to some of the crucial outbursts that have shaped history. It low-

[30] A point Professor Martines raised during the conference.
[31] J. R. Hale, "Sixteenth-Century Explanations of War and Violence," *Past and Present* (May 1971) pp. 3-26.

ers the threshold of historical inquiry to a sociopsychological level at least as fundamental as that at which Marxist inquiry can profitably begin. It is also fraught with difficulties. In our period, for instance, we cannot move from case history via computer to an understanding of crisis. Nonetheless, my hope is that the wise and imaginative conveners of this conference will follow it with others in which we can learn more from our colleagues in the social sciences about what questions to put, what links to trust, what gaps we should try to fill, what analogies from other ages and other races there are to which we may have cautious but hopeful resort.

ORDER AND DISORDER IN ROMAGNA, 1450-1500

*John Larner**

*F*ROM THE AGE of Dante the Romagna has enjoyed a
unique reputation as being that province in Italy, at
least on the mainland, in which civil disorder has most flourished. And, on these grounds, it is useful to consider its towns.
Yet there are two ways in particular in which any examination
of later medieval Romagna will differ from that made in other
areas. The first of these relates to the source material on which
one can draw. Although there was, given the size of its population, a strong tradition of chronicle writing in the province, its
archives are sparse and discontinuous, often indeed confined
to haphazard collections of notarial protocols. Logically
enough, the very violence of life here has destroyed most of
the evidence from which it could be best studied. Consequently, to consider Romagnol history is frequently an exercise
much more akin to studying, say, Anglo-Saxon England, than
fifteenth-century Florence. One cannot ask for that same depth
and detail of treatment which one can legitimately hope for in
centers where fuller sources survive, and one's conclusions often
remain fragmentary and speculative.

In the second place Romagna fits uneasily into a study of

* The preparation of this paper was greatly assisted by a grant in aid
of research from the Carnegie Trust for the Universities of Scotland. I
would like to take the opportunity here to express my gratitude to the
Trust.

specifically urban violence. Though the towns of the province were *città* in a technical sense, in size and importance they were, and by and large still are, merely *cittadine*: not true urban centers but minor marketplaces for the countryside around. Accordingly, a considerable part of lawbreaking here was not so much city crime as the overspill of rural violence, and political disorder within the towns was often merely the reflection of feuds between landowners in the *contado*.

These reservations accepted, this paper examines a few points about the character of Romagnol disorder in the second half of the fifteenth century. I exclude here consideration of Ravenna, which from 1441 had passed under the rule of Venice. I confine myself to Rimini, under the dynasty of the Malatesti; Cesena, which from 1465 was governed directly by the Church; Forlì and Imola, under various *signori*; and Faenza under the Manfredi. In the present context there are two major themes. The first of these is that the governments of these towns were unable to maintain a civil and political order in their societies. Second, obviously related to this, though not, I think, exclusively so, is the fact that the quality of everyday life in these communities was characterized by the strongest predilection to violence.

I

These five towns, set at short intervals along the Via Emilia, were incorporated within the Papal State and owed ultimate allegiance to the Church. For most of the later middle ages, however, they were ruled by *signori*, acting nominally as papal vicars, and formed independent centers of government. They had little in common with the important capitalist cities of the Italy of the day. They were poor in resources, small in population, and without any large-scale trade or industry. In each town the subjects of the *signore* consisted of peasants, some lower artisans and laborers, a handful of powerful landowners, and some twenty to thirty families forming a citizen aristocracy. This last small group of citizen families enjoyed a certain wealth based principally upon their holding of local administrative office. They farmed the taxes, they acted in the judiciary, and so on.

For all these governments two major factors threatened the establishment and maintenance of order: geography and finance. In the first place the territories over which they ruled were extremely small. More than this they were often very difficult to control. Each of their *contadi* stretched half into the plain, and half into the Romagnol Apennines, a remote area, where the decrees of the ruler could be ignored with impunity. As the Florentine administration expanded from Tuscany across the Apennines during the fifteenth century, there is a growing mass of records showing the extent of unchecked crime in the Romagnol *montagna* and a considerable part of the correspondence between the Florentine committees and the *signori* is taken up with attempts, mostly ineffective, to deal with the problems that arose there. Cattle raiding from the Val di Lamone into the Mugello was common,[1] as was bride kidnapping [2] and the usual crimes of robbery and assault.[3] From

[1] Biblioteca Comunale di Faenza (cited hereafter as BCF) Copiario dei documenti faentini, transcripts of Archivio di Stato di Firenze (cited hereafter as ASF), Signori, Missive, Registro xxxiv, fol. 36, Dec. 7, 1431). Henceforth I cite all documents in this archive from the transcripts in the BCF.

[2] *Ibid.*, Missive, Reg. xliv, fols. 137 (Feb. 8, 1463). Florence complains to Imola that thirty men of its *contado* had attacked Giovanni di Mato "to take from him by force two girls that he had in his house. They broke in, entering violently, wounded the said Giovanni, and would have snatched away the said girls, if at the sound, many persons had not approached." See also, E. Breisach, *Caterina Sforza: A Renaissance Virago* (Chicago, 1967), p. 129.

[3] ASF, Signori, Missive, Reg. xliv, fol. 115 (Oct. 11, 1463). Salvestro di Benedetto of Gamberaldo has been attacked by Gentile da Sant'Enontimo and his sons at Gattara (*ibid.*, Dieci di Balìa, Missive, Reg. xxxvi, fol. 39 (Aug. 20, 1484). Florence tells the Lord of Faenza that some of his subjects have robbed Ludovico di Perino at Modigliana and threat-

time to time private wars over boundary disputes and rights of pasturage would break out between rural communes, and even on the plains, boundary disputes at harvest time were likely to lead to killings between communities.[4] At the same time, blood feuds between families could lead to the embroilment of whole villages.[5]

The *signori* tried to bring in some elements of order here. From time to time, for instance, we see the Vicar for the Lord of Imola at Fontanalice pacifying villages and making concord between families.[6] Some attempt was made by the various governments to cooperate in the suppression of crime. Florence, for instance, wrote to the Lord of Imola in July 1466 warning him that "Mazzone da Isola, public thief, has established himself in your jurisdiction."[7] But all too easily malefactors in the Apennines could take advantage of the boundaries between governments, and cross and recross the borders of Tuscany and Romagna, when the officials of either province came to inter-

---

ened his wife (*ibid.*, Reg. xxix, fol. 81 (Nov. 10, 1486); *ibid.*, Reg. xxxix, fol. 80v [undated]).

[4] As in 1477 when the men of Casale, Fontana, and Castel Bolognese marched out against the men of Valle San Cassiano (A. Metelli, *Storia di Brisighella e della valle di Amone* [Faenza, 1869], I, 363–364, 370–375), or as between Forlimpopoli and Bertinoro in 1473 (*Annales Forolivienses*, ed. G. Mazzatinti, *Rerum Italicarum Scriptores* (cited hereafter as *RIS*), Vol. XXII, pt. ii [Città di Castello, 1903], p. 102), or between Bagnacavallo, Conselice, and Massa Lombarda in 1485 (Archivio di Stato di Modena, Cancelleria Ducale Estense, Estero, Carteggio di Principi e Signori, Imola, Busta I, May 27, 1485, June 30, 1485). Still on July 4, 1487, Girolamo Riario was complaining resignedly to Ercole d'Este of "li differentie di questi benedetti confini quali fanno intra li homini de la Massa et de Conselice et questi miei da Imola." For further, rather more acrimonious, correspondence, P. D. Pasolini, *Caterina Sforza* (Rome, 1893), III, 148–149, 156, 158–159, 160, 166–167.

[5] Metelli, *Storia di Brisinghella*, I, 382–383.

[6] As at Sassoleone in 1451 (Archivio Notarile di [cited hereafter as AN] Imola, Rogiti di G. B. Nicola di Fontanalice, Dec. 16, 1451); and in 1474, peace being made among the Galanti, Fabricini, and Torrichia families in the jurisdiction of Fontanalice (*ibid.*, June 30, 1474).

[7] ASF, Signori, Missive, Reg. xlv, fol. 83v (July 3, 1466).

cept them.[8] A certain tone of resignation enters into much of this correspondence. Its spirit is caught in a letter of Carlo II Manfredi to Lorenzo de' Medici, who had been complaining of various outrages in October 1472: "But your Magnificence, who understands the nature of the men of the Val di Lamone, Marradi, Modigliana, and those parts, will realize that they're like flies who like to buzz around corpses, and it's a great business to drive them away. However, I'll again employ all diligence so that no scandal should follow and especially from my own subjects." [9]

For the rulers of the towns, the *montagna* had another and more important aspect. These Apennines produced men who had been toughened by a hard life, who were unable to draw a living from its sparse soil, and who were often driven to become professional soldiers under their local landowners. In November 1503 it was reported to the Venetians that the Val di Lamone, for instance, a former possession of the Manfredi *signori*,[10] which extended up into the mountains from behind Faenza, had "3,000 men, all good and useful soldiers, among which are many crossbowmen and harquebusiers, and there are 30 to 40 most accomplished masters of the harquebus. If your lordships wish it, you could easily have 1,000 harquebusiers there." [11] Obviously, for a lord who could harness the energies of these men to his own purposes, these troops might be a source of strength. But once his grasp weakened, they presented a real threat to the town government.

[8] Like the counterfeiter of money, Domenico Stanghelino of Fornione (*ibid.*, Reg. xl, fol. 71v (Sept. 11, 1454).

[9] ASF, Medici Avanti il Principato (cited hereafter as MAP) Reg. xxviii, fol. 593 (Oct. 1, 1472).

[10] From 1431 the Val di Lamone had been established as a country ruled by the Manfredi separately from their jurisdiction over the town and *contado* of Faenza (see J. Larner, *The Lords of Romagna* [London, 1965], pp. 179–180). In fact between the country and the town there was considerable interdependence.

[11] M. Sanuto, *I diarii* (Venice, 1879–1902), V, 350.

The *montagna*, of course, yielded little revenue. But even the taxation of the town and of the fertile lands of the plain gave governments an insufficient income. The second burden of the *signori* was that they were continually harried by poverty. This problem was intensified in the fifteenth century by a general decline in the wealth and population of the province. Hence the revenues of Rimini declined from the equivalent of 47,000 ducats in the 1370s to 10,000 at the end of the fifteenth century.[12] In November 1499 Caterina Sforza drew £B[olognesi] 22,000 from Forlì, a sum on which, she asserted, she and her son were unable to live "as *signori*." This represented a reduction from a communal income of £B.34,700 at the beginning of the century, and makes no allowance for the devaluation of the *bolognese* pound.[13] Paradoxically enough, the problems implied for the *signori* by these figures were intensified in the fifteenth century by what seems to be a considerable growth in conspicuous consumption. It was an age of ambitious architectural projects, of extravagant employment of artists, humanists, and astrologers, of a large growth in minor arts—one thinks of lace, of medallions, of true majolica, of bronze plaquettes. There was much more on which money could be spent. Galeotto Manfredi, for instance, who ruled Faenza from

[12] P. J. Jones, "The End of Malatesta Rule in Rimini," in *Italian Renaissance Studies*, ed. E. F. Jacob (London, 1960), p. 235.

[13] A. Bernardi, *Cronache forlivesi*, ed. G. Mazzatinti (Bologna, 1895–1897), Vol. I, pt. ii, p. 251; G. Orlandelli, "Le finanze della communità di Forlì sotto il vicariato di Baldassare Cossa," *Studi romagnoli, VII* (1956), 183–192. For indications on the finances of Faenza, see nn. 14, 17, and 22 below. For Imola my own, very rough, calculations on the basis, mainly, of the *rogiti* of G. Broccardi, for 1451–1452 in the AN Imola are that the gabelles were unlikely to have yielded more than £B.9,000. On the indebtedness of Taddeo Manfredi of Imola to his own subjects, see n. 51 below. On the other hand Girolamo Riario's increase of the milling tax at Imola in 1487 is alone said to have raised 2,400 ducats (Pasolini, *Caterina Sforza*, I, 179). For financial crises among the last Malatesti of Cesena, I. Robertson, "The Return of Cesena to the Direct Dominion of the Church after the Death of Malatesta Novello," *Studi romagnoli*, XVI (1965), 137.

1477 to 1488, and whose letters to Lorenzo de' Medici are filled with complaints about his poverty,[14] kept a typically lavish court in which three hundred men found employment. He had a Jewish doctor and a Franciscan astrologer, who were perhaps considered as necessities rather than luxuries, but who were expensive, and a mistress, Cassandra Pavoni, who exacted a large endowment. In addition he had a carriage-maker, an engraver, Sperandio Savelli, to strike medallions in his honor, and a Latin poet, Angelo Lapi, to sing his provincial glories. Craftsmen in majolica produced luxurious sets of dishes, which in graceful visual imagery celebrated impartially the beauties of his wife and his mistress. He had a large library (later to be sold by Cesare Borgia). In his garden he had ten peacocks, and a lion, for whom he tried to obtain the services of a lioness.[15]

At the same time, like all the *signori*, he had inherited from past centuries the chivalric ideal of *largesse* and the instinct to put on the occasional display of magnificence which would impress his subjects. Hence such expenses as the fortnight's festivities, with jousts, banquets, and distribution of food to the people, which marked his marriage to Francesca Bentivoglio in 1482.[16] Not all this was ill-judged. It was a real function of government to provide color and pageantry to relieve the tedium of provincial life. A *signore* needed a certain style, and it was always useful to be able to give employment to the artisans of

[14] ASF, MAP, Reg. xxvi, fol. 211 (June 26, 1478); Reg. xxxvii, fol. 574 (July 25, 1478) ("non essendo io più richo de dinari che io me sia, me retrovo senza uno soldo e non so dove me movere ne le mie necessità se non da quelle persone che mi amano"—please therefore send 600 florins at once); Reg. liv, fol. 64 (April 22, 1483), ("la gran provertà e calamità dove io mi trovo").

[15] See A. Messeri, *Galeotto Manfredi* (Faenza, 1904), *passim;* C. Malagola, "Di Sperindio, e delle cartiere, dei carrozzieri, armaioli, librai, fabbricatori e pittori di vetri in Faenza sotto Carlo e Galeotto Manfredi (1468–85)," *Atti e Memorie della Deputazione di storia patria per le Province di Romagna* (cited hereafter as AMR), ser. 3, I (Bologna, 1882–1883), 377–411.

[16] Messeri, *Galeotto*, pp. 27–32.

the town. But ultimately all this expense must be seen against the background of a grim financial situation.[17]

Tenuous territories, geographical difficulties, exiguous revenues; all these made the Romagnol governments of the age, considered in isolation, unviable. They only survived at all as *accomandati*, as clients of the greater Italian powers, and indeed it could be argued that the one function of the *signori* during the second half of the fifteenth century was to disguise the fact that the local independence of their communities had been lost to larger states. The disguise was thin indeed. When in 1488 the Lord of Forlì was murdered by some of his subjects, it was proposed by the assassins that the town should continue as a free commune without *signore*. But the council invited to consider the suggestion replied, realistically enough, that once Forlì had been able to live in freedom, but that now no autonomy could, in the circumstances of Italy of the time, last for a week.[18] Either they should have a *signore* or they would be incorporated within a larger state.

Agreements of *accomandigia* (clientage) very much cut down the *signore's* capacity for independent action. Just how much is hinted at by an agreement made by Astorgio III Manfredi with Venice in 1495.[19] Astorgio, the government declared, will hold a hundred men at arms for four years, with one year's option of renewal, in return for an annual stipend of 8,000 ducats. In return, Venice will send a noble to command these soldiers, and "to deal with all things which may be arranged for the use, profit, and security" of the Manfredi family. What this in fact meant was spelled out in the visit of Astorgio to Venice in April 1500, when he thanked the senators for their protection, promised perpetual allegiance to them, and declared that

[17] *Ibid.*, p. 21; ASF, Otto di Pratica, Respons., Reg. v, fol. 495 (Aug. 8 1488). Cf. *ibid.*, MAP, Reg. liv., fol. 83 (Jan. 7 1483, Pietro Nasi to Lorenzo), ("queste poche entrate di questo signore").

[18] Pasolini, *Caterina Sforza*, I, 213–214.

[19] R. Predelli and P. Bosmin, eds., *I Libri commemoriali della Republica di Venezia: Registri* (Venice, 1876–1914), VI, 15 (Dec. 14 1495).

he was "a son of their state." So too (admittedly at a desperate moment in their fortunes) the Malatesti were to declare that "Rimini was as much a part of Venice as Ravenna." The dependence implicit in this sort of arrangement was to lead the chronicler, Sigismondo dei Conti, to declare that Rimini, Pesaro, and Faenza were governed more by Venice, Florence, and Milan, than by the papacy.[20]

On the other hand the *accomandigia* considerably enhanced the Lord's local influence. It gave a much needed element of stability to the ruling family. To plot against one's lord was now to declare oneself against the much more substantial power of his patron: Milan or Venice, or whoever it might be.[21] And the *condotte* (contracts to raise troops) that normally accompanied these arrangements, from the point of view of the maintenance of civic order, produced a whole series of benefits. In the first place—provided that payment was regular[22]—it brought wealth, probably much more wealth than these rulers could hope to gain from any other source, and certainly the only possibility of extending inadequate revenues. Money from service as a *condottiere* could be plowed back into the towns to provide the ruler with a new source of patronage. Such wealth, for instance, allowed for ambitious building projects, like the Tempio Malatestiano and Castello Sigismondo at Rimini, and Giuliano da Maiano's cathedral at Faenza. These not alone gave

[20] Sanuto, *I diarii*, III, 260, 861; Sigismondo dei Conti, *Le storie dei suoi tempi dal 1475 al 1510* (Rome, 1883), II, 227–228.

[21] In October 1480, four months after the grant of a *condotta* to count Girolamo, the Venetian senate was writing to Roberto Malatesti and the Venetian *podestà* of Ravenna, instructing them to send aid to the count if there were any insurrection against him in Imola and Forlì; Pasolini, *Caterina Sforza*, III, 71, 91.

[22] Galeotto Manfredi complains that the bad payments of his *condotta* are reducing him to desperation (ASF, X di Balìa, Respons., Reg. xxvii, fol. 197 [April 18, 1483]). Later he writes to Lorenzo de' Medici saying that the Duke of Milan had ordered him to be paid 5,000 florins, of which 2,000 will be paid in kind, only 3,000 in cash. Can Lorenzo secure him 4,000 florins in cash? (ASF, MAP, Reg. liv, fol. 65 [May 2,

employment but served as new focuses for civic and local pride.

Again the *condotte* served as a useful safety valve. In some cases they were given merely as subsidies, and the *signore* was not expected to serve as a soldier away from his town. But when the lord went in person to war on behalf of his patron power, he could take with him those men whose temperamental proclivity for violence had been sharpened by all the restrictions of provincial life. He could give status, income, and the possibility of wealth, fame, and excitement to the more brutal and unruly of his subjects, and in doing so strengthen his alliance and mutuality of interest with the aristocracy of the town. The connection between the grant of a *condotta* and the satisfaction of the pressures upon the *signore* within his own domains can be seen from a letter of the Florentine Dieci di Balìa to their commissary in Faenza, telling him of their negotiations concerning the renewal of a grant to Astorgio Manfredi in 1425.[23] Florence was being asked, they explain, for a provision of 450 "lances" and then "for the sustenance of poor men and his friends of Faenza" for an agreement for the hiring of three hundred infantry. The poor and the "friends" of *signori* were coming already to depend upon this sort of arrangement. Finally, for those *signori* who actually took part in war—as did Roberto Malatesti and Astorgio II Manfredi—it meant opportunities for enhanced status and reputation in the wider Italian scene, which in turn reflected favorably on their position within their own territories. They gained the prestige that came from being part of the great world.

1483]). In June Galeotto's *podestà* was complaining that the money still had not been paid, and in September Galeotto wrote to Lorenzo again telling him that his company was breaking up through lack of money: "No one's asking me for money any longer; only leave to go" (Messeri, *Galeotto*, pp. 107–109). The *condotta* had arranged for payments of 18,000 ducats in time of peace, and 27,000 ducats in war. Galeotto asked Lorenzo to secure him a war salary of 28,000 ducats, as his brother, Carlo, had received (ASF, MAP, Reg. liv, fol. 49 [Jan. 30, 1483]).

[23] ASF, MAP, Dieci di Balìa, Missive, Reg. ii, fol. 4 (Dec. 1, 1425).

In these circumstances two of the Romagnol towns, Rimini and Faenza, up to the 1480s, were able to preserve, however haphazardly, a certain framework of ordered rights within their governments. With the aid brought to them by external powers, their dynasties were able to satisfy the interests of those leading families within their towns, who might otherwise have been tempted to challenge their rule. Over the generations substantial grants of rights, lands, and offices could give the leading citizen families a sense of sharing in a sustained partnership with their *signori*.[24] Again, the *signore*'s intimate relation with his protecting power allowed him to appeal to it for employment and privileges for his citizens in the wider Italian world. The letters of the Manfredi to the Medici are filled with these requests, and expressions of gratitude for their fulfillment.[25] At the same time the very duration of the rule of one family gave it a charisma that attracted the loyalty of the peasant and artisan.[26]

Accordingly, at Faenza and Rimini, insofar as the evidence allows us to judge, there was a certain measure of civil order in the first three-quarters of the fifteenth century. I do not, of

[24] See Jones, "End of Malatesta Rule," pp. 230–231, 243–244; Robertson, "The Return of Cesena," pp. 136–145.

[25] E.g., Giovanni de' Manfredi to Giovanni de' Medici, asking for captaincy of Marradi for friend (ASF, MAP, Reg. ix, fol. 264 [April 27, 1457]); Astorgio II Manfredi to Giovanni de' Medici asking for office of "Mercantiali" in Florence for Giovanni Spavaldo, "mio dilecto cittadino e cara creatura e da mi molto amato" (*ibid.*, Reg. x, fol. 470 [Dec. 23, 1462]); Galeotto Manfredi asks Lorenzo de' Medici to write to Duke of Ferrara on behalf of Cesare Cassarello, "mio fidelissimo servitore" (*ibid.*, Reg. xxxvi, fol. 631 [May 20, 1473]); Galeotto asks Lorenzo for office of "jedexe ala mercantia" for Giovanni Mattioli (*ibid.*, Reg. xxxv, fol. 349 [March 1478]), for Vallambrosan abbacy of Crespino to be held *in commendam* by the Reverend Miser Luca di Pasi, "mio cittadino et cordialissimo amico et partixano" (*ibid.*, Reg. xxxi, fol. 339 [Sept. 18, 1478]), for office "del appellatione" of Florence for Tebaldo da Alba (*ibid.*, Reg. liv, fol. 68 [Dec. 3, 1483]).

[26] On the loyalty of the lower classes to Pandolfo Malatesti, C. Clementini, *Raccolto istorico della fondatione di Rimino* (Rimini, 1617–

course, imply that there was a high standard of public morality, that officials did not misgovern, that it was not difficult to obtain justice. I do not imagine that these *signori* succeeded in dominating the *montagna*. But the possibility of law enforcement existed here, and civil life was not rendered impossible by those factions or illegalities which were so prominent a feature of life in the other towns of the Romagna. By contrast, at Imola and Forlì, power passed to a series of rulers whose transitory hold upon government forbade the establishment of any traditions of a civil regimen. Ignoring minor peripeteia,[27] Forlì, for instance, was ruled from 1411 to 1422 by the Ordelaffi family, from 1424 to 1426 by the Visconti, from 1426 to 1433 by the Church, from 1433 to 1480 by the Ordelaffi again, and from 1480 to 1500 by the Riarii. Such discontinuity of rule meant that the fabric of social life was continuously in question, that plots against the government were an everyday reality, and that embittered factions sprang up among the citizen aristocracy.

Hence it would be idle to look here for any constant standards of civil justice or efficient police service. Within the town Giovanni Pedrino, the artist chronicler of Forlì, gives us the

---

1627), II, 580. For peasant loyalty to the Malatesti, see Jones, "End of Malatesta Rule," p. 237. Note, too, the rebellion of peasantry in favor of Roberto Malatesti after the fall of Cesena to the Church (*Annales Forolivienses*, p. 99) (though Dr. Robertson suggests ["The Return of Cesena," p. 137] that "the connection between commune-*contado* strife and loyalties to one regime or another appears at the most to be incidental"). At Forlì, as Breisach (*Caterina Sforza* p. 294 n. 5) has pointed out, the principal agents of plots in favor of the Ordelaffi from 1480 were "artisans, peasants, and lower clergymen."

[27] As, for instance, Giorgio Ordelaffi's expulsion of his brother, Antonio, and seizure of sole power in 1411; Pino III Ordelaffi's dispossession and murder of his brother, Cecco III, in 1460. In the same period Imola was ruled by the Alidosi to 1424; by the Visconti, 1424–1426; by the Church, 1426–1434; by the Visconti again, 1434–1439; by a branch of the Manfredi family, 1439–1472; and by the Riarii from 1473 to 1500.

occasional vignette from the *cronaca nera* of the first sixty years of the century. A peasant, sixty years old, murders his son and flees to Modigliana; a goldsmith who has sexually assaulted a young boy dies in prison before he can be burnt alive in the piazza; a prostitute is murdered by her protector. There is a robbery from a shop of eight pieces of cloth, and a "caitiff ribald friar" is carried off to the Bishop's prison after delivering a counterfeit bull at a church and asking 10 florins for his pains.[28] One gains here the impression of a limited success in the punishment of the crimes committed by the lower orders. What is lacking, however, is any evidence of the punishment of the crimes of the powerful, of the overmighty subjects, or any hint that the blood feud, characteristic of Romagnol society, has been suppressed. In 1415, for instance, two brothers of the powerful Numai family, with other associates, murdered the *podestà* of Forlì, because he had committed adultery with their sister. They fled, but after a few months were allowed to return in peace.[29] Pedrino, who tells the story, also refers quite casually and incidentally, to someone in the town who habitually wore a breastplate "because of a mortal enmity he had." [30]

II

Certainly from the beginning of the 1480s the standard of civil rule, the hold of all the Romagnol *signori* upon their towns, and so too their capacity to repress internal violence, diminished considerably. In each town the reasons for the political failure were different, and their conjunction at this particular time seems to be the effect of a series of chances rather than the consequence of any general factors common to the province or Italy as a whole. Obviously the French invasion in 1494 en-

[28] Giovanni di Mo Pedrino, *Cronica del suo tempo*, ed. G. Borghezio and M. Vattasso (Rome, 1929-1924), I, 276, 163, 193, 306; II, 353–354.
[29] *Ibid.*, I, 52–53.
[30] *Ibid.*, I, 284.

gendered new tensions and released old ones, but in most of the towns a point of crisis had already been reached by that year.

At Rimini, despite the grandiose and disastrous ambitions of Sigismondo Pandolfo Malatesti, a certain stability endured up to 1482. But from that year, with the death of Roberto Malatesti, the fortunes of the town's dynasty fell rapidly. The regents appointed to guard the interests of Roberto's heir, Pandolfo, quarreled violently among themselves. One among them, indeed, Galeotto Malatesti, had a colleague murdered, and then planned, though unsuccessfully, to seize *signoria* himself. In all monarchial societies, a regency is a period of stress, but matters did not improve when Pandolfo came of age. He was incompetent, and what was worse, burdened with a keen appetite for the wives of his subjects. In January 1498 the leading families of the town struck back in a conspiracy to murder all the Malatesti family. In fact Pandolfo escaped, and was restored to power by Venetian troops dispatched to his aid from Ravenna. But though many of the conspirators were executed, from then on plots continued. Henceforth the *signore* could summon up no real basis of power in the town. In September 1500, the Venetian commissary was reporting to the senate that "God alone and your *signoria* can help him." [31]

Within the same period the Riarii family [32] faced even graver difficulties. Girolamo Riarii had been imposed upon Imola in 1472, and upon Forlì in 1480, as a result of the nepotistic designs of Sixtus IV. He had no roots in the towns, and his principal liability in attempting to rule them was that he was an alien, incapable of focusing the local loyalties and interests of his subjects. To his new domains he brought a crowd of hangers-on from his native Liguria who received grants and offices

[31] Sanuto, *I diarii*, I, 861–862, 877, 844, 957; II, 20; III, 749. See A. Cappelli, "Di Pandolfo Malatesta, ultimo signore di Rimini," *Atti e Memorie della Reale Deputazione di Storia Patria per le Provincie Modenesi e Parmenensi*, Vol. I (1864).

[32] On whom see classical work of Pasolini, *Caterina Sforza* and more recently in English, of Breisach, *Caterina Sforza*.

which might have gone to the native citizen familes. In consequence the cause of Antonio Maria Ordelaffi (whose family had been displaced from Forlì in favor of the Riarii) was able to attract a large measure of favor from within the town, and the first four years of Girolamo's rule were distracted by the constant discovery of conspiracies in favor of the older dynasty.[33]

Thenceforward the Count's position became even more precarious. His uncle, Sixtus IV, died in August 1484; his position as papal *gonfaloniere* ended; and despite a temporary *condotta* from the Venetians, his financial condition soon grew desperate. In 1486 an emissary of Milan was sent to Forlì to invite Girolamo and his wife, Caterina, to the marriage of Bianca Maria Sforza to the King of Hungary. On this occasion he wrote an account of his mission, which for those, at least, who are moved easily by the misfortunes of the upper classes, makes painful reading. The Count, he explained, had greeted him with tears in his eyes, saying that since the Pope's death he has been desperate for money. It was impossible even to travel. If the Duke did not aid him he was lost. Caterina's jewels were in pawn at Bologna and Genoa, and though he would be willing, to please her, to let her go to the wedding, she refused to do so without them.[34] In an attempt to ameliorate the situation, the Count, in the following year, revoked the tax concessions that he had been able to grant to Forlì in 1480. Hence further unpopularity, while thenceforth a continual insolvency drove his government itself to a bizarre criminality. In order to meet debts Count Girolamo had been forced to borrow money from the castellan of his fortress of Ravaldino. As a pledge, for repayment, he had rashly made over this castle (which dominated

[33] Bernardi, *Cronache forlivesi*, I, 202–205; L. Cobelli, *Cronache forlivesi*, ed. G. Carducii, E. Fanti, and F. Guarini (Bologna, 1874), pp. 271–276.

[34] P. D. Pasolini, "Nuovi documenti su Caterina Sforza," *AMR*, ser. 3, XV (1896–1897), 95–96.

Forlì) to him. In August 1487 the only means he could see to redeem the castle was to have his creditor murdered, which he accordingly did.[35] Further Ordelaffi plots followed, and in April 1488 the count was assassinated. On this occasion the conspirators, drawn principally from the leading Orsi family, seem however to have been moved hardly at all by any particular partisanship for a rival *signore* or government, but rather by personal fears and rancors against the count.

Only one of the eight years in which Girolamo had ruled Forlì had been free from serious conspiracies against his rule. After his assassination, his wife, Caterina Sforza, was restored to control of the town by Milanese troops, and took over the government in the name of their son, Ottaviano. She too was to find it difficult to attract any native loyalty in her domains. In Forlì, Ordelaffi partisans were still active, though both here and in Imola the conspirators took as their main pretext the supposed rights of her child Ottaviano. From 1489 Caterina had taken a lover, Giacomo Feo, one of her husband's Ligurian followers, and those hostile to her rule claimed to be acting in defense of Ottaviano's interests against the dangers that might threaten him from her liaison. So in Imola in September 1491 the Tartagni and Vaini families plotted with the castellan of Tossignano to take Caterina prisoner and to murder Feo.[36] This project failed, but at Forlì in August 1495 certain families succeeded in assassinating Feo in Ottaviano's name. In this case Caterina's repression of revolt was particularly savage; twenty children of citizen families who had rebelled were slaughtered by her servants. As a result the last five years of her rule rested solely upon fear.

Lordship of this type had no hope of popular support or confidence, or of ensuring law and order. Where there was a weak

[35] Bernardi, *Cronache forlivesi*, I, 186–189; Cobelli, *Cronache forlivesi*, pp. 294–297.

[36] Bernardi, *Cronache forlivesi*, I, 324–328; Cobelli, *Cronache forlivesi*, pp. 352–354.

and criminal government, justice was seen to be obtained not
from the *signore* but by recommendation to powerful men and
to the support of their retainers, to, that is, what Andrea Bernardi, the chronicler of Forlì, calls "the hands of those wicked
men who are with the great families." [37] In consequence the
towns came to be dominated by the rivalries of their powerful
citizens and factions grew. In Imola the Tartagni, Vaini,
Codronchi, and Pighini clans claimed to be Ghibellines, and
fought the "Guelf" Mercati, Sassatelli, and Calderini.[38] In
Forlì, although there were no such strong lines of party loyalty,
the families of the Orsi, Pansecco, Paolucci, Numai, Orcioli,
Ercolani, and Maldenti were powers to be reckoned with. Private feud flourished; the casual, unexplained killings of important men went unchecked. When Francesco Sassatelli was
murdered in 1488 on the Imola road, there was speculation—
and the very uncertainty is suggestive—as to whether he had
been slain by bandits, by members of the Vaini family, or by

[37] Bernardi, *Cronache forlivesi*, I, 216.

[38] G. Alberghetti, *Compendio della storia di Imola* (Imola, 1810),
I, 258–260. The financial power of certain members of the Imolese aristocracy was made clear in the rule of Taddeo Manfredi, who was
clearly often indebted to them. In 1450 he conceded the *datia cippi
grossi, stariorum et camporum* for a year to Guido di Vaino de' Vaini
in return for £B.1,700. Of this sum, Taddeo admitted to having already
received £B.972. Vaini paid £B.352 cash, and was absolved from the
remainder for settling the debts of Taddeo to the Jew, Abraham of
Castelbolognese. In the following year Taddeo sold these gabelles again
for £B.1,700 to Guido Vaini, Nicoletto di Antonio de' Tartagni, and
Bartolomeo Gasparre. He recognized himself as already debtor for
£B.472 to the concessionaires and secured their promise to pay the
£B.100 which he owed to his castellan, Petruccio di Calabria. At the
end of 1451 again, Taddeo gave the tax on the gates of the town to
Alberico Calderini for £B.1,000 of which £B.600 was canceled for
credit of Alberico against him (AN Imola, Rogiti di G. Broccardi
[Dec. 28, 1450; Oct. 10, 1451; Oct. 27, 1451]). By 1461 Guido Vaini was
Taddeo's treasurer (*ibid.*, Rogiti di Luca dell' Antonio del Monte [Nov.
4, 1461]), and in 1463, together with Pierpaolo Calderini, Nicoletto
Tartagni, and Filippo di Beltrando Pighini, bought the milling tax for
£B.2,000 (*ibid.*, Rogiti di L. Guasconi [Jan. 5, 1463]). In 1464 Taddeo's

men in the pay of Caterina herself.[39] The *signore*, of course, tried to bring peace into these conflicts. When at Imola in February 1490 Cristofano Tartagni was wounded by a dagger blow of Giulio de' Mercati, and the Calderini took up arms against the Tartagni and Vaini "so that the whole city was aflame," Caterina Sforza came to the town with eighty horses and established an uneasy truce. Giulio Mercati was exiled for life. His family had to swear that they would have no more to do with him under pain of 1,000 ducats fine.[40] Again, in February 1499, Corbizzo, a native of Castrocaro who had been for many years captain of Castrocaro for the Florentines, was murdered by four men, possibly in the pay of the Naldi family of the Val di Lamone. At this Caterina issued a proclamation forbidding the citizens of Forlì from taking up arms in the pursuit of vengeance, "to offend any person who had offended his relatives, not even for any particular person, nor to break truce and peace with words or deeds." [41] But such decrees, of course,

---

wife, Marsibilia, conceded the exploitation of her saltworks at Mongairdino to P. P. Calderini for £B.600 (*ibid.*, Guasconi [Jan. 4, 1464]).

Many other documents testify to Taddeo's financial embarrassments. Sometime before 1452 he gave Giorgio di Romagnulo of Baffadi the castle of Cantagallo in return for the £B.700 he owed for his custody of Montebattaglia and the *rocca* of Imola. In 1452, desiring the return of Cantagallo he gave Giorgio instead lands and a house in Zulinzaga. In the same document, being unable to pay the then castellan of Montebattaglia, he gave him 12 *tornature* of land in Montebattaglia (*ibid.*, Rogiti di G. Broccardi [March 20, 1452]). In August of the same year he surrendered various lands in Bubano to a goldsmith to whom he owed £B.235 for work done for him in gold and silver (*ibid.* [Aug. 6, 1452]). In 1463 he sold his rights in the mill of Spavuglio to Giovanni de' Sassatelli for £B.400 (*ibid.*, L. di Monte [June 22, 1463]).

For the conflicts of the Vaini and Sassatelli in June 1504, see R. Ghirardacci, *Della historia di Bologna; parte terza*, A. Sorbelli, ed. *RIS*, Vol. XXXIII, pt. i, p. 331.

[39] Pasolini, *Caterina Sforza*, III, 151–152; Bernardi, *Cronache forlivesi*, I, 55–57.

[40] Bernardi, *Cronache forlivesi*, I, 305. On Giulio de Mercati, see, too, Larner, *Lords of Romagna*, p. 142.

[41] Bernardi, *Cronache forlivesi*, I, 215–216, 220–221. Caterina was also

were largely valueless. What was required here, and what was lacking, was a government that could command a true allegiance from the generality of its subjects.

If at Imola and Forlì the breakdown of consensus government led to the emergence of family rivalries, such factions, at least in this period, seem to have little connection with any fight for political power, but were entered into rather in a spirit of pure vendetta. In Cesena, however, from the 1480s, that is to say from some twenty years after the town had passed from the Malatesti to the direct rule of the Church, the leading families came forward as powerful contenders for control of government.[42] Their conflicts led to an anarchic situation which culminated, though it did not end, in the "Sicilian Vespers of Cesena" of July 1495, when in alliance with Count Guido of Bagno the Tiberti massacred ten of the Martinelli family in the church of San Francesco and nine others throughout the town.[43]

It is clear that in Cesena, Imola, and Forlì, civil justice broke down almost completely against the background of family strife and the failure of governments in mastering it. Indeed in an era when the science of criminal detection was principally conceived of in terms of the torture chamber, attempts at policing were likely to breed more serious violence in their turn. When Stasio de' Vaini of Imola was murdered in 1480, one Troilo, illegitimate son of Alessandro, was seized by the castellan on suspicion of his death. He was given thirty-five *tratti di corda* to induce a confession, but resolutely held out. At this point the governor of the town decided he must be innocent and should be tortured no more. He was kept in the castle

---

suspected of being guilty of Corbizzi's murder, Pasolini, *Caterina Sforza*, III, 367.

[42] On the families of Cesena, see Robertson, "The Return of Cesena," especially pp. 136–142, and on the Martinelli and Tiberti, pp. 157–159.

[43] Bernardi, *Cronache forlivesi*, I, 334–341, 344–345; I, 83–96; Cobelli, *Cronache forlivesi*, p. 379; Pasolini, *Caterina Sforza*, III, 227–228.

to see if there were anything else of which he could be found guilty, but was finally absolved by Count Girolamo. The treatment he had received however had embittered Troilo. When invited to a conciliatory dinner by the castellan on his release—an occasion calling for the highest social gifts—he murdered his former captor at table, and with his brothers and ten companions seized possession of the castle. At this the governor of the town roused the citizens, but was somewhat mollified when from the walls Troilo explained that he had taken the castle not as an act of rebellion, but merely as part of a private vengeance upon the castellan. Hearing this the governor allowed him and his companions to vacate the castle and leave peaceably for Bologna. The story has an uncharacteristic ending, for justice triumphed. Four days later, Troilo and his brothers returned to Imola with the intention of murdering other members of the Vaini family. But all three were captured at once and summarily dispatched on the town gallows.[44]

III

It is easy enough to state in general terms the causes for the collapse of civic order under these governments we have considered so far. Their territories were small and weak. Hence any breakdown of partnership between the *signori* and their town aristocracy spelled disaster. The *signori* and the leading citizens of the town formed an oligarchy which had to keep together if it was to survive. At Rimini the unity was broken through the character of Pandolfo Malatesti. At Imola and Forlì under the Riarii, and at Cesena under the officials of the Church, the unity was broken because the towns had now come under the rule of alien nonnative rulers. Turning to Faenza, however, one discerns the real dilemma of the Romagnol *signori*: namely, could they stay united to their oligarchy without at the same

[44] Bernardi, *Cronache forlivesi*, I, 55–57; Jacopo Gherardi da Volterra, *Diarium Romanum*, ed. E. Cerusi, *RIS*, Vol. XXIII, pt. ii, p. 52.

time alienating the affections of the mass of their subjects? It is interesting to linger on this story in that it introduces us to something unusual in Italy during the second half of the century: if not a class conflict in the Marxist sense, at least to a clash of naked class interests.

During the first three quarters of the fifteenth century the Manfredi of Faenza had been the most successful of the Romagnol *signori*, and on the death of Astorgio II in 1486 the fortunes of the dynasty were at their apogee. They had enjoyed a large confidence among the town oligarchs, and they had gained considerable wealth as *condottieri*. From this period, however, their prosperity declined sharply. First cause of this change was the dissension that arose among the sons of Astorgio II.[45] On the one side stood Carlo, to whom had been left the lordship of Faenza, and Federigo, who from 1471 was its Bishop. They found themselves at odds with their younger brothers, Galeotto and Lancillotto. The two younger men went into exile in 1476 and, encouraged by Florence, threatened the periphery of their brother's domains. In this they drew a large measure of support from popular hostility to Bishop Federigo whose ecclesiastical position ill-accorded with the character of his life or his avid search for wealth. Moreover a series of arbitrary acts by Carlo and the Bishop presented the exiles with a chance to return. Much resentment had been caused at the beginning of Carlo's rule by his decree, taken in the interest of his plans for the embellishment of the town, that porticoes that had illegally extended onto the streets should be destroyed.[46] Then in 1477 his designs for a new land assessment brought fears of higher taxation. Finally, in an attempt to raise money the brothers tampered with the communal marketing of corn.

No step could have been more rash. Some twenty years later a Florentine commissary was to write: "Almost all the changes

[45] For what follows, Messeri, *Galeotto.*

[46] B. Azzurini, *Chronica breviora*, ed. A. Messeri, *RIS*, Vol. XVIII, pt. iii, p. 241–243.

in this town are brought about by corn shortage; and when the signor Carlo and the Bishop were driven from the town, this was the principal cause." [47] On November 12, 1477, the council had fixed the price of grain at 45 shillings the *corba*. "Forestallers" among the citizen aristocracy, and most noticeably Bishop Federigo, who had cornered 8,000 *corbe*, persuaded Carlo to raise the price to 50 shillings.[48] Three days later there were riots in the piazza led by "certain poor men of the [administrative district of] Porta Ravegnana." Carlo attempted to redress the situation by promising that corn should in fact be sold at 30 shillings the *corba* until Christmas, and then at 40 shillings until harvest time. But it was too late. The men of the four districts of the town met in the cathedral, elected a captain, and presented their terms: that Carlo should make peace with his brothers, Galeotto and Lancillotto, and that the Bishop should be exiled. After renewed rioting Carlo and Federigo were forced to yield, and finding their position impossible, abandoned the town. In December Galeotto and, briefly, Lancillotto (d. February 1480) became *signori* in their place.

In its way the insurrection of 1477 demonstrated the strength of the dynasty. The *artifices* who had demonstrated against the rises in corn prices had chanted: "We want only one lord, Carlo, and not the Bishop Federigo." Only when Carlo was too slow to repudiate his brother did they turn against him. Even then the mob did not transfer its loyalties outside the family. And Galeotto's rule which was to end in personal disaster did not weaken the attachment of the lower orders of the town to the family. On the other hand it did very considerably weaken the position of the *signore*. Coming to power as the result of a popular revolution, he was forced to disown those financial practices which brought it about. When in January 1483 he summoned up courage to plan the farming of the gabelles, he

[47] ASF, MAP, Reg. xviii, fol. 317 (Oct. 7, 1494). For manipulation of corn rings see Larner, *Lords of Romagna*, pp. 129–130.
[48] Azzurini, *Chronica*, p. 244.

was compelled to withdraw by the warning of his councils that such an act would provoke disaster. Moreover he had ill-fortune in the payment of his *condotte* and as a result fell swiftly into debt.[49]

Again Galeotto's relations with many, perhaps most, of the leading families of the town, some of whom had benefited from Carlo's exploitation of the lower classes, were unhappy. "There's no *signore*," he wrote to Lorenzo de' Medici in 1488, "who isn't hated by some of his subjects." Despite the benefits he has heaped upon them, he complains, members of the Pasi and Casoli families were plotting against him "not through any lack in me, but through their ill nature." Other families whom events were to reveal as ill-disposed were the Albicelli, the Vandini, Ragnoli, Roncho, and Zuccoli.[50] Galeotto seems to have been temperamentally unbalanced, as do so many of the *signori* of Romagna—perhaps the psychological stress of their office was maiming—and he was unable to deal with these men. But, as with Pandolfo Malatesti, it was his personal passions that were the immediate cause of his fall. His wife, Francesca Bentivoglio, though young (she was married in 1482, at the age of fourteen), was ill-suited to bear patiently with Galeotto's notorious attachment to Cassandra Pavoni, or with his public insults to herself. She withdrew to Bologna, and only returned, apparently reconciled, after planning with her father to seek revenge. Giovanni Bentivoglio himself had ambitions of enlarging his seignory by the acquisition of Faenza, and was prepared to put his daughter at risk to satisfy them. Many too among the citizen aristocracy welcomed the idea of change. On the May 31, 1488, the conspirators struck. Galeotto was assassinated by four Bolognesi servants in his wife's bedroom. When the murderers faltered, the Signore's wife, then twenty years old, cried out: "You swore you'd kill him!" and thrust her own dagger in his heart.

[49] ASF, MAP, Reg. liv, fol. 83 (Jan. 7, 1483, Pietro Nasi to Lorenzo de' Medici). On Galeotto's finances see nn. 14 and 22 above.
[50] Messeri, *Galeotto*, p. 67.

The sequel to the murder was again a testimony to the hold of the Manfredi upon their subjects. The people—in particular the *artifices sordidi* (base artisans)[51]—rose against the conspirators, prevented them from seizing power, and with the aid of Florence (1488–1495) and then of Venile (1495–1500) established a regency for Galeotto's infant son, Astorgio III.[52] It was a precarious settlement, as any based upon a regency was likely to be. Almost at once the Florentine commissary, Gian Battista Ridolfi, who at this period dominated the government, realized the impracticability of excluding from it the prominent heads of those citizen families who had rebelled against Galeotto. Hence, of the six provisional "Governors" appointed on June 5, 1488, two were nobility of the Val di Lamone (traditionally hostile to the leading citizens of the town) and four were from citizen families probably, or in some cases, certainly, involved in the plot against the murdered Galeotto. Accordingly the final arrangements for the regency of Astorgio led the aristocracy of the Valle and the lower class of the town to complain that "those who are governing us are those who murdered the *signore*." [53]

At the same time, the commissary wrote: "The 300 people who used to live at the expense of the court, have now been deprived and cannot easily live, and are looking to a chance for a sack." In these circumstances, "here one can do nothing, and anyone can do anything, and only four of the older artisans need to say 'Let's go and meet in S. Pietro,' and the whole plebs will rush behind them, and whatever's decided will be done, without any remedy for it." Accordingly it had been thought advisable to halve the taxes of the gabelles in order to win the favor of the people. As a result the gabelles would probably fall to less than 1,000 ducats.[54]

[51] Azzurini, *Chronica*, pp. 248–249.

[52] See A. Missiroli, *Astorgio Manfredi* (Bologna, 1912).

[53] G. Donati, *La fine della signoria dei Manfredi in Faenza* (Turin, 1938), p. 28.

[54] *Ibid.*, pp. 193–194.

Against this background the administration of justice in Faenza seems largely to have broken down. In August 1488 the *anziani* of Faenza calculated that to guard the town and palace and to punish malefactors required a force of a hundred men. They suggested, since they could not "for the deficiency of revenues" pay for all, that they should provide for a half, and Florence for the other fifty. In January of the following year, the then Florentine commissary, Dionigi Pucci, was complaining that every week a new council or scheme was being devised to solve the problems: "The last is a Bargello with 60 employees. I don't think this will be the remedy for the ill." At the same time the Council of the Val di Lamone sent a deputation to Pucci, asking that he himself should take over the administration of justice "che in tutto si è persa," an honor he was swift to decline.[55] Nonetheless both Ridolfi and Pucci made efforts to bring peace between the major citizen families. Ridolfi reported in June 1488 that "today we've caused peace to be made for a mortal feud that has lasted many years between the house of Severoli and that of Zuccholi, who are both of the first families of this place." Again, Pucci in August 1489 made peace between the Pasi and Cavina on one side and the Cenni and one Bastino del Pescatore, "without family, but head of the soldiers."[56]

Despite this, remarkably enough, a native reverence for the Manfredi continued. When Cesare Borgia, with an army of overwhelming power, attacked their domains in 1500, the Val di Lamone surrendered at once, but the citizens of the town held out for six months in defense of their hereditary ruler. Their loyalty was in part doubtless the fruit of fear, but also compounded of a sentimental attachment to their fifteen-year old princeling and the long family and local traditions he represented. Such a conclusion must make us pause before accepting

---

[55] *Ibid.*, pp. 188–189.

[56] ASF, Otto di Pratica, Respons., Reg. v, fol. 250 (June 15, 1488); Reg. vii, fol. 53 (Aug. 26, 1489), Reg. vii, fol. 29 (Aug. 29, 1489).

fully at face value the blanket condemnation of the Romagnol *signori* made by Machiavelli in the *Discorsi*.[57] Yet the experience of Faenza, where the lower classes played a strikingly active role in the political situation,[58] strongly underlines the dilemma in which the *signori* found themselves. If they united with the citizen aristocracy to exploit the peasantry and artisans with gabelles, regrating of corn, milling monopolies, and so on, they were likely to rouse the fury of the exploited. If they failed to do this, they might ensure the loyalty of the commonality and yet incur the resentment of the town nobles, excluded from a constant source of profit. Within the Romagnol towns, by the mid-fifteenth century, there was a point where the *signore* was irreversibly committed to alienating the interests either of his leading citizens or of his subjects in general.

IV

Although the insufficiencies of governments can obviously explain much of the breakdown of civil order within the province in this period, there is another element here too: a long tradition of lawlessness which over the centuries had shaped the consciousness of the Romagnols. From the age of Dante[59]—perhaps partly as the result of the prominent way in which Romagnol crime had featured in the *Divine Comedy*—the Romagna had become a byword in Italy for crimes of treacherous violence. There were many reasons for this. In the first place the conflict of factions, naturally to be expected in a weak political frame-

[57] *Discorsi sopra la Prima Deca di Tito Livio*, III, 29.

[58] Certainly much larger than in any other of the Romagnol towns. Even under Astorgio II the mob had risen up (May 12, 1460) and burnt down the office of gabelles and *danni dati*. Astorgio and his brother treated the outburst with discretion and the incident seems to have had no repercussions (Pedrino, *Cronica*, II, 347).

[59] On which period, see A. Vasina, *I Romagnoli fra autonomie cittadine e accentramento papale nell' età di Dante* (Florence, 1965). On violence and the blood feud, Larner, *Lords of Romagna*, pp. 58–74.

work, had been enhanced by the claim of the communes to control and market the sale of all the agrarian produce of the *contado*. From this it followed that each landowning family could only hope to escape communal control and to negotiate individually when selling the produce of its estates, by seizing a position of authority in the town, either as lord, or as part of a dominating faction. Once in power, however, it could sell its produce at will, and profitably regrate.[60] Assuming the period overall to be one of falling land values and declining rents, this consideration offered a very potent stimulus for all to take part in the violence of internal politics. Moreover, these families, both by their possession of *fideles* in the *montagna*, and by their loans to artisans in the towns,[61] did not lack those bonds of clientage by which other classes—indeed the majority of adult males[62]—could be drawn into their struggles.

If under these conditions family waged war against family, the age saw, too, profound conflicts within families. In Romagna, as elsewhere in Italy, this phenomenon can often be explained by the system of inheritance *pro indiviso*: where the lands and rights of a deceased father were held in common by all his sons. Compared with inheritance by primogeniture, which reduces sibling rivalry by clearly defining roles and educating children from birth into accepting them, inheritance *pro indiviso* seems almost designed to provoke conflict between brothers. In the following generation this conflict is powerfully intensified between cousins who are co-heirs. To inherit one-eighth *pro indiviso* of an estate was to inherit also the liveliest suspicion of all those with whom one shared the property, and as each generation passed the problems of holding rights in this way grew. In these conditions suspicion supported by self-interest and fear could all too easily lead to violent conflict.

[60] Larner, *Lords of Romagna*, pp. 129–130.

[61] *Ibid.*, pp. 103–108, 111–113, 137–138.

[62] G. Fasoli, "Guelfi e Ghibellini di Romagna nel 1280–1," *Archivio storico italiano*, (1936), I, 157–180.

To attempt to explain the traditions of Romagnol violence in wholly rational terms, however, would be misleading. The province was dominated by an aristocracy who—particularly in the *montagna*—were not by and large moved so much by concepts of bourgeois rationality as by ideals of aristocratic honor. Above all these aristocrats possessed still the traditions of the blood feud. In Romagna, a few miles from the university whose task throughout the middle ages was to persuade men of the need for a *ratio* in civil life, there was, in the face of changes through the centuries, a tenacious attachment to barbarian custom. Here, in the words of Wallace-Hadrill, writing of the classical feud of the migratory period, there was "that kind of kin-hostility where there was killing in hot blood and with all publicity, for the sake of honour, most particularly in avenging an act of treachery. This was the true vengeance girt about with a magic symbolism that may have remained potent for much longer than we know." [63]

Obviously the blood feud of this age was a debased form of the earlier, more sophisticated system known to the Franks. Most noticeably it was often fought out not between but within kinship groups. Yet much of its spirit survived. Every Romagnol aristocrat could well have appreciated the words of Attila: "For the strong man, what is sweeter than to exact vengeance with one's own hand?" It is only perhaps with that sentence in mind that one can begin to understand those Romagnol acts of treachery which had featured in the *Divine Comedy*. An idle jest by some party leaders against Tebaldello Zambrasi goads him into betraying his town to the enemy, a blow leads to a mass slaughter of relatives some years later: "ex minima causa tam odiosam vindictam." [64]

[63] J. M. Wallace-Hadrill, "The Bloodfeud of the Franks," *Bulletin of the John Rylands Library*, 42 (1959), 462.

[64] Benvenuto de' Rambaldi di Imola, *Commentum super Dantis Aldigherii Comoediam* (Florence, 1887), II, 514–515 (on Tebaldello, in *Inferno*, XXXII, 122–123).

In these crimes, not only did vengeance have to be done, it had to be seen to be done. They are committed, one might say, from a love of glory; they reveal an egoism, an obsession with individual *virtù*, and with the satisfactory ordering of one's own personal esteem in society, which bring to mind all those things Burckhardt wrote about individual morality in the Quattrocento. In that morality, in fact, we see so often, not so much a rebirth of bourgeois Roman man, as the breaking free of barbarism from those chains of law which sought to shackle it. It was something, certainly, which the Church and religious opinion were unable to change. Mass attempts at exorcism of "the vengeance girt about with magic symbolism," such as the "Great Hallelujahs," even the foundation of a religious order, the Cavalieri Gaudenti, specifically designed to promote peace between factions,[65] could do nothing permanent to touch the old traditions. It is a failure easy enough to explain. The clergy themselves were too closely bound up with the lay world of the time to do anything else than reflect its character. The aristocratic composition of the cathedral chapters inevitably involved the episcopacy in the struggles of the towns, and changes in the balance of parties in the lay world were likely to be reflected in the cloister.

At a deeper level the Church failed to correct or contain the violence of the age because its own everyday morality was little different from that of the world outside. In a curious passage of his chronicle, the thirteenth-century Franciscan, Fra Salimbene, praises a man for exacting vengeance upon one opponent only, rather than two: "Sufficienter ultus est et noluit excedere modum" (He had been revenged sufficiently and did not want to exceed the just proportion).[66] This refusal to con-

---

[65] See A. de Stefano, "Le origini dei Frati Gaudenti," *Archivium Romanicum*, X (1926), 305–350. From this order came Alberico de' Manfredi, whose blood vendetta made him "peggiore spirito di Romagna" (*Inferno*, XXXIII, 109 ff.).

[66] Salimbene de Adam, *Cronica*, O. Holder-Egger, ed. *Monumenta*

demn any act of vengeance outright is a marked characteristic of a large part of north Italian didactic literature of the age. One thinks of the celebrated collection of verses written by an anonymous Genoese merchant at the end of the thirteenth century. The bulk of these deal with praises of the saints, moral teachings, and so on. Casually intermingled with this, however, there suddenly comes advice on how to secure vengeance: "Keep silent and then strike." [67]

In fact the practical theology of everyday life adapted itself to the temper of a lay morality. Sitting in the schools of Paris, the scholastics heard Saint Thomas speaking of vengeance. Was it permitted? Yes. Could it be exacted by private men who held no public office? Yes. Could vengeance be exacted upon other men than those who had actually committed a crime? Yes. Was there indeed a virtue of vindictive justice? Yes.[68] The sophisticated men who heard these judgments doubtless gathered the impression that only men of heroic virtue in pursuit of the noblest causes could exact vengeance, for "we must consider the mind of the avenger," and the permission to exact vengeance was hedged round with very many qualifications. Yet once away from the schools this teaching, as it filtered down to the lower ranks of the parish clergy, was likely to change its character. The text in Romans (12:19), "mihi vindicta, ego retribuam, dicit dominus," was likely to be thought of as meaning, not, as Christians today assume, that vengeance was forbidden to men, but that it was a Godlike act and that man's vengeance might be therefore akin to the *ultio divina*. Many passages in the Old Testament—one thinks for instance of the

---

Germaniae Historica Scriptores, Vol. XXXII, (Hanover and Leipzig, 1913), pp. 605–606.

[67] "Rime genovesi della fine del secolo xiii e del principio del xiv," N. Lagomaggiore and E. Parodi, eds. *Archivio glottologico italiano,* II (1876), 239.

[68] *Summa Theologiae,* ed. P. Caramello (Turin and Rome, 1952), pp. 507–511, pars. II^a – II^{ae}, Quaestio cviii, De vindicatione.

story of Elisha, the children, and the bears—do indeed, to minds unfortified by profound exegesis, suggest just that.

Of course it would be wrong to assume that the Romagnol attitude to violence was unchanged between the age of Dante and the fifteenth century. It was a merit of the *signorie* that emerged in the fourteenth century that they had succeeded in repressing something of the grosser lawlessness of their towns, that they had imposed some order, however fragile and temporary, upon the surface of civic life. Yet from this period a tradition of violence long survived. Old hatreds were unforgotten; the memories of clan quarrels lingered on; and popular feelings did not change. In the fifteenth century, in every town in Italy, the Franciscan Observants were waging war against the Jews, urging the people to rise up and sack their houses, not only for the crime of "usury," but also as a vendetta for the crucifixion of Christ.[69]

The law itself threw a certain mantle of protection over the blood feud. A rubric in the Statutes of Faenza drawn up in 1410 is entitled *De pena inferantis vendictam in alium quam in eum qui offenderit:* "*Item.* We order and we decree that if anyone shall be offended in his person, and shall exact vengeance on another than he who offended him, so that he shall die, and he shall fall into the power of the commune, his head shall be cut off, and if he shall not fall into the power of the commune, he shall be banished in perpetuity and his goods shall be confiscated." [70]

The sense of this statute is found earlier in Bolognesi decrees of 1252, 1265, and 1288,[71] and the clear suggestion that emerges from them is that it was legitimate to exact vengeance upon a

[69] See C. Roth, *The History of the Jews of Italy* (Philadelphia, 1946), chaps. iv and v.

[70] *Statuta faventiae,* ed. G. Rossini, *RIS,* Vol. XXVIII, pt. v, i, pp. 188–189.

[71] *Statuti di Bologna dall' anno 1245 all' anno 1267,* ed. L. Frati (Bologna, 1869–1880), I, 266; III, 609–610; *Statuti di Bologna dell' anno 1288,* ed. G. Fasoli and P. Sella (Vatican, 1937–1939), I, 209–210.

man who had wronged one, though not upon his kin. These decrees in fact serve to explain a passage in the proclamation by Caterina Sforza in February 1499 that we have already encountered: No one, she declared, should take up arms to pursue vengeance "to offend any person who had offended his relatives, *not even for any particular person.*" [72] Caterina here was seeking to prevent even the customary vendettas of one man seeking revenge from another for his injuries. In fact, here at the end of the fifteenth century the *faida* of Germanic custom still held a semiofficial position in Romagnol life.[73]

V

At the beginning of the sixteenth century the political circumstances of the Romagna were radically transformed. In two campaigns Cesare Borgia, son of the reigning pope, swept away the old *signori* and established in their place a unified Duchy of Romagna. It is one of the minor historical orthodoxies of this period that during his rule Cesare was able to bring to an end, temporarily, the habitual lawlessness of the province, and to establish in its place a *buon governo*.[74] However this may be— and it is a view deserving of reexamination [75]—with the fall of

[72] Bernardi, *Cronache forlivesi*, Vol. I, pp. 220–221: "non sia alcuna persona che diga piare l'arma per ofendre altra persona che avese ofese soi parente, nè eciam per altru' particolare persona, nè rompre nè trega e non pase nè con fate nè con parole, come se contene in li Statute dela nostra cità de Forlì, sota la pena dal dopie de hogne sova condanacione. . . ."

[73] In November 1442, in fact, two soldiers appeared before Antonio degli Ordelaffi in order to obtain permission, which was granted, to fight a duel in the piazza of the town (Pedrino, *Cronica*, II, 185).

[74] See especially W. Woodward, *Cesare Borgia* (London, 1913), which expanded the original thesis of E. Alvisi, *Cesare Borgia, Duca di Romagna* (Imola, 1878), followed by C. Yriate, *Cesar Borgia* (Paris, 1889), and thenceforward in a host of derivative works.

[75] It has been challenged only by G. Pepe, *La Politica di Borgia* (Naples, 1946) (especially pp. 253–268). My "Cesare Borgia, Machiavelli, and the Romagnol militia," *Studi romagnoli*, XVII (1966), 253–

the Borgia's government nothing of his work was to remain in the province. Nor when the Papacy finally succeeded in giving it unity did it then settle down in civil peace. This was still Romagna, in Guicciardini's words, "where there are so many wounds, and so many old and new injuries, and where men are commonly dishonest, malign, and ignorant of honor." [76]

> Terra ferox, populusque ferox ac caede frequenti
> Terribilis, semperque furens civilibus armis:

it was to remain a harsh land of unceasing violence, land of Sanfedisti and Carbonari, of Socialists and Republicans, where, even at the beginning of the twentieth century, a European poet could announce that he was assuming a university chair as an act of vengeance against the murderers of his father. [77]

The history of Romagna in fact shows that there are some societies whose basic geography determines a life for its inhabitants in which political civilization cannot be known, where the most one can expect are temporary ameliorations of basic anarchy. Only when the society itself is radically transformed, as Romagna's was in the twentieth century, can men throw off the burdensome heritage of the past. Those who have studied violence in the modern city have offered a variety of explanation for its generation and survival: overpopulation and overcrowding; technological and bureaucratic developments that serve to alienate and dehumanize the citizen; a twin affluence and materialism. Clearly none of these played any part in medieval Romagna. Here violence was almost pre-urban in character: it came from the world of the peasant and the aristo-

---

268, shows that the extravagant claims made for Cesare's military establishment in Romagna have no basis in reality. I hope to return to this general theme shortly in some other place.

[76] F. Guicciardini, *Opere inedite* (Florence, 1857–1867), III, 393.

[77] M. Biagini, *Il poeta solitario: Vita di Giovanni Pascoli* (Milan, 1955), p. 243.

crat, it was a fruit of underdevelopment rather than overcomplexity. I would conclude therefore—though, given the title of our conference, it perhaps strikes an unharmonious note—that it would be mistaken to concentrate overmuch on the city as such in this period as a leading factor in explaining the vicissitudes of human aggression.

IV

THE ASSASSINATION OF GALEAZZO MARIA SFORZA AND THE REACTION OF ITALIAN DIPLOMACY

Vincent Ilardi

*A*MONG THE MANY political conspiracies of Quattrocento Italy, that hatched by three young Milanese
patricians—Giovanni Andrea Lampugnani, Carlo Visconti, and
Gerolamo Olgiati—stands out both for its futility and its mo-
mentous consequences for the history of the Italian states and
of Europe in general. The fall at Nancy of Charles the Bold,
Duke of Burgundy, barely ten days after Galeazzo Maria had
been assassinated in the church of Santo Stefano at Milan (December 26, 1476), and the murder of Giuliano de' Medici sixteen months later, closed the decade of the 70s with three
violent events which left a legacy of uncertainty and suspicion.
The system of equilibrium among the Italian powers, which
had been fostered by Cosimo de' Medici and carefully maintained by Francesco Sforza, was dealt a crippling blow.

The story of the Milanese conspiracy has attracted the attention of novelists, playwrights, and historians alike. Among
historical works, the detailed monograph of Bortolo Belotti,
Il dramma di Gerolamo Olgiati (Milan, 1929), based on diligent archival research, can be considered definitive. It is interesting to note that the Fascist government bought up all
available copies, apparently fearing unwelcome comparison between Renaissance and modern tyranny. The book was repub-

lished posthumously in 1950 under the title *Storia di una congiura*.[1]

It has been established that the three youths plotted in secret, but they took the precaution of packing the church with about thirty of their supporters. The latter, however, were attracted to the church under various pretexts and were unaware of the plan to assassinate the Duke. The motives of the assassins have also been ascertained as much as human motivation can be revealed by surviving documents. The leader of the conspiracy, Lampugnani, had been denied justice in the disposition of certain lands attached to the Abbey of Morimondo in dispute with the Bishop of Como, Branda da Castiglione, a favorite of the Duke. Visconti, a secretary in the ducal Consiglio di Giustizia, resented Galeazzo Maria's seduction of his sister. Only Olgiati seems to have been animated not by any personal affront, but simply by a sincere passion for liberty and hatred for tyranny fostered by his humanist teacher, Cola Montano. A teacher of rhetoric in Milan since 1462, Montano had received a salary for several years from the Duke, but in 1474 he fell in disgrace, was arrested and flogged twice in public. A year later he was banished from the Duchy, and thus took no part in the actual assassination plot. It is known, however, that he had read Sallust's *Conspiracy of Catiline* with Lampugnani and Olgiati and that he had inflamed his pupils, especially the impressionable Olgiati, with a deep hatred of the tyrant.[2]

The strict secrecy observed by the three conspirators achieved the desired effect of complete surprise and gained

---

[1] Aspects of the conspiracy have also been treated by G. D'Adda, "La morte di Galeazzo Maria Sforza," *Archivio storico lombardo*, ser. 1, II (1875), 284–294; E. Motta, "Un documento per il Lampugnano, uccisore di Galeazzo Maria Sforza," *ibid.*, ser. 1, XIII (1886), 414–418, and "Ancora dell'uccisione di Galeazzo Maria Sforza," *ibid.*, ser. 4, XI (1909), 403–413. Belotti, *Il dramma*, pp. 206–212, gives an extensive bibliography.

[2] Belotti, *Il dramma*, pp. 34–96 has analyzed in detail the background and motives of the conspirators, as well as the influence of Montano.

them their immediate goal of eliminating Galeazzo Maria, but
it guaranteed the total failure of their ultimate objective—the
overthrow of the Sforza through a spontaneous popular revolt
led by Milanese patricians. The Duchy was to be transformed
into a republic, probably along the lines of the Ambrosian Republic, for the preservation of which Oldrado Lampugnani,
Giovanni Andrea's uncle, had given his life a few years earlier.[3]
But neither the populace nor the nobility made a move. On the
contrary, the relatives of the conspirators themselves, eager to
preserve their lives and property so recklessly jeopardized by
their kin, sought to prove their innocence by denouncing the
assassins to the authorities. Princivalle Lampugnani, ducal captain at La Spezia and brother of Giovanni Andrea, quickly
wrote to the Duchess condemning his brother, who had been
killed on the spot, as "that most wicked traitor and execrable
scoundrel" who had tarnished the long record of loyal service
of the Lampugnani to the Dukes of Milan.[4] Carlo Visconti, who
had managed to flee from the church, was turned over to the
authorities two days later by his uncle, Pier Francesco Visconti,
a ducal councillor, to whom he had appealed for aid.[5] Still more
tragic was the capture three days later of Gerolamo Olgiati,
whose hiding place was revealed to officials by his own father.
Subsequently Giacomino Olgiati, in accepting exile at Turin,

---

[3] *Ibid.*, pp. 76–77.

[4] "Quello sceleratissimo traditore et exacrabile ribaldo de Johanne
Andrea mio fratello" (Princivalle Lampugnani to the Duchess, La Spezia, Dec. 31, 1476, *ibid.*, doc. XII, 191). On the attitude of other members of the Lampugnani family toward Giovanni Andrea, see also
Motta, "Un documento," pp. 415–417.

[5] See the contemporary narration of these events by the Milanese
notary, Antonio da Zunico, published by Motta, "Ancora dell'uccisione," p. 410; and a copy of a letter by Orfeo da Ricavo, a ducal official of Florentine origin who was present at the assassination, written
to person or persons unknown in Florence, Milan, Jan. 1, 1477, published by E. Casanova, "L'uccisione di Galeazzo Maria Sforza e alcuni
documenti fiorentini," *Archivio storico lombardo*, ser. 3, XII (1899),
307.

thanked Duchess Bona and Duke Giangaleazzo Sforza for their clemency in allowing him to keep his possessions, and reminded them that he had offered "a thousand times" to kill his son, the archtraitor, with his own hands.[6] These demonstrations of loyalty, however, seem to be indicative more of complete hopelessness and despair than of a breakdown in the traditionally strong family ties. Nevertheless they did not deter the rulers from taking punitive measures of varying severity, including the death penalty and exile, against the relatives of the conspirators despite their proved innocence.[7]

Far from rebelling, officials and prominent members of the nobility rode through the streets of Milan immediately after the assassination exhorting the people to remain calm. Their prompt action prevented the populace, who were dragging through the streets the mutilated body of Lampugnani, from sacking the houses of the conspirators. Nothing could have been more heartbreaking for Olgiati, who from his hiding place awaited anxiously to hear the cry *libertà! libertà!* but heard instead *Duca! Duca!* These encouraging signs led the ducal court to make an early optimistic assessment, confirmed shortly after by the depositions extracted under torture from the conspirators and by the relative calm prevailing in the Duchy, that the plot had verily been the work of three youths and that no person of authority was involved.[8]

Nevertheless it was deemed wise to be cautious and take ap-

[6] "Como mille volte me offersi, mi saria stato grato con le mane proprie farli li ultimi supplicii; et ch'el sia il vero, le V. S. debono sapere se yo fu il primario a farlo pigliare et accusare il loco dove l'hera" (Giacomino Olgiati to the Dukes, Milan, Jan. 29, 1477, Archivio di Stato di Milano (cited hereafter as ASM), *Potenze Sovrane*, cart. 1462. Cf. P. Ghinzoni, "Gerolamo Olgiati e i suoi denunziatori," *Archivio storico lombardo*, ser. 2, XX [1893], 970). This outburst of parental severity, condemned by Ghinzoni, may in tact have been nothing more than the anguished appeal of a father, who thus hoped to spare his son the tormented death that was surely to follow.

[7] Belotti, *Il dramma*, pp. 130–144.

[8] These events and the mood of the court in those fateful days are

propriate steps to prevent any disorders particularly because it was known that Galeazzo Maria's government was widely unpopular. Local officials were quickly informed of the Duke's murder and were instructed to be vigilant of the public order, while prominent persons were sent to various cities to exhort the people to remain calm and faithful to the Sforza.[9] Several of the reports by these officials expressed confidence in the ultimate loyalty of their districts, but some made it clear that outbursts of violence were to be expected unless reforms were forthcoming. The Bishop of Cremona, for example, complained that peasants in particular were being victimized by greedy ducal officers, and openly urged the Duchess to end the practice of selling offices and grant them instead to persons of merit drawing sufficient salary to encourage honesty. Dishonest officials, he maintained, should be brought to trial and punished.[10]

The court was already aware of these shortcomings. On the day of the assassination it took several measures to alleviate the plight of the people—food was to enter the cities of the Duchy without payment of tolls; the onerous and hated surtax on certain basic commodities (the *inquinto*) was abolished; all per-

---

described by two participants in its deliberations, who had witnessed the tragedy at Santo Stefano—Orfeo da Ricavo and Zaccaria de' Saggi di Pisa, the Mantuan ambassador. See the former's dispatch of Jan. 1, 1477, cited above, n. 5, and the latter's dispatches to Marquis Ludovico Gonzaga, Milan, Dec. 26, 27 and 28, 1476, Archivio di Stato di Mantova (cited hereafter as ASMA), *Milano-Carteggio*, busta 1625. Cf. the account written by another eyewitness, Bernardino Corio, *Storia di Milano*, ed. E. de Magri (Milan, 1857), III, 302 ff., who also gives the text of Gerolamo Olgiati's confession. However, in a forthcoming study Prof. Riccardo Fubini will attempt to establish wider internal ramifications of the conspiracy. I am indebted to Prof. Fubini for helpful suggestions.

[9] Zaccaria de' Saggi to L. Gonzaga, Milan, Dec. 27, 1476, ASMA, *Milano-Carteggio*, busta 1625.

[10] The Bishop of Cremona to the Duchess, Cremona, Dec. 29, 1476, ASM, *Potenze Sovrane*, cart. 1462. This *cartella* contains several other replies by local officials.

sons held in prison for nonpayment of taxes were to be released; goods unjustly confiscated by the *camera ducale* were to be restored; the many debts contracted by Galeazzo Maria were to be settled; payments made to the treasury by officeholders were to be refunded and henceforth these offices were to be freely granted to persons of merit.[11] These and other measures taken clearly point to a high degree of maladministration of the Duchy under Galeazzo Maria. To be sure, not all these ills can be attributed to him, for offices were commonly sold to the highest bidder under Filippo Maria Visconti and Francesco Sforza with deleterious effects in administration.[12] The fact is that Milan had for generations been subjected to heavy fiscal demands caused by the overly ambitious and irrational foreign policy of the last Visconti ruler, the struggle for the Milanese succession, and the extensive diplomatic and military effort of Francesco Sforza to maintain himself at Milan and ensure peace throughout the Italian peninsula. A little state of no more than a million inhabitants could not sustain indefinitely a prominent role in both Italian and European politics. Even under the benevolent government of the first Sforza Duke revolts by overtaxed peasants were not unknown.[13]

Galeazzo Maria's fiscal policy aggravated an already critical situation. His efforts to create a splendid court, the envy of all Italy, entailed liberal patronage of humanists, artists, and musicians. Great sums were spent for horses, dogs, falcons, and hunting parties. His generosity to his mistresses, particularly the beautiful Lucia Marliani, is well known. By far the largest

[11] These measures are listed by Zaccaria de' Saggi in his dispatches of Dec. 26 and 27, 1476, cited above, n. 8. Cf. Belotti, *Il dramma*, pp. 150–151.

[12] See F. Cognasso, *Treccani Storia di Milano*, Vol. VI (Milan, 1955), p. 502, and C. Santoro, *Gli Uffici del dominio sforzesco (1450–1500)* (Milan, 1948), pp. xvii-xviii.

[13] For popular dissatisfaction under Francesco Sforza, consult P. Ghinzoni, "Informazioni politiche sul Ducato di Milano (1461)," *Archivio storico lombardo*, ser. 2, IX (1892), 863–881.

expenditures were devoted to the army,[14] which backed a most ambitious and expensive foreign policy designed to make Milan's influence felt throughout Italy, and perhaps transform the Duchy into a kingdom. But Galeazzo Maria was neither a good general nor an astute diplomat. Unlike his father, he never had the occasion to lead an important campaign (despite his best efforts), and his foreign policy contributed to the breakup of the Italian League into separate, competing leagues —an evil that Francesco Sforza had tenaciously avoided.[15]

It is difficult to ascertain how far popular dissatisfaction was attributable to the Duke's personal vices and arbitrary rule. No biographer has yet provided a critical assessment of the man and his government. On the one hand there is the picture of the tyrant steeped in his pleasures, impulsive and capricious in his actions, and cruel in his punishment of those who spoke or wrote against him. On the other, there is the ruler promoting trade, introducing the cultivation of rice in Lombardy, issuing decrees for the beautification and sanitation of Milan, and patronizing arts and letters.[16] It has been rightly pointed out, however, that the most damaging evidence against Galeazzo Maria is contained in an appeal which Duchess Bona directed to Sixtus IV on behalf of the soul of her husband after due

[14] See G. P. Lambertenghi, "Preventivo delle spese pel Ducato di Milano del 1476," *Archivio storico lombardo* ser. 1, V (1878), 130–134. On the resources of the Duchy, consult C. Cipolla, "I precedenti economici," *Treccani Storia di Milano*, vol. VIII (Milan, 1957), pp. 369–373.

[15] F. Catalano, *Treccani Storia di Milano*, Vol. VII (Milan, 1956), pp. 229–309, *passim*, provides the best general account of Galeazzo Maria's foreign policy.

[16] The only modern biography of Galeazzo Maria is a popular and favorable one written by C. Violini, *Galeazzo Maria Sforza* (2d ed., Turin, 1943). Summary attempts to rehabilitate him, published by Motta, "Un documento," and G. Porro, "Lettere di Galeazzo Maria Sforza, Duca di Milano," *Archivio storico lombardo*, V (1878), 108–115, are not entirely convincing. Negative is the assessment by Belotti, *Il dramma*, pp. 18–33. More balanced evaluations are supplied by C. Santoro, *Gli Sforza* (Milan, 1968), pp. 111–178, and by Catalano, *Trec-*

consultation with a group of competent theologians and canonists. Considering that the late Duke had been guilty of innumerable offenses against God and man, including unjustified wars, plunder and destruction of property, extortions, conscious negligence of justice, imposition of new gabelles even on the clergy, notorious and scandalous simony, and carnal vices (offenses that he had already confessed and for which he had at times obtained absolution and bulls of dispensation—and believing that in his last moments he had shown signs of contrition and thus had presumably died in a state of grace), the Duchess implored the Pope to apply the inexhaustable merits of Christ and the Saints to free the tormented soul from Purgatory. For her part, Bona offered to make restitution wherever possible and contribute to the projected crusade against the Turks, though she preferred to spend these funds where the crimes had been committed by making appropriate donations to churches and charity. At the same time she expressed the willingness to undergo whatever penance the Pope imposed.[17] We do not know the final disposition of this pious appeal, which, however, tends to confirm the darker side of the Duke's character.

---

cani Storia, pp. 307–309. Among the Duke's contemporaries, his faithful secretary, Cicco Simonetta, emphasized his practice of consulting frequently with the Consiglio Segreto on all important matters. See *I diari di Cicco Simonetta*, ed. A. R. Natale (Milan, 1962), esp. pp. 273–280. G. P. Cagnola, *Storia di Milano*, ed. C. Cantù, in *Archivio storico italiano*, III (1842), 179, briefly praises his government, but mentions that he "fu alquanto macchiato da la libidine, et accumulò molto tesoro." More extensive and balanced are Corio's views (*Storia di Milano*, III, 313–315), who in extolling the Duke's virtues does not fail to list his vices: "sozza libidine," cruelty, greediness.

[17] See Bona's instructions to Don Celso de' Maffei, Augustinian Canon of the Lateran Congregation, Paris, Bibliothèque Nationale, *Fonds Italien*, Cod. 1592, fols. 95r-96r, followed by the written deliberation of a group of thelogians and canonists (*ibid.*, fol. 97r). Both are undated, but appear to have been drafted in January of 1477. They were published by P. D. Pasolini, *Caterina Sforza*, Vol. III (Rome, 1893), docs. 70-71, 30-33.

The evidence above indicates that while conditions for a widespread revolt were present in the Duchy, planning, organization, and leadership were lacking. Except for the city of Parma, where rival noble families set upon each other, and minor disturbances at several other localities, the only full-scale revolt took place at Genoa in the middle of March of 1477. Here long-standing dissatisfaction with Galeazzo Maria's high-handed policies, combined with the traditional Genoese penchant for turbulence, resulted in a revolt led by Obietto Fieschi in cooperation with the Doria and the Campofregoso clans, which forced the Milanese garrison to repair to the Castelletto. A month later, the rival clans of the Adorno and Spinola, backed by a Milanese army of some ten thousand men and small contingents sent by Florence, the Duke of Ferrara, and the Marquis of Monferrato, entered the city which remained under Milanese control until the following year.[18] Milan had thus put down its only serious revolt thanks to the energetic action of the Duchess and her advisers. It remains to be seen how these events were viewed by other Italian states—the major topic of this paper and one that was summarily treated by Belotti.

On the very day of the assassination, the Duchess sent letters to all Italian rulers announcing the tragic event and asking for their cooperation in the preservation of her state and the peace in Italy. Milan was confident that it was in the interest of all Italian powers, with the possible exception of Venice, to main-

[18] For details on the various disturbances and on this struggle with the Genoese rebels, see the dispatches of Zaccaria de' Saggi to L. Gonzaga, Milan, March 18, 19, 21, 23, 25, 27, 29, 31, and April 1, 1477, ASMA, *Milano-Carteggio*, busta 1626. Savona, on the other hand, remained faithful to the Sforza (G. Filippi, "Relazioni tra Savona e Firenze nell'anno 1477," *Giornale ligustico*, XVI [1889], 161–173). In June 1476, Genoese resentment against Galeazzo Maria's oppressive government, in marked contrast with his father's benevolent rule, had resulted in an abortive uprising led by Gerolamo Gentile (M. Rosi, "La congiura di Gerolamo Gentile," *Archivio storico italiano*, ser. 5, XVI [1895], 177–205).

tain the status quo. Some fears were felt about well-known Venetian territorial ambitions in Lombardy, should revolts break out in the Duchy. This estimate proved correct on the whole.[19]

One of the first rulers to heed the Duchess's appeal was the Marquis of Mantua, Ludovico Gonzaga, a long-standing friend and *condottiere* of the Sforza, who since 1470 held the title of Luogotenente Generale of the Duchy.[20] The Marquis acted promptly. Despite a lingering illness, which forced him to be carried on a litter, he advanced with his troops as far as Canneto and Marcaria on the borders of the Duchy, whence he soon returned home after it was established that no serious threat to the security of the state existed.[21] Late in January, however, the Marquis received an urgent call to come to Milan for the purpose of settling serious divisions that had arisen within the ducal court.[22] A struggle for power had developed around Bona of Savoy, who on January 9, 1477, had assumed, with the advice and consent of the Consiglio Segreto, the Regency and the tutelage of the seven-year-old Duke, Giangaleazzo. One faction, composed of Giovanni Pallavicino da Scipione, Pietro

[19] Zaccaria de' Saggi to L. Gonzaga, Milan, Dec. 26, 1476, cited above, n. 8. The Duke of Modena, Ercole d'Este, arrived independently at the same conclusion, discounting even the threat from Venice and from the Duke's uncles (Ercole d'Este to Virgilio Malvezzi, Ferrara, Dec. 31, 1476, Archivio di Stato di Modena, *Registri di Lettere*, Reg. 4 [940], fol. 121v, published by Belotti, *Il dramma*, pp. 162–163).

[20] In announcing the death of her husband, the Duchess requested Ludovico Gonzaga to keep his troops ready in case of need, and to prevent Paolo Campofregoso, Archbishop of Genoa, exiled to Mantua since 1471 by Galeazzo Maria, from leaving the city (Bona to L. Gonzaga, Dec. 26, 1476, ASMA, *Lettere dei Signori di Milano ai Gonzaga*, busta 1607, published by Belotti, *Il dramma*, pp. 187–188).

[21] Zaccaria de' Saggi to L. Gonzaga, Milan, Jan. 1, and 4, 1477, ASMA, *Carteggio-Milano*, B. 1626; the Dukes to L. Gonzaga, Milan, Jan. 11, 1477, ASMA, *Lettere dei Signori di Milano ai Gonzaga*, busta 1608; cf. L. Mazzoldi, *Storia di Mantova*, Vol. II (Mantua, 1961), p. 27.

[22] The Dukes to L. Gonzaga, Milan, Jan. 20, 1477, ASMA, *Lettere dei Signori di Milano ai Gonzaga*, busta 1608.

Francesco Visconti, Orfeo da Ricavo, Tristano Sforza, and Pietro da Landriano, and led by Cicco Simonetta, the old councillor and secretary of both Francesco Sforza and Galeazzo Maria, dominated the government. Simonetta's power and overbearing manner were resented by another faction which included Pietro da Pusterla, Giovanni Borromeo, Antonio Marliani, and Pietro da Birago. This group was headed by the ambitious *condottiere*, Roberto da Sanseverino, who wished above all to have the command of all Milanese troops in the absence of Ludovico Gonzaga, Lieutenant General, and the Marquis of Monferrato, Captain General.[23] The impending arrival of the Duke's two most troublesome uncles—Sforza Maria and Ludovico Maria, who had been relegated temporarily to France by Galeazzo Maria—raised fears of an imminent clash between the two factions.[24] The situation was tense, and Simonetta, in fear of his life, surrounded himself with a bodyguard.[25] Under these circumstances it was agreed by all to submit the

[23] Zaccaria de' Saggi to L. Gonzaga, Milan, Jan. 21, 26, 1477, ASMA, *Carteggio-Milano*, busta 1626. For Sanseverino's demands, which he reluctantly agreed to postpone for one year, see Zaccaria's dispatches of Jan. 6, 9, 1477, *ibid.*, and *Acta in Consilio Secreto in castello Portae Jovis Mediolani*, ed. A. R. Natale, Vol. I (Milan, 1963), pp. 4–7.

[24] Galeazzo Maria had deprived his brothers, especially the turbulent Sforza Maria, Duke of Bari, and Ludovico, of any effective power in the Duchy. When the Duke fell, both were in France having left Milan on Nov. 30, 1476 ostensibly to visit Louis XI (*I diari di Cicco Simonetta*, p. 224). They returned by separate routes—probably fearing harm— Sforza Maria by the Moncenisio pass, arriving in Milan on January 25; Ludovico by the St. Bernard route, arriving two days later (Zaccaria de' Saggi to L. Gonzaga, Milan, Jan. 25, 27, 1477, ASMA, *Carteggio-Milano*, busta 1626).

[25] Zaccaria de' Saggi reported to L. Gonzaga (Milan, Jan. 21, 1477, ASMA, *Carteggio-Milano*, busta 1626) that "col Signor Roberto concorreno di voluntà tutti gli altri del Consiglio [usque ad unum], e parmi comprehendere che se Messer Cecho non muta proposito e non tiene altra via, ch'el sia in mal luoco e stia a grandissimo periculo, che se bene el sta in castello e con guardia de provisonati, non è però che non gli possi esser fatto la beffa in quelle camere, che non serà chi l'aiuti né che ne dichi parola, tanto è malvolsuto da tutti generalmente."

questions at issue to the arbitration of the old ruler of Mantua, who was widely respected for his integrity.[26]

Before Gonzaga's arrival, Sanseverino and his faction had forced Simonetta to vacate the chambers formerly occupied by Galeazzo Maria and to reside in the Chancery. Bona was made to promise that she would govern with the advice and consent of Sforza Maria and Ludovico Maria, who would have places in a reconstituted Consiglio Segreto composed of old councillors of Galeazzo Maria and members of the two factions, the Whites and the Blacks.[27]

The ailing Marquis arrived in Milan on February 6 and was housed in a suite of rooms in the Castello di Porta Giovia, where one of the chambers was large enough to hold all the members of the Consiglio Segreto.[28] On the 24th he rendered his arbitral sentence confirming the Regency of the Duchess and the tutelage of her son. Each of Bona's five brothers-in-law—Ludovico Maria, Sforza Maria, Filippo Maria, Ascanio, and Ottaviano—was granted an annual pension of 12,500 ducats, a retinue of a hundred men at arms, and the restoration of all castles and lands of which they had been deprived by Galeazzo Maria. In addition each was assigned a palace in Milan. For their part, they

[26] Simonetta had at first opposed the invitation to Gonzaga, preferring instead the presence in Milan of the Duke of Urbino, who, however, was disliked by the opposite faction (Zaccaria de' Saggi to L. Gonzaga, Milan, Jan. 11, 21, 27, 1477, *ibid.*).

[27] Among the former councillors of Galeazzo Maria were Giovanni Pallavicino de Scipione, Pietro Francesco Visconti, Pietro de Gallarate, and Orfeo da Ricavo. Among the Whites were Pietro da Pusterla, Giovanni Borromeo, and Antonio Marliani. The Blacks included the Bishop of Como, Agostino Rossi, and Giovanni Giacomo Trivulzio. Tristano Sforza, and his brother, Sforza, as well as Pietro da Landriano were also given membership in the new Council. Roberto da Sanseverino held the first place until the arrival of Gonzaga (Zaccaria de' Saggi to L. Gonzaga, Milan, Jan. 31, 1477, *ibid.*).

[28] Zaccaria de' Saggi to L. Gonzaga, Milan, Feb. 4, 1477, *ibid.* Details on the accommodations prepared for the Marquis in the castle, which reveal interesting sidelights of the internal struggle, are given in Zaccaria's dispatches of Jan. 26, 31, 1477, *ibid.*

renounced any ambition to take over the government and swore allegiance to the Regent and the young Duke. In April Ludovico and Ottaviano helped to suppress the Genoese revolt.[29] The month-long residence of Gonzaga at Milan had thus served to ward off the most serious threat to the internal stability of the Duchy. It soon became evident, however, that the opposition had sought only to buy time, for three months later the Sforza brothers and Sanseverino attempted a coup d'etat, promptly crushed by Simonetta, who remained the all powerful minister of the Regent for the next three years.[30]

At the papal court the death of Galeazzo Maria caused great concern, and it is said that Sixtus IV, upon hearing the news, exclaimed: "The peace of Italy died today." [31] There was reason for this pessimism. Despite Galeazzo Maria's tortuous foreign policy, the secret ramifications of which were not yet known, he was widely regarded as an effective obstacle to Venetian expansion in Italy and to King Ferrante's hegemonic ambitions, as well as a ready bulwark against any French intervention in the peninsula. A prolonged dynastic crisis in the Duchy could have involved all the Italian powers in a second war of Milanese succession, and retarded indefinitely papal plans for a joint effort against the ever menacing Turkish advances in the Balkans.[32] Finally any threat to the Sforza dynasty at this time was not in the interest of the Pope whose favorite nephew, Girolamo Riario, had been betrothed three years earlier to Caterina Sforza, the ten-year-old natural daughter of the late Duke.[33]

[29] See *Acta in Consilio Secreto*, Vol. I, p. 8, and Santoro, *Gli Sforza*, pp. 182, 187. Gonzaga left Milan on March 12 (The Dukes to Leonardo Botta, Milan, Mach 15, 1477, ASM, *Potenze Estere* (cited hereafter as P. E.) *Venezia*, cart. 363).

[30] Sforza Maria, Ludovico, and Ascanio were exiled (Santoro, *Gli Sforza*, pp. 187–190).

[31] "Oggi è morta la pace d'Italia" (Corio, *Storia di Milano*, III, 315).

[32] Cf. Catalano, *Treccani Storia*, VII, 311.

[33] On the background of this marriage, see E. Breisach, *Caterina Sforza: A Renaissance Virago* (Chicago and London, 1967), pp. 18–23.

The day after the news of the assassination reached Rome on December 31, the Pope ordered Girolamo Riario to place his troops at the disposal of the Duchy, and wrote to all Italian rulers to remain at peace and support the new Duke of Milan. At the same time he appointed a special envoy, Bartolomeo Marasca, Bishop of Città di Castello, to offer condolences and support to the Regent. Late in January Sixtus also dispatched to Milan a legate *de latere*, Giovanni Battista Mellini, Cardinal of Urbino, to lend more prestige to the Duchess and to celebrate by proxy the marriage of Caterina Sforza to Girolamo Riario, who was unable to leave Rome.[34]

Both the Bishop and the Cardinal had also been charged to mediate an accord between the Duchess and the brothers, Obietto and Giovanni Luigi Fieschi, influential Genoese exiles whose possessions had been confiscated by Galeazzo Maria. The Pope, who had attempted to heal this feud before the Duke's death, now intensified his efforts in the hope of preventing the Fieschi from fomenting a revolt at Genoa. He ordered Obietto to remain in Rome and refrain from any anti-Milanese activity pending the outcome of the negotiations which were being carried out at Milan by his brother.[35] But Sixtus's efforts to keep his fellow Ligurians loyal to Milan, which were vigorously promoted by Girolamo Riario and undermined by Cardinal Giuliano della Rovere's support of the

[34] For this papal activity on behalf of Milan, consult Zaccaria de' Saggi to L. Gonzaga, Milan, Jan. 5, 1477, ASMA, *Carteggio-Milano*, busta 1626; cf. Girolamo Riario to the Duchess, Rome, Jan. 1, 1477, ASM, *P. E. Roma*, cart. 83. The marriage ceremony was performed some time in April without the usual festivities owing to the official period of mourning at court. The bride left soon after for Rome where late in May a solemn celebration took place (Breisach, *Caterina Sforza*, pp. 26–31).

[35] Sagramoro Sagramori, Bishop of Parma and Milanese ambassador at the papal court, to Galeazzo Maria, Rome, Dec. 15, 20, 1476, *P. E. Roma*, cart. 82. On January 5, 1477, Obietto Fieschi wrote to the Balia and the Consiglio degli Anziani of Genoa requesting their support for his negotiations with the Regent and promising to remain loyal to Milan if his possessions were restored (*ibid.*, cat. 1202).

exiles despite strong papal admonitions,[36] failed in the end mostly because the Regent was willing to grant only a partial restoration of the Fieschi's possessions.[37] At the beginning of March, Obietto fled from Rome to Ostia whence he sailed shortly after to join the revolt already in progress at Genoa (March 19).[38] The Pope's subsequent fulminations against the Genoese rebels, including the threat of excommunication, proved to be less potent than Milanese arms.[39]

Outwardly at least a similar solicitude for Milan was publicly displayed with surprising eagerness by King Ferrante of Naples, whose recent relations with Galeazzo Maria had been anything but cordial. During the 1470s the King had in fact become increasingly estranged from other Italian heads of state, who viewed with suspicion and rancor his aggressive and shifting foreign policy. Obsessed by the ever present French threat to his throne, Ferrante resented the francophile policy of Florence and Milan, while his hegemonic ambitions clashed both with Galeazzo Maria's royal aspirations and with Venetian domination of the Adriatic. The conclusion of an alliance

[36] The Bishop of Parma and Giovanni Angelo da Firenze to the Dukes, Rome, March 27, 29, 1477, and the Bishop of Parma to the Dukes, April 11, 12, 20, 27, 1477, *ibid.*, cart. 83.

[37] The Duchess had agreed to reinstate G. L. Fieschi in some of his lands and grant him a compensation of 200 to 300 ducats. His brother, Obietto, was to receive 800 to 1,000 ducats yearly until such time as he would be granted lands producing that income (Zaccaria de' Saggi to L. Gonzaga, Milan, March 16, 1477, ASMA, *Carteggio-Milano*, busta 1626).

[38] In an effort to forestall Obietto's departure for Genoa, the Pope offered him asylum in papal territory while the agreement was being negotiated; but Obietto advanced preposterous demands, such as control of the castle of Civitavecchia or Ostia pending the release of his brother, held hostage in Milan, and these negotiations broke down (Obietto to the Pope, Ostia, March 5, 1477, ASM, *P. E. Roma*, cart. 83; Zaccaria de' Saggi to L. Gonzaga, Milan, March 23, 1477, ASMA, *Carteggio-Milano*, busta 1626).

[39] The Bishop of Parma and Giovanni Angelo da Firenze to the Dukes, Rome, March 25, 29, 1477, ASM, *P. E. Roma*, cart. 83.

among Florence, Venice, and Milan (November 2, 1474), in which the allies had reserved a place for the Pope and the King only to demonstrate their lingering attachment to the ideal of the *lega universale* (Italian League), which had been renewed in 1470 for another twenty-five year period, aggravated the antipathy between Ferrante and Galeazzo Maria.[40] Illustrative of this tension is the fact that there was no Milanese resident ambassador at Naples in 1476 though there had been one continuously from 1455 onward.[41] Nevertheless throughout 1476 there was talk of reconciliation initiated by Galeazzo Maria who, concerned over his sinking alliance with Burgundy and fearful of Louis XI, encouraged the King's son-in-law, Duke Ercole I of Ferrara, to sound out the Neapolitan court. A rapproachment with Ferrante was to be the prelude for the revival of the Italian League as the most effective weapon against the French threat.[42] Another approach was made through the Duke of Urbino in response to which the King

[40] For an analysis of Ferrante's foreign policy, see particularly E. Pontieri, *Per la storia del Regno di Ferrante I d'Aragona, Re di Napoli* (Naples, 1947), pp. 115–158. On the operation of the Italian League and its breakup into separate alliances, consult G. Nebbia, "La lega italica del 1455: sue vicende e sua rinnovazione nel 1470," *Archivio storico lombardo*, new ser., IV (1939), 115–135; and R. Cessi, "La 'lega italica' e la sua funzione storica nella seconda metá del sec. XV," *Atti del Regio Istituto Veneto di Scienze, Lettere ed Arti*, CII, p. II (1943), 158–168. Galeazzo Maria's ambivalent attitude toward the Italian League is illustrated by Catalano, *Treccani Storia*, VII, 298–299.

[41] The last Milanese ambassador was Francesco Maletta (ASM, *P. E. Napoli*, cart. 228). See also L. Cerioni, *La diplomazia sforzesca nella seconda metá del Quattrocento e i suoi cifrari segreti*, Vol. I (Rome, 1970), pp. 102–103.

[42] Galeazzo Maria made the approach through Niccolò de' Roberti, ambassador of Ferrara at Milan, following which Duke Ercole ascertained Ferrante's willingness for reconciliation and his readiness to defend Milan against all enemies (Duke Ercole to Roberti, Ferrara, March 15, April 23, and May 11, 1476, Archivio di Stato di Modena, *Carteggio degli Ambasciatori-Milano*, busta 1). Earlier the Duke of Milan had urged the Pope to revive the Italian League and allow all the members to preserve their respective alliances in Italy and elsewhere

expressed the view that an open rapprochment would have been difficult because of expected Florentine opposition and the recently concluded Triple Alliance. He proposed instead a secret understanding according to which the two rulers would agree to make the necessary military preparations, and then announce their alliance, thus confronting Florence with a *fait accompli*.[43] It is evident that Ferrante was more interested in detaching Milan from its allies than in achieving a genuine reconciliation.

The assassination put an end to these discussions, but not to the King's efforts to break-up the Triple Alliance, unless one wishes to take at face value Ferrante's public reaction of profound sorrow and concern for the preservation of the Duchy. Not only did he quickly communicate this concern to all the Italian heads of state, but he also wrote to Genoa and other cities of the Duchy, as well as to leading Milanese nobles and officials, exhorting them to remain loyal to the Regent. He announced that his troops were ready to defend Milan and that he was sending all available galleys to Genoa to be at hand for any eventuality. The Duke of Urbino was instructed to go to Milan and lend his prestige to the new rulers. The Neapolitan envoy at Ferrara was ordered to "fly" to Milan, while a special

---

since these were defensive in character (Galeazzo Maria to the Bishop of Parma, Pavia, Feb. 16, 1476, ASM, *P. E. Roma*, cart. 1202. Similar discussions were taking place in Florence among Lorenzo, Marino Tomacello, Neapolitan ambassador, and the Milanese envoy, Filippo Sagramoro, in the wake of Charles the Bold's defeat by the Swiss at Grandson, March 2, 1476 (Sagramoro to Galeazzo Maria, Florence, May 4, 1476, Paris, Bibliothèque Nationale, *Fonds Italien*, Cod. 1592, fols. 74r-75r).

[43] Ferrante's plan had been revealed in general terms to the Milanese ambassador at the Curia by the Cardinal of Naples, Olivieri Carafa, who had just returned from the royal court. The Cardinal emphasized that he had not pressed the King for details because he did not wish to interfere with the discussions already initiated through the Duke of Urbino (The Bishop of Parma to Galeazzo Maria, Rome, Dec. 24, 1476, ASM, *P. E. Roma*, cart. 82).

ambassador, Antonio Cicinello, was making hasty preparations for his journey to the ducal court.[44]

This feverish activity on behalf of Milan was interpreted by Florence and Venice as another Neapolitan attempt to detach the Duchy from the Triple Alliance.[45] The Pope, aware of these suspicions, opposed the projected trip of the Duke of Urbino, which he had favored at first, on the ground that the dual capacity of the Duke, as *condottiere* of the King and gonfalonier of the Church, added to the presence in Milan of the Cardinal of Urbino, could be regarded as a joint effort of the Holy See and Naples to break up the Triple Alliance. In vain did the Neapolitan ambassador at the papal court, Anello Archamono, attempt to allay these fears by arguing that Florence and Venice had no reason to suspect any royal design over Milan since it was common knowledge that the King was only acting out of friendship, marriage ties, and gratitude to Francesco Sforza who had saved his kingdom. Neither could they suspect the motives of the Pope who, as leader of Christendom, was interested in peace and whose legate represented only the Holy See.[46] Nevertheless the Duke never made the trip, which was quickly postponed and then canceled by the King on the ground that the situation at Milan no longer re-

---

[44] Ferrante's letters of Jan. 4, 1477, addressed to the cities of Tortona, Novara, and Alessandria, are in ASM, *P. E. Napoli*, cart. 228. His activity in support of Milan is outlined by the Mantuan ambassador, who had seen this "infinitate di littere" reaching the court (Zaccaria de' Saggi to L. Gonzaga, Milan, Jan. 14, 1477, ASMA, *Carteggio-Milano*, busta 1626). Cicinello arrived at Cremona on February 22, and was expected at Lodi on the 24th (Cicinello to Francesco Maletta, Cremona, Feb. 22, 1477, and Maletta to the Duchess, Lodi, Feb. 23, 1477, ASM, *P. E. Napoli*, cart. 228).

[45] To allay Venetian suspicions, Ferrante assured Venice through his ambassador that he would notify the Republic of any specific measures he was taking on behalf of Milan (Leonardo Botta to the Dukes, Venice, Jan. 17, 1477, ASM, *P. E. Venezia*, cart. 1062).

[46] Archamono and Agostino da Urbino to the Duke of Urbino, Rome, Jan. 25, 1477, ASM, *P. E. Roma*, cart. 83.

quired it.[47] But the suspicions continued at the papal court. The fact that the Genoese rebels had appealed to the King for aid,[48] and that Archamono continually pressed for an accord with them, pointing to the danger of French intervention at Genoa, lent credibility to rumors, largely disseminated by the Venetian ambassador, that Ferrante wished to take advantage of the Genoese revolt for his own purposes.[49] The King's alleged attempts to foment revolt at Genoa nine months earlier had not been forgotten.[50] It is also probable that by this time his secret project to dethrone the Sforza and install his second son, Federico, as Imperial Vicar at Milan through his marriage with Frederick III's daughter, Kunigunde, had leaked out.[51]

In this atmosphere of suspicion it is not surprising that the intentions of Milan's own ally, Venice, were also being questioned. Like Ferrante, the Republic was widely suspected of

[47] Ferrante to the Duke of Urbino, Tripelgulis, Jan. 7, 1477, ASM, P. E. Napoli, cart. 228.

[48] It is to be noted, however, that Archamono, who was showing all possible signs of friendship to Milan, disclosed these overtures to his Milanese colleagues (The Bishop of Parma and Giovanni Angelo da Firenze to the Dukes, Rome, March 27, 1477, ASM, P. E. Roma, cart. 83).

[49] The Bishop of Parma to the Dukes, Rome, April 3, 12, 1477, ASM, ibid. Arousing suspicion was also the fact that long-promised Neapolitan galleys were allegedly delayed by bad weather and did not reach Leghorn until March 29 (Filippo Sagramoro to the Dukes, Florence, March 30, 1477, ASM, P. E. Firenze, cart. 293). On the other hand, Ferrante had written to Obietto Fieschi and to the Otto Difensori of Genoa on April 5, 1477 (ASM, P. E. Napoli, cart. 228), urging them to reach an accord with Milan, and had instructed Cicinello to work toward that end. Did Cicinello have secret instructions to promote Neapolitan ambitions at Genoa?

[50] Rosi, "La congiura di Gerolamo Gentile," p. 193, claims that the rumors about Ferrante's involvement in Gentile's revolt have no foundation.

[51] As early as May of 1476, Galeazzo Maria had suspected such a plan, which was also promoted by Ferrante's son-in-law, Mathias Corvinus, both as an anti-French and anti-Venetian move. Kunigunde later married Albert the Wise, Duke of Bavaria. See F. Cusin, "I rapporti tra

having hegemonic aspirations. Galeazzo Maria, who had never lost hope of regaining the territories lost with the treaty of Lodi (Crema, Bergamo, and Brescia), regarded his alliance with Venice as a temporary alignment dictated by their mutual antagonism toward Ferrante. His death, therefore, aroused the fear that Venice might be tempted to resume her march into Lombardy should widespread revolts erupt in the Duchy.[52]

Officially the Republic maintained a correct and even cordial attitude toward the Regent. The Signoria promptly wrote to all Italian rulers recommending the preservation of the territorial integrity of the Duchy, and elected two ambassadors, Vittore Soranzo and Zaccaria Barbaro, to express condolences and offer aid and support to the Duchess.[53] It also summoned the Neapolitan and Estense envoys to whom it expressed its anguish for the death of its ally and "most beloved brother," for whose heirs it was ready to do as much as it would do for Venice itself.[54] As an immediate demonstration of good will,

---

la Lombardia e l'Impero dalla morte di Francesco Sforza all'avvento di Lodovico il Moro (1466–1480)," *Annali della Regia Università degli Studi Economici e Commerciali di Trieste*, VI (1934), 303–304; cf. L. Sorricchio, "Angelo ed Antonio Probi, ambasciatori di Ferdinando I d'Aragona (1464–82)," *Archivio storico per le province napoletane*, XXI (1896), 150.

[52] See above, p. 81. For the uneasy relations between Galeazzo Maria and Venice, consult Catalano, *Treccani Storia*, VII, 267–269, 298–299.

[53] The Signoria's letters to various heads of state, dated Dec. 30, 1477, are in the Archivio di Stato di Venezia (cited hereafter as ASV), *Senato Secreta*, Reg. 27, fols. 116r–117r. On December 29, two other ambassadors, Bernardo Giustiniani and Marco Barbarigo, had been designated for the mission, but they were excused on the following day and Soranzo and Barbaro took their places (*ibid.*, Reg. 27, fol. 115v and Reg. 28, fol. 118v). For their instructions by Doge Andrea Vendramin, dated Jan. 7, 1477, see *ibid.*, Reg. 28, fols. 121r–122r.

[54] "che dello horrendo caso intervenuto nella persona dello Ill.mo quondam Ducha de Milano, questo Ex.mo Dominio se ne ritrovava tanto adolorato quanto de calamità fusse potuta intervenire in questi tempi ad Italia, et che questa Republica riputava havere perso non solum uno honorevole et potentissimo consocio, ma uno amantissimo

Venice allowed grain imported from Puglia, under a special license issued by Ferrante, to be shipped to its docks, and thence forwarded to Milan, without retaining the customary third in order to relieve a serious shortage in the Duchy and thus prevent possible disorders.[55]

These assurances of wholehearted support, however, were not matched by deeds. The Senate refused to provide for the arrest of some of the Milanese conspirators, who had taken refuge in the Valley of San Martino near Bergamo, on the ground that this was contrary to Venetian laws and that in any case their conscience forbade sending people to a certain death. They agreed to expel them and deny refuge to others who might follow.[56] Likewise the Signoria turned down a request

---

et cordiale fratello, per il bene delli heredi del quale confessavano essere debitori dovere fare quanto fariano per la salute de questa propria città" (Leonardo Botta, Milanese ambassador in Venice, to the Duchess, Venice, Dec. 31, 1476, ASM, P. E. Venezia, cart. 362). This dispatch reveals that the news of the assassination had reached Venice by December 28.

[55] Milan had to pay customs duties on the grain since these were farmed out to private interests (The Duchess to Botta, Milan, Jan. 16, 1477, ASM, P. E. Venezia, cart. 1062, and Botta to the Dukes, Venice, Mar. 5, 7, 1477, ibid., cart. 363). By late April the Duchy's needs for grain had been met, and the Milanese ambassador planned to sell the surplus on the Venetian market (Botta to the Dukes Venice, April 29, 1477, ibid., cart. 1062).

[56] The Regent had communicated to Botta (Milan, Jan. 6, 1477, ibid., cart. 1062) the names and descriptions of the persons involved, and had sent to Venice an agent, Giacomino da Riva, to aid the search. The Signoria had at first authorized the apprehension of the conspirators (Botta to the Duchess, Venice, Jan. 13, 1477, ibid., cart. 1062), but it soon changed its mind (Botta to the Dukes, Venice, Jan. 20, 22, 1477, Paris, Bibliothèque Nationale, Fonds Italien, Cod. 1592, fol. 103, and ASM, P. E. Venezia, cart. 1062, respectively). It should be noted, however, that early in February the Signoria proposed a convention according to which exiles and rebels of either state would be denied refuge in their respective territories. Bona refused to negotiate the agreement for unknown reasons and ordered Botta to drop the matter

for five hundred foot soldiers to help Milanese forces suppress the Genoese revolt, pointing to the Turkish threat at their borders, and alleging that such token aid would only serve to foster Genoese unity against their old Venetian rivals. They advised the Duchess to regain the city by persuasion and negotiations, and avoid force if possible, so as to prevent the solidification of Genoese opposition to Milanese rule. This response did not convince the Milanese ambassador, Leonardo Botta, who learned through reliable sources that the Senate was divided between those who favored the request and those who were happy to see the Genoese so deeply involved in turmoil that they would have little time for commercial pursuits.[57]

It should be noted that this request for troops had actually been made to test Venetian intentions.[58] The negative response, which was contrary to the spirit and terms of the alliance, served only to revive anti-Venetian feeling in Milan and elsewhere. At the papal court the pro-Genoese faction was spreading rumors that Venice had refused to aid Milan because the Republic had from the beginning incited the revolt and was making preparations to attack the Duchy in support of the

---

(The Duchess to Botta, Milan, Feb. 12, 1477, ASM, *P. E. Venezia*, cart. 363).

[57] The Duchess made the request through Botta on March 21 (ASM, *P. E. Venezia*, cart. 363). For the ambassador's efforts to obtain the aid and for the Venetian responses, see his dispatches of March 22, 24, 26, 27, 1477, *ibid.*, cart. 363, and ASV, *Senato Secreta*, Reg. 28, March 26, 1477, fol. 4r-4v. The division within the Venetian government on this matter is illustrated by the fact that in an earlier dispatch of March 27 (ASM, *P. E. Venezia*, cart. 363), Botta reported having received assurances by the Signoria that it was willing to give more military aid than had been requested, and that it was sending a fleet to capture the Genoese island of Chios to prevent its falling to the Turks and to show the solidarity of the Triple Alliance.

[58] Officially the Regent accepted with grace the Venetian response, but in a separate note to Botta she confided the real purpose of the request and instructed him to be more vigilant about Venetian moves

rebels.[59] The fact that the rebels made overtures to Venice [60] and that the Signoria was recruiting troops in lands bordering on the Duchy (a practice suspiciously queried by the Regent) [61] lent additional credibility to the rumors. Milanese suspicion had been aroused to such an extent that when Soranzo and Barbaro signified their intention to prolong their stay at the ducal court, the Duchess instructed Botta to work diligently but discreetly to have them recalled "the sooner the better." [62] In the meantime the Regent attempted to limit their contacts to trustworthy persons and sought to prevent any unfavorable news about conditions in the Duchy from reaching them.[63] Finally the Signoria bowed to pressure exerted by the Milanese ambassador, who argued that the best way to convince the

---

(The Duchess to Botta, Milan, April 1, 1477, ASM, *P. E. Venezia*, cart. 1062).

[59] These rumors were largely spread by Bishop Urbano Fieschi and Cardinal Giuliano della Rovere (The Bishop of Parma to the Dukes, Rome, April 12, 1477, *P. E. Roma*, cart. 83). In a second dispatch of the same date (*ibid.*), the envoy reported that the Pope suspected both Venice and Naples of having had a hand in the Genoese revolt, and that he had tried to allay Sixtus's fears of an imminent Venetian attack on Milan.

[60] The Duchess to Botta, Milan, April 6, 7, 1477, ASM, *P. E. Venezia*, cart. 363 and 1062, respectively. After the revolt was crushed, Obietto Fieschi requested from Venice a subsidy of 6,000 ducats with which he planned to gather an army for the purpose of recapturing Genoa and placing it under a Venetian protectorate. The Doge rejected the proposal and so informed the Milanese ambassador (Botta to the Dukes, Venice, April 28, 1477, *ibid.*, cart. 1062).

[61] Botta to the Dukes, Venice, March 10, 1477, *ibid.*, cart. 363, and Bona to Botta, Milan, April 10, 14, 1477, *ibid.*, cart. 363 and 1062, respectively.

[62] "Questi magnifici ambaxatori demonstrano volere fare qui longa dimora, cosa che ad noi non piaceria, perché non vedemo esserli alcuno nostro proposito in lo restare loro. Unde volemo che dextramente, et non demonstrando che venga da noi, procuriati siano revocati più presto meglio, et in questo usati omne vostro ingenio ad ciò omnino sensa tardità quella S. ria gli rechiami" (Bona to Botta, Milan, Jan. 18, 1477, *ibid.*, cart. 1062).

[63] Botta to the Dukes, Venice, Feb. 17, 22, 1477, *ibid.*, cart. 362.

world that all was well at Milan was to have all ambassadors return home with Venice setting the example, and recalled its envoys on January 30, barely two weeks after their arrival.[64] On February 13 they reentered amid complaints that they had not been made welcome. The envoys made a pessimistic report predicting violent upheavals in the Duchy owing to profound divisions in the ducal court and to the fact that leading citizens had bought arms and fortified their houses.[65] This confirmed Venetian skepticism toward the optimistic reports spread by Botta, a skepticism that had prompted the Council of Ten to take exclusive charge of the Venetian mission to Milan.[66]

There seems to be no evidence, however, that the Republic had any intention, let alone plans, to invade the Duchy which would have provoked a general war in Italy at the very time when she was facing a serious Turkish threat at her eastern frontiers. Throughout 1476 Venice had suffered heavy losses through Turkish incursions in Albania and in the Friuli region, and massive attacks were expected in the spring of the following year.[67] In the West the final triumph of Louis XI over Charles the Bold not only aggravated the danger posed by the

[64] The Venetian ambassadors arrived at Milan on January 15 and they were given an audience the following day (Bona to Botta, Milan, Jan. 18, 1477, *ibid.*, cart. 1062). They planned to leave Milan on February 6 (Zaccaria de' Saggi to L. Gonzaga, Milan, Feb. 3, 1477, ASMA, *Carteggio-Milano*, busta 1626). Botta's efforts to have them recalled and the Senate's decision on this matter are related in his dispatch of Jan. 31, 1477, ASM, *P. E. Venezia*, cart. 362.

[65] Botta to the Dukes, Venice, Feb. 13, 17, 22, 1477, ASM, *P. E. Venezia*, cart. 362. The Signoria's charges that the ambassadors had been mistreated by a Milanese official, Giuliano da Varese, and that they had been poorly received, were denied by the Duchess (Bona to Botta, Milan, Feb. 7, 1477, *ibid.*, cart. 363).

[66] Botta to the Dukes, Venice, Jan. 28, 1477, *ibid.*, cart. 362. Venetian skepticism in reference to conditions in the Duchy is particularly illustrated in Botta's dispatch of March 2, 1477, *ibid.*, cart. 363.

[67] On Venetian fears of the Turkish threat and the preparations being made to meet it, see particularly Botta to the Dukes, Venice, March 13, 31, 1477, *ibid.*, cart. 363, and April 29, 1477, *ibid.*, cart. 1062.

French fleet against Venetian convoys in the Atlantic, but raised fears over that King's aggressive intentions in Italy itself. The Signoria and leading patricians confessed these fears to the Milanese ambassador, pointing out that Italy was threatened by two dragons—the Turks and Louis XI—and warning that Italy should remain at peace and keep them away from its borders imitating nature that had placed steep mountains in their way.[68] A strong Duchy could have provided protection against the western threat, but Venice knew from past experience that she would have to face her eastern enemy alone as indeed happened in the autumn of 1477 when the fires of the invaders in the Friuli could be seen from the bell tower of St. Mark's.[69] Under these circumstances, the Venetian denial of military aid against the Genoese rebels seems to have been dictated more by the Republic's own needs to protect its borders than by any desire to gain commercial advantage over the Genoese.

With her other ally, Florence, Milan enjoyed more cordial

[68] In a dispatch of February 17, 1477, *ibid.*, cart. 362, Botta reported the exact words of the warning as follows: "Ambassatore, ell'è necessario che nuy tuti siamo molto savii e che se may Italia stete in pace, che la stia al presente, perché essendo manchato el Duca de Burgogna et facendossi grande el Re de Franza, como el sarà, la natura del quale è inquieta et avida de havere de quello del compagno, potremo dire che Italia haverà duy draghi alle spalle, uno da uno canto et l'altro da l'altro, videlicet el Turco et dicto Re, li quali non expectariano altro se non che li celi gli offeresseno una comodità de potere satisfare alli loro appetiti. Siché lasciamoli luntani piú che potemo et imittemo la natura, la quale per monti asperrimi gli ha distincti et divisi da nuy." Portions of this dispatch were published by E. Motta, "Cassandra nel 1477," *Archivio Veneto*, XXXVI (1888), 377–378. On January 9, 1478, Venice signed a peace treaty with Louis XI which put an end to several years of French harassment of Venetian convoys in the Atlantic. On Franco-Venetian relations at this time, consult P. M. Perret, *Histoire des relations de la France avec Venise du XIIIᵉ siècle à l'avènement de Charles VIII*, Vol. II (Paris, 1896), pp. 1–115.

[69] F. Babinger, *Maometto il Conquistatore e il suo tempo*, trans. E. Polacco (Turin, 1957), pp. 526–529.

relations, the basis of which had been laid by Cosimo de' Medici and Francesco Sforza. This tradition of friendship was continued by Lorenzo and Galeazzo Maria, though not to the same degree of intimacy owing mostly to the inconstant nature of the latter.[70] Thus when the news of the assassination reached Florence on December 29, the saddened Signoria took only one hour and a half to appoint Tommaso Soderini and Luigi Guicciardini as ambassadors charged to convey condolences and offer assistance to the Duchess, and ordered that letters be addressed to various heads of state inviting them to support the new rulers.[71]

The ambassadors left the next day. In the quickly drafted instructions, they were charged to convey to the Regent the profound grief of the Republic and its resolve to do all in its power for the protection of Milan as provided in their alliance. They were also to recommend Cicco Simonetta to the Duchess, a clear indication that the Florentines wished to preserve the leading role of the faithful councillor who for so many years had been friendly to Florence.[72] Lorenzo wrote in his own hand, promising to do all in his power for the Duchy, "as long as he had life in his body, and if that failed, he would leave instructions in his will for his sons to do the same." [73]

[70] For relations between Lorenzo and Galeazzo Maria, see Catalano, *Treccani Storia*, VII, 263–309 *passim*, and C. B. Uricchio, "I rapporti fra Lorenzo il Magnifico e Galeazzo Maria Sforza negli anni 1471–1473," *Archivio storico lombardo*, ser. 9, IV (1964–1965), 33–49.

[71] Filippo Sagramoro, Milanese ambassador in Florence, to the Duchess, Florence, Dec. 29, 1476, ASM, *P. E. Firenze*, cart. 291. The Signoria's letters to Bona, Sixtus IV, Ferrante, and Venice were published by Casanova, "L'uccisione," docs. I-IV, pp. 310–313.

[72] The instructions are dated December 29, but the note of recommendation for Simonetta bears the date of December 31 (Casanova, "L'uccisione," docs. XI-XII, pp. 316–317).

[73] "Finché gli durerà la vita, e manchando quella, lasserà per testamento a suoi figliuoli che facenio el medesimo." The contents of Lorenzo's letter are related in Zaccaria de' Saggi's dispatch to L. Gonzaga, Milan, Jan. 5, 1477, ASMA, *Carteggio-Milano*, busta 1626.

This time the promises of an ally were backed up by deeds. At the request of the Regent, the Signoria promptly ordered its troops stationed at Sarzana to cooperate with Milanese forces in keeping order in the Genoese riviera. Transit through Florentine territory was denied to Genoese exiles and orders were given for their arrest should they attempt to cross the frontier.[74] At the same time Lorenzo attempted unsuccessfully to mediate an accord between Milan and one of the powerful Genoese clans in exile, the Campofregoso.[75] When the revolt finally broke out, the Signoria quickly dispatched the Commissary, Antonio Ridolfi, with more troops than had been requested and placed them under Milanese command.[76] Although these measures were partly prompted by reports that the Genoese were planning to give the city to their enemy, Ferrante, they nonetheless display an intelligent, if not altruistic conviction

[74] Bona to Sagramoro, Milan, Jan. 13, 1477, and Sagramoro to Bona, Jan. 8, 10, 1477, ASM, *P. E. Firenze*, cart. 292 and 293, respectively; the Signoria of Florence to Soderini and Guicciardini, Florence, Jan. 8, 1477, in Casanova, "L'uccisione," doc. XVI, pp. 320–321.

[75] Through his kinsman, Giovanni Galeazzo, Lodovico Campofregoso demanded a settlement that included the cession of Corsica, Pietrasanta, La Spezia, and Carrara. The fortresses in Corsica were to be ceded immediately pending the outcome of the negotiations. These excessive demands precluded any agreement (Sagramoro to Bona, Jan. 16, 1477, postcript, ASM, *P. E. Firenze*, cart. 292).

[76] On March 18, Guicciardini left Milan for Florence bearing a proposal that Florence take Ludovico Sforza into its service and pay half of the *condotta* of Roberto da Sanseverino, an obvious attempt to remove these two troublesome figures from the Duchy. Presumably he also carried the request for five hundred foot soldiers and some cavalry to be sent to Sarzana (Bona to Sagramoro, Milan, March 23, 24, 1477, *ibid.*, cart. 292; the Signoria to Soderini, March 22, 1477, in Casanova, "L'uccisione," doc. XXVI, p. 329; Soderini and Guicciardini to the Signoria, Milan, March 17, 1477, Archivio di Stato di Firenze (cited hereafter as ASF), *Archivio Mediceo avanti il Principato*, busta 89, no. 328). Few days later the Signoria decided to send three thousand men (Sagramoro to the Dukes, Florence, March 26, 27, 30, ASM, *P. E. Firenze*, cart. 293).

that the peace of Italy demanded the preservation of the Triple Alliance.

Florence in fact became the focus of discussions on the future of that alliance. Late in January Venice instructed its ambassador, Pietro da Mulino, to inquire whether Florence shared its view that the treaty remained in force despite the death of Galeazzo Maria as indeed the treaty itself provided.[77] The Signoria's response was prompt and unqualified. The alliance was intact and if not, it was ready to renegotiate it. In discussions with the Milanese and Venetian ambassadors it was agreed by all that the Triple Alliance was the best means of preserving peace in Italy and keeping the ultramontanes out of the Italian peninsula. In a private audience with the Signoria, Mulino revealed the real reason for raising the question. Venice suspected that Ferrante's persistent public demonstrations in support of Milan were a prelude to his resumption of earlier efforts to effect a division among the allies.[78] He refrained, however, from expressing an even darker suspicion, previously communicated to the Regent, that Milan and Florence had already contracted a new alliance with the King against Venice.[79] There is no doubt that Florence's tactful role in dispelling these suspicions, despite its own misgivings about Venetian coolness

[77] The Doge to Pietro da Mulino, Venice, Jan. 24, 1477, ASV, *Senato Secreta*, Reg. 28, fol. 127r-127v.

[78] Sagramoro to the Dukes, Florence, Jan. 29, 1477, ASM, *P. E. Firenze*, cart. 292 and 293; cf. Mulino to the Doge, Florence, Jan. 28, 1477 (copy), *ibid.*, cart. 953.

[79] Ferrante, on the other hand, in a transparent attempt to detach Milan from her ally, was complaining to the Regent that she was placing more faith on Venice than on Naples (Bona to Sagramoro, Milan, Jan. 28, 1477, *ibid.*, cart. 292). Later the Duchess informed Venice that since the death of her husband she had in fact repulsed several times Ferrante's proposals for an alliance with the excuse that they were already connected by ties of marriage and friendship (Bona to Botta, Milan, April 29, 1477, *ibid.*, cart. 363).

and Ferrante's disruptive maneuvers, was at least as valuable to Milan as its military assistance.

Sixteen months later to the day Lorenzo himself was to benefit from Milan's diplomatic and military aid when the dagger of the assassin struck down his brother in Santa Maria del Fiore in Florence. Like the Milanese conspirators, the Pazzi counted mistakenly on a spontaneous popular uprising, but unlike them and perhaps because of their failure, they took the precaution of securing outside support probably from the very beginning of their deliberations. Documents in the Archivio di Stato in Milan, which apparently have escaped the attention of historians, reveal that as early as the middle of January 1478 Venice warned Lorenzo, through the manager of the Medici Bank in Venice, Giovanni Lanfredini, that Florentine exiles at Ferrara were plotting to harm him and his brother, and that these exiles had made contact with Ferrante who seemed to know of the plot.[80] The names of the plotters do not appear in the docu-

[80] "Io ho per bona via inteso, che circha doi dì sono, questa Sig.ria mandò secretamente per Iohanne Lamferdino [sic] et li disse con parole molto affectionate, che essendo questo Dominio desyderoso del bene et salute del M.co Lorenzo et del fratello, essa voleva significarli quanto l'haveva de presenti dal suo Visdomino da Ferrara; et hiis dictis, li monstrò una littera per la quale dicto Visdomino li scriveva, como l'haveva noticia che alcuni delli forausciti de Fiorentia erano in praticha de fare offendere el prefato Mag.co Lorenzo et Iuliano, suo fratello, nelle persone proprie; et che per dicta casone uno delli dicti forausciti era andato a Napoli alla M.tà del Re, il quale Re pareva fusse conscio de dicta praticha. Delle quale parole et adviso sento ch'el prenominato Iohanni, et mediatamente [?], per uno fante aposta dette subito noticia al dicto M.co Lorenzo" (Botta to the Dukes, Venice, Jan. 18, 1478, ibid., cart. 363). On January 21, the Duchess instructed Sagramoro to relay this warning to Lorenzo, who revealed that he had already received a similar message from Giovanni II Bentivoglio, lord of Bologna, and from Tommaso Soderini, Florentine ambassador at Milan (Sagramoro to the Dukes, Florence, Jan. 24, 1478, ibid., P. E. Firenze cart. 294). Lorenzo thanked the Signoria for the warning, and suggested that the allies press the Duke of Ferrara and Siena to expel the Florentine exiles. The suggestion did not please some Venetians, who feared that the exiles

ments, and further research will be necessary to establish if this is indeed the origin of the Pazzi conspiracy. It may well be that the Florentine conspirators received their inspiration from their Milanese counterparts. The two plots, in fact became intimately connected in the minds of some Florentines, such as Piero di Marco Parenti[81] and Alamanno Rinuccini, the latter even bestowing praises on both groups of assassins as worthy emulators of ancient tyrannicides.[82] It appears that political assassinations, then and now, are highly suggestive.

Another Florentine, Machiavelli, had a more realistic view of tyrannicide. He maintained that as a method of restoring liberty it was bound to fail in states such as Naples and Milan, where the public spirit had been thoroughly suppressed and

---

might then seek refuge in Venetian territory and thus create a dilemma for the Republic in view of its traditional liberal policy toward political refugees (Botta to the Dukes, Venice, Feb. 4, 1478, *ibid.*, cart. 363).

[81] "El precedente facto a Milano animò ' nostri Fiorentini," Parenti, *Storia fiorentina*, fol. 7r, published in Angelo Poliziano, *Della congiura dei Pazzi (Coniurationis commentarium)*, A. Perosa, ed. (Padua, 1958), Appendix I, p. 69 n. 1.

[82] See N. Rubinstein, *The Government of Florence under the Medici (1434 to 1494)* (Oxford, 1966), p. 196. Unfortunately we still lack a comparative study of the numerous Renaissance conspiracies as well as a detailed treatment of the Pazzi conspiracy, which could establish the exact roles played by Ferrante and Sixtus IV both in the attempted overthrow of the Medici and in the plot to assassinate Lorenzo and Giuliano. Venice retained the Pope and the King guilty on both counts according to the Milanese ambassador: "Questa Signoria tene per certo, et cosí publice senza reguardo alcuno se dice, ch'el Re Ferdinando col mezo del Conte Ieronimo [Riario] ha menato questa praticha de Fiorenza et de amazare Lorenzo de' Medici, et ch'el Papa è stato consentiente del tuto" (Botta to the Dukes, Venice, April 28, 1478, ASM, *P. E. Venezia*, cart. 365. Girolamo Riario's responsibility for the entire affair has been universally accepted, although in an apparently unknown letter to the Dukes of Milan he vehemently denied any knowledge of the assassination plot: "Inteso el nefando caso successo in Firenze, ne ho presa tanta a[ma]ritudine et displicentia che me ha facto esser fuor de la mente. Il che me ha facto tardare sino in hora lo

corrupted by centuries-old tyranny.[83] One may add that, as he was writing, this spirit was past reviving in Florence itself. In Renaissance Italy the overthrow of a tyrant was normally followed by the rise of another. The populace, apathetic and alienated from the circle of power, generally played little or no role in the periodic purges, though it was ready to share in the spoils when opportunity arose. Examples of an enraged people in revolt against tyrannical masters are rare in this period. Nor could the people look for guidance to the intellectuals, who at the beginning of the fifteenth century were by no means united on the relative merits of Florentine "liberty" and Visconti "tyranny," and who ultimately retreated into contemplation while enjoying the fruits of courtly patronage. It is no wonder that conspirators, though always hoping for a spontaneous popular revolt, preferred more often than not to secure outside support, thus entangling their private quarrels with the foreign policy of princes. The records of Renaissance diplomacy are full of this kind of intrigue by plotters and exiles everywhere at a time when political opposition could neither be loyal nor legal. This intimate connection btween threats to internal peace and external aggression is vividly demonstrated once again by the fearful attitude of Italian rulers following the assassination of Galeazzo Maria, even though it was soon

---

scrivere. Et perché so certo per li malivoli me porria esser data qualche gravezza, per esserne trovati alcuni de mei, ad chiarezza de V. Illustrissime Signorie et purgation mia, intendano che io sapia che quisti tali haviano li animi loro molto pregni verso Lorenzo, como dicevano haverlo Lorenzo contra di loro; ma che sapesse né fusse conscio de morte de alcuno, non se troverà mai cum verità; et de questo sieno chiarissime V. Illustrissime Signorie, che essendome dato caricho, sappiano questa essere la mera verità" (Riario to the Dukes, Rome, May 5, 1478, ASM, *P. E. Roma*, cart. 1202). On Riario's role, consult L. von Pastor, *Storia dei Papi dalla fine del Medio Evo*, new Italian trans. by A. Mercati, Vol. II (Rome, 1961), pp. 506–509.

[83] *Discorsi*, Bk. I, chap. xvii.

established that the conspiracy uncharacteristically had no out-side support. In the long run these fears were justified. The sudden elimination of the Duke brought in its wake the gradual usurpation of power by Ludovico il Moro, himself a target of another assassination plot (1484). His insecurity and estrange-ment from Ferrante turned out to be important links in the chain of events leading to the debacle at the end of the century.

V

CRIME AND PUNISHMENT IN FERRARA,

1440-1500

Werner L. Gundersheimer

*T*HE PROBLEM of urban violence and civil strife may
be timely, but the present generation of Renaissance
scholars is not the first to perceive its centrality to an adequate
understanding of the period from 1200 to 1500. In fact, it has
traditionally been one of the issues that has succeeded in elicit-
ing theories and generalizations from the giants upon whose
shoulders we stand. To reflect on their views of this subject is
to realize very quickly the extent of the historian's dependence
on his own culturally and environmentally determined per-
spectives. Consider, for example, the first chapter of that lu-
minous and evocative masterpiece by Johan Huizinga, *The
Waning of the Middle Ages.*[1] It is called "The Violent Tenor
of Life." Perhaps its most serious point is the view, rather passionately urged, that *homo sapiens* was in many ways a different
kind of animal in the fifteenth century than he is now. Volatile
in temperament, feverishly excitable, and passionately self-
righteous, full of extreme and exaggerated responses, Huizinga's late medieval man seemed to him different almost in kind,
rather than degree, from the repressed products of what he
called "the complicated mechanism of social life" in the modern
world.

None of us would be at a loss, one assumes, to think of ways
in which, since the appearance of Huizinga's book in 1924, this

[1] New York, 1956 (first published in 1924).

"complicated mechanism" has managed to revivify, nurture, institutionalize, and perhaps even intensify the violent tenor of life. Yet, the men, or perhaps it is better to say the characters whom Huizinga describes, were in perhaps misleading respects unlike us. They would seem bizarre indeed to the citizen of an industrialized Western country. Their behavior, according to Huizinga's description would appear little short of schizophrenic, at the very least manic-depressive. Their inhibitions would be few, their superstitions many and diverse, and their actions would in no way correspond to our social or legal norms. It would be difficult, if not impossible, to accommodate them to existing forms of social order, except for special institutions designed to seal them off from the rest of humanity, and they might be a trial even then.

There is a grain of truth in Huizinga's view of the difference between medieval and modern men, but it has only a small kernel. It does seem, for example, that society has found some ways to localize its more violent groups, and their activities. The main contemporary loci are athletic fields, campuses, the poorer sections of cities and towns, and distant battlefields in the lands of less "developed" people. It appears, though, that even in these regions violent behavior is ultimately intolerable, except according to certain well-defined rules of the game. And these modern groups are not comprised of individuals strongly resembling Huizinga's medieval man, though there are some interesting parallels that the author could not have anticipated. Such possible parallels aside, one may be permitted to doubt that the human differences between these ages were nearly as great as Huizinga believed. Even in the best of times, the veneer of restraint and civility in human behavior has always been, and remains, thin and fragile. Even today, we know very little about the causes of violent criminal behavior, how it can be prevented or reformed, what the goals and purposes of criminal punition should be, and how they may best be achieved. By and large, with the necessary changes being made, we are work-

ing within some of the same intellectual constructs in this area
as did our Italian Renaissance forebears. Thus, if we no longer
fine people for blasphemy, much less cut out their tongues,
we may incarcerate and fine them for mailing publications
which are adjudged to appeal to "prurient interest." [2] If it does
not constitute lèse majesty to criticize or malign one's govern-
nors, it is still possible to attempt to enforce the consent of the
governed through oaths of loyalty (which used to be called
fealty) and men convicted of treason have in 1969 perished
more or less in the manner prescribed by early statute books.[3]

Conversely, it may be argued that men in the fifteenth century seldom behaved in ways generically different from ours,
and this is perhaps particularly true of criminals. The chronicles often have a disturbingly familiar content, despite their
archaic form. And one need only ride the New York subway,
glancing from time to time at the avid consumers of tabloids
full of crime and astrology, to realize that Huizinga's description of the "cruel excitement and coarse compassion" engen-
dered by executions in medieval Burgundy have their analogue
today.

It is interesting to contrast Huizinga, writing optimistically

[2] The first major codification of Ferrarese law is that of 1288, for
which see C. Laderchi, *Statuti di Ferrara dell'anno 1288*, Monumenti
Istorici della Provincia della Romagna, IV (Ferrara, 1864); also W.
Montorsi, *Statuta Ferrariae anno MCCLXXXVIII* (Ferrara, 1955), and
I. Farneti, "Riflessi di diritto pubblico e di teorie politiche medioevali
negli statuti di Ferrara del 1288," *Atti dell'Accademia delle Scienze di
Ferrara*, XXVII (1949–1950). The statutes were revised in the 1450s
and published for the first time in 1476. The most accessible early edition, in which the criminal provisions remain very close to those of
earlier redactions, is that of G. B. Pigna, *Statuta Ferrariae nuper re-
formata* (Ferrara, 1567). For a discussion of Ferrarese criminal law,
especially in the sixteenth century, see D. Zaccarini, "Delitti e pene
negli Stati Estensi nel secolo XVI: Contributo allo studio della delinquenza," *Atti e Memorie della Deputazione Ferrarese di Storia Patria*,
XXVII (1928), 3–66.

[3] In the Iraqi spy trials, for which see *The New York Times*, Jan.
27–28, 1969. Of course it could be argued that in some sense Iraq might
be considered "medieval," but that is precisely the point.

in the aftermath of the war to end all wars, with Jacob Burck-hardt, so full of foreboding for the future of Europe. In his brief chapter on morality, the author of *The Civilization of the Renaissance in Italy* views the fifteenth century as a tumultu-ous, violent age. "It cannot be denied," he says, "that Italy at the beginning of the sixteenth century found itself in the midst of a grave moral crisis, out of which the best men saw hardly any escape." [4] But, with customary shrewdness, Burckhardt carefully disavows any intention of forming generalizations, and aspires only to present some fragmentary evidence, "a string of marginal notes." Yet, this section does not lack inter-pretive concepts. For Burckhardt, the "unbridled egoism" of the Italian individualist is informed and rendered terrifying by the psychic quality of "imagination." This concept, never de-fined, is used to explain the vendetta, gambling, political crimes, and above all, what the author calls "the illicit intercourse of the two sexes." [5]

The result is that for Burckhardt's reader, Renaissance vio-lence becomes in a sense dignified and idealized by a new di-mension of intellectual energy and power. An anticipation of the Nietzschean reverence for strength appears in such pas-sages as this: "In the imagination, then, which governed the people more than any other, lies one general reason why the course of every passion was violent, and why the means used for the gratification of passion were often criminal. There is a violence which cannot control itself because it is born of weak-ness; but in Italy what we find is the corruption of powerful natures. Sometimes this corruption assumes a colossal shape, and crime seems to acquire almost a personal existence of its own." [6] One can hardly criticize Burckhardt for making such assertions in an age innocent of sociological and psychological

---

[4] *The Civilization of the Renaissance in Italy*, Vol. II (New York, 1958), p. 427. I have used the translation by S. G. C. Middlemore, made from the fifteenth German edition of the work, first published in 1865.
[5] *Ibid.*, p. 432.
[6] *Ibid.*, p. 437.

theories of criminal behavior, but it is evident that the combination of awed fascination and horrified distaste with which that scholar viewed Renaissance crime could be applied to almost any period or people in European history. As regards such occurrences as the paid assassination of political figures, violent sexual assaults, and political insurrection, all specified by Burckhardt, a chapter on contemporary American morality might be written so as to read as a fairly exact paraphrase of his discussion.

What we obviously need is a much more precise knowledge of the nature, frequency, social origins, and human motives for crime in Italian city-states. Only with such information at our disposal can we ever hope to go beyond impressionistic generalizations to more sophisticated theories based on extensive evidence. Earlier historians were certainly correct in observing the frequency with which chroniclers report important crimes. But the question remains open of how violent, by some statistical standard, the fifteenth century was, as compared with the tenth, the thirteenth, or the seventeenth. Such hard information may not be easy to come by, and its results, once obtained, might not even justify the time and trouble needed to get it, but it is certain that we have to know much more than we do at the present time. I have accumulated some very crude statistical data for capital crimes punished in Ferrara between 1441 and 1500. Since that city clearly had its share of sensationally violent activity in this period, it may be helpful to begin by trying to discern some patterns.

I

The Biblioteca Communale Ariostea in Ferrara contains a manuscript book listing the executions that were performed there between 1441 and 1557. This book, called the *Libro de' Giustiziati*, was most probably kept up to date either by a religious confraternity or by a notary in the service of the *podestà*.[7] It provides a wealth of information on such subjects as the identity of criminals, the crimes punished by execution, and the methods of execution used in specific cases. It is, of course, of no help in the case of capital crimes that never came to trial, or in which the death sentence may have been rejected or commuted to banishment and confiscation of goods, or punished by retaliation outside the courts. Nor does it provide information on the frequency or seriousness of noncapital crimes, which, owing to their less disruptive nature, also tend to be noticed less by the chroniclers. Still, a study of the *Libro de' Giustiziati* of Ferrara for the second half of the fifteenth century yields some interesting information.

Owing to the frequency with which executions are cited in one of the three principal Ferrarese chronicles of the fifteenth century, it has for some time been assumed that there was a tremendous crime wave toward the end of our period, especially in the 1490s. One scholar has attempted to explain this on the basis of the large number of foreigners (i.e., non-Ferrarese Italians) who allegedly flocked into the city to aid in the construction of the Herculean Addition, a new section, laid out and circumvallated by the architect Biagio Rossetti, for Ercole I D'Este.[8] At the same time, there is good reason to believe that the authorship of the chronicle in question may have changed

[7] MS Cl. I, 404, cod. mem. in—4⁰, fols. 44. Fols. 16v-17r of this book has a miniature depicting a beheading in Ferrara, with the Palazzo della Ragione in the background. The MS was noticed by Zaccarini, *op. cit.*, p. 15, who made little use of it. The *podestà*, typically was a distinguished citizen or noble from one city, trained in the law, and elected to serve a fixed term as chief magistrate or executive of another city. For details, see D. Waley, *The Italian City-Republics* (New York, 1969), pp. 66-74.

[8] On the *Addizione Erculea*, see now B. Zevi, *Biagio Rossetti: Il primo urbanista moderno europeo* (Turin, 1960), and the remarks in W. L. Gundersheimer, "Toward a Reinterpretation of the Renaissance in Ferrara," *Bibliothèque d'Humanisme et Renaissance*, XXX (1968), 268.

hands about that time.[9] If so, one could suppose that an author more concerned with crime had replaced someone who took it in stride. Study of the *Libro de' Giustiziati* strongly suggests not only that foreigners did not commit a larger percentage of Ferrarese crimes in the 1490s than in earlier decades, but also that, unless the reporting of executions in the *Libro* is wildly unreliable, there was no significant increase over the preceding period; and therefore that the crime-wave theory may be a myth. At the risk of some tedium, it should be helpful here to introduce, as briefly as possible, some numerical data.

For the sake of precision, let us look more closely first at the annual figures on executions, and then consolidate them into twenty-year periods. From 1441 to 1460, 79 people were executed in Ferrara. In the following twenty years, there were 110 victims, and in the subsequent period, 104. These figures, totaling 293 executions in sixty years, include, however, the years in which there were more or less wholesale executions for treason. If one subtracts the figures for those years, the results are even closer. Thus, there were 57 for the first two decades, 62 for the second two decades, and 66 for the third two decades, a total of 185. This small increase over twenty-year periods is not a statistically significant one for the lengths of time involved, in terms of a population of 30,000 to 35,000.

In the entire sixty-year period, there were only nine years in

---

G. Pardi has attempted to interpret this phenomenon in his preface to the anonymous *Diario Ferrarese dall'anno 1409 fino al 1502*, in L. A. Muratori, ed., *Rerum Italicarum Scriptores* (cited hereafter as *RIS*) (rev. ed.; Bologna, 1900–   ), XXIV, pt. 7, fasc. 4, p. xii: "La venuta di tanti individui, per lo piu miserabili, senza casa ne tetto . . . deve aver cagionato un grave perturbamento e peggioramento dei costumi. . . . De allora [the beginning of the enlargement in 1492] il *Diario* si riempie dei racconti di violenze, dirisse, di ferimenti, di omicidi e sopratutto di furto."

[9] The problem of authorship of the *Diario Ferrarese* will be discussed in a subsequent publication.

which more than six people were executed. Of these nine, all
but three were years in which the total was swelled by executions for crimes against the state. All these big years occur in
the first half of the period. The first, 1454, witnessed eleven
executions, of which eight were for theft, one each for homicide and sodomy, and one on a combined charge of theft,
homicide, and rape.[10] The second, 1458, had seven executions,
of which five were for theft and two for homicide.[11] The final
year in the high-execution, nontreason category was 1465, in
which eight people were put to death, six of them for theft and
two for homicide.[12] In general, the Ferrarese criminal code
called for harsher punishments for foreign than for domestic
evildoers. This is reflected in such years as 1465, where four of
the six thieves executed were foreigners, including two Germans and two gentlemen from Verona (a city that seems to
have more than its share of victims in the Ferrarese *Libro*).[13]
One may safely assume that there were also some local thieves
who got off with a stiff fine, imprisonment, some sort of mutilation or torture, or banishment. As for the homicides that year,
one was in the case of a woman convicted of having poisoned
her husband, and the other, a thwarted attempt, involved a man
convicted of supplying poison to a woman so that she might
murder her husband and son.[14] There is much evidence to suggest that poisoning, especially by women, was one form of
murder toward which the authorities took an exceptionally dim

[10] *Libro de' Giustiziati* (cited hereafter as *Libro*), fols. 2v-3v.

[11] *Ibid.*, fol. 4r-4v.

[12] *Ibid.*, fol. 5v.

[13] Most foreign thieves executed in Ferrara were from neighboring
cities, especially Bologna, Padua, Mantua, Verona, Vicenza, and Venice.
The only non-Italians were Germans and Slavonians, but there are occasionally examples of Italians from more distant parts. Thus, a man
from Ancona was burned for sodomy (March 1468), a thief from
Viterbo was hanged in July 1467.

[14] *Libro*, fol. 5r-5v.

view. Its punishment involved decapitation, a method regarded as more serious, if not more final, than hanging, which was the fate of many thieves and murderers.[15]

To offset these years of many executions, there were others in which only one or two people are listed. Leaving aside crimes against the state, over the sixty-year period with which we are concerned, the average number of people executed each year was three. This figure may well be fantastically high by the standards of Western cities of comparable size in the more modern periods, even before the decline of capital punishment, but it must be remembered that Italian cities used the death penalty for a much wider variety of offenses. Thus, a number of this magnitude, in relation to population figures, does not in my judgment support, or perhaps even suggest, an appreciably more violent tenor of life than in, say, Kansas City in the 1860s, or Los Angeles in the 1960s.

But if the averages are expanded to include treason, the situation looks very different for Ferrara in this period. There are no fewer than eleven years out of our sixty in which there were executions for treason or conspiracy against the Estensi rulers. In 1476, in the wake of Niccolò di Leonello d'Este's unsuccessful coup against his half-uncle Ercole, 27 men were hanged or decapitated, including 6 individuals referred to only as "uomini maligni." [16] In 1482, 18 men were executed, most of them for espionage, sedition, and arson, which, in the circumstances, may at least be suspected as a political crime. For that was the

---

[15] Generally, methods of punishment were selected for their efficacy as examples to other potential evildoers. They also reflect the gravity of the criminal's total activity. Thus, hardened murderers, or those who combined several serious offenses, were often made to suffer the capital punishment in several different forms. Of course, they would have already died as a result of the first of these. It is perhaps here that one observes the most extensive use of "imagination" in relation to crimes of violence.

[16] *Ibid.*, fols. 7v-8r.

year in which the war with Venice began.[17] Such figures as these complicate the crime situation in an unexpected way. If one includes political crimes, the average number of people executed per annum from 1441 to 1500 rises to 4.88 from the figure of 3 cited before. It means that the inclusion of crimes against the state drives the average upward by over 50 percent. Yet, these crimes occur in fewer than 20 percent of the years in question (eleven out of sixty), almost half of them are concentrated in two of these years, namely 1476 and 1482, and these are years of very special historical and political significance. It may be reasonable to conclude from this that the annual rate of capital crimes remains relatively constant throughout this period, except for the very dramatic and atypical fluctuations introduced by political disorders. Thus, to proceed a step further, the 1490s, which Giuseppe Pardi has characterized as a period of particular criminality, includes forty-one executions.[18] In the 1460s I count forty-three. If the *Libro de' Giustiziati* is roughly accurate, and if there is any more or less constant ratio between the frequency of capital and other kinds of crimes, there can be no substance to his view. If the Herculean Addition, which more than doubled the land area of the city, was in fact a response to increasingly crowded conditions in Ferrara, which is very likely according to other demographic data, these figures suggest a relative decline (as

[17] *Ibid.*, fols. 8v-9r. During this year, many outsiders seem to have been active in Ferrara. In June, some Slavonians, probably mercenaries, were hanged for arson and espionage. Other hangings for sedition, espionage, and homicide follow, including that of "uno chiamato el priete." For the Venetian war, see now the useful bibliography in L. Chiappini, *Gli Estensi*, (Milan, 1967), pp. 526–527, as well as the *Diario Ferrarese*, pp. 98–120, the other Ferrarese chronicles (see nn. 21, 35), and above all Marino Sanudo, *Commentarii della Guerra di Ferrara* (Venice, 1829).

[18] *Op. cit.*, p. xii. These figures are based on the *Libro*, which I find to be more reliable than the chronicles.

well as an absolute decline) in the criminality of the Ferrarese people around the turn of the century.

II

Besides providing much information on the dates and numbers of executions in Ferrara in the second half of the fifteenth century, the *Libro de' Giustiziati* also gives some interesting and fairly detailed insights on various types of crime and punishment. It takes us beyond the technical and prescriptive vocabulary of the statute books, which are remarkably similar from one city to the next within a given time period, to a more intimate view of the actual relationship between criminal violence and legally sanctioned violent punishment. In presenting a general view of violence and civil disorder in Ferrara, it may be most useful now to consider the nature of crime, and then of punishment.

People were executed in Ferrara for seven principal crimes, including (in order of descending frequency) theft, homicide, theft and homicide together, counterfeiting, rape, sodomy, and arson.[19] Treason, the importance of which has already been noted, is considered separately. Therefore it is not included in what follows, though it would take third place in the foregoing list if it were. In the entire period under discussion, the *Libro* lists 118 persons executed for theft alone, 70 for homicide, 21 for theft and homicide together, 17 for counterfeiting, 10 for rape, 8 for sodomy, 4 for arson, and a small number for unspe-

[19] There were, of course, other crimes that called for the death penalty, such as witchcraft, heresy, some of the less common offenses against morality. But the Ferrarese situation is not far different from that in Siena 150 years earlier, according to William M. Bowsky, "The Medieval Commune and Internal Violence: Police Power and Public Safety in Siena, 1287–1355," *American Historical Review*, LXXIII:1 (Oct. 1967), 2, who gives as the enormous crimes "homicide, treason, arson, kidnapping, rape, poisoning, mutilation, torture, highway robbery, perjury, wounding and drawing blood, and breaking into a home for the purpose of theft."

cified crimes. This breakdown suggests that crimes against property constituted by far the gravest single law enforcement problem in Ferrara, especially since the percentage of homicides executed must have greatly exceeded the percentage of thieves put to death, assuming reasonable adherence to the statutes. If that line of reasoning is correct, it follows that most violent crime in this society partakes of little more imagination, and derives from essentially similar sources as in other urban societies.

Some rather arresting correlations emerge if one tabulates the incidence of these various kinds of offenses over the sixty-year period. In the case of executions for theft, for example, there is a small decline, from 43 in the years 1441 to 1460, to 39 in the years 1461 to 1480, to 36 in the years 1481 to 1500. This decline has its parallel in the areas of counterfeiting and sexual offenses. There are only half as many counterfeit cases in the last twenty years as in the first, though there are more in the middle. Executions for rape decline from 5, to 3, to 2 over the three twenty-year stretches, while sodomy starts at 4, drops to 1, and then rises to 3. Little can be made of such differences because the numbers are so small as to reflect normal variations. But there is some indication that serious sexual offenses are either much less frequent than has traditionally been assumed, or that they were often handled outside the legal system, or that they were taken much less seriously by the authorities than one might expect. I am inclined to favor some combination of the first two of these possibilities.

The numbers that may be tentatively interpreted to suggest a relative decline in theft toward the end of the period are not borne out, however, by the statistics concerning homicide. For that crime, there were 17 executions between 1441 and 1460, 23 between 1461 and 1480, and 30 between 1481 and 1500. Though the total numbers involved do not admit of any degree of statistical rigor, there is a very clear suggestion that murder was on the rise, especially in relation to other kinds of crime. There are almost twice as many murders in the last twenty years as in the first. It seems likely that much of the explanation here has to do with population growth.

The extreme severity of criminal punishments is a notorious aspect of early modern judicial systems, and Ferrara is no exception. In view of the fact that in almost all Italian cities the official entrusted with the administration of criminal justice was the podestà, and that this office was usually reserved by statute for foreigners serving a term of one year or less, it is not surprising to find that there is a certain uniformity in criminal codes from place to place.[20] Ferrara's law held that the podestà had to be a native of a city in which Ferrarese citizens were eligible for similar service, and also stipulated that a newly appointed podestà had to spend his first three working days studying the statutes of the city. By the late fifteenth century, however, these would have contained few surprises for any Italian on what might be called the podestà "circuit." But within these statutes were some tightly circumscribed areas of discretionary authority, and one may perhaps detect the exercise of this authority in the administration of capital punishments.

A very striking feature of the period is the steady decline of such methods of execution as decapitation and burning, and the correspondingly dramatic increase in the use of hanging. Here, the statistics are more or less unequivocal, but their meaning is not as clear as the factual situation. In the latter part of the period, decapitation comes to be used almost exclusively for homicide, or extreme sexual offenses, whereas in the early

[20] I claim no detailed knowledge of early statute books, but having perused several dozen of them in the Henry Charles Lea Library of the University of Pennsylvania, for the purposes of ascertaining how unique Ferrara's laws were, I think it safe to say that there is a broad base of similarity, despite regional and local differences. The sociology of the legal profession should help to explain this. For many useful insights, see L. Martines, *Lawyers and Statecraft in Renaissance Florence* (Princeton, 1968), esp. pt. 1, "The Profession."

years it was quite commonly used for armed robbery.[21] This change seems to have occurred between 1450 and 1465, and there is no convincing explanation for it. Similarly counterfeiting, which in the early years was commonly punished by burning, comes to be dealt with by hanging later. Burning becomes increasingly a penalty only for arson and for crimes with strong religious overtones—sodomy, incest, and witchcraft. Such crimes are rare indeed.[22]

It is notable that summary executions were almost unknown. There are only two instances of truly impromptu treatment of a suspect in these years, and the more interesting of them is unique also as the only case in which the Duke is directly involved by name, and the only possible instance of execution by defenestration. Upon confronting the suspected murderer, "lo duca ercole lo fece butare zo de la fenestra immediate sensa lezere condanaxon." [23] The court chronicler Bernardino Zambotti agrees that the execution was summary "zenza son de la campana," but says the murderer was hanged from the window.[24] The man in question was an intarsia artisan from Mirandola, who in a financial quarrel had killed his partner, a Piedmontese. Ercole was so upset by this incident that he had

[21] Over the sixty-year period, 213 hangings occurred, distributed over the three twenty-year portions as follows: 48, 80, 85. There were only 64 beheadings, distributed thus: 27, 22, 15. It is evident that in the period from 1441 to 1460 there were more than half as many decapitations as there were hangings, whereas for the years 1481 to 1500 there were almost six times as many hangings as beheadings.

[22] There were twenty-one executions by fire in the period, and they decreased by 50 percent in each twenty-year section, from twelve, to six, to three.

[23] *Libro*, fol. 10r, Sept. 1488.

[24] B. Zambotti, *Diario Ferrarese dall'anno 1476 sino al 1504*, ed. G. Pardi, *RIS* XXIV, pt. 7, 200: ". . . fu prexo de commissione del duca e incontinenti, zenza son de la campana, fu impicato a le fenestre del palazo. Tal caxo miserando rincrescie a tuta questa citade, che dui compagni longo tempo de une botega, de bona fama, habiano finiti la vita e loro compagnia, e tuta la robba perduta in doe hore. Et herano de anni 25."

the suspect removed forcibly from a church in which he had taken asylum. A possible reason for Ercole's rapid action was the fact that only a week before a distinguished Ferrarese legist was killed in a quarrel with a member of the nobility, "et hera persona vertuosa e costumata." [25]

III

The most convenient general way of classifying violence in Ferrara, as much of the foregoing may have suggested, requires a distinction between violence directed against persons or property on the one hand, and violence directed at political change on the other. It is useful to discuss and contrast some important examples of each. In the first category, which subsumes what one may call ordinary criminal violence, it is impossible at the present state of my knowledge to discern any distinguishing social patterns, beyond those that are intuitively obvious. Thus, for example, it is not surprising to find that most thieves and burglars are not men of high social position. But in the case of violent crimes in which there is no clear economic or social rationalization, a random pattern seems to prevail. Homicide, for example, does not follow class, guild, or other lines.[26] Thus, we read in the chronicles of soldiers being executed for mur-

[25] *Ibid.*

[26] In this sense, the *Libro de' Giustiziati* provides a very useful corrective to such sources as chronicles, where the prominent are most likely to receive notice, and also to such interpretations as Burckhardt's, based almost entirely on upper-class crime. That is the kind of personality, both in its criminal and noncriminal forms, which intrigued the Swiss scholar. He refers often to "the more highly developed Italian" and "the cultivated and highly placed Italian," though he has trouble in limiting the range of his comment, and soon begins to refer to "Italians" in general, and even to "the lowest of the people." Still, the examples with which he deals are drawn mostly from the upper classes, where, in all societies, one might begin to look for the most "imaginative" crimes. What would Burckhardt have made of Genet?

der;[27] of a renegade priest who, after celebrating his first masses, killed at least five men, married two women, violated others, and then terrorized the entire Ferrarese countryside until he was finally hunted down and condemned; [28] of a woman condemned for killing a baby; [29] of *contadini* hanged for theft, rape, and homicide; [30] of members of the ducal household being involved in theft; [31] of occasional attacks on priests; [32] and of crimes by, or directed against, students at the university.

The Studium of Ferrara, though not a large institution, was perhaps the most unified and conspicuous collection of foreigners within the city. Given the propensity of students to become involved in compromising situations, it is not surprising to find their names in the grim rolls both of the sinned against and the sinning. Thus, in October of 1486, a Ferrarese citizen was dragged through the city, then decapitated, quartered, and displayed for having killed two German students.[33] Such punishments were reserved for cases in which a strong example had to be set. On the other hand, there was the execution of a young man from Padua, "giovane dotto e intelligente," who was convicted of stealing chalices and tabernacles from churches.[34] There are also incidents of brawling within the university community.[35] Nor were professors immune. Zambotti tells us that

[27] *Diario Ferrarese*, p. 161.
[28] *Ibid.*, p. 162.
[29] *Libro*, fol. 1r.
[30] *Ibid.*, fol. 2r.
[31] *Ibid.*, fol. 5r.
[32] *Ibid.*, fol. 5v.
[33] *Ibid.*, fol. 9v. It was the beginning of the academic year, which may have something to do with the nature of the punishment.
[34] *Ibid.*, fol. 11r. Two of the youth's companions were also hanged.
[35] Thus Ugo Caleffini describes a brawl among some medical students, which resulted in one student's being wounded, and four others barricading themselves in the campanile of the Church of San Domenico, where the fight occurred. The autograph of this extraordinary chronicle is among the Chigi MSS of the Biblioteca Apostolica Vaticana (I.I. 4) (cited hereafter as Vat. Chig.). There is a useful paraphrased

on Sunday, December 8, 1482, "Maestro Ludovico de Sivero, doctore de Leze nostro Ferrarexe, siando sta' ferito a li di passati suxo la testa da uno Ferrarexe, hozi he morto e sepelito con honore." [36] In September of 1491, another Ferrarese law professor, Zilfredo Caballo da Verona, was murdered at night in his own house, while sitting by the fire, by several disguised housebreakers. Their motive was robbery. They were apprehended, and turned out to be not only students, but also members of the Ferrarese nobility, and nephews of the victim. Two of the three, including a member of the Duke's entourage, were decapitated in the piazza, but the third, a scholar of canon law, being a priest, had his sentence deferred.[37]

That example suggests that a considerable amount of violence was committed by young people, and other cases support such a conclusion. Thus, there is the son of a Ferrarese notary who, though repentant for a murder, was decapitated; [38] and the young man burned to death for having violated a boy in Church on Good Friday night ("e mori valorosamente"); [39] and the sixteen-year-old girl, "galante et bela," who was burned for arson; [40] the list could be continued.

Females, incidentally, played a very subordinate role in the commission of violence, except as objects of it. To the crimes by women already cited, however, it is possible to add a single instance of witchcraft, tried in November 1454, in which "Una

---

abridgment by G. Pardi, *Diario di Ugo Caleffini (1471-1494)*, in Monumenti della R. Deputazione di Storia Patria per l'Emilia e la Romagna (Sezione di Ferrara), 2 vols. (Ferrara, 1938). The incident is noticed in II, 357. Further references are to the Vatican manuscript.

[36] Zambotti, *op. cit.*, p. 122.

[37] *Ibid.*, p. 223.

[38] *Libro*, fol. 12r. At the same period, around 1491, there are several instances of the bodies of executed people being given over to the medical school, "per fare la nottomia." Thus, see *Libro*, fols. 11v, 14v.

[39] *Ibid.*, fol. 13v.

[40] *Ibid.*, fol. 15v. The bystanders are said to have shed many tears, because of her valiant behavior.

Orsolina che fu de Antonio dentone diabolica affatinazione et incantatrice fu in uno caxon de cana brusata." [41]

To cite all these instances of various kinds of crimes—and they could be multiplied even without taking into account the occasional eruptions of vendettas—is perhaps to invite misunderstanding. For, as the statistics show, the most prevalent of all crimes was theft. I would even hazard a speculation that a very significant proportion of all homicide in Ferrara was related to the desire to acquire property. It was based often on need or greed, and not necessarily passion or hatred. Given the penal code, to be identified as a burglar was tantamount to a death warrant in many cases. It presented a built-in invitation to murder any witness to crime against property. Thus the chronicler Ugo Caleffini, a notary at the court, had the good fortune to be out of his house when it was burglarized. He narrates the incident in a tone of incredulity: "Mi, Ugo Caleffini, notaro publico ferrarexe, fu' malamente robato in Ferrara in casa mia . . . . li ladri ropeno li ferri de la fenestra ferrata de la cusina, ove che erano in dui gran mastelli le bugate, et ogno cossa porto via." [42] Often, of course, such crimes were committed by people in disguises, and there are frequent ducal edicts attempting to limit the practices of wearing masks and of bearing arms.[43]

[41] *Ibid.*, fol. 3r.

[42] Vat. Chig. I, I, 4, fol. 279. On the same day, according to Caleffini, a Jewish moneylender was killed by masked people.

[43] The practice of wearing masks was especially prevalent during Lent and led to all sorts of abuses. So, too, did the bearing of arms, which the Estensi often tried to control. Thus, Archivio Storico Communale di Ferrara, Commissioni Ducali, 9, 30, cart. 8 (April 12, 1476) is a Herculean decree that no one may appear in public with the face covered in such a way as to be unidentifiable, at a penalty of 25 lire. Another decree, prohibiting the bearing of arms by people of any station is dated August 25, 1471 (Proclami Ducali, 7, 10, p. 109). A similar decree is issued in 1490 (Archivio di Stato di Modena, Archivio Segreto Estense, Cancelleria, Gride manoscritte, Oct. 16, 1490). The measure

Despite some notable exceptions, most thieves appear to have been men of low social and economic status. But there does not appear, in Ferrara, to be any particular correlation between periods of scarcity or famine and outbreaks of crime by individuals. Stealing was a fairly constant feature of the urban scene, though a regime ruled and supported by men of property dealt with it as harshly as possible. Nor is there any doubt that the poor were as numerous in Ferrara as elsewhere. They are mentioned in the chronicles, a medical writer refers to them in a treatise on poisons presented to Ercole I, and new institutions are founded to help them during this period.[44] Such humanitarian endeavors, however, were never on so large a scale as to have had appreciable effects on the problem of law and order. Nor could they have achieved much with regard to one of the chief areas of urban disorder—civil strife based on political disagreements.

IV

The most dangerous violent attempts against the authority of the lords of Ferrara came neither from townspeople nor outside enemies, but from rival claimants within the family. Such attempts to depose the dukes were serious, but relatively infrequent, as compared with other crimes of lese majesty and perhaps to similar attempts in other cities. The most common offenses against the state involved counterfeit money, and for

---

must have been unsuccessful, for similar decrees were issued in 1491 and again in 1497. They are in the same *busta*.

[44] I intend to deal with the subject of Ferrarese poverty in my forthcoming book, *Ferrara: The Style of a Renaissance Despotism*. The MSS in question are in the Biblioteca Communale Ariostea di Ferrara, Cl. I, nos. 352 and 346. Number 352, by Baptista Massa da Argenta, is a treatise "De Venenis"; no. 346 is also an elegant illuminated MS entitled "Capitoli della compagnia chiamata la scola de' poveri vergognosi sotto la protexione di S. Martino," and dated 1491. It attributed local poverty to the ravages of war.

all but six of the eleven years in which political offenses figure in the *Libro de' Giustiziati,* counterfeiting is the only stated crime. I shall rapidly survey the principal seditious attempts on the ducal authority, and then attempt some tentative conclusions.

The first instance, in 1460, resulted in the execution of Uguccione dell'Abbadia, the principal secretary of the ducal chancery, who was decapitated at night, in the castle, in the presence of Borso d'Este's principal advisers.[45] His crime was failure to inform the Duke that one Pietro Paolo, an acquaintance of his, had said six times that he wanted to murder Borso, whereupon Pietro Paolo informed the Duke that Uguccione had heard these plans and done nothing about them. The hapless secretary's defense against what looks very much like a frame-up, was that he did not take Pietro Paolo seriously, considering him "puocho savio." [46] In the aftermath, Uguccione's very considerable estate was divided up among the Duke's intimates and the family were dispersed to remote prisons. The incident seems to suggest a good deal about the methods used by the Duke to maintain the fidelity of his associates.

In 1469, a more serious attempt to unseat Borso was nipped in the bud. Some members of the house of Pio, the lords of Carpi, in retaliation for an alleged insult, plotted either to depose or murder Borso, and bring his younger half-brother Ercole, then governing Modena, to power. They gained support from Borso's enemies in other cities, and then sought Ercole's complicity. Ercole, however, did not commit Uguccione's folly. Instead he revealed the general lines of the plot to Borso, who instructed him to play along and learn the rest of it. After Ercole had done so, he had all the principals in the plot arrested. and then transported, with a guard of four hundred horsemen, from Modena to Bondeno, whence they

---

[45] *Libro,* fol. 4v.
[46] *Diario Ferrarese,* p. 43; it gives a complete account.

took boats to Ferrara. There, they were given a state trial, and condemned, some to execution, others to life imprisonment, all to confiscation of goods by the ducal *camera*. A month later the sentences were carried out. The two brothers Pio, nephews of Borso, were decapitated in a splendid public ceremony, and so was one of their chancellors. The other conspirators were spread around various castle dungeons in the duchy, from which many later escaped or were ransomed.[47] Among the contemporary accounts of the event is one by the important courtly scribe and ducal librarian, Carlo di San Giorgio, published only a few weeks after these events, and rapidly translated into the vernacular so that Borso could understand it.[48] It is, predictably, strongly biased, but it nonetheless adds considerable detail to the chronicler's account. We learn, for example, the suggestive fact that when the prisoners were brought into Ferrara, they had to wear hoods over their faces, to prevent the outraged populace from recognizing individuals and tearing them into "mille pezzi." [49] This would have been a form of civil disorder which, while flattering to the Duke, would have set a perilous precedent.

[47] *Libro*, fol. 6r-6v. For the Pio plot, see also *Diario Ferrarese*, pp. 60–61; Chiappini, *op. cit.*, pp. 136–137; and A. Cappelli, "La congiura dei Pio signori da Carpi contro Borso d'Este," *Atti e Memorie della Deputazione Modenese di Storia Patria*, II (1864), 367–416, the most complete account, with accompanying documents.

[48] Biblioteca Estense di Modena, MS Alpha G. 6, 12, also known as MS Ital. 1004, "Storia del tradimento fatto verso il duca Borso da Gio. Lod. Pio e Andr. da Veregnana," cod. mem. in–fol., ff. 19, with an illuminated frontispiece. Text published by Cappelli, *op. cit.*, pp. 377–393: "Quando il mio libretto at te presentare feci, . . . represo et quasi calonniato fui, . . . havesse a scrivere cotale facenda in latino et non nel nostro vulgare parlare" (fol. 1).

[49] Cappelli, *op. cit.*, 393. Instead of allowing this to happen, even though to do so would have been permissible under the circumstances, "il divo Borso non di meno se despose et ordinoe, per conservatione de la iusticia, secundo le nostre lege li iudici ver loro malfactori di ragione precedesseno, et secundo la lege et la consuetudine de la nostra patria li iudicasseno."

When Borso died in the summer of 1471, Ercole's succession, while smooth, and fully supported by the communal government and the populace, was contested by his nephew Niccolò, the son of Leonello d'Este and Margherita Gonzaga. The latter based his claim on his status as the legitimate heir of Leonello, and could draw upon predictably strong Mantuan support. Accordingly, only a few months after his accession Ercole condemned Niccolò and about eighty-five of his followers and partisans as rebels, and confiscated all their goods and feudal privileges.[50] At the same time, two of Niccolò's party were hanged for treason. They had come from Mantua to the Ferrarese stronghold at Ficarolo, and had attempted to suborn its captain. The chronicler emphasizes that their hanging was public, and that they were left in place for a day and a half.[51]

It was not until September 1, 1476, that Niccolò di Leonello finally made his real move, the biggest attempt at a coup in fifteenth-century Ferrara. That summer, Ercole had been given a male heir, Alfonso, by Eleanora of Aragon, and Niccolò must have felt that he could delay no longer. Accordingly, on that Sunday afternoon, having learned from an informer that Ercole was leaving the city that morning for his pleasure house of Belriguardo, the so-called "Versailles of the Estensi," ten miles southeast of the city, Niccolò invaded with a force of at least 650 armed men.[52] Catching everyone completely off guard, they quickly made themselves masters of the center of the city, and raised their party cry "Vela, vela," to rouse the population to their support. Niccolò also rode around promising a 33 1/3 percent reduction in the price of grain, then rather high, and

[50] *Diario Ferrarese*, pp. 76–78.

[51] *Ibid.*, p. 78; *Libro*, fol. 6v.

[52] The three major chronicles all contain interesting accounts of the attack. A. Cappelli has written authoritatively, and added invaluable documentary evidence, in "Niccolò di Lionello d'Este," *Atti e Memorie della Deputazione di Storia Patria per le antiche Provincie Modeneis, V* (1870), 413–438. The incident is also well if summarily described in E. G. Gardner, *Dukes and Poets in Ferrara* (London, 1904), pp. 142–146.

immediately released all prisoners.[53] Eleanora and her company took refuge in the *castello*, guarding the infant Alfonso. While the Veleschi milled around the piazza, swaggering and carousing, the populace held its peace, and couriers went out to Ercole, bearing the news that Niccolò had captured the city. As the Duke approached the walls, another messenger reached him, estimating that Niccolò had a force of fourteen thousand men, and that three German students had already been killed in the piazza for refusing to say "Vela, vela." [54] Ercole then withdrew to assemble more troops, but his brothers Sigismondo and Rinaldo, who were in the city and saw the weakness of Niccolò's position, launched a counterattack. Niccolò fled, and the populace rallied to the cry of "Diamante, diamante," Ercole's emblem. The reprisals against the first captured Veleschi were, the chronicler says, "una crudel cosa da vedere." [55] Eventually, Niccolò and many of his followers were captured at various points around the city, and brought back to prison. The next day, Ercole made his entry, "cum grande alegreza del popolo." By September 3, the reprisals were well under way. The *Libro de' Giustiziati* gives the names of seventeen people who were hanged from the windows of the Palazzo della Ragione, and five more who merited similar positions on the battlements of the castle. More followed over the next few weeks. On the evening of the next day, in the castle, Niccolò and his cousin Azzo were beheaded. Ercole, whose sense of *pietas* toward his family was equal to his outraged sense of justice, had Niccolò's head sewn back on, and gave him a dignified funeral. "On that day," Zambotti writes, "the decree went out that each gentleman, doctor, citizen, and official must, on behalf of our duke, go to honor the body of messer Niccolò da

[53] *Diario Ferrarese*, p. 91; Vat. Chig. I, I, 4, fol. 64v.
[54] *Diario Ferrarese*, p. 91; Zambotti, *op. cit.*, p. 17, makes them Hungarians. Both chroniclers agree that the students simply did not understand what it was that they were expected to do.
[55] *Diario Ferrarese*, p. 92.

Este, even to the burial." [56] He was buried with the rest of the family, in the church of San Francesco, and with all honors. Subsequently, the Duke commuted the sentences of a great number of people in Niccolò's company, who had been condemned to various types of bodily mutilation. For this, he received much praise.[57]

A few months later, on December 26, Galeazzo Maria Sforza fell victim to the knives of three assassins in the Church of San Stefano in Milan, and died in the arms of the Ferrarese ambassador, Roberti. This violent deed produced a more serious threat to Ferrara's security than any of the attempts from within, which I have reviewed. Ercole had been strengthening ties with Milan. Now, the heir to that powerful duchy was a boy of seven, his guardian a lady of no political acumen, and Milan was no longer in a position to appear as Ferrara's bulwark to her enemies. The Venetians, jealous of their salt monopolies on which Ercole was infringing, and covetous of the fertile Ferrarese *terra ferma* around Rovigo, were not slow to realize this. By 1482, a costly and destructive war was the result. Or, as the great Muratori put it, "con esso lui morì anche la pace e quiete d'Italia." [58]

V

It is all too easy, after pondering such a sustained recitation of some of the violence and civil disorder in a single medium-sized Italian city in the fifteenth century, to imagine the age as one

---

[56] Zambotti, *op. cit.*, pp. 19–20.

[57] *Ibid.*, p .20: "Et remaxeno incarcerati in Castello, messi in cippi in lo cortile del Xastello, Molti de la compagnia. A li quali havendo deliberato il prefato messer Agustino di Bonfranceschi, ducale commissario, di farli cavare uno ochio et talgiare una mano e bolarli in fronte de uno diamante, il parse a la Excellentia del duca usarli clementia e misericordia a quelli che non sapeano che venesseno a fare e cusi non volse che fossero altramente puniti."

[58] *Antichità Estensi ed Italiane* (Modena, 1717, 1740), II, 235

of more or less constant tumult, stress, and strife. So, in concluding, I think it is worth emphasizing the fact that I have been dealing with only a very limited range of social and political expression, and concentrating on the most dramatic events within that circumscribed category. In the period from 1440 to 1500 there were many years of real tranquility and considerable well-being in Ferrara, many periods when people labored together to solve common problems in agriculture, in urban construction, in defense, in hydraulics; many people who strove to obey the letter of the law in times of want and stress, and who attempted to effect ducal and communal decisions with words rather than deeds. The significance of political as well as other forms of criminal violence in Ferrara may easily be exaggerated. Many acts appear graver and more sanguinary to us because of technological differences in the modes of destruction, or because of the graphic descriptions of the chroniclers. Some crimes seem to have been virtually encouraged by the Draconian provisions of the criminal law, and its traditionally rigorous enforcement by noncitizens, who naturally preferred arousing the displeasure of the people to incurring the wrath of the prince.

More fundamentally, it seems clear that the political and social structure of a Renaissance signory like Ferrara was sound enough to weather all but the most serious political uprisings without any real strain. Ducal institutions remained viable all through the sixteenth century, and recurrent efforts were made to elaborate and improve upon them. The legal and judicial systems are not exceptions. Changes within their form and content reveal at least a flexible receptivity to innovation within continuing and accepted structures. Though Ferrara never solved the problems of violence and civil disorder, her generally unflinching application of a *modus moriendi* for the few would seem to have preserved a *modus vivendi* for the many.

VI

SOME PSYCHOLOGICAL AND SOCIAL ROOTS OF VIOLENCE IN THE TUSCAN CITIES

David Herlihy

*I*N THE FIRST decade of the fifteenth century, the Florentine Dominican, later cardinal, Giovanni Dominici declared that public order had all but vanished from the world. "There is no other justice," he affirmed, "but deceit, force, money and factional and family ties; all the other books of every law might as well be burned."[1] Dominici, to be sure, cultivated a distinctly somber view of his times, but his remarks may still help define for us the problem of social disorder in the cities of Renaissance Tuscany, and in some measure of Renaissance Italy. As his statement implies, that problem has both psychological and social dimensions. Dominici attributed the alleged triumph of lawlessness to the dishonesty, greed and ambition of individual citizens. But he perceptively discerned a social factor too, in the power exercised by family alliances and factions. Through their interventions, and the nefarious "law" by which they lived, even trivial incidents could ignite protracted social conflict.

[1] *Regola del governo di cura familiare*, ed. Donato Salvi (Florence, 1860), p. 178: "la quale [iustizia] oggi è sbandita per simili difetti dell' universo mondo; e non è altro iustizia che inganni, forza, danari e amicizia, e parentado; tutti gli altri libri di ciascuna legge si possono abbruciare." The *Regola*, one of the most interesting tracts on household management, was written between 1400 and 1405.

In this paper I examine some factors, both psychological and social, which seem to have contributed to what contemporaries would have called the *furori* and the *rumori* of the Tuscan city —the violent temperaments of many of its citizens and the frequent disruptions of its social peace through riots and factional battles. In prudence, I must emphasize that here can be considered only a few of the sources of violence in urban society. The magnitude of the problem, and the limitations imposed by time, space, and competence, exclude any pretense at a rigorous, not to say exhaustive, survey. In prudence too, we must recognize that the Tuscan cities were highly complex societies, and it is hazardous to advance generalizations that would supposedly be valid for all of them over several centuries of their history.

The obstacles to a thorough analysis of violence are real, but they need not completely overawe the social historian and cow him into silence. He can still take comfort and find help in this facet at least of the problem: the extraordinary documentary wealth that the age has left us. Writers of the period, who show little reluctance to generalize, produced numerous, extensive, and often perspicacious tracts on the formation of good citizens, the education of children, the management of households, and the governance of the commonwealth.[2] They commented at equal length on the civic vices—anger, irascibility, hate, dis-

2 William Harrison Woodward, *Vittorino da Feltre and Other Humanist Educators* (Cambridge, 1897), pp. 180–181, gives a partial but useful bibliography of the principal educational tracts written between 1374 and the closing fifteenth century. For more extended comment, see the study by Augustin Rösler, *Kardinal Iohannes Dominicis Erziehungslehre und die übrigen pädagogischen Leistungen Italiens im 15. Jahrhundert* (Freiburg im Breisgau, 1894). In this present survey of opinion concerning the sources of violence, I have included some excerpts from later works, notably the *Della ragion di stato* of Giovanni Botero (1589; see n. 26) and "Il cittadino di repubblica" of Ansaldo Ceba (1617) in *Scrittori politici*, Biblioteca encyclopedica italiana (Milan, 1839) pp. 389–448. For an English translation of Ceba, see *The Citizen of a Republic, What Are His Rights, His Duties and His Privileges and*

cord, and others—which undermined social order. In seeking explanations for the *furori* and *rumori* of the cities, we can, in other words, let contemporaries shoulder for us the risk of generalizations. Moreover, the Tuscan town is illuminated not only by a rich social commentary, but by huge sources of a statistical character. Through them and in them, we can hope to test with some precision the validity of these contemporary explanations for the violence in urban life. We can even in some sense measure the social weight of the factors, to which the writers of the age direct our attention, as being partially responsible for social disorder.

One of the most famous of these large statistical compilations, and the one I make principal use of here, is the Florentine *Catasto* of 1427.[3] It combined the features of a census and an inventory of all the possessions owned by Florentine citizens and subjects. All areas of Tuscany then subject to Florentine rule were included in this magnificent document, and it therefore records the names and describes the wealth of some 250,000 people, residing in some 60,000 households. Scholars associated with my own University of Wisconsin and with the École Pratique des Hautes Études at Paris are currently engaged in editing and analyzing by computer a considerable portion of this data. We hope to finish the analysis in 1972 or 1973.

How then did contemporaries explain the psychology and

What Should Be His Education, trans. C. Edwards Lester (New York, 1845). These authors do not of course have the authority of contemporary witnesses of town life in the Quattrocento, but their comments are nonetheless instructive. In several places, they develop with remarkable perspicacity ideas present in the earlier writers, and it is for this reason that they are cited here.

[3] On the character of the Catasto, see most recently Elio Conti, *I catasti agrari della Repubblica fiorentina e il catasto particellare toscano (secoli XIV-XIX)*, La formazione della struttura agraria moderna nel contado fiorentino, III, pt. 1, sect. 1 (Rome, 1966) pp. 21–130. Cf. in English the comments of Lauro Martines, *The Social World of the Florentine Humanists, 1390-1460* (Princeton, 1963), pp. 99–105.

deportment of the bad and disruptive citizen? The common opinion was that the antisocial personality was marked by psychological perturbations, and by the subservience of the rational faculties to the power of the passions. According to Francesco Patrizi of Siena, who has left us one of the longest disquisitions on the civic vices, those unsettling perturbations included greed (*indigentia*), anger, irascibility, volatility (*excandescentia*), hate, discord, desire, and lust, and these were all subspecies of cupidity.[4] In turn, cupidity was one of four principal passions that threatened the reign of reason in the human soul. Patrizi gives the following description of the personality and behavior of the passionate citizen:

> "Whatever citizen labors under this perturbation of the soul [the vice of discord] is useless to the commonwealth and is recognized as disruptive in human assemblies. He disagrees with others; he gives in to no one; he destroys all human society; he creates disorders in the halls of princes; and he corrupts all things with quarrels and divisions. From this arise plots and conspiracies, murders, destruction, poisonings and those black plagues, which are wont to undermine all public and private establishments." [5]

In a physiological sense, the power of the passions rested upon a certain unbalance in the elements that formed the human temperament. Like the world itself, the human personality was thought to be composed of four elements—hot, cold, dry, and moist—and various combinations of these elements produced

---

[4] *Francisci Patricii senensis de regno et regis institutione libri IX* (Paris, 1567), pp. 123 ff. The work was first printed in 1494.

[5] *Ibid.* p. 127: "hac animi perturbatione quicumque civis laborat, inutilis est reipublicae, et in hominum coetu importunus habetur. Dissidet sequidem ab aliis, nemini cedit, omnemque humanam societatem dirimit, principum aulas perturbat, seditionibus ac partibus omnia inficit. Hinc conspirationes coniurationesque oriuntur, hinc caedes, direptiones, veneficia, et pestes illae teterrimae, quae status omnes publicos privatosque labefactare soleant."

the four classical psychological types—phlegmatic, sanguine, choleric, and melancholic.[6] Heat was the element most closely connected with the passions, and our writers mention many factors and influences that could give the element of heat a disordered prominence within the personality. For convenience, we can group these factors and influences under three broad headings: heredity, age, and the social circumstances attending the education and the life of the citizen.

Intemperate parents, especially fathers, could easily pass on their own "furies" to their children. According to Maffeo Vegio of Lodi, young men should avoiding siring sons before the age of 36, when time was finally allaying their own passions.[7] The mother should be younger (but at least 18) to assure a healthy child. She should be peaceful, humble, reasonable, and intelligent, insofar—another writer noted—as that is possible for a

[6] A good summary of contemporary ideas concerning the psychological humors or complexions and their physiological basis is provided by the thirteenth-century Florentine encyclopedist, Brunetto Latini, *Li livres dou trésor: Edition critique*, ed. Francis J. Carmody, University of California Publications in Modern Philology, 22 (Berkeley and Los Angeles, 1948), pp. 84–85: "Des .IIII. complexions de l'ome et des autres choses."

[7] Cf. *Maphei Vegii laudensis De educatione liberorum et eorum claris moribus libri sex*, ed. Sister Maria Walburg Fanning and Sister Anne Stanislaus Sullivan, Catholic University of America, Studies in Medieval and Renaissance Latin, 1 (Washington, D.C., 1933), p. 19: "Quare recte maiores nostri feminas non ante octavum et decimum, viros vero sextum et tricesimum annum, conubio iungendos esse censuerunt." Maffeo Vegio, who came from the town of Lodi in Lombardy, published this tract in 1444. For the fear that young fathers would produce violent children, see Leon Battista Alberti, *I libri della famiglia*, in *Opere volgari*, ed. Cecil Grayson, Scrittori d'Italia, 218 (Bari, 1960), I, 109: "A tutti prima che XXV [anni] pare che sia dannoso accostare la gioventù volenterosa e fervente a simile opera [the procreation of children]." The date of the composition of Alberti's Books on the Family is uncertain, but it was probably written in the 1430s, though subjected to later revisions. Cf. the comments of Cecil Grayson in *ibid*. pp. 379–380.

woman.[8] Our moral counselors further laid a great and curious stress on the circumstances that should accompany the act of procreation. A man who carelessly plants a tree, noted Vegio, cannot expect good fruit.[9] Children were best conceived in the spring and fall, while the hot season of summer was distinctly unsuitable. The husband should not be upset, ill, tired, hungry, sated, or drunk. He should not approach his wife with too much passion, as if she were a prostitute. Giovanni Morelli, author of some spirited family memoirs in the early fifteenth century, warned that the babies conceived in such passionate unions were likely to be weak, stunted, and female.[10] Bad milk as well as bad seed could injure the temperament of the child. Preferably, the mother should nurse her own baby, but if this was not possible, the father should give careful attention to the selection of a young, healthy, and calm woman to feed his baby.[11]

Inheritance could incline the child to passion and excess, but it could not alone assure the formation of good citizens. "We have seen," wrote Leon Battista Alberti, "abroad and at home children of most worthy citizens who showed from their tenderest years the best character, who manifested a most attrac-

[8] Giovanni di Pagolo Morelli, *Ricordi*, ed. Vittore Branca (Florence, 1956), p. 209: "E arai riguardo ch'ella sia donna pacefica e non altiera o superba, e ch'ella sia, secondo donna, ragionevole e intendente. . . ."

[9] *De educatione liberorum*, p. 17: "Caput III: Quomodo recte filii generari . . . debeant." For similar comment concerning "quanto al procreare de' figliuoli si richiegga," see Alberti, *Libri della famiglia*, in *Opere*, I, 116.

[10] *Ricordi*, p. 213. From too frequent or too passionate sexual relations, Morelli warns his descendants that "Tu guasterai ancora lei, ma non come te, tu non n'arai figliuoli se none a stento, tu l'arai femmine, tu l'arai tisichi e mai non parrà che vadino innanzi, tu viverai tedioso e ontoso e maniconico e tristo. . . ."

[11] For characteristic comments on nursing, see Alberti, *Libri della famiglia*, *Opere*, I, 36–38; Vegio, *De educatione*, pp. 20–26; Matteo Palmieri, *Della vita civile*, in *Scrittori politici*, Biblioteca enciclopedica italiana, 6 (Milan, 1839), p. 335.

tive air and aspect, full of gentleness and good manners, who then turned out badly. . . ." [12]

Age, even more powerfully than heredity, affected the temperament of the child or young man and influenced his behavior. More specifically, passions were thought to rule the years of adolescence, which extended from puberty to 25, 28, or 30 years, according to various writers.[13] Some authors seem to suggest that a temperate, reasonable, virtuous young man was hardly to be found in all of society, outside of the religious life. In the early fourteenth century, Giles of Rome flatly affirmed that the morals of the young were abominable, and he went on to offer a lengthy proof and illustration of his proposition.[14] In the course of this indictment, he argued that the young were followers of the passions, that they were by nature insolent, and that they kept no moderation but were given to excess in their actions. A century later, a participant in Alberti's dialogue on the family similarly contended that the appetites of young men were insatiable, and their vices innumerable; they were themselves volatile and unstable, and could be given no firm instruction.[15] Ludovico Ariosto, who in his Orlando posed

[12] *Opere*, I, 17: "come abbiamo altrove e nella nostra terra veduti figliuoli di valentissimi cittadini da piccioli porgere di se ottima indole, avere in se aere e aspetto molto ornatissimo, pieno di mansuetudine e costume, poi riusciti infami. . . ."

[13] Dante, in *Convivio*, IV, xxiv, extends adolescence to age 25 (*Le opere di Dante: Testo critico della Società Dantesca Italiana* [2d ed., Florence, 1960], pp. 279-293). Palmieri, "Della vita civile," p. 339, gives the age of 28 for the end of adolescence, and Ansaldo Ceba, "Il cittadino di repubblica," in *Scrittori politici*, p. 419, mentions 30.

[14] *Aegidii romani archiepiscopi bituricensis ordinis fratrum eremitarum sancti Augustini de regimine principum libri III ad Francorum regem Philippum IIII cognomento pulchrum* (Rome, 1556), I, 114: "Quod mores iuvenum sunt vituperabiles."

[15] *Opere*, I, 64: "Segue la gioventù sempre volubile le voluntati; gli appetiti dei giovani sono infiniti, sono instabilissimi, e credo io sia quasi impossibile in animo giovenile fermare certa alcuna instituzione. . . .

a kind of model of the passionate young man, similarly attributed to youth a certain fury, which did not recede until the age of 30. The young, he stated, were lamentably quick to decide, and quick to repent.[16]

Of all passions, the sex urge was recognized to be among the most powerful sources of youthful volatility. "There is no passion," wrote the Genoese Ansaldo Ceba, "by which the citizen is more impeded in acquiring and exercising the virtues needed to render happy his republic, than the storms of sensual love." [17] Although most writers were opposed to the marriage of men before the age of 30, they still recognized the wisdom of the advice of Saint Paul or of Saint John Chrysostom, that marriage could cool the hot temperament of the young.[18] "So wonderful," wrote Maffeo Vegio, "is the force of the marriage bond, that although it frequently is wont to bring the wise to stupidity, it always makes the stupid wise." [19] The father should therefore seek to find a wife for a son who appears too much disturbed by sexual urges. Leon Battista Alberti provided his reader with a list of arguments, to be used in persuading young men to marry. The reluctant young men were to be shown "how many prodigal and misguided men were brought to a

---

Chi potrebbe in tanta incertezza tenere certo ordine a modo a correggere ed emendare e' vizii innumerabili quali d'ora in ora nella gioventù ti pare vedere?"

[16] Le satire di Lodovico Ariosto, ed. Cirillo Berardi (Campobasso, 1918), Satira V, 11. 193–195: "Però vorrei che'l sposo avesse i suoi / Trent' anni, quella età che 'l furor cessa, / Presto al voler, presto al pentirsi poi."

[17] "Il cittadino di repubblica," Scrittori politici, p. 428: "non è passione, onde possa essere tanto impedito il cittadino dall' acquisto e dall' esercizio delle virtù necessarie, per render felice la sua repubblica, come sono i tumulti dell' amore sensuale."

[18] Cf. Vegio, De educatione, p. 47, who cites the ninth homily of St. John Chrysostom.

[19] Ibid., p. 119: "tanta enim tamque mira est vis coniugalis vinculi, ut cum sapientes ad stultitiam plerumque redigere soleat, stultos tamen semper sapientes efficiat."

better life once they had a wife at home."[20] Several writers sharply contrasted the life of the bachelor who pursued his amours outside of marriage, avoiding the responsibilities of wife and children, with that of the responsible married man. "There is madness, here is reason," wrote Alberti, "there shame, here praise; there vice, here honesty; there cruelty, here loyalty."[21] Much later, in his portrait of the perfect citizen, Ansaldo Ceba included a lengthy condemnation of the young men who pursued the pleasures of illicit love, delaying marriage until old age or rejecting it altogether. He saw them as reckless, prodigal, shameless, immoral, and unstable; they were useless if not destructive members of the commonwealth.[22]

Social status could also affect the temperament of the citizen, and dispose him to arrogance and violence. Many authors commented that the very wealthy, especially those who had recently amassed their riches, were given to pride and insubordination. In Dante's *Inferno*, the Florentine sodomite Jacopo Rusticucci attributed the moral excesses of his city to the pernicious influence of the *nouveaux riches*.

> New people, and sudden profits
> Have produced pride and excess,
> Florence, in you, so that you already are weeping.[23]

Giles of Rome similarly asserted that the wealthy were gov-

---

[20] *Opere*, I, 168: "Sarà utile ancora ramentare a' giovani quanti prodighi e sviati sieno a miglior vita ridutti poichè ebbono in casa la moglie."

[21] *Ibid.*, I, 96: "Ivi furia, qui ragione; ivi biasimo, qui lodo; ivi vizio, qui onestà; ivi crudeltà, qui pietà."

[22] "Il cittadino di repubblica," *Scrittori politici*, pp. 427–436, cap. 47. According to Ceba, these unattached young men gave little thought to marriage or the procreation of children: "Di generare, e di nutricar figliuoli per benefizio della repubblica, non possono essere molto solleciti gl' innamorati . . . e trovansi alcuna volta di quelli che per questa cagione, o non prendono moglie del tutto, o la prendono fuor di stagione . . ." (p. 432).

[23] *Inferno*, XVI, 73–75.

erned by their passions rather than their reason; he attributed their lack of self-discipline to their soft and luxurious manner of living.[24] Ansaldo Ceba reaffirmed this opinion that the rich were proud and ambitious, arrogant in their behavior, and impatient under the rule of others.[25] And if their wealth had recently been achieved, they were especially disruptive and recalcitrant.

But perhaps the most perceptive analysis of the relationship between social classes and violence is provided by an author of the late Cinquecento, Giovanni Botero, whose *Della ragion di stato*, published in 1589, is one of the most original political tracts of the age. Discoursing on "the way to avoid riots and uprisings," Botero stated that cities were composed of three types of persons: the rich (*opulenti*), the members of the middle classes (*mezzani*), and the poor.[26] Like Giles of Rome and others, Botero believed that the rich were especially difficult to govern. Their luxurious habits and permissive upbringing did not accustom them to self-discipline, and their pride made them contemptuous of the authority of others. But the poor too did not live easily under the law. Their desperate straits prepared them for any adventure, and they had almost nothing to lose by

[24] *De regimine principum*, p. 126.

[25] "Il cittadino di repubblica," *Scrittori politici*, p. 417: "Coloro adunque che soperchiano nella possessione delle ricchezze, sogliono ordinariamente essere superbi ed oltraggiosi; siccome quelli a cui pare d'esser padroni di tutti le cose in quanto i danari sono, secondo essi, il prezzo ond' elle si comprano: son delicati nel vivere, per far mostra della loro felicità: arroganti nelle opinioni, perchè veggono molti aver bisogno d'essi; somiglianti a chi ha più dovizia di fortuna che di senno, impazienti dell' imperio degli altri; e se le lor ricchezze son nuove, dice Aristotile, che per l'ignoranza d'esse, sono molto peggiori degli altri."

[26] Giovanni Botero, "Della ragion di Stato libri dieci con tre libri delle cause della grandezza e magnificenza delle città," Book IV, "Del modo di ovviare a' romori ed a' sollevamenti," in *Scrittori politici* (Milan, 1839), pp. 475–478; English translation, *The Reason of State*, trans. P. J. Waley and D. P. Waley, and the *Greatness of Cities*, trans. Robert Peterson (1606) (London, 1956).

armed revolt. In contrast, the middle classes were the stablest component of society and the only part of it with a real stake in social peace. They were immune both from the extravagant ambitions that motivated the rich and the desperation that drove the poor. Violence threatened their livelihood and their small capital, and they were usually therefore lovers of peace and order. Large cities, concluded Botero, because they had many inhabitants of middle rank, were thus less subject to disturbances than small towns, which lacked the stabilizing influence of a large middle class.[27] The prince who wanted a peaceful regime should keep close watch on the very rich and very poor, and seek to advance the interests of the *mezzani*.

Finally, to most of these authors, education played a critical role in the formation of good citizens and the inculcation of the civic virtues. The rich were, as we have seen, repeatedly accused of spoiling their children through their permissive attitudes toward child rearing and their delicate manner of life. The writers also discussed at considerable length the roles of both father and mother in the education of the children. The father was repeatedly warned against neglecting his children through political and business concerns; a boy with insufficient paternal guidance would likely turn out badly.[28] The writers looked with similar disfavor upon an education or upbringing too much dominated by the mother. She was more likely than her husband to spoil the children, give in to their whims, and impart to them soft and effeminate habits. Maffeo Vegio claimed that the excessively attentive mother was apt to smother any sign of good character or manly strength in her children.

---

[27] *Ibid.*, p. 474: "di qua viene, che le città grandi (perchè hanno gran numero di persone mediocri di fortuna) sono meno soggette alle sedizioni che le picciole."

[28] Cf. Alberti, *Opere*, I, 40: "molti pochi savi padri che si straccano e scalpestano la sua vita tutta in arti faticosissime, in viaggi e travagli grandissimi, e vivono in disagii e servitù per lassare gli eredi suoi abondanti d'ozio, delizie e di pompa."

Mothers, he wrote, "say 'no' to no request; they let [their children] have their way; they take their side when they complain about the hurts of their playmates or the blows of their teachers, just as if they believed that they themselves were injured. Finally, they allow them complete license for whatever they may want. What is more foolish? What could be called more monstrous than this easy and permissive education, which mothers in particular are wont to follow?" [29]

The young, the unmarried, the spoiled rich, and the desperate poor, those too much neglected by their fathers and pampered by their mothers—these are the groups that contemporary moralists identify as the chief perpetrators of violence and disorder. In describing the actual *rumori* that plagued the cities, the chroniclers frequently make similar observations, or lay the blame on similar types. The famous dispute between the Blacks and the Whites, which was the occasion of Dante's exile from Florence in 1302, provides us some ready illustrations. According to most chroniclers, this factional war had its origins in a feud between two branches of the Cancellieri family of Pistoia. One contemporary attributed the disastrous feud to the ambition, the wealth, and the overweening pride of this prominent house; "there was no one," he observed, "whether in the city or the countryside whom they did not despise." [30] Probably

[29] *De educatione*, p. 45: "quare vana quadam et feminea teneritudine, si qua indoles probitatis, si qua imago generositatis in filiis elucebat, si quid eis virilis roboris nerat, confundunt extenuant minuunt quae gaudentibus illis collaetantur, maerentibus condolent, ridentibus applaudunt, flentibus collacrimantur, quin et lacrimas abstergunt, crebra insuper iungentes oscula atque amplexus; petentibus ne denegant quicquam, recusantibus acquiescunt, conquerentibus vel aequalium iniurias vel praeceptorum plagas favent ac tanquam seipsas laesas existimantes assentiuntur licentiam denique illis omnem quorumcumque voluntas fuerit permittunt. quid stultius? quid prodigiosius hac tanta, qua praecipue matres uti solent, educandi facilitate et indulgentia dici possit."
[30] *Storie pistoresi*, ed. S. A. Barbi, *Rerum Italicarum Scriptores* (hereafter cited as *RIS*), new ed. 11, pt. 5 (Città di Castello, 1927), p. 3: "e

in 1286, two young cousins of the Cancellieri house fell to brawling in a tavern, and from this small spark, struck by irresponsible youths, a war began which eventually engulfed the major cities of Tuscany.[31] The prominence of the young in precipitating this battle is evident also at Florence. There, the Donati and the Cerchi families led the Black and White factions, respectively. At a public dance, held in welcome of the first of May, gangs of young men from the two factions traded insults and blows, and turned the rivalry into open war. The devil, reported the chronicler Dino Compagni, inspired them, "because the young are more easily deceived than the old." [32]

The history of Pistoia, which abounds in factional fights, gives further examples of the role of young men, most of them unmarried, in these violent episodes. In 1401, the Cancellieri faction took up arms against their opponents the Panciatichi and the Florentines who supported them. For more than a year, operating out of mountain strongholds, they devasted the countryside. The leaders of this uprising were Ricciardo Cancellieri, age 28; Lazzero his brother, age 20; and two cousins, both age 22.[33] In 1499, a young man only 23 years old assassinated the head of the Panciatichi and provoked another civil war, which was not suppressed until 1502, and then only partially.[34] Here too it is worth recalling the famous assassination of the Duke of Milan, Galeazzo Maria Visconti, in 1476. The murderers were

---

per loro grandigia e ricchezza montano in tanta superbia che non era nessuno sì grande nè in città nè in contado che non tenessero al disotto."

[31] See the reconstruction of these events presented by Silvio Barbi in *ibid.*, p. 40.

[32] *Cronica di Dino Compagni*, ed. I del Lungo, *RIS*, new ed. 9, pt. 2 (Città di Castello, 1916), pp. 66–67: "Perchè i giovani è più agevole a ingannare che i vecchi, il diavolo . . . si fece. . . ."

[33] Their ages are given in the *Cronache di ser Luca Dominici*, ed. Giovan Carlo Gigliotti, Vol. II, *Cronaca seconda*, Rerum pistoriensium scriptores, 3 (Pistoia, 1939), p. 13.

[34] *Ricordi storici di Francesco Ricciardi detto "Ceccodea,"* ed. Alfredo Chiti, Rerum pistoriensium scriptores, 2 (Pistoia, 1934), p. 5.

young students; Girolamo Olgiati, who was executed for the crime, was 22.[35]

At Pistoia too, the destructiveness of the factional feuds was substantially augmented by the ability of the prominent families to call to their aid even—or perhaps especially—the poorest classes. Nearly the entire city took sides on the often petty or obscure issues that divided the great households.[36] The factions recruited supporters even in the countryside. Of all rural areas, the most tumultuous was also the poorest—the high mountains.[37]

These then are some of the explanations offered by contemporaries for the endemic violence in urban society. Some of the alleged factors—such as the milk supplied by bad-tempered wet nurses—are completely beyond evaluation by, not to say the credence of, a modern historian. But we ought not to dismiss lightly those factors which our writers emphasized even more strongly—age, marital status, social position, home life, and education. Moreover, the statistical sources of the epoch allow us to investigate with some precision the numerical size and social weight of the groups that our commentators accused of violent inclinations. The young, the unmarried, the very rich, the very poor, and the products of a permissive education—these allegedly volatile persons we shall seek to find, and partially at least to count, within the Florentine population of 1427.

Age, all writers agreed, strongly influenced behavior. The age distribution of the Florentine population in 1427 was quite distinctive, and it also shows some few but pronounced resem-

[35] Pietro Verri, *Storia di Milano* (Florence, 1963), p. 69.

[36] Cf. Luca Dominici, *Cronache*, II, 14: "quasi tucte famiglie di Pistoia e di gentiluomeni e popolani fosseno divise." See also D. Herlihy, *Medieval and Renaissance Pistoia: The Social History of an Italian Town, 1200–1430* (New Haven, 1967), p. 199.

[37] For the participation of the communes of the mountains in the factional battles, cf. M.-A. Salvi, *Delle historie di Pistoia e fazioni d'Italia*, Vol. I (Rome, 1656), p. 263, referring to the feud between the Blacks and Whites. Mountain towns were also the chief supporters of the revolt of Ricciardo Cancellieri in 1401.

blances to the spread of ages within our own society. In 1427, the population of Florence was heavily weighted in favor of the young. The average age of the male Florentines was 26 years.[38] Fully one-half the entire population was 22 years of age or younger. In 1966, the median age of the American male population was also quite low, only 26.5 years.[39] The moralists of the fifteenth century, as we have seen, considered that young men between puberty and the early 30s, especially if they were not married, were likely to be the most volatile and unstable members of society. At Florence, one-half the male population older than 14 was also younger than 35.[40] The comparable figure for the American male population in 1966 was 41 percent.

Today, of course, the skewing of the age distribution toward the younger years is the direct result of the high birth rates during and following World War II. The youthful orientation of American society is therefore a passing phenomenon, inevitably to be changed as the population bubble pushes toward ever higher levels of age. At Florence in 1427, the age distribution reflected the high mortalities and comparatively high birth rates characteristic of a traditional society, and thus remained a continuing trait of the city. But whatever the reason, Florence and all the Renaissance cities remained remarkably young communities. Their quality of youth was further emphasized by a distinctive generational balance. Fathers were very old in relation to their sons; few men married before the age of 30, and the average baby born in the city in 1427 was received by a father already nearly 40 years of age. Well before their sons reached adulthood, death was ruthlessly thinning the genera-

[38] Males for whom ages are given number 19,690. Females were slightly older, with an average age of 27.27.

[39] These and subsequent figures concerning the American population are taken from *The World Almanac and Book of Facts, 1966*. ed. L. H. Long (New York, 1967), p. 262.

[40] Of males in the population, 12,512 were 15 years of age or over, and of these 6,316 were less than 35.

tion of the fathers, muting the counsel and weakening the moral guidance they might have offered their children.

Although youth was characteristic of the entire urban community, the young were, in relative terms, particularly numerous in the wealthiest households. In those homes with a tax assessment after deductions of more than 3,200 florins, the median age of males was only 16, as against 22 for the entire population.[41] Among the very rich, young men between ages 15 and 30 constituted more than 50 percent of the adult male population; in the city as a whole, youths in the same age bracket constituted only 41 percent of the adult males.[42]

Two factors seem to have increased the relative proportion of the young within the wealthiest households. Of all urban males, the rich were the tardiest to marry, and thus they fathered their children later in life.[43] Many wealthy fathers died when their children were still young, and this may have helped skew the age pyramid still more in favor of youth. But most important, in spite of later marriage, the richest males were the most prolific group in society in producing and rearing children. In 1427, the average baby born in the entire population had 2.2 older brothers or sisters. The baby born to the richest parents had 3.1 older siblings.[44] This is not the place to discuss at length whether the many children of the rich primarily reflects higher fertility or better care of their offspring. But the plenitude of children among the wealthy sharply lowered their average age. In the entire city, 60 percent of the population of both men

[41] Similarly, the average age of males in the richest category was 21.9 years, and 26.0 in the population as a whole.

[42] Of 932 men age 15 or over in the richest households, 468 were between 15 and 30. Of 12,135 men in the entire population, 4,997 were in that age range.

[43] See below, n. 48.

[44] In the richest households, 81 babies born in 1427 had 253 older brothers and sisters up to age 14; 1,005 babies born in all households had 2,235 older brothers and sisters.

and women were age 16 or over, and only 50 percent of the richest.[45] Even with the high mortalities, the comparatively high fertility of the wealthy, or perhaps the better survival rates enjoyed by their children, made them the youngest group within the city.[46] The very rich, as we have mentioned, gained among contemporaries a particular notoriety for their volatility and violence. Perhaps one reason for this was the preponderance of young men among them.

According to our writers, not only the age but also the marital status of the male population affected its behavior. As we have already noted, the urban male married extraordinarily late. For the city as a whole, only slightly more than a quarter of the men between ages 18 and 32 were certainly married or were widowers.[47] Not until the middle 30s was more than one-half of the male population certainly married. Again, males in the wealthiest households, who were relatively more numerous than in the entire population, were also the most reluctant to marry. Between the ages 23 and 27, in all households, 25 percent of the males were married; less than 17 percent of the richest males in the same age range had taken a wife.[48] At every social level, urban society was flooded with large numbers of young men, unable or unwilling to marry for two decades after puber-

[45] In the entire population, 21,591 out of 36,196 persons were age 16 or over, and 1,482 out of 2,957 in the richest households.

[46] "Birth rates, and not death rates, are the major determining factor of population structure." Cf. Ralph Thomlinson, *Population Dynamics: Causes and Consequences of World Demographic Change* (New York, 1965), p. 434.

[47] The total of men in this age range was 4,456, and those certainly married were 1,097; widowers were 86. Unfortunately, it is impossible to distinguish for technical reasons single men from childless widowers. Our figures are thus not precise, but the number of childless widowers in this age range was surely very small.

[48] In all households, 339 out of 1,468 males were married, and 24 were widowers (24.72 percent). Among families with an assessment of more than 1,600 florins, out of 275 men, only 39 were married and 6 were widowers (16.35 percent).

ty, and these were especially numerous among the wealthy. This could only have heightened what we might call the erotic tension within the city, and helped give it a probably merited reputation for vice and sexual disorders.

One other social peculiarity made the rich distinct within the urban population: the sex ratio, or relative numbers of men to women. For the city as a whole, men outnumbered women by a ratio of 116 to 100. But a careful examination of the city's population shows that this shortage of women was primarily characteristic of the years of young adulthood, and was especially pronounced within the richest classes. For the city as a whole, the sex ratio between ages 18 and 32 was 132; all young men within the city would have difficulty finding contact and companionship with girls their own age. Perhaps there is little wonder that we hear of riots and brawls at the public dances held to welcome spring. But among the wealthiest households, the sex ratio over these same years was a nearly incredible 150— three young men for every two young women.[49] The principal reason for this shortage of girls seems to be this: urban parents, and especially the wealthy, were eager to settle the future of their daughters at an almost desperate speed. The most common age of marriage for girls in the city was only 15 years; by the age of 20, nearly 85 percent of the girls appearing in the *Catasto* were already married.[50] Among the rich, the brides were younger at marriage (and the grooms older) than among the other classes. Girls who lacked a sufficiently large dowry or physical beauty, and who had slight hope of finding a husband, were placed in convents with equal haste. They were thus largely lost to our records, and largely lost to lay society. The kind

[49] For the city as a whole, there were 20,116 men and 17,304 women. Between the ages 18 and 32 there were 4,455 men and 3,363 women; in the richest homes, men in the same age bracket numbered 407 and women 271.

[50] Of 1,228 women in the age category 18–22, 1,035 were married and 9 were widows.

of moderating influence which young women are likely to exert over young men was similarly diminished.

The marital habits of the Florentines thus had pronounced effects for the moral life of the city. Economic pressures and family customs discouraged young men, especially the rich, from marrying until they were well into their 30s. "I counted the other day," complained a participant in Alberti's dialogue on the family, "no less than 22 young Alberti males, living alone without a mate, not having taken a wife, none of them younger than 16 and none older than 36 years."[51] For an extended period, young men such as these were deprived of all legitimate outlet for their sexual energies; their behavior was also unrestrained by any responsibility for a wife or children. Moreover, the haste to settle the future of young girls through early marriage or the convent largely deprived these men of even the companionship of women their own age. Unless the strictures of the contemporary moralists and the plots of numerous novelle deceive us, many of these unattached young men, blocked from marrying, relentlessly pursued women in hope of seducing them—married and widowed even more than single girls. The presence of so many bachelors within the urban population offered fertile grounds too for the practice of prostitution and for sodomy, for which the Renaissance town had a notorious and deserved reputation.

Educational practices also helped shape the character of the urban male. Our writers warned that the neglect or absence of the father was likely to have a pernicious influence upon the upbringing of his sons. But several factors worked to curtail the father's influence within the household, and these factors were again most prominent among the rich. In the entire population, husbands were some 13 years older than their wives, and

[51] *Opere*, I, 34: "Che è questo a dire?—che io annoveravo pochi di fa non meno che venti e due giovani Alberti vivere soli senza compagna, non aver moglie, niuno manco che sedici, niuno più che anni trenta e sei."

in the richest households the average age difference was 15 or 16 years.[52] This remarkable age differential between the spouses limited the duration of marriage and threatened the stability of the household. Although we cannot here make exact calculations, it appears that the average father had a less than even chance of seeing his babies reach adulthood.[53] The possibility that a child would lose one at least of his parents before maturity was of course even greater.

Some Florentine fathers recognized that age and death might well silence their voices, and deprive their sons of paternal counsel during the difficult years of adolescence and young manhood. Advice that they might not personally be able to convey they therefore included in family memoirs or *ricordi*, which their sons could at least read and consider after their own demise. Giovanni Morelli, for example, whose *ricordi* are among the most colorful of those composed in the fifteenth century, himself had lost his father while a baby. To avoid this unhappy situation, he strongly urged his own descendants to take a wife between ages 20 and 25—extraordinary advice quite opposed to the usual practice of the times.[54] He listed in minute detail seven injuries ("danni") that the child deprived of his father must suffer, and among them was the lack of paternal instruction.[55]

The moral counselors of the age similarly frowned upon an education too much dominated by women. The mother was more likely than the father to spoil the child, impart to him

[52] Married men in the highest wealth category had an average age of 44.64 years, and their wives 30.31 years. In households with an assessment of from 801 to 1,600 florins, the husbands averaged 47.06 years, and their wives 31.79.

[53] Calculated on the basis of this single census, life expectancy for men at age 39 (the average age of parenthood for men) was 17 years. Because of immigration and other factors which influence age distributions, this estimate can be considered only roughly approximate.

[54] *Ricordi*, p. 207: "E fatto questo pensiero, e tu dilibera torla da' venti anni insino ne' venticinque. . . ."

[55] *Ibid.*, pp. 202–285.

effeminate habits, acquiesce in his whims, and convey to him the impression that he could always have his way through tears and tantrums. Sociologists today point out that a woman who alone or with little help from her husband assumes the heavy burdens of child rearing is apt herself to develop tensions and anxieties. These in turn may influence the atmosphere of the home, and the personality and behavior of her children. But again, the domestic customs of the Florentines tended to tip the balance of parental responsibilities for the child toward the mother. The older husband was often occupied by affairs of business or of politics, which kept him physically away from home or only remotely involved in its problems. His much younger and often physically more vigorous spouse enjoyed a more intimate, and usually a longer contact with her children. One marked result of the large age differential between the spouses was the proliferation of widows within Florentine society. By age 50, one-half the women in Florence were widows.[56] Most lived with their married sons, aided in the management of their homes and the raising of their children. The *nonna* was a familiar person to Florentine children, but few of them would have known their grandfathers.

These then seem to be some of the social factors that contributed to urban violence in the Renaissance city. The urban population contained large numbers of young males forced to delay marriage for some two decades after puberty. They were free from responsibilities of managing a household and supporting a family, but they were simultaneously denied any legitimate outlet for their sexual drives. Even the companionship with women their own age and their own station in life was restricted for them. Moreover, some of them at least lacked a strong paternal presence in their own upbringing. Most of them were poorly counseled and poorly restrained by the much older and rapidly thinning generation of their own fathers. There

[56] In the age bracket 47 to 52, 502 out of 899 women were widows.

seems little wonder that the tensions within them often found release in the perpetration of violent deeds.

But our picture is still not complete. The tremendous upheavals in the cities, though often provoked by the thoughtless acts of the young, were aggravated and sustained through organized factions. As Giovanni Botero noted with keen perspicacity, certain classes were especially prone to factional allignments and factional violence. Both the very rich and the very poor tended to favor violence—the rich to advance their limitless ambitions and the poor to escape their crushing misery. The rich had the wealth to grant favors or the power to win them, and inevitably they attracted friends and clients from the lower levels of society, especially the humblest. The middle classes, alone among the major social divisions of the city, associated their own interests with peace and stability. Botero's stress on the peaceful preferences of the *mezzani* fits in well with the comments of the Quattrocento moralists. Giovanni Morelli, for example, who himself derived from the middle ranges of Florentine society, urged his descendants to assume a very cautious attitude toward the "sects" as he called them, which divided society.[57] They should preferably seek and maintain the friendship of all factions. If this was not possible, one should prudently support the stronger or the strongest side, in order to be associated with its victory. Still, one should act justly in regard to all men, and should even avoid excessive displays of enthusiasm in the support of one's own party. Reason, moderation, and extreme caution should govern the behavior of the prudent citizen in regard to the factions.

The stability of a community was thus in considerable measure determined by the relative strength of its various classes and the balance that existed among them. We have some indication of what that balance was through the distribution of taxable wealth. Urban society was marked by extraordinary contrasts

[57] *Ricordi*, p. 280.

between the very rich and the very poor. At Pistoia in 1427, the richest 10 percent of the population owned nearly 60 percent of the city's wealth, and nearly 30 percent had, after deductions, no wealth at all.[58] At Florence in the same year, the highest 1 percent of the households owned a substantial quarter of the city's taxable wealth, and 31 percent owned nothing.[59]

The pronounced contrasts between rich and poor made for an unstable society, but Botero is probably also correct in his assumption that large cities were usually more peaceful than the small towns, because they possessed a larger population of *mezzani*. In spite of the huge wealth owned by few families, Florence did possess considerable numbers of small shopkeepers and merchants, with some wealth to defend. If we ignore deductions allowed in the *Catasto*, 15 percent of the Florentine population had no possessions. In contrast, at the small, neighboring town of Prato, 25 percent of the households were without any taxable asset.[60]

Botero's analysis further seems to offer an excellent explanation for the contrasting social histories of the two neighboring towns, Florence and Pistoia, in the late Middle Ages. Florence, for all the tumult of its history, seems a paradigm of peace in comparison with its much smaller neighbor.[61] Contemporaries believed that the men of Pistoia were descended from the followers of the Roman conspirator Catiline, and this bad seed explained their violent deportment. But perhaps a stronger influence was exerted upon them by the sharp contrasts between rich and poor, and by the lack of a population of small shopkeepers able to offer stability to the city.

To combine both parts of our analysis, we would suggest that

[58] Herlihy, *Pistoia*, p. 188.
[59] The total tax assessment borne by the city (after deductions) was in round figures 7,638,000 florins. The richest 99 families had a combined assessment of 1,910,046 florins.
[60] Out of 958 households, 240 had no tax assessment after deductions.
[61] Cf. my further comments in *Pistoia*, pp. 198–207.

the proclivity to violence so characteristic of the Tuscan cities seems to be related to certain distinctive features of both the urban family and urban society. In regard to the family, perhaps the most important single factor was the extraordinarily late age at which most men became husbands and fathers. Delayed marriage flooded society with numerous unattached and sexually repressed young men, cut short the duration of the marital union, diminished masculine influence in the rearing of children, and weakened the restraints that the older male generation could exert upon the exuberance of the young. In regard to society, the few numbers of middle-class *mezzani* meant that the tone of urban life tended to be set by the very rich and very poor—groups more inclined to violence than the small shopkeepers and merchants.

These features of the urban family and society seem evident enough in our statistical sources of the Quattrocento. Had they always marked the Tuscan communities? In some measure, probably yes; but it does appear that the bad economic times of the fourteenth century aggravated both aspects of urban society. Unfortunately, the sources of the thirteenth or earlier centuries, when the medieval prosperity was at its height, do not permit a rigorous comparison with the later epoch. But it is certain that writers of the Quattrocento at least believed that their own marital practices were much different from those of their distant ancestors.[62] In particular, they noted that girls married much later in the past; presumably, the age difference between the spouses, so marked in the family of the Quattrocento, would not have been as large.[63] While we cannot prove this statistically, it does appear likely that the hard times of the four-

[62] Cf. Morelli, *Ricordi*, pp. 111–112, in regard to the marriage age of girls, noted that "le fanciulle si maritavano allora nell'età d'anni ventiquattro o venzei" in the twelfth century. See also "Anonymi Itali breviarium italicae historicae," in *RIS*, ed. L. Muratori (Milan, 1730), XVI, 259.

[63] In *Paradiso* XV, 104–105, Dante similarly condemns the desperate haste with which fathers were marrying their daughters.

teenth century obstructed and delayed marriage for the urban male, with important consequences for the character of the urban family and society.

It further seems that the disrupted economy of the fourteenth century weakened the social weight of the middle ranges of urban society. The small shopkeeper and merchant was, on the whole, less able than his richer neighbors to weather the economic storms of the age. Bad times, in other words, helped polarize society into classes very rich and very poor. Unfortunately, this cannot at present be proved for any Tuscan city, but it can be illustrated for small rural communities. Both at Impruneta in the Florentine *contado* and at Piuvica, a suburb of Pistoia, the contrasts between rich and poor seem to have sharpened considerably between the thirteenth and fifteenth centuries.[64]

In conclusion, it may be appropriate to draw some analogies between the problem of violence in the Tuscan city and the similar problem in the cities of our own society. Obviously, there is no social group today which could be considered analogous to the haughty and turbulent magnates of the Renaissance town. But clearly there are groups analogous to the poor and the destitute in Quattrocento society. Botero's observation, that the poor have little to lose by violence, seems applicable to urban communities in both ages. In recommending that the way to stability is to strengthen the numbers and the influence of the middle ranges of society, that is, the small shopkeepers and artisans with an economic interest in social peace, he seems to be speaking very much to our own times. Perhaps there is also some analogy, although admittedly more distant, between the family structure of the Quattrocento towns and that characteristic of many households in the inner core of our own cities.

[64] Cf. Herlihy, *Pistoia*, pp. 182–183, and *idem*, "Santa Maria Impruneta: A Rural Commune in the Late Middle Ages," *Florentine Studies: Politics and Society in Renaissance Florence*. ed. Nicolai Rubinstein (London, 1969), pp. 242–276.

The moralists of the fifteenth century agreed that a stable and durable family, in which fathers and mothers took equal responsibility for the rearing of children, was the best means for producing cooperative members of the community. But the men of the Renaissance were themselves not always able to realize their own ideals. In particular, the late marriage age for males introduced an element of instability into the urban family; it curtailed the duration of the marriage, weakened the male presence within the home, and tended to give prime responsibility for the training of the children to the mother. It is well known that many households today in the inner city lack a masculine presence and influence on the rearing of children, although desertion plays the role that death assumed in the fifteenth century. Still, both then and now, the principle of the Quattrocento moral counselors seems valid: unstable homes and marriages of short duration do not provide the best atmosphere for educating peaceful, responsible citizens.

VII

THE FLORENTINE *POPOLO MINUTO* AND ITS POLITICAL ROLE, 1340-1450

Gene A. Brucker

*T*HE HISTORY of urban society in medieval and Renaissance Italy has been primarily a study of organized groups. Scholars have concentrated upon those associations—*consorterie*, clans, guilds, Parte Guelfa, Parte Ghibellina—which were strong enough to win a share (and sometimes a monopoly) of political power. Moreover, these organizations kept records, some of which have survived. But we know relatively little about those segments of the urban community which were never organized—the occupations and professions, for example, which were not incorporated into guilds—or which so antagonized the authorities that their organizations were suppressed and their records destroyed: the textile workers and the heretics. It is true that the clothworkers have aroused scholarly interest, and Marxist historians in particular have investigated their efforts to organize, and their participation in the disorders that broke out in many Italian cities during the fourteenth century.[1] Yet even in a city like Florence, with its large textile industry,

---

[1] For a recent example, see E. Werner, "Probleme städtischer Volksbewegungen im. 14. Jahrhundert, dargestellt am Beispiel der Ciompi-Erhebung in Florenz," in E. Englemann, ed., *Städtische Volksbewegungen im 14. Jahrhundert* (Berlin, 1960), pp. 11–55. The Marxist viewpoint is summarized in G. Brucker, "The Ciompi Revolution," in *Florentine Studies*, ed. N. Rubinstein (London, 1968), pp. 315–317.

these laborers constituted only a part of the *popolo minuto*. This study defines this lowest stratum of Florence's urban society in terms of occupation, economic status, behavior patterns, aspirations, and then examines its political role.

The basic problem is definition: who were the *popolo minuto*? We receive very little help from contemporaries who employed the phrase very loosely, and modern scholars have not been much more precise. In his analysis of the city mob in *Primitive Rebels*, Eric Hobsbawm includes in this category not only the "scum" but also artisans, apprentices, and those engaged in menial trades and occupations outside the guild structure: porters, stevedores, peddlers, and unskilled laborers.[2] This definition is roughly applicable to Florence's *popolo minuto* in the fourteenth and fifteenth centuries.[3] The clothworkers formed the most homogeneous group, comprising carders and beaters who performed the least skilled tasks in the cloth *botteghe*, as well as apprentices and assistants who worked in the dye shops and in other subsidiary trades in this large and complex industry. Indeed, some of the operators of these shops —the shearers, burlers, menders—were themselves so poor and so dependent upon (and exploited by) the cloth manufacturers that they also belong to this category.[4] Forming a second group were the journeymen, apprentices, and helpers in the craft guilds, as well as the poorest artisans in such trades as stonema-

---

[2] *Primitive Rebels* (New York, 1959), chap. 7.

[3] Hobsbawm is primarily interested in mobs that inhabited European capital cities without large industries: Rome, Naples, Palermo, Vienna. For a definition of the poor in sixteenth-century Lyon, see Natalie Davis, "Poor Relief, Humanism and Heresy: The Case of Lyon," *Studies in Medieval and Renaissance History*, VI (1968), 221–229. In his article, "La vie et la lutte des Ciompi de Sienne," *Annales*, XX (1965), 103, V. Rutenburg has stated that the terms "*popolo minuto*" and "Ciompi" in Florence applied only to the salaried laborers in the cloth industry, a definition that is too narrow and limited, in my judgment. The category was broader, similar to that which Rutenburg describes for Siena.

[4] Brucker, "Ciompi," pp. 319–325.

sonry, carpentry, and metalwork. A third category consisted of those inhabitants who eked out a marginal existence in menial occupations: servants, grooms, carters, messengers, peddlers, fishermen. And at the bottom of the social scale were the dregs of this human community: vagrants and vagabonds, beggars, prostitutes and their pimps, and the criminals (both professional and amateur) who inhabited the shadowy precincts of Florence's underworld. The distinctions between these groups are not economic or social but occupational, and since the poor moved easily from one unskilled job to another, the categories are not sharply defined.

A statistical analysis of the heads of households in a tax survey (*estimo*) drawn up in 1379 for one district (Rota in the quarter of Santa Croce) provides some data on the numerical proportions of the Florentine poor who fit into these four groups.[5] This survey was unusually thorough and complete; it included such unlikely sources of tax revenue as Masa of Arezzo and the widow Lisabetta, who were each assessed 7 denarii, or approximately 1/15 of the average daily wage of an unskilled laborer. But criminals, beggars, and vagabonds were not represented in any substantial number (or at least not identified), since the tax assessors would not waste their time reporting the wholly destitute, or those individuals with no fixed abode. I have arbitrarily designated certain households, those with assessments of 10 soldi or less, as belonging to the *popolo minuto*. This group comprises nearly 60 percent of the total: 302 of 547 households.[6] The livelihood of approximately one-half of these poor families (140

[5] *Archivio di Stato di Firenze* (cited hereafter as *ASF*), *Prestanze*, 367, fols. 48r–61v. On this *estimo*, see N. Rodolico, *La democrazia fiorentina nel suo tramonto (1378–1382)* (Bologna, 1905), pp. 40, 296–297.

[6] In the 1352 *estimo*, the percentage of households in the Rota district receiving assessments of 10 soldi or less was 61 percent (261 of 426); the ratio was 61.09 percent for the entire city; B. Barbadoro, "Finanza e demografia nei ruoli fiorentine d'imposta del 1352–1355," *Atti del Congresso internazionale per lo studio dei problemi della popolazione* (Rome, 1931), IX, 624–629.

of 302) came from the cloth industry, while another 47 family heads were artisans, either members of a craft guild or employees working in a shop. Another group of households was subsidized by the paltry earnings from menial occupations. These breadwinners were identified as porters, couriers, cooks, market women, gardeners, laborers in brick kilns and flour mills. Nearly one-quarter (78 of 302) of the poor heads of households were not identified by occupation; many doubtless earned some income from part-time labor in the cloth *botteghe*, or by spinning and weaving in their cottages.

Since this *estimo* is very comprehensive, it is an exceptionally good source for measuring the geographical mobility of the urban poor. A year before its compilation (April 1378), a forced loan had been levied upon the inhabitants of the Rota district; a total of 469 households (compared with the *estimo*'s 547) were recorded in this *prestanza*.[7] Just over one-half of the poor households (237 of 469) in the 1378 survey were headed by living males. But 45 percent of these taxpayers were not listed in the more complete *estimo* survey compiled just twelve months later. One must naturally make allowance for misinformation and clerical errors, and for deaths during the year that separated the surveys. These were also very troubled times; the Ciompi revolution and its aftermath undoubtedly contributed to social dislocation. Nevertheless, this data indicates that the Florentine poor were very mobile. They moved from district to district within the city in search of lower rents and more lucrative jobs; they moved back to their native hamlets in the *contado* when the cloth factories shut down, or when seasonal fluctuations in economic activity reduced the opportunities for employment. The lowliest of these poor inhabitants—beggars,

---

[7] *Prestanze*, 333, fols. 87r-121v. For the entire city, the 1379 *estimo* listed 13,372 households (Rodolico, *Democrazia*, p. 40), and the 1378 *prestanza*, 8,430 households. The latter figure corrects an error in my *Florentine Politics and Society, 1343–1378* (Princeton, 1962), p. 316 n. 71, and repeated in "Ciompi," p. 324 n. 5.

vagabonds, criminals—were also the most mobile; they were constantly shifting from place to place in their search for alms, or a day's wage, or the opportunity to steal.

Concerning another type of movement involving the poor, the upward thrust in the social hierarchy, the sources are not very informative. The old myth about the serfs fleeing to the cities to make their fortunes has been exploded, for Florence, by Plesner and Fiumi. We know that most urban wealth was built upon rural foundations and that Florence's patriciate had descended from Tuscany's rural bourgeoisie.[8] Still, the records do reveal the exceptional cases of large fortunes being amassed by artisans of modest wealth and status. The Martelli, Fioravanti, Gaddi, and Vespucci families can all be traced back to artisan origins; those prominent merchants, Francesco Datini and Gregorio Dati, descended from shopkeepers.[9] Did some artisans, whose descendants became wealthy merchants and industrialists, themselves come up from the ranks of the clothworkers or the menial trades? The evidence for tracing such careers might be found for the years after 1350 when tax records, guild protocols, and other pertinent sources become abundant. By this later period, however, and particularly after 1380, the Florentine social structure had become more rigid, and the opportunities for upward mobility more limited.[10] There may have been some poor wool carders and peddlers

---

[8] J. Plesner, *L'émigration de la campagne à la ville libre de Florence au XIIIe siècle* (Copenhagen, 1934); E. Fiumi, "Fioritura e decadenza dell'economia fiorentina," *Archivio storico italiano*, CXV (1957), 385–439.

[9] On the Martelli, see L. Martines, "La famiglia Martelli e un documento sulla vigilia del ritorno dall'esilio di Cosimo de' Medici (1434), *Archivio storico italiano*, CXVII (1959), 31–41. The Gaddi were painters who became merchants; the first well-known member of the Fioravanti family, Neri, was a stonemason and builder. On the Vespucci, see G. Brucker, *Renaissance Florence* (New York, 1969), p. 95.

[10] See the comments of L. Martines, *Lawyers and Statecraft in Renaissance Florence* (Princeton, 1968), pp. 403–404.

who themselves, or whose children, became prosperous merchants and founders of patrician families, but their number was certainly not large.

"One may safely assume that the living conditions of the poor were wretched," writes Raymond de Roover in his recent article on labor conditions in Florence around 1400.[11] The degree of wretchedness naturally varied from family to family, from year to year, even from month to month. The variables are so numerous (income, property holdings,[12] professional skills, windfalls from inheritances, business conditions, taxation) and so poorly documented that generalizations are extremely hazardous. One fact, however, is obvious: the precariousness of life among the Florentine poor. Even in times of high employment and cheap bread, their income was barely above the subsistence level; only the skilled workers could earn enough to build up reserves for hard times.[13] Bad harvest, epidemics, and wars were common and recurring experiences in the century following the Black Death, and the poor suffered most from inflated prices, hunger, and unemployment. Until more is known about price and wage levels for these decades, we can only speculate about the long-term trends in the living standards of the poor. Charles de la Roncière's researches on Florentine gabelles prove that taxes on food products rose very sharply from the late thirteenth century to 1380, so that a progressively larger share of the poor family's budget went into the commu-

[11] R. de Roover, "Labor Conditions in Florence c. 1400," *Florentine Studies,* ed. N. Rubinstein (London, 1968), p. 303.

[12] On property ownership by Florentine clothworkers in the fifteenth century, see *ibid.,* p. 304. Professor David Herlihy informs me that only 15 percent of the households listed in the 1427 *catasto* were propertyless.

[13] On the income differences between skilled and unskilled workers, see de Roover, *op.cit.,* pp. 303, 306–307; Brucker, "Ciompi," p. 320 n. 4, 324 n. 2; C. de la Roncière, "Indirect Taxes or 'Gabelles' at Florence in the Fourteenth Century: The Evolution of Tariffs and Problems of Collection," *Florentine Studies* (London, 1968), p. 186.

nal treasury.[14] Wages certainly did not keep pace with this gabelle increase; indeed, the wages paid to unskilled laborers apparently declined in the decade (1368–1378) prior to the Ciompi revolution.[15] With respect to prices and wages, the years after 1380 are still uncharted.

In addition to the tax records, with their fragmentary data on economic conditions, occupations, and mobility,[16] other sources furnish clues to a very significant aspect of urban poverty, namely debt. Most poor Florentines owed money to their employer, or their pawnbroker, or both. No thorough study has yet been made of these credit relationships which are so important for comprehending the economic and social milieu of Renaissance Florence. Much of the extant data from communal and guild records describes the efforts of creditors to recover their loans. In the protocols of the Lana guild, for example, are hundreds of cases of cloth workers being prosecuted for debt. Occasionally, their creditors would petition the guild consuls for authority to imprison their clients; more frequently, they sought a license authorizing guild officials to sequester their

[14] De la Roncière, "Indirect Taxes," pp. 140–192, especially his summary, pp. 186–187. Only the wheat gabelle remained stable and low, at 12 denarii per *staio* (*ibid.*, p. 152). The gabelle on oil increased fivefold between 1326 and 1360; that on hogs, sevenfold between 1333 and 1365; that on wine imported in casks, fivefold between 1320 and 1360 (*ibid.*, pp. 152–155). Between 1359 and 1380 (and probably later), the gabelle accounted for one-half of the retail price of wine sold in taverns and wineshops. The retail price of wine had increased tenfold between 1285 and 1358 (*ibid.*, p. 168).

[15] *Ibid.*, p. 186. De la Roncière describes the living conditions of the Florentine poor on the eve of the Ciompi revolution in bleaker terms than I have done (Brucker, "Ciompi," p. 324). His evidence on price and wage trends is not yet published (see De la Ronciere, "Indirect Taxes," p. 171 n. 2; 186 n. 3) but his data concerning the increasingly heavy gabelle burdens is very persuasive.

[16] David Herlihy and Christiane Klapisch have begun a statistical analysis of the *catasto* records, which will provide solid and detailed information about the economy and demography of the Florentine poor.

property: the tools by which they earned a meager livelihood, their beds, clothing, or kitchen utensils.[17] The records of the civil courts are filled with the petitions of licensed usurers for judgments against their delinquent clients.[18] Although treated contemptuously by the authorities and disliked by the populace, Christian moneylenders performed a valuable service for this community by providing consumer credit at a reasonable price. The commune established the maximum interest rates and required these lenders to pay a substantial fee for engaging in usury.[19] I have found no evidence of riots or mob attacks upon licensed pawnbrokers before the establishment of the Jewish community in 1435. Either their social utility was universally recognized by the poor, or they were well protected by the authorities. When, in the 1430s, these men could not provide sufficient capital for their poor clients, the government reluctantly permitted a group of Jewish moneylenders to settle in Florence, "so that the necessities of the poor may be satisfied at a low rate of interest," which was fixed at 20 percent annually.[20]

As Niccolò Rodolico discovered seventy years ago, the crim-

[17] Brucker, "Ciompi," pp. 321–322. For examples of cloth workers imprisoned for debt, see *ASF, Lana,* 84, fols. 10v, 39v; 85, fols. 43r, 50r, 109r. Examples of the seizure of a laborer's property to satisfy debts are in *ibid.,* 101, fols. 3v, 6v, 15r, 17v, 45r, 49v, 51v. These cases are very common.

[18] See, e.g., *ASF, Atti del Esecutore degli Ordinamenti di Giustizia* (cited hereafter as *AEOG,* 811, fols. 12v-14r, 18v-21r, 23r-24r, 26v-27v, 34v-38v; *ASF, Atti del Podestà* (cited hereafter as *AP*), 3087, fols. 156v-157r.

[19] For a 1379 provision that licensed usurers, see Rodolico, *Demoerazia fiorentina,* pp. 137–138; see also M. Becker, "Nota dei processi riguardanti prestatori di danari nei tribunali fiorentini dal 1343 al 1379," *Archivio storico italiano,* CXIV (1956), 746–747.

[20] U. Cassuto, *Gli ebrei a Firenze nell'età del Rinascimento* (Florence, 1918), pp. 17, 364–365. To engage in pawnbroking without a license was prohibited; for examples of such illegal loan activity and the penalties, see *ASF, Giudice degli Appelli* (cited hereafter as *GA*), 79, fol. 320r-320v.

inal court records contain much information about the *popolo minuto*. Most scholars who have exploited these records have emulated Rodolico in searching for material on conspiracies, on riots and disorders, and on any form of lower-class activity with political implications.[21] I discuss those problems later in this paper, but here I wish to consider the court records as a source for perceiving the life style of the Florentine poor. The cases are sufficiently numerous to permit statistical analysis, of the kind now being employed by French scholars in studying the history and sociology of crime during the *ancien régime*.[22] It is true that the records are incomplete and often biased. So universal in Western experience is judicial prejudice against the poor, and a consequent lack of objectivity in describing their world, that the phenomenon does not require elaborate documentation. It appears, in blatant form, in a rector's judgment (1382) against one Nanni di Cione, convicted of assault. Condemning Nanni to the amputation of his left hand, the judge announced that he was applying the maximum sentence because the culprit was obviously too poor to pay a fine (the normal penalty) and thus merited corporal punishment.[23] These flaws and limitations notwithstanding, the criminal court records do contain valuable if sketchy data about their clients, including the poor. Sentences always included the Christian name of the accused (as well as his patronymic and nickname), occasionally

[21] N. Rodolico, *Il popolo minuto* (Bologna, 1899); Brucker, *Florentine Politics and Society*.

[22] See F. Billacois, "Pour une enquête sur la criminalité dans la France d'Ancien Régime," *Annales*, XXII (1967), 340–347; Y. Bercé, "Aspects de la criminalité au XVIIe siècle," *Revue historique*, CCXXXIX (1968), 33–42. For one attempt to compile statistics on Florentine crime, see U. Dorini, *Il diritto penale e la delinquenza in Firenze nel secolo XIV* (Lucca, 1923).

[23] ASF, *Atti del Capitano del Popolo* (cited hereafter as *ACP*), 1428, fols. 21r-22v. Nanni was described in these terms: "hominem vilis abiecte et male condictionis"; his left hand was to be amputated "cum deficiat sibi dextrum."

his occupation, and invariably his place of origin: the parish if he was a native of the city or *contado*, the province or kingdom of his birth if a foreigner. In describing the crimes, the notaries sometimes divulged information concerning social mores and behavior, even attitudes and perceptions. Anonymous denunciations are particularly revealing about sentiments and prejudices, if frequently unreliable for events. We may be skeptical about the facts, while accepting the hostile spirit that motivated this accusation against the magnate Niccolò Tosinghi, who allegedly threw filthy water from his tower onto the property of his neighbor: "And this he has done to me because he is a powerful man and I am a poor and impotent *popolano*, and I must earn my living with my hands, and I am not strong enough to resist him." Another example from this category is a document submitted to the Conservators of the Laws in 1431, describing the origins and upbringing of an artisan named Niccolò, accused of being the bastard son of a priest named Pazzino, and therefore ineligible for communal office:

> This Pazzino, son of Ser Cristoforo, was a priest in the church of S. Piero a Quaracchi, . . . Pazzino's mother is still alive; she lives in that church of S. Piero a Quaracchi with her other son, a priest named Ser Domenico . . . who being a bastard, cannot hold the benefice in his own name, but it is held by others. And if you want to be informed about this, ask the patrons [of the church] who are the Pigli. . . . This Pazzino was born in San Marco . . . and then Ser Cristofano arranged to have the mother married to a tiler named Niccolò . . . so that Pazzino was present at his mother's wedding, his father being the priest. Then Niccolò died and the girl went back to live with Ser Cristofano. . . . When Pazzino was eleven years old or thereabouts, he was denounced as the bastard son of a priest and so he left and stayed away for some time. Then the priest died and he returned and married a girl named Margherita. . . .[24]

[24] *AEOG*, 499, fol. 75r, March 29, 1367 (the accusation against Tosinghi), *GA*, 79, fols. 116r-117r, Nov. 15, 1431.

While judicial documents are most revealing about the underworld and the criminals and vagabonds who inhabited it, they also throw light upon the mores of respectable citizens. In sharp contrast with the pattern in our cities today, every social class in Renaissance Florence (and not only the poor) was well represented in the criminal courts. This was the result, in part, of a much broader network of controls and prohibitions, and also of a strong though diminishing penchant for violence, which could motivate the rich and the prominent as well as the poor and the lowly. Some rough patterns in the sociology of crime can be discerned in these records. Individuals from all classes were convicted of physical assault, but the incidence was greatest (at least in the fourteenth century) at both extremes of the social scale: among the prepotent magnates, and among the very poor. Merchants and artisans, the Florentine men of property, were somewhat less violent in their behavior. Petty theft was almost exclusively a lower-class phenomenon; those apprehended and convicted were either identified as vagabonds, immigrants from the *contado*, or menials: servants, porters, messengers, apprentices, slaves. First offenders were normally punished by fines, but habitual thieves were imprisoned, branded, whipped, and even hanged. In higher levels of society, the delicts involving property were more sophisticated. Among the wellborn criminals were businessmen who absconded with money entrusted to them, notaries who forged wills and deeds of sale, landowners who seized a neighbor's farm or crops by force.

But we are concerned here with the poor and their involvement in criminal activity. Inhabiting the Florentine underworld were those individuals who were not gainfully employed and who were engaged, more or less regularly, in illicit activities for their livelihood. The category may be divided roughly into professionals and amateurs. The latter were the more numerous, and they included those indigents who committed crimes when they were unemployed. When they were hungry, they stole and then sold their loot to dealers of old clothes (a legitimate, respected profession in Florence) or took it to the pawnshops.[25] Incidental, petty theft tended to increase when the cloth industry was depressed, or in winter when certain occupations (building, gardening, transport) were not active. But Florence also attracted professional criminals. Brought to justice in 1405 by the *podestà* was the pickpocket Antoniello from the Abruzzi, who confessed to crimes committed in Rimini, Fermo, Prato, Assisi, Siena, and Empoli. A native of Poland, Bartolomeo alias Griffone, went to the gallows in 1443 for robberies committed in Florence, Bologna, Venice, Rome, and Siena.[26] A large proportion of these professionals migrated to Tuscany from the poorer Italian provinces (Piedmont, Friuli, Abruzzi, Sicily, Sardinia) and from ultramontane areas (Germany, Flanders, Hungary, Spain). Since these foreigners had no kinsmen and few friends to help them to hide or escape, they were more easily caught by the authorities than native criminals, and more likely to pay for their misdeeds on the gallows or in the communal prisons. In one period of seventeen months, from February 1382 through June 1383, the judges pronounced death sentences against eleven foreigners, of whom seven were executed. Between 1409 and 1413, seven others were hanged for robbery in Florence: Andrea of Budapest, Johannes of Vienna, Biagio of Hungary, Giovanni di Francesco from Friuli, Piero de Giovanni from Piedmont, Clemente of Zagreb and Johannes, a native of Moravia.[27]

[25] An example: Antonio di Paolo of Bologna, who stole a coat worth 4 florins and pawned it for 4 lire; *AEOG*, 960, fol. 111r-111v, Sept. 5, 1384.

[26] *AP*, 4038, fols. 83r-87v; 4732, fols. 17r-22r.

[27] In my definition of foreigners, I have included natives of distant provinces: Friuli, Venezia, Lombardy, and Piedmont, and the regions south of Rome. The condemnations of foreigners in 1382–1383 are in *AP*, 3084, 3112, 3113, 3147, 3150; *AEOG*, 919; *ACP*, 1428, 1496. The cases for the years 1409–1413 are in *AP*, 4193, fol. 41v; 4261, fols. 68v-

In terms of numbers involved and capital invested, the two major industries of the Florentine underworld were gambling and prostitution. Although these professions were condemned by the authorities as immoral, they were not technically illegal, but tolerated as necessary evils. Periodically, a wave of moral fervor would sweep the city and inspire the authorities to enact regulatory legislation and to intensify the state's control over these corrupting activities. In 1401, for example, the councils enacted a provision that prohibited certain games of chance,[28] but this law was not rigorously enforced.

The commune maintained a public brothel and also tolerated soliciting in the streets, as long as the prostitutes wore the hats and gloves that identified their profession. The business could be lucrative. One prostitute rejected an offer by her neighbors to provide her with a weekly basket of bread if she would give up her trade, declaring that she earned much more from her clients, and that she enjoyed her work.[29] But these women had to pay exorbitant rents for their lodgings, and many were coerced into turning over their earnings to pimps. Since the underworld's economy benefited substantially from prostitution, its members recruited labor for the brothels. Court records indicate that many of the city's prostitutes came from abroad, particularly Germany and the Low Countries. But others were poor country girls, seduced by promises of fine clothes and a comfortable life, persuaded to work as prostitutes in an inn or tavern, and then placed in public brothels. Described in the condemnation of a procurer named Niccolò di Giunta was his proposition to Monna Riguardata who lived with her husband

---

69r; *AEOG*, 1762, fols. 67r-70v; 4279, no pag., June 10, 1413; *ACP*, 2523 *bis*, fol. 19v.
   28 *Biblioteca Nazionale di Firenze* (cited hereafter as *BNF*), *Panciatichi*, 158, fol. 199r.
   29 See the testimony of Bartolo Gadini in the trial of Angela, wife of Nofri di Francesco, *GA*, 66, no pag., Dec. 9, 1398.

Meo—"an honest couple of good reputation"—in a rural district near Florence:

> Monna Riguardata, I have great sympathy for your youth, since you are a very beautiful girl and have not married well. . . . You know that Meo is crippled in one arm and one leg so that he is not really a man. Of the things of this world, he has none. . . . You are poorly dressed and badly shod. You have little bread and wine and there is neither meat nor oil in your house. I have never seen such a pretty girl living in this poverty and misery. I have the greatest compassion for you, particularly since your husband is the ugliest and most wretched man in the world and you are so beautiful. So I have decided to take you away from this misery and arrange matters so that you will lack for nothing, and you will be well clothed, as your youth and beauty require. . . .[30]

Riguardata finally succumbed to these blandishments and was taken to an inn near Trespiano, where Niccolò slept with her. He was planning to place her in Bologna's public brothel when he was captured by police officials. In the activities of the pimps and white-slave operators who recruited these poor creatures, we can discern the outlines of a criminal network linking all the major cities of central Italy.[31]

Like prostitution, gambling had a large and socially diverse clientele, and provided a livelihood for many Florentines. Wealthy merchants and even clerics mingled with wool carders and gravediggers around the tables. These were scattered throughout the city, in the loggias of the Canigiani and the

[30] *ACP*, 1198, fols. 70r-72r. Niccolò engaged in this activity as a profession: "quod dictus Nicolaus tanquam publice et famosus leno . . . induxit et subduxit diversas mulieres maritatas et viduas civitatis Florentie ad peccandum et adulterium commictendum cum variis et diversis hominibus et nobilibus civitatis Florentie et forensibus in domo ipsius Niccoli. . . ." He was hanged.

[31] For evidence of the white-slave traffic in Tuscany, see *GA*, 82, part 2, fols. 412r-414v; *ASF, Provvisioni*, 117, fols. 54v-55r. Some girls were sold to procurers; *AEOG*, 475, fol. 59r; 662, fol. 11r.

Buondelmonti, near the piazza of Santa Maria Novella, outside
the Porta San Piero Gattolino. Citizens frequently complained
about these gambling dens which allegedly blighted the neighborhoods in which they were located. One witness described
the scene in the Via de' Servi where gamblers congregated outside the Macigni palace, and impeded the passage of pilgrims
on their way to the church of Santissima Annunziata.[32] Those
who operated the gaming tables were often accused (and
sometimes convicted) of introducing loaded dice and marked
cards into the games. According to an anonymous denunciation of 1445, a certain gambler named Domenico operated a
table near Santa Maria Novella where "he keeps a gang of
ruffians who use loaded dice and rob many poor people." [33]
Both rich and poor gambled, but the latter could less afford to
lose. Many of the complaints recorded in the judicial protocols
deplored the effects of gambling upon the young, and also on
poor laborers who lost both time and money at the tables. One
denunciation identified a group of artisans and workers who
played regularly in the parish of San Piero Gattolino: Antonio
di Paolo, a dealer of old clothes; Nenno di Gherardo, a cloth
stretcher; two weavers named Stefano and Antonio; Cecco di
Nanni Giubetti, an oil vendor; Ridolfo, a stocking maker; and
Piero di Zanobi whose occupation was not identified. "When
Francesco di Gaddo wants to work, he is an excellent stocking
maker, and he is healthy and virile," declared an anonymous
citizen to the Conservators of the Laws in 1448, "but he is a
miserable and wicked poltroon, so given to evil ways that he
does nothing but operate a gambling den. . . ." [34]

This cursory sketch of Florence's *popolo minuto* provides
a fragile context for examining the political role of these poor

---

[32] *GA*, 82, fol. 275r-275v. Others complained about the gamblers'
penchant for blasphemy; e.g., *ibid.*, part 2, fols. 173r-174r.

[33] *Ibid.*, 81, no pag., Nov. 13, 1444. Gambling quarrels often led to
assault and even homicide; e.g., *BNF, Panciatichi*, 158, fol. 143v.

[34] These cases are described in *GA*, 79, fol. 21r; 82, fol. 275r.

inhabitants. They were not represented in the communal government, nor were they allowed to organize even for social or religious purposes. Had the authorities granted that privilege to the poor, the precarious and unstable conditions of their existence would still have inhibited the formation of guilds or confraternities. Even rioting might call for a greater degree of social cohesion than the Florentine poor normally possessed. The majority were people without roots, with no deep attachment to an urban neighborhood (although perhaps to a *contado* village), and no genuine link to any urban collectivity. Meaningful participation in guilds, confraternities, and parish assemblies was limited to the affluent, the socially prominent, and the occasional artisan or small shopkeeper. Clothworkers and beggars might visit their parish church (one wonders how frequently), and they certainly witnessed the public ceremonies and celebrations on feast days. But they were essentially spectators; they did not belong. Some did enroll in the craft guilds and were registered in their district or *gonfalone* as taxpayers and militiamen, but they had no effective voice in these societies, which were controlled by men of status and substance.[35] The one system to which many of the poor did belong was the administration of charity. Florentines imposed order and coherence upon almsgiving, as upon all their other activities. Those societies which succored the destitute made an effort to identify the worthy recipients of their charity, and then assumed responsibility for providing these *miserabili* with their weekly ration of bread and wine, or subsistence payments.[36]

[35] For a list of 25 parishioners (including 7 artisans but no laborers) assembled to elect a priest of the parish of San Piero Bonconsiglio, see *ASF, Carte Strozziane,* ser. 2, 11, fol. 99v. For an interesting comment on the size of a *gonfalone* assembly, see *ASF, Consulte e Pratiche* (cited hereafter as *CP*), 44, fol. 110v, statement by Cino Nobili: "Conatus est habere quot homines potuit de vexillo suo et quod habere non potuit nisi circa XX. . . ."

[36] Brucker, *Renaissance Florence,* pp. 208–209.

Some historians have argued that the clothworkers developed a strong sense of solidarity, and even after their initial efforts to organize were crushed in the 1340s, they kept alive their ideal of a laborers' guild.[37] But given the instability of the poor and the wave of epidemics that periodically decimated the urban population, this does not seem credible. Did the Ciompi in 1378 recall the martyrs of an earlier generation, men like Ciuto Brandini who was hanged in 1346 for attempting to organize the clothworkers? More plausible is the argument that these laborers lived and worked in a climate of contemporaneity; they responded to their immediate needs and circumstances, and not to any tradition of grievance extending back over decades. Another inhibiting factor was the diversity of economic conditions and interests among these operatives. Some of the Lana *sottoposti* who participated in the Ciompi revolution were petty entrepreneurs, who were themselves employers of labor. These artisans tended to be more conservative than the salaried workers; in late August 1378, they fought alongside the men from the greater guilds to suppress the uprising of the radical Ciompi.[38]

I have stressed the lack of organization and common purpose within the ranks of the *popolo minuto* and by implication, have denied this group any possibility of an active role in Florentine government. Yet, the poor did exert some indirect influence in communal politics, even though they were excluded from office. Their potential capacity for disorder was an important factor in the formulation of the republic's grain policy, and in its exercise of police powers and the administration of justice.

There is a discrepancy between the stereotype of Florence as a violent, disorderly city in the fourteenth and fifteenth centuries, and the reality that can be glimpsed—however imper-

[37] Rodolico, *Democrazia fiorentina*, pp. 87–128.
[38] Brucker, "Ciompi," pp. 319–322, 346–352.

fectly—in the chronicles and documents. Violence was endemic in late medieval Florence, but it was more characteristic of relations between individuals than groups.[39] There were few mass disorders in the city after the Black Death. Only once between 1343 and 1450 did the city experience a total breakdown of authority, during the Ciompi revolution in the summer of 1378. Ten years earlier, the one large grain riot in these decades occurred, although Florence suffered periodic grain shortages, and the city's poor were often without work and bread.[40] There were other moments of crisis, after a coup or an abortive revolt, when nervous and fearful crowds gathered in the streets and squares, when the city "was under arms." And during these tense periods, quarrels and altercations occurred, and some blood was shed. But except for the Ciompi episode, the authorities were able to maintain a tenuous control, and to prevent massacres of the inhabitants and widespread destruction of property.[41] A *pratica* debate in June 1417, during a time of plague and famine, provides some clues to the commune's ability to maintain order in difficult circumstances.[42] The speakers in this debate did not mince words about the gravity of the peril.

[39] An exception to this generalization: the gang brawls of Florentine youths which frequently disturbed the peace; CP, 26, fols. 3r, 23r, 26v-27r; 28, fol. 38v; 30, fol. 22r. For a valuable study of violence in Siena, see W. Bowsky "The Medieval Commune and Internal Violence: Police Power and Public Safety in Siena, 1287–1355," *American Historical Review*, LXXIII (1967), 1–17.

[40] Rodolico, *Popolo minuto*, pp. 150–152.

[41] For mob disorders in the 1340s, see Brucker, *Florentine Politics and Society*, pp. 107–111; and during the Ciompi revolution, Brucker, "Ciompi," pp. 315–316, 333–334, 344–351. For two months following the revolution of January 1382, Florence was extremely tense, and the government's control of the city was perilously close to breaking down; *Cronaca fiorentina di Marchionne di Coppo Stefani*, ed. N. Rodolico, in *Rerum Italicarum Scriptores*, new ed., Vol. XXX, part 1 (Città di Castello, 1903–1955), rub. 901–923; BNF, *Panciatichi*, 158, fols. 140r-146r.

[42] CP, 43, fols. 151v-154r.

"The poor earn nothing and they are dying like dogs," so Bar- tolomeo Valori appraised the situation. The remedy was sug- gested by Antonio Alessandri: "We must provide for the con- servation of our regime on account of the plague which threatens us, recalling the actions and measures which were taken during similar times in the past. And considering the number of paupers, we must show our gratitude to God by distributing alms to the destitute. . . . But since not all [of the poor] are peaceable, and to fill these with terror, we should have troops (neither citizens nor *contadini*) who will obey the commune and not private individuals." The general willingness to provide alms for the poor was certainly encouraged by the belief, expressed by Salomone Strozzi, "that on account of our pride and other vices, God has smitten us with the plague." The dispensation of charity might assuage God's wrath, but feeding the poor was a political issue, as important for the re- gime's security as stationing troops in the Piazza della Signoria. Any sharp rise in grain prices was immediately noticed and dis- cussed in the palace of the Signoria. After gauging the impact of this increase upon the stomachs and tempers of the *popolo minuto*, the authorities would authorize the purchase of grain in Sicily or Naples, and its shipment to Florence.[43] While bread prices did rise and the indigent did suffer in these famine periods, the additional reserves of foreign grain were usually adequate to provide a subsistence diet for the poor.

In the course of the 1417 debate on the emergency created by famine and plague, Buonaccorso Pitti proposed that a certain

[43] References to famine conditions from 1340 to 1378 are in my *Flor- entine Politics and Society*, index, p. 419. After 1378, the problem is mentioned frequently in the *Consulte e Pratiche* protocols: *CP*, 18, fols. 69v, 71v; 22, fols. 60v-61r, 67r, 87r-88r; 27, fols. 99r, 101r; 29, fol. 9v; 41, fols. 32r, 35r; 43, fols. 72r, 185r; 44, fols. 13v-14v, 37r, 43v, 48v-49r, 54v, 114r. Treasury records also contain data on communal expenditures for grain. On this question, see E. Fiumi, "Sui rapporti economici tra città e contado," *Archivio storico italiano*, CXIV (1956), 56–61.

number of poor inhabitants "who are prone to evil acts" be
hired as militiamen and sent off to fortified places where other
troops are stationed. Apparently, this ingenious scheme did not
win favor with other counselors. But it does reveal another approach to the problem of urban poverty, one that had been
initiated briefly during the Ciompi regime in 1378, and again
in 1383, when Florence was stricken by a plague. In July of
that year, a spokesman for the sixteen *gonfalonieri* had recom-
mended that a hundred Ciompi be hired as soldiers to guard
the dominion, "placing six or eight in each place so that they
do not become a threat." Two months later, however, another
collegiate group expressed a contrary view: "See to it that the
Ciompi do not receive any stipend from the commune, but dis-
charge them all!" [44] Thus, an early version of the modern slogan, "Do not reward the rioters," became an axiom of communal policy.

The program adopted by the government in June 1417 was
a version of that classic policy of the carrot and the stick which
Italian governments have pursued since Roman times. The poor
would be fed, and those with evil intentions would be deterred
by five hundred soldiers in the Piazza della Signoria. This regime did rely upon troops for its defense, and it had to calculate
security needs with care. The goal was to strike a balance between adequate protection on the one hand, and expenditure
and public tolerance on the other. Disliking large and costly
police guards which inhibited their freedom of action, Florentines preferred only the minimum force necessary to maintain
a precarious order. [45] In this sphere, too, the *popolo minuto* influenced public policy. Officials of the *podestà* were greeted
with no more affection in the working class quarter of San

[44] CP, 22, fols. 67v, 87v. On the hiring of Ciompi militia in 1378, see
Brucker, "Ciompi," pp. 334–335; and in June 1382, CP, 21, fol. 12r.

[45] For opposition to the appointment or reappointment of rectors
with broad police powers, see, e.g., CP, 28, fols. 123v–124v; *ASF, Libri
Fabarum*, 41, fols. 72r–75v; 43, fol. 114r; 45, fols. 10r–12r.

Frediano than the *sbirri* receive there today.[46] An excessive show of force, an imprudent act by a nervous official, could spark a riot. In November 1383, officials of the Inquisition accompanied by members of the *podestà*'s entourage attempted to seize a suspected heretic, Lorenzo Puccini. Lorenzo's son Angelo urged the residents of the neighborhood to rescue his father and the cry went up: "Stone those buggering friars and the police!" So enthusiastically did the crowd respond to this appeal that the officials had to flee for their lives.[47]

Whenever the regime's security was seriously imperiled, it mobilized all its resources to defend itself. "Punish the guilty so that they will be an example to others" was the motto of those who believed that rigid enforcement of the laws was the key to security. But a contrary opinion, favoring justice tempered with mercy, was also voiced in council deliberations. "Let justice be done with moderation," counseled Maso degli Albizzi in November 1400; in developing his argument, he stated that he preferred excessive clemency to extreme severity. Speakers frequently urged the rectors to mete out the most severe punishment to organizers of conspiracies, and to treat their followers more leniently.[48] But judges rarely accepted this counsel; the poor and the ignorant paid for their indiscretions more frequently, and more severely, than did citizens with money and influential friends. But in certain areas involving the Florentine poor, the commune moved very circumspectly. The Fraticelli heresy, for example, had gained many adherents from the ranks of the *popolo minuto* in the fourteenth century, but the authori-

[46] For examples of attacks upon police officials, see *AEOG*, 934, fols. 33r-33v; 992, fols. 15r-16r; 1034, fol. 50r; *AP*, 3147, fols. 47r-48r; 3268, fols. 51v-52r; *ACP*, 1608, no pag., Aug. 19, 1385.

[47] *AP*, 3178, fols. 136r-136v, 153v-154v.

[48] Maso's statement is in *CP*, 34, fol. 132r. For similar views, see *ibid.*, fol. 145v; 20, fol. 127r; 30. fol. 87v. For examples of a more severe attitude, cf. *CP*, 41, fols. 27v-28v, 58r. On distinctions between leaders and followers, and *grandi* and *minuti*, see *CP*, 16, fol. 75r; 18, fol. 53v.

ties never launched a massive campaign against this movement. The fact that only one member of this sect, Fra Michele of Calci, was executed in Florence is evidence of the commune's tolerance and perhaps of its unwillingness to alienate the poor.[49]

In yet another sphere, involving war and peace, the *popolo minuto* exerted a sporadic influence. Even though the poor never appeared in council meetings to voice their opinions, patrician counselors were always aware of the popular mood. As lengthy and debilitating wars continued with no end in sight, speakers would bolster their arguments for ending hostilities by describing the deleterious effects of the conflict upon commerce and industry, and the welfare of the poor. During the Genoese war of 1411–1412, for example, Agnolo Pandolfini made an emotional plea for peace, asserting that "trade is at a standstill, and the artisans and manual laborers can earn nothing, and there is widespread hunger. . . ."[50] At other times, the xenophobic passions of the mob encouraged the adoption of bellicose postures by the republic. Neighboring cities—Pisa, Siena, Lucca—were the particular targets of popular hostility. In 1385, a Sienese ambassador noted the antipathy of the Florentine *vulgo* toward his government which, so he argued, contributed to the difficulties he encountered in negotiating with the government. The popular hatred of Lucca was certainly a factor in Rinaldo degli Albizzi's decision to push Florence into war with that city in 1429, just as it later hampered the regime's efforts to extricate itself from that disastrous enterprise.[51]

Thus, in their potential capacity for destruction, the Florentine poor exerted a certain influence, an oblique pressure,

[49] Brucker, *Renaissance Florence*, p. 207.

[50] *CP*, 41, fol. 55r, Nov. 20, 1411.

[51] The comments of the Sienese envoy are in *Archivio di Stato di Siena, Concistoro*, 1816, no. 28 (May 10, 1385); 1817, no. 3 (July 2, 1385); and 1819, no. 24 (May 20, 1385). On popular hostility to Lucca, see C. Bayley, *War and Society in Renaissance Florence* (Toronto, 1961), p. 99.

upon the city's politics. Yet, in the century following the Black Death, the *popolo minuto* never rioted spontaneously, but only after some segment of the patriciate, the governing class, had first promoted disorder for its own ends. In 1378 the mob burned and pillaged palaces under the direction of aristocratic politicians; in 1397, in 1400 and in 1412, patrician exiles sought to use the *popolo minuto* as the instrument for recovering their political rights. Once aroused, for whatever selfish purpose and by whatever means, the mob was a dangerous force which could literally destroy the city. And when normal restraints and inhibitions had dissolved in the act of rioting, the poor did not return quickly to their normal quiescent state. The tremors emanating from the Ciompi revolution of 1378 continued to reverberate through the working-class districts of Florence for more than a decade. During those rare occasions when the poor were aroused and active, we can learn something about their methods, objectives, and aspirations.

Save for the absence of women, the mobs that surged through Florentine streets in times of crisis were quite representative of the *popolo minuto*. The majority of those convicted of opposing the regime after the fall of the Ciompi were cloth-workers: the carder Antonio Pacini, the dyer Niccolò di Giovanni del Segna, the doublet-maker Niccolò Bacchi, the comber Clemente. Although the textile workers formed the core of these revolutionary movements, they did receive substantial support from laborers in other crafts and occupations. Among those condemned in the wake of a 1383 plot were a pork butcher, Marco di Feo; an armorer, Coso di Jacopo; a tailor named Niccolò di Bartolomeo; a stocking maker, Antonio di Domenico; two wine sellers, Feo Coveri and Miliano Morelli; a gravedigger named Cazzano della Zera; a coppersmith named Benedetto Datini; a road mender, Michele del Forza; and a cook, Benedetto di Guido.[52] Some of the plotters not identified

[52] These were some of the 106 men condemned to death (only one

by profession may have been criminals attracted to the movement by the prospect of mass violence and the opportunity for
looting.

Judicial records provide the most detailed accounts of the
internal histories of these conspiracies, even though the evidence (frequently extracted by torture) is not wholly reliable.
The formats of these lower-class plots were all quite similar,
and they suggest a common approach to rebellion. Underlying
every conspiratorial movement was the conviction that a hostile
populace would rise up to overthrow the tyrannical regime
which oppressed the poor, if they received some signal or act
of encouragement. Flags with Ciompi slogans were smuggled
into the city, to be unfurled at the opportune moment and
paraded through the working-class districts of San Frediano,
San Piero Gattolino, Camaldoli, San Ambrogio, San Lorenzo.
Very important was the recruitment of potential supporters,
always the most dangerous stage in the organization of conspiracies. By any criterion, the methods employed by Florentine revolutionaries to enlist recruits for these uprisings were
crude and haphazard. Exile groups sent agents into Florence to
contact friends and acquaintances, to arrange secret meetings
in taverns where conversations of this nature might be over-
heard:

> "I have good news for you [said Tommaso di Bartolo to his
> friend, Stagio di Dino]. Very shortly there will be another
> regime in place of this one. Aren't you pleased?" To which
> Stagio replied: "Of course." Then Tommaso said: "Be assured
> that these events are going to happen, and there will be so
> many people [involved in the plot] that if you knew how

was caught and executed) for conspiring to overthrow the regime in
July 1383: *AEOG*, 950, fols. 17r-18v, 25r-27v, 29r-30v, 33r-34r, 35v-
36r. Most of the Ciompi convicted of conspiracy between September
1378 and January 1382 were identified as clothworkers. Fewer artisans
and representatives of the menial trades were involved in these plots;
e.g., *ACP*, 1198, fols. 47r, 54v.

many you would be delighted." And Stagio said: "Who are they?" Tommaso replied: "They are all your friends: Priore di Feduccio of the parish of S. Niccolò . . . Piero di Lapozzo of the parish of S. Romolo, Luca di Agostino Bruni, a cloth manufacturer of the parish of S. Felice. And Luca has many sworn men with him, so that we are so numerous that we can easily accomplish this. If you want to join us, then speak with Piero." And Stagio replied: "I am content." [53]

The most striking features of this conversation are the stress on personal bonds, the use of the oath as a means of ensuring complicity, and the lack of concern about security. These characteristics are all present in other Ciompi conspiracies which were foiled by the authorities. Matteo Cerbelleri encountered Ardingho di Lorenzo in the Piazza de' Nerli and, after describing a plot organized by exiles to gain control of the city, asked him to join the movement. While passing through the Mercato Nuovo on his way to mass in the cathedral, Leoncino Francini met Guerriante Marignolli who told him that "a large number of us have taken an oath together and tomorrow night we are going to stage a revolution in this city . . . and I want you to be a member of our company. . . ." Enroute to Florence from Venice, Andrea Sali met a group of thirty Florentines in Bologna and inquired of their plans. They replied: "We are going to a place where we will all be rich, and if you promise to keep our secret and follow us and become a member of our company, we will tell you." After agreeing to their conditions, Andrea learned that they were plotting to overthrow the Florentine republic. "We will kill and rob all of those fat ones who have driven us from our homes, and we will be lords of that territory, and we will govern it to suit ourselves, and we will all be rich!" [54]

[53] *AEOG*, 900, fols. 29r-30v, Oct. 15, 1381, printed in Rodolico, *Democrazia fiorentina*, p. 476.

[54] These cases are in *AEOG*, 870, fols. 13v-14r; *ACP*, 1197 *bis*, fols. 99v-101r, 130r-132r. Cf. Rodolico, *Democrazia fiorentina*, pp. 376–384.

Perhaps the unhappy experiences of exile had so embittered these proletarians that they could think only of revenge and material gain, of their personal interests. The surviving evidence, nearly all from hostile sources, may not reveal their deeply felt hopes and aspirations, which were doubtless more "political" than these documents indicate.[55] From the annals of the Ciompi revolt and its aftermath, we can determine, roughly, what the *popolo minuto* hoped to achieve. First, they demanded their own guild, which would give them representation in the communal government, and also a stronger bargaining position vis-à-vis the manufacturers. Secondly, they wanted a more equitable fiscal policy: the abolition of forced loans which harmed their interests and benefited the rich; the gradual elimination of the funded debt (*Monte*); and the imposition of a graduated, direct tax on income (*estimo*). They favored more lenient and humane treatment of debtors, and the abolition of the Lana guild's authority over workers and artisans in the cloth industry. They certainly hoped for cheaper bread, higher wages and (possibly) an annual production quota of 24,000 pieces of cloth.[56] None of these demands seem particularly radical to modern eyes, but they frightened the Florentine merchants and industrialists, the men of property, who excoriated "these Ciompi, robbers and traitors and assassins and gluttons and malefactors." [57]

[55] These laborers tended to formulate their political goals in specific and concrete (and not in general or abstract) terms; see Brucker, "Ciompi," pp. 347–348, 355. Many of the Ciompi exiles cooperated with magnates in organizing plots to overthrow the regime between September 1378 and January 1382: *ACP*, 1198, fols. 47r, 54v-59r; *AEOG*, 870, fols. 37r-38v.

[56] Brucker, *Florentine Politics*, pp. 382–384, and "Ciompi," pp. 347–348, 353–354; De Roover, *op. cit.*, pp. 309–312. One chronicler stated that the Ciompi demanded that the industrialists promise to produce at least 2,000 pieces of cloth per month, but the evidence is not conclusive (Brucker, "Ciompi," p. 341). On the surprising indifference of the Ciompi to the heavy gabelle burden, see De la Roncière, *op. cit.*, pp. 191–192.

[57] Brucker, "Ciompi," pp. 351–352.

Discontent among the Florentine poor was most intense in the decade following the Ciompi revolution, and then subsided. Two significant manifestations of lower-class unrest did occur in 1393 and in 1411–1412; they furnish some clues to the conditions of the poor and to their mood in those years. The origins of the 1393 disorders are obscure.[58] Spokesmen for the regime claimed that the riots were instigated by the Alberti family, while other sources have suggested that Maso degli Albizzi organized them to implicate the Alberti, and to provide an excuse for banishing them from the city. From whatever source these disturbances derived, they spread quickly to the *popolo minuto* who marched through the streets with banners and arms shouting: "Viva il popolo e le arti!" and defying the supporters of the government whose slogan was: "Viva il popolo e la Parte Guelfa!" After a week of street fighting and some bloodshed, the regime restored order and prosecuted the ringleaders. The Alberti were fined and exiled, while the rebellious poor were sentenced to death. Most of the convicted rebels were not laborers but artisans who were demanding a larger political role in the regime for lower guildsmen. Among those convicted of participating in the disorders were three butchers, four old-clothes dealers, a druggist, a baker, a purse maker, a wine seller, an innkeeper, a brickmaker, and only two textile workers: a weaver and a washer.[59] The rebels did not favor (or so it appears) the incorporation of the clothworkers into the guild community; consequently, the laborers were unwilling to join a movement that did not promote their interests.

In 1411 and 1412, when the Alberti were actively engaged

---

[58] The main chronicle sources for this upheaval are *Cronica volgare di anonimo fiorentino dell'anno 1385 al 1409 già attribuita a Piero di Giovanni Minerbetti*, in *Rerum Italicarum Scriptores*, new ed., Vol. XXVII, part 2, ed. E. Bellondi (Città di Castello, 1915), chaps. 22–25; *BNF, Panciatichi*, 158, fols. 172v-176v. For the opinion that the disorders were planned by Maso degli Albizzi, see *ASF, Manoscritti*, 225, fol. 122v.

[59] *ACP*, 1998, fols. 5r-11r.

in conspiratorial activity, the danger of revolution was much greater. From Bologna where they were living in exile, the Alberti sent agents into Florence to recruit supporters, both among the discontented members of the patriciate, and from the ranks of the *popolo minuto*. The city was in a parlous state. Commerce and industry were paralyzed by the Genoese war, which cut off Florence's access to the sea; workers and artisans were unemployed, hungry, and desperate. The judicial sentences against Bindaccio Alberti and his supporter, Cola di Maestro Piero, contain some revealing fragments of evidence concerning the popular mood in these months. When Bindaccio secretly visited Florence in June 1411, he met a friend who urged him and his family to organize a revolt: "There are many more malcontents than [citizens who are] satisfied, and the *popolo minuto* complain loudly . . . and there is so much discord that a small uprising will accomplish our objectives." [60] While contacting men who might join his conspiracy, Bindaccio fell into the hands of the police and died on the scaffold in August 1411. Three months later, a group of Alberti sympathizers met secretly in the *contado* to lament his death. One said: "Bindaccio Alberti . . . was the finest young gentleman in Florence, and I have proof of that statement, for I was with him in Pisa. . . ." Later in a tavern, Cola denounced the leaders of the Florentine government: "Those traitors who rule us have taken grain from the poultry and fed it to us; by God, we shall eat the good [grain] in their houses shortly; we don't deserve to be treated like chickens!" Cola recruited a dozen men for his plot, but he and two of his associates were captured before the scheduled date of the uprising. They did reveal the details of their abortive coup before they went to the gallows.[61]

By the fifteenth century, the *popolo minuto* had ceased to

---

[60] *AEOG*, 1759, fols. 103r-108r.

[61] *AEOG*, 1763, fols. 3r-4r. For sentences against others implicated in this conspiracy, see *ibid.*, fols. 13r-13v; *AP*, 4254, fols. 15r-17r.

be a revolutionary force in Florentine politics. Since we know so little about the life of the poor in these decades, we must be very tentative in formulating an explanation for this development. Certain contributory factors seem obvious and plausible, while others are more dubious. In Florence, public and private violence gradually subsided in the fifteenth century. Street riots and disorders became less common, just as the incidence of private vendettas and personal assaults declined in these years.[62] The main deterrent was the ability of the state to enforce its laws and to punish the unruly; this was most clearly demonstrated in the area of internal security. With monotonous regularity, the authorities exposed one plot after another, those organized by prominent citizens, as well as the conspiracies hatched in taverns where workers congregated. This dreary record of failure quenched the revolutionary impulses of all but the most determined conspirators. The connection between a more powerful state and the subsidence of proletarian unrest is definite; more problematical is the influence of social and economic conditions upon the mood and temper of the poor. Students of Florentine demography agree that the city's population declined in the early fifteenth century, falling from approximately 60,000 in 1380 to 40,000 in 1427.[63] This may have created a labor shortage, and perhaps raised wages in the cloth industry and in other trades and occupations.[64] But like so many other aspects of Florentine poverty, this problem of living conditions has not been thoroughly studied. The *popolo di Dio* [65] still await their historian.

[62] Brucker, *Renaissance Florence*, pp. 126–128.
[63] A. Molho, "Politics and the Ruling Class in Early Renaissance Florence," *Nuova Rivista Storica*, LII (1968), 405.
[64] For a summary of trends in the Florentine economy between 1380 and 1430, see Brucker, *Renaissance Florence*, pp. 79–88.
[65] On this phrase, see N. Rodolico, *I Ciompi* (Florence, 1945), p. 150.

VIII

CRIME, PUNISHMENT, AND THE
TRECENTO VENETIAN STATE

Stanley Chojnacki

I

*U*RBS . . . solidis fundata marmoribus sed solidior etiam fundamento civilis concordie stabilita. . . ." A more flattering description of a Trecento Italian state can hardly be imagined than Petrarch's nicely phrased comment on Venice.[1] In a century of endemic political turbulence in Italy, a state enjoying "civil concord" was a monument of wisdom, prosperity, or immense good luck. But Petrarch was scarcely unique in his admiration of Venetian internal order. Indeed, by his time praise for the stability of Venice and for its corollary, Venetian civic loyalty, was developing into a political convention which subsequent centuries would see elaborated into a full-blown historical myth, the "mito di Venezia" of the Renaissance.[2]

Moreover Venice's reputation for governmental sagacity and civic loyalty has proved hardy enough to outlive the Vene-

---

[1] *Lettere senili*, book IV, no. 3, quoted in F. Gilbert, "The Venetian Constitution in Florentine Political Thought," in *Florentine Studies: Politics and Society in Renaissance Florence*, ed. N. Rubinstein (London, 1968), p. 467 n. 3.

[2] See for example the observation of Albertino Mussato: "Felix . . . Venetiarum comune: cum cives illi in agendis suis omnibus adea ad comunitatem respiciant, ut Venetiarum nomen iam habeant quasi numen et iam fere jurent per Venetiarum reverentiam et honorem," quoted in H. Kretschmayr, *Geschichte von Venedig*, 3 vols. (Gotha, 1905–1934), II, 663. For a discussion of the early development of this convention see G. Fasoli, "Nascita di un mito," in *Studi storici in onore di Gioacchino Volpe*, 2 vols. (Florence, 1958), I, 455–479. See

tian Republic and to maintain an insistent grip on the sensibilities of modern historians as well.[3] And although lately a tendency to deflate the myth has begun to assert itself, notably in the studies of younger Italian scholars, it is safe to say that the consensus of historians is still a largely positive assessment of Venetian government and its record in preserving domestic tranquillity during the Middle Ages and the Renaissance.[4]

It is not my intention here to add to the growing literature on the myth of Venice, nor to suggest that Venetian historiography since the fall of the Republic has been charmed into a romanticized view of the Venetian past.[5] What does seem to me worth discussing is a tendency, common to Renaissance and modern writers alike, to gloss over some important questions in considering the Venetian political order and its successes.

One question involves a chronological distinction. By now it is scarcely controversial to observe that social and political con-

---

also N. Rubinstein, "Marsilius of Padua and Italian Political Thought of His Time," in *Europe in the Late Middle Ages* (cited hereafter as *ELMA*), eds. J. R. Hale et al. (London, 1965), pp. 60, 63. Recent literature on the *mito* is extensive. A chronological complement to Fasoli's article is F. Gaeta, "Alcune considerazioni sul mito di Venezia," *Bibliothèque d'Humanisme et Renaissance*, XXIII (1961), 58–75.

[3] For representative instances cf. works as diverse as S. Romanin, *Storia documentata di Venezia*, 10 vols. (Venice, 1853–1861); P. Molmenti, *Storia di Venezia nella vita privata*, 3 vols. (7th ed., Bergamo, 1927); Kretschmayr, *Geschichte;* and R. Cessi, *Storia della Repubblica di Venezia*, 2 vols. (Milan and Messina, 1944–1946).

[4] Both at home and in subject territories: see P. Pieri, *Il Rinascimento e la crisi militare italiana* (Turin, 1952), p. 181: "verso il 1494, la repubblica di San Marco presenta un affiatamento fra le classi sociali entro la capitale, e un accordo fra la dominante e il territorio quale non è dato riscontrare altrove in Italia." Even Machiavelli, no friend of Venice, marveled at the loyalty of the mainland subjects; see the references in A. Ventura, *Nobiltà e popolo nella società veneta del '400 e '500* (Bari, 1964), pp. 167–168. This book and that of G. Cracco, *Società e stato nel medioevo veneziano* (Florence, 1967), represent important reconsiderations of traditional postulates in Venetian historiography.

[5] This seems in fact to be the suggestion in Fasoli, "Nascita," p. 447.

ditions in north and central Italy underwent significant changes between the thirteenth and sixteenth centuries. The nature and degree of change still provoke varying interpretations, but few would maintain that the Tre-Quattrocento was a socially and politically static period in Italian history.[6] Yet with an occasional rare exception scholars have avoided applying this perspective to Venetian history during these centuries.[7] Among the main reasons is the constitutional orientation of much of traditional Venetian historiography. Thus despite different interpretations of the closing (in Venetian, and conventionally, "Serrata") in 1297 of the Venetian Maggior Consiglio to all but some two hundred families (who thereby became the hereditary Venetian aristocracy), scholars have by and large agreed that this measure was definitive. Since the institutional framework of the Venetian sociopolitical order did not change essentially after 1297, goes the argument, the substantive reality of Venetian politics and society did not change either.[8] The result has been an implicit, or explicit, linking of the Serrata of the Maggior Consiglio with the qualities celebrated in the myth of

[6] Although the emergence of the signori still provides the central focus, several authors have in recent years suggested alternatives to the traditional configuration of the entire question of the medieval commune and its changes. See E. Sestan, "Le origini delle signorie cittadine: Un problema storico esaurito?" *Bullettino dell' Istituto Storico Italiano per il Medio Evo*, LXXIII (1961), 41–69; P. J. Jones, "Commune and Despots: The City State in Late-Medieval Italy," *Royal Historical Society, Transactions*, 5th ser., XV (1965), 71–96; D. M. Bueno de Mesquita, "The Place of Despotism in Italian Politics," in *ELMA*, pp. 301–331.

[7] The most important recent exception is Cracco, *Società e stato*.

[8] The titles of Giuseppe Maranini's two volumes on Venetian constitutional history are indicative: *La costituzione di Venezia dalle origini alla Serrata del Maggior Consiglio* (cited hereafter as *Costituzione I*) (Florence, 1927) and *La costituzione di Venezia dopo la Serrata del Maggior Consiglio* (cited hereafter as *Costituzione II*) (Venice, 1931). On the Serrata see, in addition to the introduction to Maranini, *Costituzione II*, the observations in Kretschmayr, *Geschichte*, II, 72–73; Cessi, *Storia della Repubblica*, I, 265–270; and Molmenti, *Storia*, I, 65.

Venice—a configuration that in effect ignores the two centuries of history between 1297 and the myth's emergence at the end of the Quattrocento. And specifically, it has all but prevented analysis of the Venetian involvement in the political, social, and economic crises afflicting Italy generally during the Trecento and consideration of the implications of this involvement for the subsequent development of Renaissance Venice.

A second distinction is more substantive, but it is closely related to the chronological question. In explaining Venice's internal stability the traditional view has stressed, in Gina Fasoli'a words, the "political wisdom and moral force" that, institutionalized in Venice's constitutional and legal structure, kept the aristocracy dedicated and the populace contented.[9] Earlier writers on the question were especially inclined to emphasize the constitutional factor, perceiving in the "mixed-state" order of Venice and the freedom it afforded all Venetians the key to internal harmony. Scholars in recent times have rather pointed to the respect and protection Venetian law extended to the popular classes.[10] In either case the distinctive, farsighted civic

[9] Fasoli, "Nascita," p. 447. Characteristic is this statement by a thoughtful Venetian of the Cinquecento: "nulla [civitas] tamen fuit, quae institutione ac legibus ad bene beateque vivendum idoneis, cum hac nostra conferri potest. . . ." Gasparo Contarini, *De Magistratibus et Republica Venetorum*, Book I, quoted in F. Gilbert, "Religion and Politics in the Thought of Gasparo Contarini," in *Action and Conviction in Early Modern Europe*, eds. T. K. Rabb and J. E. Seigel (Princeton, 1969), p. 111 n. 72.

[10] On the constitutional factor, see Gaeta, "Alcune considerazioni," pp. 65 ff. This view still finds acceptance (H. G. Koenigsberger, "Decadence or Shift: Changes in the Civilization of Italy and Europe in the Sixteenth and Seventeenth Centuries," *Royal Historical Society, Transactions*, 5th ser., X [1960], 10). On Venetian equality see the paradigmatic statement of Molmenti, *Storia*, I, 71: "Se la costituzione veneziana rinvigoriva la potenza dei nobili, proteggeva d'altra parte e guarantiva d'ogni torto i popolani, così che patrizi e plebei si sostennero a vicenda, cooperando al bene comune." Similarly Maranini *Costituzione II*, p. 73: "Ben sapeva il borghese ed anche il plebeo veneziano come otteneva ascolto e giustizia. . . ."

spirit of the patriciate in erecting such institutions receives high praise. But underlying all such views—which at bottom cannot be disputed—is a negative perspective: Venetian policies and institutions are deemed praiseworthy, in the final analysis, because they prevented upheavals. The logic of this approach leads to a conception of popular contentment, or internal stability, essentially as a means of preserving the Venetian establishment—the patrician regime—an end that the wily patricians were flexible enough to serve by bestowing upon the *popolo* tokens of equality before the law, security from outside attack, and a share in the state's prosperity.[11]

The difficulty with this view is the passivity it ascribes to the Venetian *popolo*. In the first place, it postulates patrician capacity to dispense such political largesse at a time when Venice was beleaguered by a variety of pressures and required the active engagement of the *popolo* in withstanding them. Moreover, and more profoundly, it presumes that the institutionalization of legal guarantees could satisfy by itself the needs of the people and thus establish civil concord. What it fails to consider is that in Trecento Venice the government faced formidable obstacles to the successful implementation of the internal order which made the legal guarantees meaningful. There can be no question that legal rights did much to enlist popular support of the regime; but first the regime had to provide the elementary conditions of urban order. Venetians, like other Italians, craved " 'pax et quies': a good and peaceful life, a quiet and good governance."[12] The test of governmental sagacity in the early Renaissance would be its ability to achieve internal order not only in the population but for the population, and to do so

[11] To my knowledge only one work has recognized this logic and carried it to its rather unflattering conclusion: Cracco, *Società e stato*, cf. esp. pp. 454–455.

[12] Cf. the observations on "pax et quies" as a justification for despotic rule in Mesquita, "Place of Despotism," pp. 322–323.

without violating the rights upon which popular toleration of the patrician regime rested.

In the following pages I consider internal order in Trecento Venice, attempting to indicate the kinds of problems the establishment of order had to overcome and to examine the government's response to them. It is my hope that such a discussion of what amounts to Venetian crime and punishment can provide not only a more intimate look at the Trecento Venetian experience but also an insight into the political achievement represented by the Venetian state of the Renaissance and by the "mito di Venezia."

II

The "pax et quies" of Trecento Venetian society was challenged above all by two sets of circumstances, one political in origin, the other economic. I treat them in turn, considering the particular kinds of disorder generated by each; then 1 examine the provisions the government made to deal with the disorder and the principles underlying the governmental response.

The first source of civil disturbance—and indeed the foremost problem of early Renaissance Venetian politics and society—was the status of the patriciate after the reform of the Maggior Consiglio in 1297.[13] By giving a juridical finality to patrician, or noble, political supremacy, the measure of 1297, along with subsequent legislation that refined it, involved the articulation of a new patrician ethos, one in which patrician behavior, individual and collective, would conform to the re-

[13] This formulation of the Trecento patrician problem runs counter to both traditional historiography and recent revisions such as that of Cracco, *Società e stato*. I hope to complete in the near future a book-length study of the patriciate in the Tre-Quattrocento. In the present context I deal only with such aspects of the patrician problem as bear directly on Trecento order and disorder.

strictions that the new order imposed on the noble at the same time that it assured him political dominance. As early as the first decade of the Trecento, however, political tensions deriving from the restiveness of certain noble families under the new order had issued into confrontations between individual patricians and governmental authority.[14] Even more significant is the continued patrician rejection, well into the Trecento, of the post-Serrata political order's basic postulates. Noble conspiracies of 1310, 1328, and 1355 each represented, in one way or another, a refusal to accept the fundamental requirement of collective discipline that the aristocratic regime demanded.[15]

To these and other Trecento political crises the government responded sternly and—very characteristically of Venice—institutionally, adopting in their wakes new measures to ensure the security of the regime. The classic example of institutional response to an internal political threat was the creation of the Council of Ten, the Dieci, whose original mandate from the Maggior Consiglio empowered them to "make provision, to order and to do all that appears appropriate to them" in bringing to justice the members of the Tiepolo-Querini conspiracy

[14] The most notorious instance is the scuffle between Piero Querini and Marco Morosini, who as a Signore di Notte—i.e., a member of Venice's most important police force—sought to search Querini on the street and received a beating for his efforts: Marin Sanudo, *Le vite de'duchi di Venezia*, in *Rerum Italicarum Scriptores*, ed. L. A. Muratori, Vol. XXII (Milan, 1733), col. 590.

[15] On the famous Tiepolo-Querini plot of 1310 see the classic account in Sanudo, *Vite*, cols., 581–591. Cf. also the accounts and interpretations in Romanin, *Storia documentata*, III, 25–37; Kretschmayr, *Geschichte*, II, 181–183; Cessi, *Storia della Repubblica*, I, 284–285; and Cracco, *Società e stato*, pp. 364–373. The plot of 1328, apparently a carry-over of the 1310 conspiracy, has yet to receive a thorough treatment; see Sanudo *Vite*, col. 599, and Romanin, *Storia documentata*, III, 48. The conspiracy of the Doge Marin Falier, in 1355, seems not to have involved any patricians other than the Doge himself and some members of his immediate family. The fullest account is V. Lazzarini, *Marino Faliero* (Florence, 1963).

of 1310.[16] And the Dieci were themselves kept busy throughout the fourteenth century, taking institutional steps to deal with actual or potential threats to the government from within the patriciate. In the months and even years following the 1355 plot involving the Doge Marin Falier, for example, they added so substantially to the Venetian police forces that the city must have fairly bristled with armed patrols walking the streets and plying the canals and "rii" in boats.[17]

These noble uprisings and the government's reactions to them are evidence of Venice's unsettled political situation throughout much of the century following the Serrata. On the one hand, they reveal the unwillingness of certain elements of the patriciate to abide the limits on political virtuosity implicit in the laws of 1297 and after; on the other, they show that the governmental structure of Trecento Venice was in a process of development. Viewed from this perspective, Venetian internal political activity in that century was something more than simply "maintaining the constitution and the administration."[18] The moral force underlying the civil concord

---

[16] ". . . possint . . . omnia . . . providere, ordinare et facere que eis videbuntur . . ." reproduced in F. Zago, ed., *Consiglio dei Dieci: Deliberazioni miste, Registri I-II (1310-1325)*, Fonti per la Storia di Venezia, Section 1, Archivi pubblici (Venice, 1962), p. 247.

[17] Archivio di Stato di Venezia (cited hereafter as *ASV*), *Consiglio dei Dieci, Deliberazioni Miste* (cited hereafter as *Dieci, Misti*), Reg. 5, fol. 52v, July 1, 1356: authorization for the various police forces— Signori di Notte, Capi Sestieri, and others—to pool their resources and increase waterborne patrols around the city; *ibid.*, fol. 53r, July 20, 1356: Capi Sestieri ordered to initiate all-night patrols of twelve men in each *contrada*; *ibid.*, fol. 54r, Aug. 8, 1356: Capi Sestieri authorized to increase their personnel by four patricians and four *popolani* in each *sestiere*, "pro maiori custodia"; *ibid.*, fol. 66r, Dec. 28, 1357: election of six more nobles for each *sestiere*, each of whom to be given a retinue of four *popolani*, "pro meliori custodia fiendi de nocte."

[18] "Verfassung und Behördensorganisation zu behaupten. . . ." The phrase is Kretschmayr's, who refers to the Trecento as "das goldene Jahrhundert" (*Geschichte*, II, 281).

which figures so prominently in the myth was less than a universally effective imperative among the fourteenth-century nobility; and the vaunted political order which would so impress Europe two centuries later was still in significant measure developing in response to events rather than shaping them.

Important as political rebellion was, however, it represents only one dimension of the noble problem of the Trecento, and not necessarily the most important one. Another dimension with profound implications for the patrician's place in the sociopolitical order had to do with the double nature of his status as a noble. On one hand he clearly was a privileged individual. At the same time, however, he belonged to a ruling class whose success in ruling depended in considerable measure upon its ability to impose discipline upon its members. The way in which the ruling class dealt with the tension between these two aspects of noble status was a critical factor in determining the social climate of Renaissance Venice.

By the 1320s the nobility was legally closed and hereditary, and in the following century continued to render entrance into its ranks ever more difficult. Its exclusive tenure of political power was virtually unchallenged and its domination of society complete.[19] But precisely this unmistakable supremacy contained a potential threat to the patriciate's enjoyment of it in a congenial social atmosphere. Collective patrician supremacy

[19] A concise account of the legislation that between 1297 and 1321 completes the Serrata can be found in M. Merores, "Der grosse Rat von Venedig und die sogenannte Serrata vom Jahres 1297," *Vierteljahrschrift für Sozial- und Wirtschaftsgeschichte*, XXI (1928), 75–81. For further legislation in the Tre-Quattrocento, see Maranini, *Costituzione ll*, pp. 44–49. The only significant attack on the regime from outside the patriciate came almost immediately after the Serrata, in 1300: the conspiracy of Marin Bocconio and his followers, who apparently resented their exclusion from the newly defined patriciate. See Sanudo, *Vite*, cols. 581–584; also Kretschmayr, *Geschichte*, II, 71; Romanin, *Storia documentata*, III, 5–6; and Cracco, *Società e stato*, pp. 355–356.

could lead to individual patrician arrogance. And in circumstances that required active governmental solicitude of nonnoble sensibilities—prompted, as we shall see, by concrete economic motives as well as by fear of popular upheaval—excessive noble assertiveness could be critically self-defeating.[20] Thus while patrician legal status occasionally degenerated into the *superbia* of individual nobles, the broad requirements of society dictated its energetic repression by the government. The result was a sharp demarcation between the patriciate in its public, governmental personality and the patriciate considered as a collection of individuals whose interests and inclinations had to be subordinated to the requirements of internal order, or civil concord. The relationship between these two aspects of Trecento Venetian nobility is well illustrated in the records of patrician crime and punishment during that century.

For purposes of discussion it is useful to mark off two categories of crime by noblemen: acts that derived from the special status of the patrician—or his conception of it—and acts that might be committed by a nonnoble as well. The distinction is worth making because each category involved a particular kind of policy decision by the government. In the first instance the issue was whether an individual noble could flout the institutionalized consensus of his class; in the second, whether as a noble he received preferential treatment from the police and courts.

---

[20] The overbearing behavior of certain nobles was a factor in the popular participation in the Falier conspiracy of 1355. Moreover, one of the tactics used by the plotters—exacerbating popular resentment of patricians by addressing one another by noble names while assaulting *popolani* in the Piazza San Marco—suggests a patrician practice which was fair game for the plotters' exploitation. ". . . adiunctis sibi [i.e., the Doge Falier] quampluribus complicibus et plebeis . . . cum sua fatione vulgari insultum faceret in plateam, civitatem pariter ac vitam nobilibus ablaturus" (*Venetiarum Historia vulgo Petro Iustiniano Iustiniani filio adiudicata*, eds. R. Cessi and F. Bennato, Deputazione di Storia Patria per le Venezie, *Monumenti Storici*, n.s., XVIII [Venice,

One thing is clear from the outset: the law and its institutions do not appear to have inspired great reverence among four-teenth-century patricians.[21] An especially vivid way in which many expressed their disdain for the judiciary was the physical violence they sometimes visited upon its representatives. In one week in 1361, for example, the Quarantia—Venice's highest court—convicted two nobles of beating the bailiffs who had ar-tempted to deliver court summonses to them.[22] Upon occasion such violent tendencies could extend to the court precincts themselves, as they did in the case of the noble who in the heat of an inheritance dispute in court attacked his opponent with his fists flying.[23]

But a tendency toward fisticuffs was not the only manifes-

1964], p. 243). See also Lazzarini, *Marino Faliero*, pp. 166–167; Romanin, *Storia documentata*, III, 185.

[21] The basis for this and other general observations is examination of the records of two Venetian magistracies, the *Raspe* of the Avogaria di Comun (cited hereafter as AC *Raspe*) and the *Processi* of the Signori di Notte (cited hereafter as SN Processi), both in the ASV. It should be noted that most of the references are from the 1360s: I selected this decade because unlike some others in the Trecento it was not particu-larly characterized by internal turbulence. Accordingly it seemed to me a good period in which to seek patterns of ordinary police and judicial activity.

[22] AC *Raspe*, Reg. 3, fols. 8v, 9r, decisions of June 16 and 23, 1361. Each was fined 50 lire *di piccoli*. The procedure in most cases was for the Avogadori di Comun to act as prosecuting attorneys, presenting the evidence in criminal cases to the Quarantia, Venice's highest tribunal, for determination of guilt or innocence and sentencing. See Molmenti, *Storia*, I, 102–103, for a clear description of criminal procedure.

[23] AC *Raspe*, Reg. 3, fol. 52r, Sept. 27, 1363. His sentence was a fine of 50 lire *di piccoli*. In 1376 one ducat equaled 3 lire, 14 soldi *di piccoli* (cf. F. C. Lane, *Venetian Ships and Shipbuilders of the Renaissance* [Baltimore, 1934], p. 252). What this and other fines meant in real terms can be gauged by the fact that a Venetian housemaid's yearly salary in 1343 was 3 ducats (G. Luzzatto, "Il costo della vita a Venezia nel Tre-cento," in *Studi di storia economica veneziana* [Padua, 1954], pp. 285–286).

tation of aristocratic disrespect for judicial and legal institutions. More subtle threats to the rule of law were attempts to influence or undo judicial decisions. They sometimes took the form of trying to persuade a judge to render a favorable verdict or, once the court had decided, of importuning a court clerk to alter the transcript. In an extreme case a noble might simply refuse to pay a fine levied upon him and indignantly threaten the officials sent to dun him.[24]

Through all these cases runs a current of patrician intolerance of legal restraint. Though far less violent—and ultimately less of an obstacle to institutionalized civil order—than the flamboyant lawlessness of Lombard and Tuscan magnates, Venetian noble interference with the administration of justice nevertheless sprang from a similar source, the aristocratic tendency to translate dominance in political institutions into personal superiority to them.[25] This impatience with restraints on personal and factional interests underlay not only the Tiepolo-Querini conspiracy of 1310 but—in considerable measure—the struggles within the upper class which had led to the Serrata.[26]

[24] AC *Raspe*, Reg. 3, fol. 220r, Oct. 15, 1375: Zanino Morosini not only tried to persuade the judge but threatened him as well; his sentence was three months in prison and a fine of 25 lire. *Ibid.*, fol. 61v, July 5, 1364: Francesco Contarini detto Rizzo threatened to put out the eyes of a court clerk who refused to alter the transcript of a trial; he was fined 50 lire. *Ibid.*, Reg. 4, fol. 49v, Oct. 10, 1382: Luca q. Maffeo Morosini told the officials seeking payment of the fine "quod errueret eis ocullos," among other things; this brought him an additional fine of 100 lire *di piccoli*. (All monetary references are in lire *di piccoli* unless otherwise noted.)

[25] See the discussion of the elaborate principles underlying factional or familial organization—a sort of law code of the *parte*—in Jones, "Communes and Despots," pp. 83–84. For a description of enduring partisan autonomy in mid-Trecento Florence, see G. A. Brucker, *Florentine Politics and Society, 1343–1378* (Princeton, 1962), pp. 194 ff.

[26] For a statement of this interpretation of the Serrata, see Maranini, *Costituzione I*, pp. 335–351; a dissenting view in Cracco, *Società e stato*, pp. 290–350.

Now, in the fourteenth century, it still found expression in patrician opposition to the law when the law proved inconvenient.

Another type of patrician offense involved the abuse of noble status or of its political responsibilities. Only with great aplomb and luck, for example, could a nonnoble walk into a police station, pass himself off as a Signore di Notte—an office reserved to patricians—and be issued a sword of a kind reserved to policemen. But what mere patrolman would challenge the credentials of a well-known noble falsely making the same claim? [27] And nobles actually in office not infrequently yielded to the temptations of power as well. It would be inaccurate to depict noble officeholders as generally corrupt. But it is also a misrepresentation to characterize them all as dedicated and selfless public servants. Among Venetian public officials, as among officials of every government, there were those who took advantage of their positions to line their pockets.[28]

The problem that these infractions—all deriving in some way from the special status of nobles—posed to the government was a difficult one, since at bottom the regime rested upon precisely that status. Obviously the problem could not be attacked at its source. The Serrata had been a response to social and political turmoil as well as to threats against the hegemony of the communal upper class, and no amount of aristocratic contempt for the courts or peculation in office could induce the government, that is, the collective patriciate, to reverse that measure. The alternative then was to provide that individual noble bumptious-

[27] AC *Raspe*, Reg. 3, fol. 106v, May 31, 1368. The patrician guilty in this case of impersonating a Signore di Notte was Marco di Fantin Morosini, a member of one of Venice's most prestigious families and thus quite capable of cowing an ordinary patrolman.

[28] AC *Raspe*, Reg. 3, fol. 187r, Sept. 16, 1373: Marco q. Zanino Morosini convicted of buying gold cheap and selling it dear to the mint, of which he was an official. *Ibid.*, fol. 130v, Jan. 11, 1370: Piero Morosini convicted of engaging in commerce while an official on Crete —in violation of the rules of his office.

ness be kept within limits and at the same time to prosecute individual noble malefactors firmly and consistently. The preventive measures are typified by the government's provisions against armed factions. A specific manifestation, very revealing of the kind of threat the government still feared, was a concern that armed officials might turn their weapons to private use. Although certain officials were required to go about their duties armed, it was made quite clear that their armed retainers were to have no private relationship, familial or economic, with the officials they served.[29]

But prevention of armed factions was in any case an indispensable objective of governmental policy; prosecution of offending nobles was more complex. Clearly in matters directly affecting the government, such as the offenses against the courts or violations of public responsibility which we have discussed, there could be no alternative to meting out penalties: the validity of the state demanded it. But disturbances of the peace of one kind or another, involving no direct assault on the regime or its judicial institutions, were another matter. It is in this general area that the patrician regime's attitude toward the privileges of individual nobles—with all its implications for general social morale—find clearest expression. The critical question is, did nobles escape prosecution for crimes for which other Venetians were punished? [30]

[29] ". . . filii fratres vel nipotes filii filiorum vel fratrum vel . . . famuli [qui] habitent in domo "—a measure of the Dieci, Dec. 5, 1328 (F. Zago, ed., *Consiglio dei Dieci: Deliberazioni miste. Registri III-IV (1325-1335)*, Fonti per la Storia di Venezia, Section 1, Archivi pubblici [Venice, 1968], p. 102). The same restriction had been written into the capitulary of the Signori di Notte in 1299, two years after the Serrata (M. Roberti, *Le magistrature giudiziarie veneziane e i loro capitolari fino al 1300*, 3 vols. [Padua and Venice, 1906–1911], III, 100).

[30] For a perspective on this question from outside Venice, see the discussion of Florentine upper-class exemptions from the law in the early Trecento in M. B. Becker, *Florence in Transition, I, The Decline of the Commune* (Baltimore, 1967), pp. 19–25, 207–211.

The answer is a qualified no, and the qualification reflects not so much on judicial leniency as on the proclivities of the nobles. The crimes of greatest social importance in Trecento Venice may be gathered under three headings: violence against persons, violence against property, and outraging public decency. Fleshing out these categories we can focus on homicide and rape, on larceny and robbery, and on socially obnoxious sexual behavior as the offenses that kept the criminal courts of Trecento Venice most busy.[31] And a comparison of incidences of noble and popular indictments for these crimes reveals significant trends. To judge from indications in the records of the Signori di Notte, patricians were not given to homicide or theft, two kinds of crime into which Venetians of lesser status fell with considerable frequency. Of some ninety trials for homicide in the late 1350s and the 1360s, only two involved noble culprits. Of sixty theft trials during the same period, not one involved a noble.[32]

At first glance these figures might suggest not so much the disinclination of noblemen toward bloodletting and theft as an effective governmental policy of not prosecuting patrician killers and thieves. In addition to the few cases that reveal governmental prosecution of nobles, however, there is ample evidence from other criminal proceedings that the government was not indulgent toward disorderly patricians.[33] What the evidence

[31] The two tribunals with jurisdiction in criminal cases were the Signori di Notte and the Quarantia. Generally crimes of violence against persons and property came under the competence of the former magistracy. The Quarantia, however, adjudicated all cases involving violence against governmental officials, crimes against the family, carnal violence, and thefts of church or state goods—"insomma tutti quei reati soggetti a sanzione penale, che potevano direttamente o indirettamente comprendersi nella formula *contra Deum et civitatis et populi Veneciarum honorem et utilitatem* . . ." (Molmenti, *Storia*, I, 102). The Dieci also exercised jurisdiction over criminal offenses, but only those with clear political overtones.

[32] SN *Processi*, Regs. 8, 9, *passim.* Neither figure represents the total of trials for the respective crimes during this period.

[33] For an example of the prosecution of violence by a noblemen, see

also demonstrates is that if nobles were not especially inclined toward homicide and theft, they made up for it by their tendencies toward more casual violence and more subtle theft—such as exploiting their official positions—as well as by an occasional willingness to disregard conventional morality. In these areas they were at least a match for their popular counterparts.

The largest percentage of patrician crimes of violence seems to have had a sexual object. One is led to speculate on the constraints of Venetian mores in the light of the great number of sexual assaults committed by nobles.[34] They ranged from outright rape, for which the penalty was very heavy, to attempted rape, which drew a lighter sentence, to what might be called effusive flirtation.[35] In some cases erotic ardor could lead to a compounding of enormities, as it did for Piero Capello one night in 1385. Bent on seducing a young nun, he stole into her quarters while she lay sleeping. When two of her companions

---

SN *Processi*, Reg. 8, fols. 50r-52r: Piero q. Zaneto Lando sentenced to the loss of his left hand and eye for killing another young patrician, Naufosio Morosini, in 1365.

[34] Molmenti (*Storia*, I, 484) observes that in the Tre-Quattrocento "il costume veneziano si allontanava dall' antica semplicità, e il senso morale si abbassava col crescere della civiltà," an observation that strikes me as missing completely the point of increased governmental sensitivity to the requirements of society and consequent implementation of measures to respond to them in late medieval and early Renaissance Italy.

[35] E.g., the rape case of Andreolo Baffo, sentenced to a year in prison for violating a young girl (AC *Raspe*, Reg. 3, fol. 59r). Two cases of attempted rape, in 1362 and 1363, illustrate the judicial tendency to mete out sentences in proportion to the gravity of the offense: Marin Tron was fined 50 lire for attempting to rape a widow; Marco Grimani was fined 300 lire for attempting to rape a young virgin, and one-third of his fine was to go to the girl's dowry (*ibid.*, fols. 32v, 47r). In each of these cases the victim was a *popolana*. For an example of violent flirtation, see the case of the two young nobles who attacked the boat of a young patrician woman in the Grand Canal, inspiring the would-be victim to leap overboard and swim to safety; for this escapade they were sentenced to 15 days in prison and a 50 lire fine (*ibid.*, fol. 109v).

discovered his presence, he first demanded that one of them submit to his desires; then, upon their declining this suggestion, he proceeded to beat and kick them till the entire building was roused by the tumult. For this adventure Piero was sentenced to two years in prison and a fine of 500 lire.[36]

Even in instances where the young woman yielded herself willingly the courts could be stern, particularly if the circumstances were sufficiently grievous. Seducing a nun, for example, as Lorenzo Morosini did in 1381, luring her out of her convent by night and into his home for the purpose—"in contemptum supreme maiestatis" reads the indictment, and one imagines the Avogadori di Comun fairly quivering with indignation as they recited it—could result in a very heavy sentence. In this case it was not only eight months in prison and a fine of 600 ducats for Lorenzo, but provision for a fine of 1,000 ducats to be levied upon anyone seeking clemency for him.[37] Clearly the government frowned severely upon such scandalous violations of the public morality even when they were committed by patricians.

These few cases prompt some general considerations. First, the trial records suggest that noble disorderliness took different outlets than did that of their *popolani* neighbors. Although on occasion they could react as violently to provocation as the most insignificant waterfront vagabond,[38] on the whole patri-

[36] AC *Raspe*, Reg. 4, fol. 82v.

[37] AC *Raspe*, Reg. 4, fol. 34v. The indictment also assures us that once Lorenzo had got the girl to his house, "[illam] pluries carnaliter cognovit." Petitions for clemency (*gratia*) were frequently granted to convicted malefactors of all classes. See Elena Favaro, ed., *Cassiere della Bolla Ducale, Grazie, Novus Liber (1299–1305)*, Fonti per la Storia di Venezia, Sec. 1, Archivi pubblici [Venice, 1962], and especially the lengthy discussion of procedure and practice by C. G. Mor which serves as introduction to the volume.

[38] E.g., the case of Leonardo and Benedetto Morosini, who in 1371 thrashed the doge's wine steward while he was on official business in the meeting room of the Maggior Consiglio. Each was fined 100 lire (AC *Raspe*, Reg. 3, fol. 146r). On the vagabonds see below.

cians confined their violent outbursts to actions that satisfied their carnal desires or their self-esteem, as in the case of the beatings administered to court officials. These tendencies further suggest that by the Trecento the patriciate had evolved an ethos of individual assertiveness tamed by the civilizing demands of orderly social intercourse essential to the commercial world in which most of them dwelt. In the last analysis they were not *grandi* on the mainland model.[39] To be sure the vigilance of the government against factional conflict, visible in the care exercised to prevent the appearance of armed bands of nobles, erected an external impediment to sanguinary violence. But the habits of the nobles themselves seem not to have included the easy recourse to homicide which characterized other Venetians, particularly those of the lowest economic groups.[40]

At the same time the crimes that patricians characteristically committed did not go unpunished. The prerogatives of membership in an exclusive ruling class did not include superiority to the law; individual patricians did not possess immunity from the judicial process. Why was this so? Why were nobles forced, like *popolani*, to submit to the rule of law? A brief answer is that the essential functioning of government in Trecento Ven-

[39] See the discussion of the conditions leading to factional and social conflict in medieval Pistoia in D. Herlihy, *Medieval and Renaissance Pistoia* (New Haven, 1967), pp. 198–199. For a late Quattrocento Lombard model of the magnate proclivity to violence and factors contributing to it, D. M. Bueno de Mesquita, "Ludovico Sforza and His Vassals," in *Italian Renaissance Studies*, ed. E. F. Jacob (London, 1960), pp. 184–216. In both cases the upper-class ethos is rather different even from that which underlay the factional struggles of the Venetian Dugento.

[40] In a sense this is an incomplete generalization, based mainly on the visibility of noble names in the court records. It ignores the various gradations among non-nobles, and thus should be extended to include the economically substantial bourgeoisie among the *cittadini* whose level of civilization was doubtless just as high as that of the mercantile patricians. The difference, of course, lay in the special problems presented by the noble political position.

ice, its capacity to respond to the social and economic problems of the age, required circumscription of noble prerogatives. But this brief answer leads into a more thorough discussion of the problems of Trecento Venice and their effect on the development of the state.

III

The second set of circumstances challenging the government's capacity to establish "pax et quies" arose from the distinctive nature of the Venetian economy and particularly from its vicissitudes in the fourteenth century. Here as in the case of the problem posed by the patriciate's newly defined status, the peculiarities of the Venetian experience forced the regime to formulate and implement responses to complex realities that had evolved over the course of centuries, but which in the Trecento acquired significant new dimensions.

There is no need to rehearse the elementary facts of Venetian economic life in the Middle Ages. At the very basis of the Venetian economy—indeed, in Henri Pirenne's words, "the very condition of [Venice's] existence"—was maritime commerce. And it was trade that made Venice an international power of the first magnitude in the high Middle Ages.[41] The vast influence of its commerce made Venice not only an entrepot for goods traveling from east to west but an important center of activity for large numbers of foreign merchants. Their presence

[41] H. Pirenne, *Economic and Social History of Medieval Europe*, Eng. trans by I. E. Clegg (New York, 1937), p. 17. The literature on the Venetian economy in the Middle Ages is enormous. The best survey, containing an excellent bibliography, is G. Luzzatto, *Storia economica di Venezia dall'XI al XVI secolo* (Venice, 1961). For Venice's role in the European commerce of the thirteenth and fourteenth centuries, see R. S. Lopez, "The Trade of Medieval Europe: The South," in *The Cambridge Economic History of Europe*, II, *Trade and Industry in the Middle Ages*, eds. M. M. Postan and E. E. Rich (Cambridge, 1952), pp. 291–301.

in the city was necessarily of long duration since it was strict governmental policy to require foreigners to buy and sell in Venice, restricting rights of overseas commerce to Venetians. The result was the establishment of foreign merchant colonies whose members became more or less permanent fixtures on the Venetian scene.[42] The most famous and most elaborately organized foreign commercial community was that of the Germans and Austrians, whose headquarters, the Fondaco dei Tedeschi, was regulated by the Venetian Consoli dei Mercanti —an institutionalized testimony to the essentially commercial character of the foreign presence.[43] But the Germans were only one of many foreign groups whose presence in Venice was testimony to and a bulwark of Venetian commercial prosperity.

Merchants, however, were not the only foreigners in the city. In addition to the pilgrims, crusaders and tourists who passed through because of Venice's location and transport facilities, there were large numbers of that footloose community to be found in any thriving seaport: sailors, day laborers, unemployed men-at-arms, and vagabonds pure and simple, some in transit,

[42] Luzzatto, *Storia economica*, p. 58: "La politica veneziana, che ha sempre mirato, per ragioni economiche e fiscali, a fare della città un attivo centro di scambi . . . ha sempre preteso . . . che gli stranieri vendessero o scambiassero le loro merci a Venezia, e che i rischi ed i profitti del commercio marittimo, in particolare con l'Oriente, fossero riservati ai suoi cittadini." On the foreign communities, *ibid.*, pp. 58–61; Kretschmayr, *Geschichte*, II, 152, 162; also the description by the thirteenth-century chronicler, Marino da Canale: "s'en aloient les Venisiens parmi la mer sa et la, et dela la mer et en tos leus, et achetoient les merchandies, et les condusoient en Venise de totes pars. Si les venoient acheter droitement en Venise Alemans et Baviers, Franceis et Lombars, Toscans et Ongres, et totes gens qui vivent de marchandies," quoted in H. Simonsfeld, *Der Fondaco dei Tedeschi in Venedig und die deutsch-venetianischen Handelsbeziehungen*, 2 vols. in 1 (Stuttgart, 1887), II, 8.

[43] In 1284 the Maggior Consiglio gave the Consoli "libertatem addendi, minuendi et mutandi in capitulari vicedominorum fontici Teotonicorum quicquid eis videbitur pro melioramento mercadantie" (Simonsfeld, *Fondaco dei Tedeschi*, I, 2, doc. 3). On the Consoli dei Mercanti, see Kretschmayr, *Geschichte*, II, 152.

others resident for long periods of time. Even the policemen, by mid-century, seem to have been mostly foreigners.[44] The numbers of the foreign population are difficult to calculate, but some sense of their impact on the city can be gathered from the elaborate regulations governing hotels and inns, extending even to the number of beds and the cost of a night's lodging.[45]

Finally there was the servant and slave population, the majority of whom were foreign born. Domestic servants and household slaves generally came from Friuli and the Balkans, respectively, and thus did not present as exotic a spectacle as the large numbers of Circassian and Tartar slaves who passed through the Venetian slave market or who remained in Venice as the property of Venetians.[46]

All these groups of foreigners, resident and transient, represented in one way or another the wealth and international im-

[44] SN *Processi*, Regs. 7, 8, 9, *passim*. Most appear to have come from northern Italy. The capitulary of the Signori di Notte expressly provided that the *custodes* be either native Venetians or Venetian residents for ten years. Exceptions were so frequently made, however, that this regulation seems to have been honored in the breach (Roberti, *Le magistrature*, III, 25, for the capitulary provision). The practice of hiring foreign policemen obtained in other Italian cities as well (cf. W. M. Bowsky, "The Medieval Commune and Internal Violence: Police Power and Public Safety in Siena, 1287–1355," *American Historical Review*, LXXIII [1967], 7).

[45] Kretschmayr, *Geschichte*, II, 303.

[46] On domestic help, *ibid.*, II, 162. On Venice as a source of slaves for Italy, I. Origo, "The Domestic Enemy: The Eastern Slaves in Tuscany in the Fourteenth and Fifteenth Centuries," *Speculum*, XXX (1955), 329 and *passim*. The notarial records of the ASV are full of slave transactions among Venetians, many involving importation, but many also clearly demonstrating domestic consumption. An indication of the pervasiveness of slave-owning in Venice is the quittance of "nobilis et religiosa domina Zanina Mauroceno [i.e., Morosini] monialis monasterii Sancti Zacharie de Veneciis" to ser Benedetto Sartor of Venice for 25 ducats which he paid her for "unam suam sclavam vocatam lingua Tartarorum 'Altum' . . . gratia baptismi vocata Anna, de progene Tartarorum, etatis circa annorum xiii" (ASV, *Cancelleria Inferiore*, Busta 35, notary Pietro de Carrozati, protocol 1, fol. 8v).

portance of Venice. At the same time, however, they represented a difficult problem for the forces of public order. The
very cosmopolitanism of medieval Venice meant that there
were at all times in the city large numbers of unassimilated persons, unfamiliar with Venetian mores and law and in many cases
competing economically with Venetians. Although Venice
was far from unique in having a large foreign population, the
importance and the maritime aspect of the Venetian economy
meant that the foreign presence there was particularly heavy,
and that it occupied the government, as attempts to regulate
foreign residents' activities indicate.[47]

To this residual fact of Venetian life the events of the Trecento added qualitatively significant new dimensions. Two
impulses in particular contributed to a growth of the city's
foreign element, in influence if not in numbers: the demographic problems that Venice shared with other Italian cities
and tendencies toward economic diversification, notably in the
direction of industry.[48]

Although the most persuasive study of late medieval Venetian population has argued that Venice's recovery from the
demographic losses of the mid-Trecento was comparatively
rapid,[49] the main factor seems to have been not so much re-

[47] See a Maggior Consiglio act of 1314, requiring all German merchants to register at the Fondaco dei Tedeschi—thus coming under the
controlling scrutiny of the government—and assessing a fine of 200 lire
on anyone, "Venetus vel forensis vel habitator Venetiarum [qui] receperint aliquem mercatorem Theotonicum vel aliam quamcumque
personam in domo, habitatione vel volta vel statione suis vel aliquid de
suo receperint, antequam descendant sic ad fonticum . . ." (Simonsfeld,
Fondaco dei Tedeschi, I, 14, doc. 40).

[48] For a view of these two phenomena as different manifestations of
the same general development in Italy in general, see R. Romano,
"L'Italia nella crisi del XIV secolo," Nuova rivista storica, L (1966),
582–588. Their relationship in the present Venetian context is discussed below.

[49] K. J. Beloch, Bevölkerungsgeschichte Italiens, 3 vols. (Berlin, 1937–
1961), III, 3–4. Estimating the proportion of nobles to popolani, he uses

newed biological vitality among Venetians as governmental encouragement of immigration. In the wake of heavy mortalities, and especially of the epidemic of 1348, the government enacted legislation to attract new blood—and financial resources—into Venice.[50] These measures fell into two categories: easing the requirements for citizenship and granting exemptions from communal obligations.[51] Each aimed at a particular kind of immigrant. Since one of the main attractions of Venetian *cittadinanza* was the right it gave of engaging in overseas commerce, it appealed primarily to foreigners of some economic substance; and the response indicates that significant numbers of foreign-born merchants found the opportunity attractive.[52] But the postplague needs of Venice included labor as well as capital,

---

a 1379 list of nobles in Venice to arrive at a total population figure of 100,000 for that year—approximately the same as 1338. This method strikes me as risky; yet earlier attempts at fixing the Trecento population are scarcely more reliable. See A. Contento, "Il censimento della popolazione sotto la Repubblica Veneta," *Nuovo archivio veneto*, XIX (1900), 5–42.

[50] The impact of the Black Death in Venice has yet to receive a thorough study. The two-part article of M. Brunetti, "Venezia durante la peste del 1348," *Ateneo veneto*, Anno XXXII (1909), I, 289–311, II, 5–42, deals primarily with governmental responses to the plague without analyzing the epidemic's long-range effects.

[51] For a discussion of these measures, particularly the relaxation of *cittadinanza* requirements, M. Kovalesky, "Die wirthschaftlichen Folgen des schwarzen Todes in Italien," *Zeitschrift für Social- und Wirtschaftsgeschichte*, III (1895), 421–423. Some of the legislation is reproduced at length in Molmenti, *Storia*, I, 74n; also Brunetti, "Venezia durante la peste," II, 20–27.

[52] See the decrees of citizenship in R. Predelli, ed., *I libri commemoriali della Repubblica di Venezia. Regesti*, Deputazione Veneta di Storia Patria, *Monumenti Storici*, ser. 1, Documenti, 8 vols. (Venice, 1876–1914), VII, *passim*; for some examples from the 1360s, see nos. 81, 93, 218, 250. For some comments on the German *cittadini*, B. Cecchetti, "La vita dei veneziani nel 1300," *Archivio veneto*, XXIX (1885), 31–33. On *cittadinanza* in general, Molmenti, *Storia*, I, 72 ff.; and M. Ferro, *Dizionario del diritto comune e veneto*, 2 vols. (2d ed.; Venice, 1847), I, 396–397.

and specific provisions were enacted to encourage artisans, sailors, and unskilled workers to take up Venetian residence. Among the lures the government offered were waivers of matriculation fees in the various guilds and an increase in the limit of money a sailor could invest in trade while on a voyage. In the latter case the sailor had to leave his wife and family in Venice as an earnest of his residential intentions.[53]

The same open encouragement of immigration to fill population gaps occurred after the critical War of Chioggia, 1378–1381, against the Genoese and their allies.[54] But these two critical moments, postplague and postwar, were only the most important instances of governmental response to demographic need. Adjusting *cittadinanza* requirements was a constant of governmental policy throughout the Trecento, and the result was continued renewal not only of the foreign presence, but also of the economic privileges enjoyed by the immigrants.[55] And from the perspective of civic order this fact involved a task of considerable delicacy for the Venetian government: to restrain the potential for disorder these new arrivals represented while recognizing their great importance for the Venetian economy.[56]

But the demographic crises were not the only causes of Trecento immigration. A factor ultimately of more profound im-

[53] Brunetti, "Venezia durante la peste," II, 20–27. On June 13, 1348, a commission was appointed to look into the feasibility of "prestandi immunitates, libertates et franchisias venientibus habitatum terram nostram et absolvandi eos ab honeribus" (*ibid.*, p. 20).

[54] Cf. Luzzatto, *Storia economica*, p. 146.

[55] On the employment of *cittadinanza* as a demographic weapon, see Ferro, *Dizionario*, I, 396–397, which cites the relevant fourteenth-century legislation.

[56] For a negative assessment of the Venetian Trecento in general, see Cracco, *Società e stato*, pp. 353–458, *passim*. A persuasive discussion of one phase of the commercial problems is R. Cessi, "L' 'officium de navigantibus' e i sistemi della politica commerciale veneziana nel sec. XIV," in *Politica ed economia di Venezia nel Trecento. Saggi* (Rome, 1952), pp. 23–61.

portance was the growing industrial activity of Trecento Venice. While commerce maintained its hegemony in the Venetian
economy throughout the Tre-Quattrocento, industry, particularly in wool and silk, was establishing itself as an important
new activity.[57] The significance of this fact in the present context is twofold. In the first place the demands of industry on
manpower resources contributed substantially to the demographic difficulties of the century. This is apparent in the trib-
ulations of the Arsenale, the state-owned shipyards, during
much of the Trecento. So keen did competition for skilled labor
become that the government frequently had to enact legislation to combat the drain of shipworkers—carpenters, caulkers,
and the like—into private industry. Thus the demographic
losses we have noted only intensified an existing need, making
all the more urgent the governmental provisions to attract
foreign artisans into Venice and to lure back those who had
left.[58]

The contribution of Trecento industrial growth to the foreign presence had, however, a more direct manifestation. The
wool and silk industries specifically required skilled labor that
could only be supplied from outside Venice. This is clearly the
case of Venetian silk manufacture, for which the political

[57] On the broad developments of the late Middle Ages and Renaissance, there is G. Luzzatto, "L'economia veneziana dopo l'acquisto della
Terraferma," *Bergomum*, XXXVIII (1964), 59–61; also his *Storia economica*, pp. 164 ff. On industrial development, one author observes, "Dal
1316 fino al 1359 . . . è . . . il periodo in cui l'Arte [della Lana] raggiunge
il massimo sviluppo . . ." (N. Fano, "Ricerche sull'Arte della Lana a
Venezia nel XIII e XIV secolo," *Archivio veneto*, 5th ser., XVIII [1936],
90–91). See also R. Broglio d'Ajano, "L'industria della seta a Venezia,"
in *Storia dell'economia italiana: Saggi di storia economica*, I, *Secoli
settimo-diciassettesimo*, ed. C. M. Cipolla (Turin, 1959), p. 231.

[58] On the effects of private industry, G. Luzzatto, "Per la storia delle
costruzioni navali a Venezia nei secoli XV e XVI," in *Studi di storia
economica veneziana*, pp. 38–42. The incentives to foreigners to come
to—or remain in—Venice continued to appear through the 1370s and
1380s (*ibid.*, p. 42; Broglio d'Ajano, "Seta," p. 241).

tumults in Lucca during the first half of the Trecento proved an enormous blessing, since they led to an influx of Lucchese *setaiuoli* into Venice. Less indebted to one particular region but equally dependent upon imported labor was the wool industry, whose practitioners—entrepreneurs and laborers alike —were attracted to Venice by substantial advantages.[59] The fact of foreign origins together with the economic difficulties afflicting Venice throughout the century necessitated continued governmental solicitude of these economically important resident aliens, since they often demonstrated a disinclination to remain in Venice during periods of hardship and consequently had to be lured back by further privileges.[60]

Thus, under the pressure of Trecento economic conditions, the government was forced into assuming important new initiatives in the economic sphere. These various steps to promote prosperity involved severe social strains. We have already noted the potential for friction the newcomers carried by reason of the cultural diversity they introduced into the Venetian scene. But to make the social situation even more explosive they entered Venetian society possessing privileges at precisely the time when the economic difficulties meant special hardships for the native population. Especially rankling must have been the governmental policy of responding to crisis by raising customs duties, with its effect on price levels. And on the most elementary level it is possible to speculate on native Venetians' reaction to the newcomers' privileges while even grain was in short domestic supply.[61] In these tense circumstances civil con-

[59] On silk, see Broglio d'Ajano, "Seta," p. 231; Romanin, *Storia documentata*, III, 102. On wool, see Fano, "Arte della Lana," pp. 133–136. The registers of the SN *Processi* reveal a large number of Germans involved in the wool industry.

[60] Fano, "Arte della Lana," pp. 132, 138–139; Broglio d'Ajano, "Seta," p. 241.

[61] The governmental response to economic crisis must have been especially painful for the lower classes, since these measures were adopted in large part to protect the public funded debt and to promote

cord would be a governmental achievement of no small dimensions.

But the task of preserving public order confronted an even more formidable obstacle: the lower classes' chronic impulses toward violence. If patricians did not characteristically seek physically destructive outlets for their individual assertiveness, the popular classes were far less subtle. The Trecento was indeed a time of violence at the most elementary levels of social relations and in nearly all types of situations.

In common with their patrician neighbors, Venetian *popolani* vented their sexual desires with destructive exuberance. The varieties of rape encountered in court records are innumerable, but they all attest in one way or another to the readiness of smitten males to resort to force to attain their objective. Servant girls were especially vulnerable to their masters' advances.[62] But the danger they faced seems to have arisen less from their servant status than from the willingness of men in all situations to take advantage of a woman's defenselessness. A landlady might be the victim of her lodger, a passenger of her boatman, a pedestrian of a lurking assailant, or a housewife of a stranger breaking into her house.[63] These are the circumstances of sexual assault in all ages, but there could be more elaborate procedures as well. In one case before the Quarantia in January, 1343, indictments were handed down not only to a man who had committed a rape but also to a female neighbor of the victim who

---

the interests of certain mercantile interests, neither of which involved the lower classes (Luzzatto, *Storia economica*, p. 136; Cessi, "Officium de navigantibus," pp. 26–28 and *passim*). On the grain problems, see Brunetti, "Venezia durante la peste," I, 306.

[62] AV *Raspe*, Reg. 3, fols. 5rv, 10v, are examples. The penalties were not light: in these cases thirty days plus 500 lire and six months in prison, respectively.

[63] AV *Raspe*, Reg. 3, fol. 12v; A. Lombardo, ed., *Le deliberazioni del Consiglio dei XL della Repubblica di Venezia I, 1342–1344*, Deputazione di Storia Patria per le Venezie, *Monumenti Storici*, n.s., IX (Venice, 1957), p. 41, nos. 144–145; *Raspe*, Reg. 3, fols. 7r, 8v.

had provided her house for the purpose, a friend of the rapist who had helped arrange the assault, and "others implicated in this matter." [64]

Sexual assaults were not visited only on women, however. Sodomite rape also could involve mayhem and even murder.[65] Young boys were particularly apt victims of this kind of violence, which could occur on board the merchant ships that sailed under the Venetian flag or in the Ducal Palace itself.[66] Such offenses were viewed with particular horror, and men convicted of them were nearly always burned at the stake. Bestiality, though not strictly a crime of violence, was also considered an "ignominiosum et abhominabile peccatum," although extenuating circumstances might lead to a milder punishment. They did in the case of Simone Furlan, who persuaded the Signori di Notte that his congress with a goat was the only libidinous outlet available to him owing to certain physiological defects rendering him incapable of normal human intercourse. Thus he was sentenced only to the loss of his hands and a branding.[67]

Acts of sexually inspired violence such as these constituted a disturbing fact of the urban milieu, and the government's assiduity in prosecuting assailants, noble and popular, is testi-

[64] ". . . et alios culpabiles de dicto facto . . ." (Lombardo, *Deliberazioni dei XL*, p. 23, no. 72, Jan. 22, 1343).

[65] As it did in the case of Giacomello de Bonaldo who stabbed Marin q. Piero "vagabundus" to death after forcing him into the act (Lombardo, *Deliberazioni dei XL*, pp. 13–14, nos. 40–41).

[66] SN *Processi*, Reg. 8, fol. 55r–55v, April 20, 1365: Roberto de Marchesio found guilty of forcing a twelve-year-old shipboy to commit sodomy with him during a voyage. *Ibid.*, fols. 81v–82r, May 6, 1368: Benedetto, a government herald, found guilty of first forcing then cajoling—at 2 denarii a meeting—a certain Antonio, aged thirteen, into a sodomite affair lasting three years. One tryst occurred on the steps leading to the meeting room of the Maggior Consiglio.

[67] SN *Processi*, Reg. 8, fol. 58r. To determine the validity of Simone's claim, the court called in two "peccatrices" to "facere multa experimenta" which evidently persuaded the judges.

mony to its concern over the problem. In the last analysis, however, violence stemming from lust presented far less a problem than violence stemming from anger. The greatest obstacle to social tranquillity came from the *popolo's* quick resort to arms. Here, as in the case of sexual assaults, insult, injury, and especially violent death could occur in almost any social circumstances.

The domestic situation was a frequent setting for bloodshed; indeed family ties seem particularly to have inspired violent impulses. A chance encounter on a street at night could lead to an impulsive fratricide in the rough-and-ready atmosphere of the time.[68] The heat of family arguments could grow so great that even would-be peacemakers could be killed.[69] Not surprisingly the most frequently encountered kind of familial bloodshed occurred in disputes between husband and wife. One source of it was estrangement between the spouses. This situation could lead to an attack on both wife and mother-in-law by an unhappy husband. More common were uxoricides arising out of wifely infidelity.[70] Husbandly rage could go to unusual lengths: in 1361 one Jacopo da Perugia murdered his wife Giuliana with a sword specially made for him, since he was

[68] SN *Processi*, Reg. 8, fols. 45v–46r, Feb. 24, 1365. In this case homicide appeared unintentional: the victim struck his head upon being pushed by his brother.

[69] SN *Processi*, Reg. 7, fols. 16v–18r, Oct. 30, 1357: When Giuliana, wife of Francesco Belcapuzo, sought to stop a knife fight between her husband and his cousin, an argument erupted between the two spouses which ended in Francesco's stabbing Giuliana to death.

[70] SN *Processi*, Reg. 9, fol. 43r–43v, Jan. 16, 1365: Lorenzo Calegher stormed the house where his wife and mother-in-law were living and stabbed them both. *Ibid.*, fols. 49r–50v, Jan. 10, 1365: Maddelena, wife of Guglielmo de Rovereto, was killed by her husband for running off to Florence with a lover. *Ibid.*, fol. 55r, June 8, 1366: Donato Pellegrino killed his wife, Colletta, because, in the words of a neighbor's testimony, she was "mulier malle fame et vite inhoneste."

"mutillatus ambos manos." [71] The other side of this coin also turned up on occasion; husbands too were killed by their wives' lovers.[72]

Domestic violence also extended outside the family circle. Servants and masters appear to have shed each other's blood pretty reciprocally.[73] The former occasionally employed their kitchen responsibilities to poison unloved employers, but an impatient master could be equally dangerous for an inefficient servant.[74] Dislikes among neighbors also degenerated into fatal attacks. This was perhaps a natural consequence of the close quarters in which Venetians lived.[75] But it provides further indication of the low threshold of violence in the Trecento.

The threshold was easily reached outside the family and neighborhood as well. Disputes over money were a frequent cause of bloodshed. It is not altogether surprising that gambling losses could inspire murderous tendencies, as they frequently did.[76] But the records of the courts are also full of homicides

[71] AC *Raspe*, Reg. 3, fol. 9r.

[72] AC *Raspe*, Reg. 3, fol. 8r-8v, June 2, 1361: In this case the lover killed the husband and was hanged. The guilty wife's sentence was that she be led along the Grand Canal, a herald crying out her crime, then be given fifty lashes and released.

[73] E.g., SN *Processi*, Reg. 9, fols. 6r–6v, 23r–23v.

[74] SN *Processi*, Reg. 8, fols. 40r–42r, April 26, 1364: Jacopo Saraceno, slave of Maffeo da Mosto, put rat poison into the chicken soup. *Ibid.*, Reg. 9, fols. 23v–24r, June 25, 1364: Giovanni Coltelliere hurled a pair of pliers at a slowly moving servant.

[75] The accused in the SN *Processi* are generally identified as living in the *palazzi* of noble families. On residential conditions in general, see B. Cecchetti, "La vita dei veneziani nel 1300," *Archivio veneto*, XXVII (1884), 20–29. For some examples of neighborly bloodshed, SN *Processi*, Reg. 9, fols. 17r–18r, 47r–48r.

[76] SN *Processi*, Reg. 8, fols. 78v–79r; Reg. 9, fols. 11r–11v, 41r–41v. The gambling atmosphere lent itself to violence in other ways. When Michelino Aqualea one night in 1365 reproached a shipmate for taking advantage of a youth with whom the latter was gambling he received a knife-thrust in the ribs for his efforts (*ibid.*, fols. 44v–45r).

resulting from such minor matters as a dispute over a boat fare, a customer's low opinion of a vendor's wool stock, an innkeeper overcharging his guest or a tailor his customer.[77]

But although domestic and financial disagreements were common causes of violence, by far the majority of *popolano* killings were the result of completely chance encounters, such as two boats ramming into each other. A casual jostle on the street might lead to the same sanguinary conclusion.[78] Even such banal matters as an argument over whether fish or meat should be served at the seamen's mess, the obstinacy of two claimants to a chair in a public place, or a groom's offense at a passerby's use of his stable as a privy could culminate in killings.[79]

Such disputes did not inevitably end in loss of life, but the effect of less than lethal violence could be grave too. On October 10, 1361, fourteen members of the carpenters' and caulkers' guilds were sentenced for their participation in a riot in the Ducal Palace on the occasion of their annual ceremonial visit to the doge. One of them had fallen into an argument with a gold-leaf worker who was decorating the Palace. Words gave way to fighting and soon a wholesale riot had developed between the carpenters and the decorators—an egregious affront to the ducal dignity but also a clear indication of the brawling spirit of the epoch.[80]

And the extent to which the violent impulses of quick-tempered Venetians combined with the highly visible foreign presence is apparent in the foreign representation in the criminal

[77] SN *Processi*, Reg. 8, fols. 48v–49r; Reg. 9, fols. 33v–34r, 54r–54v, 48v–49r.

[78] For some encounters in the *rii*, SN *Processi*, Reg. 8, fols. 80v–81r; Reg. 9, fols. 7v–8r. For encounters on the street, *ibid.*, Reg. 8, 42v–44r; Reg. 9, fols. 31v–32v, 34v–35r.

[79] SN *Processi*, Reg. 9, fol. 15r–15v; Reg. 8, fols. 52v–53r; Reg. 9, fols. 46v–47r.

[80] AC *Raspe*, Reg. 3, fols. 16v–17v. The sentences in this case ranged from one month in prison and a 20 lire fine to a fine of 50 lire.

records. A few crude statistics may convey an initial idea of the foreigners' impact on Venetian disorder. Of ninety homicide cases before the Signori di Notte during the 1360s, thirty-two, more than a third, involved foreign defendants. Of sixty convictions for theft during the same period more than half, thirty-eight, were handed down to foreigners.[81] Although it is impossible to determine the proportions of native and foreign-born Venetians in the general population, it is unlikely that the latter constituted anything like one-third—some 30,000.[82] Thus even making allowance for the meagerness of the sample, the incidence of foreign crime is striking.

Equally striking is the wide variety of social conditions among the foreign-born criminals. Indeed, the records of the Signori di Notte offer a very revealing insight into the kinds of resident aliens who were in Venice, the professions they exercised, and the peculiar social problems they created.

Probably the most important and respectable foreign residents were the merchants, and especially the Germans. The importance of their commercial activity in Venice gave rise in the Trecento to rivalries among merchants of different German cities for *locum supremum* in the Fondaco dei Tedeschi. And these rivalries sometimes degenerated into violence.[83] But the merchants could be violent for less chauvinistic reasons too, as was Mathias of Neustadt (?), who in 1364 asked a Venetian carpenter working in the Fondaco to plane an ax for him. When the carpenter refused, Mathias proceeded to beat him to death

---

[81] SN *Processi*, Regs. 8, 9, *passim*.

[82] The figure of 100,000 for the Venetian population in the 1370s is in Beloch, *Bevölkerungsgeschichte Italiens*, p. 4.

[83] ". . . zwei Regensburger . . . wehrten sich für das Recht ihrer Stadt mit den Stöcken in der Hand" (Simonsfeld, *Fondaco dei Tedeschi*, II, 86–87). The special status of merchants is illustrated by the trial of one Jacobus Theotonicus before the Quarantia for falsely impersonating a merchant (*ibid.*, p. 56, no. 146, Nov. 7, 1348).

[84] SN *Processi*, Reg. 9, fol. 12r–12v. The trial record does not include the sentence in this as in all other cases recorded in Reg. 9.

with both his own ax and the offending plane.[84] This is clearly a case of national and class lines coming into conflict in the same situation.

Except for an occasional outburst of this kind, however, the merchants did not constitute a particularly violent element in the population, most likely for the reason that kept a check on Venetian noble violence. But the same cannot be said of less economically substantial foreigners. The highly prized workers in the wool and silk industries, for example, followed the same violent impulses that characterized their Venetian neighbors. In fact the conditions of their work appear to have given rise to violent conflicts; in cases involving wool- and silk-workers both killer and victim frequently worked in the same shop.[85] But their involvement in bloody fights was by no means confined to disputes with colleagues.

The strongest penchant for violence lay not with the skilled artisans, who after all constituted a sort of established element in the economy, but rather with the less solidly rooted foreigners. Sailors, for example, seem to have been a particularly tough group, as were the boatmen, many of whom came from the northeastern Italian mainland.[86] And the vagabond element, from all indications a very sizable group, was a constant source of internal disorder.[87]

The vagabonds indeed represented a problem not only because of the potential for violence their social disorientation encouraged, but also by reason of their uncertain economic situations. Slaves and servants were frequently arrested for

[85] E.g., SN *Processi*, Reg. 9, fols. 30v–31r, 33r. The first case involved Tuscan silk workers, the second a Lombard and a Ferrarese wool worker. In another case, both killer and victim were unemployed German wool workers (*ibid.*, fol. 55v).

[86] SN *Processi*, Reg. 8, fols. 32v–33v, 34r–35r; Reg. 9, fol. 14r–14v.

[87] E.g., Giorgio da Friuli, convicted in 1366 of killing another *furlan* while both were at work cleaning privies—precisely the kind of pickup work characteristic of the *vagabundi* (SN *Processi*, Reg. 8, fols. 69v–70v).

robbing their masters, and the court records are full of convictions of Circassians and Tartars for domestic theft.[88] But far surpassing them were the thieves with no apparent occupation. These vagabonds, from such exotic places as Hungary and Poland, Dalmatia and Crete,[89] as well as from every part of the Italian peninsula,[90] likely came to Venice in search of opportunity, but could find none other than that of picking a pocket, robbing a money changer's counter, or burgling a house left open. By far the largest number of foreign thieves came from Germany and Austria, presumably following in the wake of their respectable and well-heeled merchant countrymen.[91] The presence of such large numbers of rootless individuals—so unassimilated that the police had frequently to resort to interpreters while questioning suspects [92]—was a constant menace to the property not only of Venetians but of foreigners of substance as well. And in a city dedicated to property this was a source of deep concern to the government.[93]

Thus the government found itself forced to respond to challenges to internal order from a number of quarters. And the

[88] E.g., SN *Processi*, Reg. 8, fols. 47r, 64r, 78r, 84rv, 86v–91v, 93r–93v.

[89] SN *Processi*, Reg. 8, fols. 39r, 54r, 68r–69r, 44v–45v, 65r–66r.

[90] SN *Processi*, Reg. 8: Johanes Centilinus de Tarvisio, fols. 35v–36v; Jacobus Zerbini de Padua, fol. 62v; Lodovicus de Pensauro, fol. 75r–75v; Petrus de Arecio, fols. 61v–62r; Angellus Bertholucii de Missina, fol. 83v.

[91] SN *Processi*, Reg. 8: Renaldus Theotonicus de Vienia, fol. 63r; Martel Theotonicus, fol. 63v; Fredericus de Austria, Theotonicus vagabundus, fol. 77v; Henricus de Colonia, Theotonicus vagabundus, fol. 54v; Thomas Theotonicus, fol. 76r–76v—all indicted for burglary or theft.

[92] The formula encountered frequently in the SN *Processi* was "quia ignorabat linguam latinam fuit interrogatus per . . . interpretem."

[93] An indication of how concerned the government was to protect property can be found in an act of the Quarantia in 1343. Noting that a safe belonging to some Slavonic merchants and containing 50 lire had been stolen, the officials posted a reward of 500 lire for information leading to the thieves' apprehension, with an additional 200 for each culprit brought bodily to the authorities (Lombardo, *Deliberazioni dei XL*, pp. 44–45, no. 154).

two main problems, regulating the patriciate and regulating the foreigners, were complicated by the political importance of the first and the economic value of the second. Faced with the intricacies of the situation the government had to devise clear-headed and sophisticated solutions to the problems of public order. It is in these solutions that the civil concord underlying the Venetian Renaissance state was rooted.

IV

To the intricate demands of Trecento "pax et quies" the Venetian government responded in two ways that reflect a general juridical policy with significant political and moral implications. Briefly put, the responses were elaboration of police and judicial institutions and evenhandedness in the dispensation of justice.

The institutional adjustments were dictated by the severe pressures Trecento developments put on the previously existing police and judicial system. As such they must be viewed in the light of a general tendency of late medieval Italian states to assume more responsibility for the prevention and punishment of crime. In the case of Venice the government's increased activity arose from the need for social and economic stability in an increasingly complex age. The Serrata itself had been a prime example of this kind of response.[94] Indeed this same impulse had led, in the course of the thirteenth century, to the first strict ordering of the state's juridical system; this ordering in turn provided the basis for the further elaborations of the Trecento.[95]

One very visible manifestation of the institutional reform

[94] On the general Italian development, Jones, "Communes and Despots," p. 86. On the Venetian institutional growth in general, cf. Cessi, *Storia della Repubblica*, I, 270 ff.; Kretschmayr, *Geschichte*, II, 72 ff.

[95] Molmenti, Storia, I, 86: "Sotto l'impulso di una crescente attività, il bisogno di una disciplina, più rigida tutrice di vasti e complessi

was the redefinition of the competences of the various magistracies. The clearest example was the creation of the Council of Ten. The Dieci's essential function was to protect the regime by ferreting out and suppressing potential plots against it. It was not long, however, before the broader implications of this mandate became clear: already by the 1320s the other courts were deferring to the Dieci.[96] And even though this rapid acquisition of power must be seen in the context of the anxious circumstances of the time (the conspirators of 1310 were still at large and another plot was being hatched in the 1320s), the impact of the new magistracy on the entire system of criminal justice was to be permanent and profound.

But it is a mistake to view the growth of the Dieci's influence in a vacuum. Indeed, in the ordinary administration of criminal justice, their activity was relatively modest, in comparison with the other criminal courts.[97] What the Dieci's emergence signifies in a larger context is a more general systematic approach to

---

interessi, creava gradatamente un ordine politico e giuridico nuovo, promovendo anche uno studio esegetico meno empirico di quello dei primi interpreti, guidati più da senso pratico che da conoscenze teoriche." In addition to the political reordering of which the Serrata was part, the thirteenth century saw the first comprehensive codifications of Venetian law and the redaction of the capitularies of the various magistracies (Kretschmayr, *Geschichte*, II, 110–112; Roberti, *Le magistrature, passim*).

[96] In 1326 the Curia del Esaminador refused to approve a property transaction—normally within its jurisdiction—between two members of the Barozzi family, referring the case instead to the Dieci. The Barozzi were at the time in exile on Crete because of their complicity in the 1310 conspiracy and consequently were under the jurisdiction of the Dieci or so the Giudici del Esaminador thought: the Dieci decided instead that the Curia del Esaminador could exercise jurisdiction in this matter (Zago, *Consiglio dei Dieci, Registri III–IV*, p. 28, no. 65). On the Dieci in general, see Romanin, *Storia documentata*, III, 52–79; Kretschmayr, *Geschichte*, II, 103 ff.; Maranini, *Costituzione II*, pp. 455 ff.

[97] In contrast with the records of other magistracies, the *Misti* of the Dieci demonstrate that this council characteristically occupied it-

the problems of law and order. If the Dieci came to exercise broad jurisdiction in matters affecting the state's security, the responsibilities of other magistracies were also receiving further elaboration in a general attempt by the state to render the administration of justice more efficient and more responsive to the needs of the age.

This tendency to streamline the magisterial framework is apparent in the frequent Trecento measures defining the jurisdictions of various courts. In 1321, for example, the Maggior Consiglio authorized the Signori di Notte to try all assault and homicide cases. Up till that time such competence had been divided among several different offices.[98] On the other hand the Avogadori di Comun, prosecutors before the Quarantia, had their mandate narrowed to enable them better to concentrate on criminal trials.[99] And the Quarantia itself was split into two branches, criminal and civil, in 1400—a measure clearly designed to improve its activity in both spheres of justice.[100]

All these measures were inspired by the government's resolve to deal more effectively with criminal activity in Venice. The same resolve is apparent in the provisions to make the streets safe and in general to regulate public behavior. Already in the 1270s and 1280s the Signori di Notte, in their capacity as Venice's main police force, had received a broad mandate to deal with crime. Their responsibilities included a stop-and-frisk authority, inspections of taverns at least once a week, keep-

---

self exclusively with subversions, conspiracies, and so on, sometimes spending months on the ramifications of a single case.

[98] Ferro, *Dizionario*, II, 693; also Roberti, *Le magistrature*, I, 208–209, III, 15–16; and Molmenti, *Storia*, I, 97, no. 3.

[99] Ferro, *Dizionario*, I, 213–215. An act of the Maggior Consiglio in 1352 limited the competence of the Avogadori to criminal cases.

[100] Kretschmayr, *Geschichte*, II, 102–103; Cessi, *Storia della Repubblica*, II, 16–17. The increased importance of criminal justice as a factor in the Quarantia's political eclipse is a question that has yet to be studied in depth.

ing prostitutes in their special ghetto, the "Castelletto," and keeping track of all "homines male fame" in the city.[101]

In the new century further refinements, as well as increased manpower, were added to these duties. The prohibitions against gambling, for example, were stiffened and—very significantly for our general inquiry—the police were urged to keep themselves informed of all new arrivals in the city. The importance attached to police activity was evident in the sternness with which the government punished those who interfered with or injured patrolmen in the course of their duties.[102]

These and other provisions enhancing the government's capacity to achieve order and dispense justice in a period when increased social complexity meant greater potential for disorder represent a major element of the Renaissance political order which would inspire the myth. If the patriciate was restrained and the popular classes tolerant of the aristocratic regime, it was due in significant measure to the development of police and judicial institutions that evoked respect and a sense of security. The confidence Trecento Venetians reposed in the judicial system is evident in the frequency with which they appealed to it. The appropriateness of their confidence is indicated by the fact that these appeals were satisfied.[103]

[101] Roberti, *Le magistrature*, III, 18–21, 36, 60–61. The government's concern with private weapons is reflected in continued legislative activity on the question (*ibid.*, pp. 51, 67, 72–74, 98–99). On the Castelletto, see Molmenti, *Storia*, I, 478. Anyone convicted of harboring a prostitute in his own house was to be fined 10 lire (Lombardo, *Deliberazioni dei XL*, p. 56, no. 186).

[102] In 1343 Zanino da Porto was sentenced to six months in prison for inflicting injury on an official of the Cinque di Pace (another police agency). In 1344 Francesco Natal was sentenced to two months because "dixit obprobria officialibus Quinque a Pace occasione sui officii" (*Lombardo, Deliberazioni dei XL*, pp. 34, 76). On the additional police responsibilities in the Trecento, see the act of the Dieci of 1319 ordering the duties of the Capi Sestieri and the Capi Contrade, in Zago, *Consiglio dei Dieci. Registri I–II*, pp. 25–28.

[103] E.g., SN *Processi*, Reg. 9, fols. 1r–1v, 25r–30r, 49v–50r. In these

But institutional effectiveness in dealing with crime was by itself insufficient to restrain the potential for discontent inherent in the conditions of Trecento Venetian society. With so many different elements in the population and all of them essential to Venetian prosperity, the posture of government toward society had to be based on a principle that responded to the needs of all of them. What was needed was a principle of government regulation of society which would acknowledge patrician supremacy without suffering patrician license; encourage the foreign presence while enforcing conformity to Venetian law; and evoke loyalty from a native populace that had no political influence, endured many economic hardships, yet played an essential role in the achievement of Venetian prosperity.[104]

The principle answering all these requirements was the just application of the law. Only firm and fair dispensation of justice could provide both an effective means of maintaining public order and a principle for treading the narrow path among the conflicting interests in Venetian society. And the official recognition of this fact is apparent in the criminal procedures of the Venetian courts.

It is apparent first in the scrupulousness of criminal investigation, extending even to the principles governing arrest. When one of the Signori di Notte made an arrest, for example, he was required by law to justify it to his colleagues within the week.

---

cases the relatives of *popolano* homicide victims pressed the Signori di Notte to investigate the circumstances of the deaths of their relatives. In each instance the Signori undertook a thorough inquiry, ranging outside Venice to gather testimony in two of them.

[104] This view of the *popolo* differs substantially from that of Cracco, *Società e stato*, p. 454. For him, the *popolo* in the latter Trecento was a "corpo morto," lacking any influence in the Venetian social or economic order. This view seems to me to ignore the implications of governmental acts like those of 1374 and 1377, which offered carpenters and caulkers from the Arsenale who had left the city special terms for

If the other Signori did not approve of his action he was required to release the prisoner.[105] While there is every reason to believe that collegial solidarity would reinforce the discretion of each Signore, this provision at least demonstrates the official intention of protecting individuals from capricious arrest, and especially from vendetta. Moreover, even when an indictment had been issued the accused had the right to select his own defender; if he declined the court would select one for him.[106]

Judicial scruples are apparent also in the conduct of the trial. Although by law only one witness was necessary to determine guilt or innocence in homicide trials, in practice the courts went to great pains, and often long distances, to register the testimony of as many witnesses as possible. In one group of seventy homicide trials before the Signori di Notte, all but six included testimony by at least two witnesses, and nearly half, thirty-three, had three or more. In this connection it is notable that the court consistently enlarged its number of witnesses as a result of testimony by previous witnesses; whenever a witness testified to the presence of another person at the crime, the latter was inevitably summoned to testify.[107]

The importance attached by the courts to testimony is evident in a somewhat different way in cases involving theft. Suspected thieves, unlike suspected homicides, were subjected to torture in the course of their questioning; the object was the recovery of the stolen goods. Resort to torture, however, was governed by careful procedures. Authorization required the

---

payment not only of the fines they had incurred by their unauthorized departure but also of their private debts, in an effort to bring them back (Luzzatto, "Per la storia delle costruzioni navali," p. 42).

[105] Four of the six Signori had to approve each arrest (Roberti, Le magistrature, III, 95). For a general discussion of Venetian criminal procedure, cf. Molmenti, Storia, I, 110 ff.

[106] Roberti, Le magistrature, I, 285.

[107] SN Processi, Regs. 7, 8, 9, passim. For the rules governing the taking of testimony, Roberti, Le magistrature, I, 285.

unanimous consent of the six Signori di Notte; and the presence
not only of two of them, but of two ducal councillors, one
Capo of the Quarantia, and an Avogador di Comun was necessary to make the torture legal.[108] While this may not have eased
the suspect's pain, it at least suggests that the government's use
of torture was not altogether blithe and that even in the torture
chamber the defendant had at least the protection of formality.
But the most significant aspect of the use of torture was that
the information it yielded had to be corroborated by other
sources. This means that the suspect could not confess simply
to escape the rack; it would not be admitted without verifica-
tion of both the kind of theft committed and the amount
stolen.[109]

Procedural practices such as these attest to a strong judicial
commitment to determining the actual facts of a case; and that
in turn suggests a general commitment to justice in criminal
trials. The best indication of such a commitment is to be found
in the principles governing sentences. Here two variables must
be considered: the gravity of the offense and the social status
of the offender. By considering the sentences of particular social groups for particular crimes we may arrive at a clearer indication of the equitability, or lack, of Venetian justice.

Detailed analysis of twenty-five homicide cases yields the
surprising information that only twelve of them resulted in
capital sentences, but there appears to be no social or economic
determinant of the lightness or heaviness of the sentences. Of
the nine executed killers whose occupations are listed, three
were boatmen, two were city officials, and the remaining four

[108] Roberti, *Le magistrature*, II, 49, III, 91–92.
[109] SN *Processi*, Regs. 7, 8, 9, *passim*. Torture was used only when
the accused refused to admit an offense of which there was strong reason to suspect his guilt. Of seventy theft trials studied, torture was used
in exactly half. It should be noted also that female suspects were tortured as readily as were their male counterparts (e.g., *ibid.*, Reg. 7, fols.
2r–3r; Reg. 8, fols. 39r, 64r).

were a workman, a vagabond, a prisoner who had killed another prisoner, and a galley oarsman. Of the thirteen who received lighter sentences—that is, loss of hands or eyes—the nine whose occupations are listed included four boatmen, three workmen, one patrician, and one vagabond.[110] There seems to be no essential difference between the two groups—with the exception of the patrician; the principle underlying the determination of sentences must then have been something other than class or occupation. In fact in all but two of the capital cases testimony had established that the convicted killer's victim had been unarmed and the act itself unprovoked, at least relative to the killing. But in each of the noncapital cases extenuating circumstances mitigated the gravity of the crime. Either the victim also had drawn a weapon; the victim had provoked the quarrel; the assailant shared his guilt with others or—in one case—the victim had been the killer's wife.

Analyzing sentences for theft is less illuminating, since by definition most thieves were not among the solid citizens of Venice. In fact in over half the cases studied the convicted thieves were foreigners. But it is still useful to compare the situations of thieves sentenced to death with those of thieves let off more lightly. Of fifty sentences for theft in the 1350s and 1360s, seventeen involved hanging; the other thirty-three resulted in maiming.[111] Of the seventeen sentenced to hang, fourteen were

---

[110] The twelve capital cases are: SN *Processi*, Reg. 7, fol. 12r–12v; Reg. 8, fols. 48v–49v, 52v–53r, 57r–57v, 60v–61r, 73r–73v, 74r–74v, 78v, 79r, 80v–81r, 96v–97r, 98r. The thirteen other cases are: *ibid.*, Reg. 7, fols. 10r–11v, 14r–16r, 16v–18r; Reg. 8, fols. 32v–33v, 34r–35r, 42v–44v, 50r–52r, 58r–60r, 66v–67v, 69v–70v, 71r–72v, 85r–86r, 94r–96r.

[111] The death sentences are in SN *Processi*, Reg. 7, fols. 1r–1v, 5r–6r; Reg. 8, fols. 35v–36v, 37r–38v, 53v, 65r–66r, 68r–69r, 75r–75v, 79v–80r, 83v, 84r–84v, 87v–88v, 89r–89v, 90r–90v, 91r–91v, 92r–92v; Lombardo, *Deliberazioni dei XL*, p. 40, nos. 142–143. Lighter sentences are in SN *Processi*, Reg. 7, fols. 2r–3r, 3v–4v, 6v–7r, 7v–8r, 8v–9r, 9v, 13r–13v; Reg. 8, fols. 39r, 39v, 44v–45v, 46r–46v, 47r, 47v, 48r, 54r, 54v, 56r–56v, 61v–62r, 62v, 63v, 64r, 64v, 76r–76v, 77r, 77v, 78r, 82v, 83r, 86r–87r, 93v, 94r.

foreigners, of whom three were officially designated vagabonds and five were slaves. This might suggest that heavy sentences were more readily handed out to the outcasts of society. The thirty-three who received lighter sentences, however, included twenty-eight foreigners, of whom six were listed as vagabonds and three as slaves. Thus there seems to be no discrimination in sentencing based on social status in theft trials either.

What does seem to have determined the sentence was the kind of theft involved and the value of the goods stolen. Of the seventeen hanged thieves, ten had confessed to multiple thefts; of the other seven, one had robbed a church, four were slaves who had robbed their masters, and the remaining two had stolen large amounts of money. By contrast only five of the thirty-three spared the gallows were guilty of more than one theft.[112]

Even on the basis of so few cases it seems fair to observe that the criminal courts of Venice operated on the principle of the gravity of the crime determining the sentence, with no apparent partiality to one or another social group. Although patricians were not given to homicide or theft, the sentences they received for crimes of sexual violence were no greater or smaller than those meted out to their popular counterparts. The one patrician among our list of convicted homicides who were not condemned to death had killed his victim, another noble, in a fight with knives drawn on both sides; thus he got off with losing his left eye and hand.[113] In the dispensation of justice, the govern-

---

[112] Generally thieves were sentenced to the loss of one or both eyes and/or hands, depending on the gravity of the crime. In cases of attempted or very minor theft, a whipping and a branding was the usual sentence. Women convicted of theft, however, generally suffered the gruesome sentence of having their lips and noses cut off. All of which prompted Molmenti to observe that "sembra esservi stata quasi una gara tra la ferocia del delitto e quella dei gastighi" (*Storia*, I, 106).

[113] SN *Processi*, Reg. 8, fols., 50r–52r. The victim was actually killed by a brick thrown by a servant of the convicted noble.

ment appears to have acted according to a principle of equal justice to all segments of the population.

Thus the judicial posture of the Venetian government in the Trecento was marked by an institutional reordering and a practical commitment to enforcing equality before the law. The one enabled the government to respond to the threats to public order generated by an increasingly complex social order; the other provided a rationale and a justification for the effective application of the strengthened institutious. If the law was effective it was also fair; and no one, noble or popular, Venetian or resident alien, need feel that his craving for "pax et quies" was ignored by the government or that his craving for justice would be sacrificed in the state's pursuit of order. Thus, in its administrative and substantive aspects, justice was the cement holding together, under the rule of the state, the diverse elements of a complex society. As a Florentine of a later epoch would observe, "Justizia ha in se ogni cosa"—everything necessary for the flourishing of a republic.[114] In fourteenth-century Venice justice had in itself the essential ingredient of civil concord.

V

The Venetian government's commitment to order and justice was above all a pragmatic response to Trecento conditions. If there was "love of justice with clemency" pure and simple, it arose from the mundane requirements of ruling a cosmopolitan state in a century of tension and innovation.[115] Justice and clemency held the society of that state together.

[114] Quoted in F. Gilbert, "Florentine Political Assumptions in the Period of Savonarola and Soderini," *Journal of the Warburg and Courtauld Institutes*, XX (1957), 212. The Florentine speaking here was, like his countrymen, intensely conscious of the Venetian example (*ibid.*, pp. 210–211).

[115] The phrase is from Albertus Magnus: "de gentis Venetorum . . .

But the manner in which the commitment was made has implications beyond mere Venetian pragmatism. The very creation of more efficient administrative machinery for achieving order and justice bespeaks the bureaucratic factor in the emergence of the Renaissance. As Federico Chabod has pointed out, the "element of administrative organization" is what distinguishes Renaissance—and modern—states from their medieval predecessors.[116] But as he also observes, what gave life to the new institutions was a "corps of officials" whose orientation was to the State and the State alone.[117] Thus underlying both institutions and officers was a sense of the state.

In Venice, already in the fourteenth century, the government was manifesting the rudiments of this sense in its implementation of order and justice. It was a conception of the state as bearing responsibility for the well-being of the entire society that prompted the government to establish limits on the activities of society's privileged elements and to enforce conformity among the foreign benefactors of the Venetian economy. Thus the very conditions of the Trecento, in their complexity and difficulty, provided the stimulus to the development of policies guaranteeing social concord. In that sense, it was these conditions that led to the Venetian Renaissance state and the myth of Venice.

---

unitate civium et concordia et amore totius iustitiae cum clementia omnibus fere nationibus iam sit notum" (quoted in Fasoli, "Mito," pp. 467–468).

[116] F. Chabod, "Y a-t-il un état de la Renaissance?" in *Actes du Colloque sur la Renaissance organisé par la Société d'Histoire Moderne* (Paris, 1958). I use the Eng. trans. in H. Lubasz, ed., *The Development of the Modern State* (New York, 1964), p. 40.

[117] "Y a-t-il un état?" p. 36.

IX

THE ANATOMY OF REBELLION
IN FOURTEENTH-CENTURY SIENA:
FROM COMMUNE TO SIGNORY?*

William M. Bowsky

*T*HANKS in large part to Ferdinand Schevill's well-
known popularization, *Siena: The Story of a Mediaeval
Commune*,[1] the Tuscan city of Siena, nestled on a westward
spur of the Chiana mountain range south of Florence, emerges
as a center of violence, civil disorder, and rebellion *par excellence*. Its uprisings appear as illustrative of broad and basic class
divisions that seared medieval and early Renaissance Italian
communes—and illustrative of a communal society imbued with
a highly developed class consciousness.

His analysis and strictures concentrate with greatest force
upon the regime of the Nine Governors and Defenders of the
Commune and People of Siena, a government that ruled the
city-state from the late thirteenth century until the *calata* of
the Emperor-Elect, Charles IV, in 1355. During this period
"conspiracy followed conspiracy, chiefly among the nobles
and the more enterprising of the excluded guilds"[2]—nobles and

* The archival research in Italy necessary for this study was made
possible in part through the generous assistance of a John Simon Gug-
genheim Memorial Foundation Fellowship and a Social Science Research Council Faculty Research Fellowship. All unpublished documents
cited below are housed in the Archivio di Stato of Siena unless otherwise specified.

[1] London, 1909.
[2] Schevill, *Siena*, p. 198.

guilds constitutionally and systematically excluded from government, according to Schevill. "Repression," he wrote, "became one of the constant preoccupations of the [government]. . . . In addition to minor tumults, more or less dangerous to the government, the chronicles report three serious conspiracies against the Nine. . . ." [3]

Siena, he reported, was ruled by an oligarchy of "merchants and manufacturers, the mezza gente . . . [who had] converted [public] offices into a private monopoly. Not only the nobles, but the professional classes of lawyers and doctors, as well as such petty guildsmen as butchers, bakers, barbers, and carpenters, and, of course, the proletariat of day-laborers, were declared ineligible to rule Siena." [4] Conspiracy and rebellion were the efforts of those excluded classes, united in their attempts to oust the regime in power and replace it with one of their own.

But is this the best interpretation of the violence and rebellion in Siena, or in any other city-state? Is it sufficiently nuanced to be of any value? I would suggest that more interesting and valuable lessons are to be learned from a study of the conspiracies that racked the Sienese commune during the regime of the Nine.

It is commonplace that the Tuscan republics enacted much legislation designed to preserve or maintain "the good and pacific state of the city" or "the tranquil and pacific state" of the commune or city. Almost every historian of Florence from Gaetano Salvemini to Niccola Ottokar to our colleague, Professor Gene A. Brucker, has reminded us that "All Florentines realized that the survival of republican government depended upon the maintenance of a certain type of internal peace and harmony. . . . A theme reiterated in the legislative provisions was that the law was designed to promote 'the good and peaceful state of the commune and people of Florence.' " [5]

[3] *Ibid.*, pp. 198, 205.
[4] *Ibid.*, p. 195.
[5] The quotation is from Gene A. Brucker, *Florentine Politics and*

In Siena such statements were almost ubiquitous. They preface measures insuring military preparedness, initiating cavalry expeditions and full-scale wars, and related to the various police forces of the city.[6] Prisoners released in honor of the major religious festivals were freed "so that God and the . . . Virgin Mary may conserve the city and people of Siena in a good and pacific state. . . ."[7] Even antisodomy legislation was enacted not only for fear of divine wrath, but in the hope that "because of these ordinances and the aforesaid holy provisions the Lord our God Jesus Christ, and his purest mother and always glorious Virgin Mary, the special advocate and defender of the city, commune, and people of Siena, by their piety and mercy she [sic] will remove scandals from the same city and take away perils, and the more swiftly lead that same city and its citizens to a state of tranquillity and peace, and by her grace will conserve it in that same state." [8] An undated rubric of the Sienese constitution of 1309–1310, entitled De la pena di chi turbasse el pacifico stato de la città di Siena, provided that at his discretion the Podestà fine £100 or more anyone of the city, contado, district, or jurisdiction of Siena who said, counseled, wrote, or

---

Society, 1343–1378 (Princeton, 1962), p. 85. See also Nicola Ottokar, Il Comune di Firenze alla fine del dugento (Florence, 1926), p. 245 n. 5, and Marvin B. Becker, "A Study in Political Failure: The Florentine Magnates, 1280–1343," Mediaeval Studies, XXVII (1965), 246–308, at p. 250 (and the quotation there from Gaetano Salvemini, Magnati e popolani in Firenze dal 1280 al 1295 [Florence, 1899], p. 384). Cf. Gina Fasoli, Le compagnie delle armi a Bologna (Bologna, 1933), p. 4.

[6] See, e.g., William M. Bowsky, "The Medieval Commune and Internal Violence: Police Power and Public Safety in Siena, 1287–1355," American Historical Review, LXXIII (1967), 1–17, at pp. 9 n. 27, 16 n. 61; Consiglio Generale, Deliberazioni (cited hereafter as CG), 45, fol. 55v (Feb. 28, 1293), 102, fols. 59r-63r (Sept. 27, 1325); Statuti, Siena, 15, fol. 171r (Aug. 7, 1302); 8, fol. 194r (May, 1319).

[7] CG, 48, fol. 44r (Aug. 14, 1295); see also the City Council deliberations cited in Bowsky, "Police Power," p. 3 n. 7.

[8] CG, 101, fol. 85r (Sept. 13, 1324). On antisodomy legislation, see Bowsky, "Police Power," p. 5.

did anything that might even indirectly "disturb the pacific state of the city and of the district of Siena, or might suscitate or create any discord among individual persons. . . ." In order to arrive at the true facts the Podestà was even granted that rare authority to torture suspects, if any were accused by six hearsay witnesses of good reputation who themselves were not suspect.[9]

The heaviest emphasis, in fact, on "the good and pacific state" of the city and commune occurs in relation to any possible threats to internal peace, and, most specifically, conspiracies and rebellions within the city itself. This is the theme of the final eighty rubrics of the third distinction of the major Sienese constitutional redaction of the late 1330s.[10] So crucial were they considered that rubric 408 specifically enjoined that "Statutes speaking of the good and pacific state of the city of Siena, of the societies and companies or of the vicariates [of the contado] are to prevail over each and all other statutes of the said city. . . ." [11]

The first twenty-three of these rubrics (r. 332–354) "On the Good and Pacific State of the City of Siena" treat problems of rebellion, capture, or betrayal of contado communities and fortifications, and conspiracies within the city and state—with the members of the casati, the magnates specifically excluded by law from membership on the bimonthly magistracy of the Nine, being singled out for special attention.[12]

---

[9] Alessandro Lisini, ed., Il costituto del comune di Siena volgarizzato nel MCCCIX-MCCX, 2 vols. (Siena, 1903), Dist. V, r. liii.

[10] Statuti, Siena, 26, Dist. III, r. 332–411, fols. 181r-195v. For the dating of this constitutional redaction see William M. Bowsky, "Medieval Citizenship: The Individual and the State in the Commune of Siena, 1287–1355," Studies in Medieval and Renaissance History, IV (1967), 193–243, at pp. 239–243.

[11] Statuti, Siena, 26, Dist. III, r. 408, fol. 195r.

[12] Ibid., fols. 181r-184v. For the magnates, see, e.g., r. 335, fol. 181v (". . . Si aliquis potens de casato" etc.); r. 342, fol. 183r, "Quod de populo non sint homines de casato, et manutenendo populum [apostil]."

The next fifty-seven rubrics (r. 355–411), "On the societies and companies for the fortification of the good and pacific state of Siena," [13] are particularly revealing. They deal primarily with the organization, functioning, and regulation of the urban Sienese military companies, and to a lesser extent with special military units composed of selected *contadini*—residents of the bulk of the state lying outside the city proper and its immediate environs (the Masse or Masse and Cortine of the city). [14] From them we learn that the companies' principal functions were to suppress acts of aggression committed by powerful urban magnates against their fellow Sienese, especially *popolani*, and to quell riots and battles, particularly those that threatened the government itself. (When not qualified, the term *popolani* in Siena might comprehend both the *popolo grasso* or upper bourgeoisie and the *popolo minuto*, including small businessmen and artisans and salaried workers. [15]

In Siena, as in Pisa, the fourteenth-century urban military companies seem to have resulted from a fusion of the early thirteenth-century military companies with the companies of the Society of the People or the Popolo. [16] But while the Captain of the People still retained the major share of jurisdiction over the companies, the Podestà and the newly created War Captain actively participated in their supervision. [17]

For magnates, and some who actually served on the Nine, see William M. Bowsky, "The *Buon Governo* of Siena (1287–1355): A Mediaeval Italian Oligarchy," *Speculum*, XXXVII (1962), 368–381, esp. p. 375, and *idem, The Finance of the Commune of Siena, 1287–1355* (Oxford, 1970), pp. 6–7, 27.

[13] Statuti, Siena, 26, fols. 184v-195v.

[14] For the communities of the Massa, see esp. Bowsky, *Finance*, p. 375, and *idem*, "Medieval Citizenship," pp. 227–230.

[15] See Bowsky, *Finance*, pp. 82–87; cf. Victor Rutenberg, "La vie et la lutte des Ciompi a Sienne," *Annales. Économies, Sociétés, Civilisations*, XX (1965), 95–109, at p. 103.

[16] See Bowsky, "Police Power," p. 11 n. 37.

[17] See, esp., Statuti, Siena, 26, Dist. III, r. 333, 340, 348–352, fols. 181r, 182r-182v, 183v-184v.

That the Sienese companies displayed expected similarities with those of other towns did not preclude them from possessing their own peculiarities, differences intimately related to and reflecting Siena's own sociopolitical and socioeconomic situations. Unlike the Bolognese companies, for example, those of Siena were not called Companies of the People or even Military Companies, but simply "the companies" or "the societies" of the city.[18] Nor was their Guelf quality much emphasized—not unnaturally in a city where the so-called Guelf Party was a minor and almost vestigial institution, especially as compared with its powerful and influential Florentine counterpart.[19] The Sienese companies were not organized by guilds, again commensurate with the lack of prominence of the overwhelming majority of the guilds in Sienese constitutional life. Rather they were the companies of the *contrade*, wards or precincts, the relatively small territorial and administrative units into which the city was divided. (A measure of 1302, repeated in an earlier portion of the constitution of the late 1330s, specifically stated that a person's *contrada* was to be understood as being a distance of 100 *braccie* [slightly less than 200 feet] from his house.[20])

According to law each *contrada* was to contain one company, although the possibility was admitted that this might not always be the case. And, indeed, I have found that throughout the regime of the Nine there always were more *contrade* than companies. There seem to have been only some eighteen companies in 1255, while by 1317 there were at least thirty-seven. From about 1339 to 1349 the number fluctuated between forty-one and forty-three. After the Black Death of 1348 they

[18] For Bologna, see Fasoli, *Le compagnie* (cited above, n. 5).

[19] See, e.g., Bowsky, *Finance*, pp. 3, 72. I shall treat the subject of Sienese Guelfism, the Guelf Party, and Ghibellinism more extensively in a separate study.

[20] Statuti, Siena, 15, fol. 142r (May 7, 1302); 26, Dist. III, r. 7, fol. 128r.

were about halved, while, interestingly, the *contrade* (or *lire* as they also were called when being treated as tax and administrative districts) remained some fifty-odd in number much as they had been throughout the first half of the fourteenth century.[21]

Not all of the men of the *contrade* were eligible for membership in the companies. According to statute they were to be composed of "good and faithful *popolani*," and of those foreigners and *contadini* who resided in the city, owned property there and in the *contado* that was registered in the urban tax rolls, and performed the customary obligations for the commune. Excluded were persons against whom a vendetta was be-

[21] Provisions of May 22, 1310, already ordered that there be a company for each *contrada* (Statuti, Siena, 15, fol. 404r); but for recognition that this was not always the case, see, e.g., Statuti, Siena, 26, Dist. III, r. 399, fol. 194r, "Et si iniuriatus vel vim vel violentiam substinens esset de contrata ubi non esset sotietas vel compagna. . . ." Giuseppe Canestrini ("Le compagnie del popolo di Siena e suo distretto," *Archivio storico italiano*, XV [1851], xviii-xix, 13–25, at p. xviii) clearly errs in stating that there were seventeen military companies in the early fourteenth century. For the number of companies and *contrade*, see, e.g., Lodovico Zdekauer, ed., *Il constituto del comune di Siena dell'anno 1262* (Milan, 1897), pp. xxxxv, lxxv; William M. Bowsky, "The Impact of the Black Death upon Sienese Government and Society," *Speculum*, XXXIX (1964), 1–34, at pp. 8, 18; MS C 46 and the Estimo volumes cited in Bowsky, *"Buon Governo,"* 375 n. 31; Lira, 385 (ca. 1312–1316); Lira, 423, fols. iir-iiir (1348–1364); Gabella [G], 19, fols. 59v-60v (Jan.-June 1334); G, 20, fols. 47v-48v (July-Dec. 1334); Concistoro, 2, fols. 62v-67r (Dec. 22, 1347); Biccherna [B], 133, fols. 145r, 145v; 155, fol. 64v; 174, fol. 79r; 176, fol. 108r; 201, fols. 98v-100r; 202, fols. 150v-152r; 206, fol. 72r; 209, fols. 163r-164r; 217, fol. 147r; 220, fols. 130v, 131r (July-Dec. 1347, 42 *ridotti* and 64 *sindaci* of *lire* or *contrade*); 223, fols. 156v-157r (Jan.-June 1348, 43 *ridotti* and 65 *sindaci* of *contrade*); 692, fols. 12r-12v, 25v-26v (July-Dec. 1348, 41 *ridotti* and 58 sindaci of *contrade*); 224, fols. 187r, 188v; 225, fols. 107r, 108r; 226, fol. 91r; 228, fols. 137v, 145r; 230, fols. 137v, 139v; 231, fols. 208v-209v. [*NB:* several of the *lire* or *contrade* listed in the Biccherna volumes lay outside the city proper]. Cf. also Orlando Malavolti, *Dell' Historia di Siena*, 3 vols. in one (Venice, 1599), II, 64r.

ing waged and magnates of the *casati*. The official composition of the companies had to be approved by the Nine and the other "Orders" or principal magistracies of the commune.[22]

Each company had a storeroom (*ridotto*) equipped with a minimum of ten war axes, ten crossbows, ten shields, and four lanterns, equipment that could only be removed "in defense of the city of Siena . . . [or] when the commune of Siena shall make an army. . . ." [23]

Every "*contrada* and company or society" was headed by a captain, a standard-bearer, and three councillors, all of whom were at least thirty years old and were selected by the Nine and the other Orders. These company officials had to be men of some substance, each owning at least a house located within his own *contrada*.[24] By 1314 each company also had its own notary, who served as its treasurer—this because too many captains had embezzled company funds![25] Most particularly was the notary to safeguard the five lire a semester given each company by the commune for the rental of its storeroom and other expenses. Two books were kept recording the membership of each company, the captain and the treasurer each having a copy that they were bound to show to the Podestà, the Captain of the People, and their courts on demand.[26]

All men receiving offices in the companies had to "swear that they are Guelfs and lovers of the pacific state of the city and jurisdiction of Siena," while at the wish of the Nine all mem-

[22] Statuti, Siena, 26, Dist. III, r. 357, fol. 184v. The other Orders of the city were the Four Provveditori of the Biccherna (the leading financial magistracy), the Consuls of the Mercanzia (Merchant Guild), and the Captains of the (Guelf) Party or Consuls of the Knights; for these see, esp., Bowsky, *Finance*, p. 3.

[23] Statuti, Siena, Dist. III, r. 370–371, fol. 186r–186v.

[24] *Ibid.*, r. 358, fol. 185r.

[25] *Ibid.*, r. 376–377, fol. 187r–187v; Capitano del Popolo, 1, fols. 45r, 174r–175r; Statuti, Siena, 23, fols. 499r–500v.

[26] Statuti, Siena, 26, Dist. III, r. 378, fol. 187v.

bers of the companies might be compelled to take the same oath. It was the duty of the Captain of the People to make certain that "useful Guelfs be placed in those same companies and that useless persons and Ghibellines be removed." He too saw to it that men moving from one *contrada* to another swore membership in their new *contrade* and were absolved of obligations to their former ones.[27]

Most valuable is a surviving membership list of the officials of the thirty-nine companies appointed to serve during that ill-fated first semester of 1348. At least fifteen of the thirty-nine captains and five of the standard-bearers can definitely be identified as belonging to the Noveschi or families whose members served on the Nine. So, too, did many of the company councillors. These Noveschi included members of noble families as well as men of bourgeois origin. Nine other officials of 1348 had occupations that might have placed them among the Noveschi. (And while several of the company officers may have pertained to excluded magnate families, this cannot be proved conclusively.)[28]

The total picture to emerge is that the companies were headed by persons most trusted by and loyal to the ruling oligarchy, and that the Nine maintained absolute control over those organizations.

Stricter still was the regime's hold over a special elite corps composed of eight men from each company, "lovers of the pacific state of the city of Siena," who at times of disturbance were to hasten to the palace of the Nine (the communal palace) and not leave without the Nine's express permission. So crucial was their role that each member of this group had to leave behind in his own company at least one close relative, and the special corps was renewed annually by two men from each company

[27] *Ibid.*, r. 366, fols. 185v-186r.
[28] Concistoro, 2, fols. 62v-67r.

personally chosen by the Nine. Each group of eight had its own banner, and a list of its members was kept by the Nine.[29]

I suspect that this elite corps was created sometime after up-risings of 1318 and 1325, perhaps replacing an earlier elite body in existence since at least 1299, and probably earlier—a body of four-hundred men from each Terzo or third of the city. (The membership was 1,000 per Terzo by 1306, and seems to have been disbanded just a few years before the 1318 uprising, pos-sibly between 1315 and 1318.) Little is known of these earlier groups of 400 and of 1,000 per Terzo other than that they were composed of "good men *de medio Civitatis*" and were the only Sienese permitted to go to places where members of the *casati* were brawling or fighting.[30] Possibly like Bologna,[31] Siena had

[29] Statuti, Siena, 26, Dist. III, r. 374, fol. 187r.

[30] Giugurta Tommasi, *Dell' Historie di Siena*, 2 vols. in one (Venice, 1625–1626), II, 129–130, contains a reference to a group of 1,000 per Terzo dissolved in 1289 which is not confirmed by other sources and is less clear than believed by Romolo Caggese, "La Repubblica di Siena e il suo contado nel secolo decimoterzo," *Bullettino senese di storia patria*, XIII (1906), 3–120, whose discussion of this corps and of the military companies (pp. 93–102) is confused and unsatisfactory. The comments of Alessandro Lisini on the special corps and the companies confuse the two and are partially erroneous: Alessandro Lisini and Fabio Iacometti, eds., *Cronache Senesi* (cited hereafter as CS), in *Rerum Italicarum Scriptores*, n.s., XV Part VI (Bologna, 1931–1937), on pp. 86 n. 1, 242 n. 1. For the elite bodies of 400 or more men per Terzo, see esp. Statuti, Siena, 4, fols. 398r-400r (May 5, 1299); CG, 55, fols. 101r-102v (May 5, 1299); Statuti, Siena, 15, fols. 141r-143v, esp. fol. 142v (May 7, 1302—when the body numbered 500 per Terzo); Statuti, Siena, 15, fols. 276r-278v (Feb. 21, 1306); CS, 86 (the report of an anonymous chronicler that the corps was increased to 1,000 per Terzo in 1306). Provisions of May 26, 1310 (Statuti, Siena, 15, fol. 404v) and Statuti, Siena, 26, Dist. III, r. 361, fol. 185r, noted that the office of the 1,000 per Terzo was canceled, but an anonymous chronicle reports activities of the 1,000 per Terzo in 1312, 1314, and 1315 (CS, 96, 102, 105, cf. 103 n. 1), as does the relatively reliable chronicle of Agnolo di Tura del Grasso (cited hereafter as Agnolo) for 1312 (in C.S., p. 325).

[31] For the Bolognese "Società di giustizia," see Fasoli, *Le compagnie* (cited above, n. 5), p. 27. Cf. Becker, "Florentine Magnates" (cited above, n. 5), 253, esp. his citation from Salvemini, *Magnati e popolani*.

found that such a large, separate elite corps was impractical, but had decided to reconstitute it as a smaller corps (the groups of eight per company) and to maintain it in an intimate relationship with the military companies.

At times of such uprisings, as in general military campaigns, the companies from each Terzo of the city could be requested to act as a group, and to rally around the one general standard-bearer for each Terzo, either at the palace of the Nine or at such other locations as the Nine might order themselves or through the Podestà or Captain of the People. (The general standard-bearer of each Terzo, who carried a banner of the commune, was appointed by the Nine to serve a six-month term, and was assisted by three councilors, also selected by the Nine.)[32] Each of the military companies was assigned specific tasks to perform at times of tumults or rebellions. Those of San Salvatore, Salicotto di Sopra, Campanile, and Casato, located close to the Campo or principal piazza, were to go armed to the palace of the Nine and there remain until released by the Nine themselves. Twenty other companies guarded designated gates of the city, a most delicate task. (Depending upon the circumstances either the entire company or a minimum of ten men protected each gate.) Within three days after such a disturbance the captains of each company were to furnish the Captain of the People with the names of any men who had failed to appear at their *ridotti*, so that they could be fined up to £25 each.[33] These detailed regulations were not elaborated, I believe, until the late 1320s or early 1330s.

The defense of the city in times of trouble was not left solely to the military companies and to various bodies of foreign mercenary soldiery and police. Selected *contado* residents also were called upon. A special force was created for this purpose in 1302, composed of 2,000 *contadini*, "*fidelibus* and lovers of

[32] Statuti, Siena, 26, Dist. III, r. 355–356, fol. 184v.
[33] *Ibid.*, r. 375, 379, fols. 187r, 188r-188v.

the sacrosanct Roman church and of the pacific state of the city of Siena," chosen from among the nine vicariates or military districts of the *contado*. In addition to helping to quell *contado* uprisings, they were to come to the city of Siena at times of turmoil at the bidding of the Nine and to do the bidding of that magistracy. In 1310 their number was increased to 5,000 —not surprising in view of the imperial *calata* of Henry VII— with their special task being defined as going to Siena "in the service and defense of the office of the lords Nine and of the pacific state of the city of Siena." (This force was supplemented by a far smaller one from the Masse, a group of communities immediately adjacent to the city and jurisdictionally distinct from the *contado*.) But the *contado* forces were captained by urban Sienese *popolani* selected by the Nine and the other Orders, and were generally commanded by the Captain of the People. Nor was it uncommon for those captains to be Noveschi. These special *contado* forces still existed at the time of the major Sienese constitutional redaction of the late 1330s, even though the urban force of 1,000 per Terzo had been abandoned. The continuance of the *contado* force of 5,000 may be explained in that while the urban military companies and the forces of the leading foreign magistrates employed by the commune could be utilized during emergencies within the city, the commune wished to insure that only selected *contadini*, known to be loyal, would be called upon to participate in such actions. It remains significant, nonetheless, that the regime believed that it could rely upon men from the *contado* at such perilous and sensitive moments.[34]

[34] For the provisions of May 7, 1302, and the 2,000 *contado* infantry see Statuti, Siena, 15, fols. 141r-143v, esp. 142r-142v; for the 5,000 of 1310, cf. Caggese, "Contado" (cited above, n. 30), pp. 104–105, 116. (Caggese was unaware of the earlier force of 2,000.) The principal rubrics of Statuti, Siena, 26, Dist. III, pertaining to the vicariates and the special force of 5,000, are r. 381–398, fols. 188v-194r; r. 384–392, fols. 189v-193r, lists the communities in each of the nine vicariates; r. 393,

The first major conspiracy to confront the regime of the Nine has hitherto escaped the notice of historians, and was, in fact, nipped in the bud. Certain of its facets, however, help to illuminate the general nature of the problem of internal violence and allow us to place it in a broader framework than that solely of Sienese history.

On October 4, 1311, at a meeting of the City Council, the treasurer of the Biccherna (the leading Sienese financial magistracy), Friar Bernard, of the Humiliati, declared:

As it was told and related throughout the city of Siena that some persons of the city of Siena, in a not moderate number, both nobles and magnates and *popolani* (*in non modica quantitate tam de nobilibus et magnatibus quam de popularibus*) had made and composed a sect, sworn plot, and conspiracy or company (*sotietatem*) . . . by reason of which the state of the city of Siena and of the people could be disturbed. And it is said that the Podestà and his court intend to proceed to conduct an investigation concerning the aforesaid persons, who are said to be very numerous (*qui dicuntur multi esse numero*) and to condemn them severely; because of which things scandal and great discord can easily arise in the city of Siena— *quod deus advertat!* And it pertains to the commune of Siena and to the office of the lords Nine principally, who are the head of the same commune (*qui sunt capud ipsius communis*), to provide that the aforesaid things at no time occur, and especially now because of the conditions and great novelties

---

fol. 193r, is "De quinque milibus hominibus bene armatis eligendis et vexilliferis fiendis." As late as February 27, 1303, the *contado* had been divided into only three vicariates (CG, 62, fols. 83v-84v). A deliberation of the signory of Dec. 22, 1347, names the captains of eleven vicariates of the *contado* and 3 of the Masse (one for the Massa assigned to each Terzo of the city): Concistoro, 2, fol. 62r-62v. By Sept. 8, 1310, there already were separate vicariates for the Masse, as a provision of that date declared that beginning on Jan. 1, 1311, those communities need no longer pay the salaries of the captains, notaries, and messengers of their vicariates, but that the funds would be supplied by the Sienese commune (Statuti, Siena, 15, fols. 421r-423r, esp. 422r-422v).

that continually are seen to proceed and the greater ones in the offing, especially in the province of Tuscany, that desire and require great remedies and opportune councils and deliberations and provisions for the defense of the liberty of persons and goods (*bonorum*) and for the conservation of the pacific state of the aforesaid [commune], in which matters it is not possible to move conveniently unless there is unity and full concord among the men of the whole Sienese commune (*nisi unitas et concordia sit intotum inter homines universitatis comunis Sen.*).[35]

He further explained that the Nine, meeting with many secret councils of wise men, agreed that the Podestà should proceed no further with this matter, even though they already had selected a commission to write ordinances providing for the severe punishment of persons doing similar things in the future so that others might not disturb "the pacific state of the city." Friar Bernard therefore proposed that the City Council agree that all proceedings be stopped, and this it did by the large majority of 240 to 28, despite the *pro forma* objection of the Maggior Sindaco.[36]

What would appear to have occurred, then, was that a large and disparate group of men had plotted the overthrow of the government, probably encouraged by the approach of the imperial candidate, the future Emperor Henry VII, on his way to his coronation in Rome with an army swelled by exiled Ghibellines—among them at least one powerful Sienese noble, Niccolò di Bonifazio dei Bonsignori. That army would pass temptingly close to Siena, and it would have been the hope of the conspirators that the imperial forces would assist any attempted internal conspiracy.[37]

[35] CG, 79, fols. 106r–108r; quotations on fols. 106r, 106v.
[36] For the Maggior Sindaco, see William M. Bowsky, "The Constitution and Administration of a Tuscan Republic in the Middle Ages and Early Renaissance: The *Maggior Sindaco* in Siena," *Studi senesi*, LXXX (1968), 7-22.
[37] See William M. Bowsky, *Henry VII in Italy: The Conflict of Empire and City-State, 1310–1313* (Lincoln, Nebr., 1960), pp. 124–130.

The decision not to punish the conspirators of 1311 was made not despite their large number, but because of it. The government feared to exacerbate the feelings of many who might have tended to oppose it, and through harsh punishment to create just the link between revolutionaries and imperial forces for which the conspirators hoped.

This leniency was not unique. Although communes generally treated conspirators severely, we need only recall Giovanni Villani's account of a Florentine conspiracy of 1323. On that occasion even though many magnates were implicated punishment was mild, "in order," wrote the chronicler, "that scandal not grow, from which there might be born a change in [the government of] the city. . . ." [38]

As a result of its scare of 1311 the Sienese government did enact strict measures to head off future plots. Conspirators' property was to be confiscated and they themselves executed, or, at the government's pleasure, exiled. Normal legal restraints and safeguards did not apply in the investigation of such plots: the Podestà could not only use torture, but could also generally proceed in those ways that seemed best to him, "*tam iure comune quam iure municipali.* . . ." Any official, including a member of the Nine, who impeded justice was subject to an enormous £1,000 fine for each violation. Informers were promised anonymity and sizable rewards if they themselves were not implicated, and immunity if they were. Any judge or notary who revealed the name of a witness was to be treated as a forger and burned alive.[39]

Nor were these treated as commonplace statutes. They were to be read at the first City Council meeting held after each new Podestà took office, and that magistrate and his judges swore a special oath (apart from their ordinary oaths of office) to main-

[38] *Cronica di Giovanni Villani a miglior lezione ridotta,* 4 vols. in 2 (Florence [Magheri], 1823–1825), IV, 197 (Book IX, chap. 219).

[39] Statuti, Siena, 15, fols. 459r-462r (Oct. 15, 1311); quotation on fol. 460v.

tain them. Each Podestà was to have them proclaimed publicly throughout the city at least once while he held office. The orders were declared to have the validity of statutes, and to be "perpetual" and irrevocable. Anyone who presumed to try to remove or derogate them was subject to a fine of £1,000—and removal from the protection of the commune. And finally, so that there might be no mistake, within eight days of their passage these provisions were to be written "*in lictera grossa in corpus statutorum comunis sen.*"[40]

Seven years later, after the death of Henry VII and the quelling of a series of rebellions by *contado* lords, the government faced its next major crisis, the most serious to confront it until its final overthrow in 1355: the uprising of October 26, 1318.

In June of 1318 Siena sent several sizable military contingents against the town of Massa Marittima with which it was engaged in a dispute over the ownership of the Maremma castle of Gerfalco.[41] The Nine themselves were in charge of the composition of the Sienese forces. For reasons unknown to us they did not merely dispatch Sienese companies, units based on the wards or precincts (*contrade*) and thus to some degree heterogeneous. Instead, one large contingent contained some 400 cavalry, 400 crossbowmen of the companies, *and*, as the chronicle of Agnolo di Tura del Grasso rightly notes, "600 infantry, all from the city, that is, 200 infantry from the Wool Guild, 100 from the Arte del Fuoco [a guild that included smiths and other metal workers], 100 *carnaioli* [butcher–animal dealers], and many masters of wood and large-scale retailers (*pizzicaioli*). . . ."[42]

This special arrangement of infantry by occupation may

[40] *Ibid.*, fols. 461r-462r; quotation on fol. 461v.
[41] This was, of course, but the immediate casus belli; the larger issue was that of Sienese expansion into the Maremma. For Siena and Massa Marittima, see esp. the material cited in Bowsky, "Medieval Citizenship," pp. 222 n. 72, 223 n. 73.
[42] Agnolo (cited above, n. 30), p. 371; cf. *C.S.* (cited in full above, n.

have been made in the hope that such units would fight particularly well because of long-standing friendships and associations. But it presented the danger of uniting into armed groups men holding common economic, social, and political interests; men who might harbor grievances against a regime that excluded them from the highest seats of power and closely regulated their activities—or, as with the butchers, indeed controlled their every action.

These troops soon were recalled, whether because of hints of conspiracy or merely as a result of a rapid Massan surrender. But the military combination had been combustible. On Friday, July 21, the butcher–animal dealers and the smiths "with other *populari minuti*" milled about in the Campo of Siena. They quickly began to shout against officials of the regime and to hurl stones.[43] And while this was but a brief disturbance that wrought little harm the situation was sufficiently serious to close the court of the Captain of the People for at least twelve days.[44]

Allegedly disappointment over the failure to sack Massa touched off that brief tumult. But its roots ran much deeper. The relations of the butchers with the government of the Nine had been strained from its inception. Often men of more than average wealth, the *carnaioli* chafed under the restrictions placed upon them, restrictions that forced them to sell in Siena

---

30), p. 171 (anon. chronicle). For the role of the Nine in the selection of the military contingent, see CG, 90, fols. 134r-137r (June 7, 1318), and esp. 143r–144v (June 20, 1318). Biccherna payments of July 29, 1318 (B, 135, fol. 72v, 136, fol. 80v) lend credence to much of Agnolo's account. They include £660 paid to 200 infantry of the Wool Guild for eleven days' service in the army ending July 21, 1318; £330 to 100 infantry of the "arte del fuocho" and £330 to 100 infantry of the "arte della carne" for the same service and at the same rate; and £1,389/6/– paid to 421 "balestrieri delle compagne" for the same eleven days.

[43] Agnolo, pp. 371–372, and two anonymous chronicles, *C.S.*, 113–114, 171.

[44] CG, 91, fols. 66r-68r (Aug. 2, 1318), esp. fol. 66r-66v.

large numbers of animals that would have brought them higher prices outside the Sienese state. They deeply resented the communal policies of price-fixing and the strict supervision of their *"male opere,"* their "evil deeds," such as selling rotten meats, passing one meat for another, and giving false weights. Relations had been so strained that for some years around the turn of the century the government had deprived them of their guild. And it is most interesting that at least one governmental commission of 1307 entrusted with the custody of the city had as its second charge the supervision and regulation of the butchers.[45]

It was probably the tumultuous conditions following the Massan campaign that emboldened one of the most powerful groups in Siena to bring novel pressure to bear upon the government during the ensuing months: the judges and notaries. Their social and economic advantages recently have been well described by Professors J. K. Hyde and Lauro Martines.[46] These

---

[45] For relations between the butchers and the Sienese commune, see, e.g., Bowsky, *Finance* [cited above, n. 12], pp. 141 ff. For the outlawing of the butchers guild, for the present see CG, 51, fols. 30v-32r (Jan. 10, 1297) and Statuti, Siena, 15, fols. 98v-99r (Dec. 19, 1300). The guild did, however, exist and have rectors during some of the intervening period; see, e.g., Statuti, Siena, 4, fol. 320r-320v (Dec. 19, 1298). The commission of six "uficiali del chomune di Siena sopra ala guardia dela cita e sopra al fatto de charnaiuolo" for the first semester of 1307 included the Noveschi, Petruccio Bianchi, and one "Zero Fino orafo"—one whose occupation was among those represented on the Nine (B, 120, fol. 379v). For the goldsmith, see, e.g., Bowsky, *"Buon Governo"* [cited above, n. 12], p. 374. Petruccio di Bianco, from the Terzo of San Martino, served on the Nine May-June, 1300 (Diplomatico Riformagioni [cited hereafter as DR], May 20, 1300). I shall treat the role of the butchers in Siena more directly and extensively in a forthcoming separate study.

[46] J. K. Hyde, *Padua in the Age of Dante* (Manchester and New York, 1966), pp. 121-175, esp. pp. 174-175; Lauro Martines, *Lawyers and Statecraft in Renaissance Florence* (Princeton, 1968), esp. chap. ii, "The Guild," pp. 11-61, and chap. iii, "Backgrounds and Foregrounds," pp. 62-115.

men had splendid opportunities in governmental posts and access to information that helped them to bid for the most lucrative farmed taxes and auctioned properties. The notaries received fees for their legalization of a host of private transactions, and, like their Florentine counterparts, gained from being joined in the same guild with the socially and intellectually more prestigious judges. I suspect that it was, in fact, in part because of the sensitive positions that they held that Siena's judges and notaries were specifically excluded from membership on the Nine.[47] Men needed for delicate consultations, service on key embassies, required for the redaction of every sort of official document, they were privy to the commune's innermost secrets and already enjoyed immense power out of proportion to their number.

But an economic motivation seems to have been at least as important as exclusion from the Nine in bringing the judges and notaries to pressure the government during the summer of 1318. For their fees were becoming the subject of increasing regulation during the regime's opening decades. Not untypical was a measure of 1310 that lamented the high prices charged for the services of judges, advocates, and procurators, "*qui ultra modum antiqum et consuetum hodie maxime extorquent salaria. . . .*"[48]

Their present requests, however, produced even more repressive legislation. On September 13, 1318, by a margin of five to one the City Council approved a key measure that drastically limited the independence of the freewheeling judges and notaries and perhaps even deprived them of their guild. And this despite strong support for their position by such nobles as Giovanni Paparoni and Cino Saracini, and, even more important,

[47] For this exclusion, see Bowsky, "*Buon Governo*," pp. 370, 374–375.
[48] Statuti, Siena, 15, fols. 391r–395r (March 30, 1310); quotation on fol. 391r. For this paragraph see esp. MS F 23: Massimo Fabio, "La posizione di diritto pubblico dei Notai nella costituzione politica del comune di Siena" (Anno accademico 1955–56), pp. 58–67, 82–84.

the urgent request of messer Sozzo di messer Deo Tolomei (a leader of the powerful Tolomei clan) that the City Council delay its action so that the guild and its consuls might have another week in which to come to an agreement with the Nine.[49]

The judges and notaries were not men to yield without a struggle. They responded with what can only be called a general strike. "They do not give legal opinions, do not advocate, do not serve as procurators, do not write contracts or draw up any instruments," reads a City Council deliberation of October 9.[50] Some openly threatened members of the government.[51] But under increased pressure they capitulated by October 19, and promised to do "anything that pleased and satisfied the Sienese commune and the lords Nine." [52] The Nine then were empowered to appoint a commission to set the fees that judges and notaries could charge, and, significantly, to provide for the personal safety of those making the provisions and of those favoring them.[53]

The kettle was boiling, and another vital ingredient soon was added: the active opposition of some members of great magnate clans. Foremost were the Tolomei, holders of numerous *contado* castles and lands, members of prominent banking and commercial firms, possessors of valuable urban real estate—and men well supplied with armed followers in Siena, and with noble connections in Florence and elsewhere. The Tolomei and other nobles had still another advantage: they were *not* ex-

[49] CG, 91, fols. 91v-94r; which does not include the specific provisions of this measure, whose necessity for consideration the City Council approved 252 to 51, and that it finally passed 257 to 46. For literature concerning the Tolomei, see, e.g., Bowsky, *Finance*, p. 7 n. 19.

[50] CG, 91, fols. 116v-117v; quotation on fol. 116v.

[51] *Ibid.*, fol. 116v.

[52] CG, 91, fols. 126r-127r; quotation on fol. 126v.

[53] *Ibid.*, fol. 126v. For a paragraph in a measure of Oct. 1318 (no day) that provided for this protection, see Statuti, Siena, 18, fols. 416r-417v, on fols. 416v-417r.

cluded from government. Although denied places on the Nine, the magnates served on each of the other Orders of the city and as Executors of the Gabella—another key magistracy; they commanded communal forts, held key *contado* posts, led Sienese military contingents, and represented the commune itself in the most sensitive diplomatic missions.

Judges, and to a lesser degree notaries, enjoyed similar roles in government. Nor were powerful guildsmen like the butchers excluded from political life. They too served on the City Council and were appointed to legislative and administrative commissions, including important tax assessment boards.[54]

Yet only three months after the Massan episode, and but a week after the capitulation of the judges and notaries, all these groups played key roles in the crucial events of October 26, 1318. Late that Thursday afternoon several hundred well-armed men burst into the Campo. With shouts of "Death to the Nine!" they tried desperately to storm the communal palace, the residence of the Nine and the Podestà.

But the government was ready. Bells rang out to summon support. The commune's defenders were well served by huge catapults and by a contingent of the military companies specially skilled in the use of the crossbow. The hundred mercenary infantry or police (*birri*) of the Nine fought bravely. And the government was fortunate in still having within the city several hundred mercenaries, whom it had hired to serve King Robert of Naples at Genoa.

Nor were the conspirators united. Deo di messer Guccio Guelfo and Sozzo di Deo, leading Tolomei, withheld the bulk of their forces in the courtyard of the chief Tolomei palace, in Piazza San Cristofano, only about a block from the raging battle, probably waiting to see how the tide would turn. This

[54] Numerous illustrations and examples for all the statements in this and the preceding paragraph can be found in Bowsky, *Finance, passim.*

tactic contributed to the rebels' defeat—for defeated they were.[55]

A handful were captured and the remainder fled the city. And, we are told, judges, notaries, and butchers—leaders of the rebellion—as well as "artisans and [the] *popolo minuto*" greatly blamed the Tolomei and other magnates (the Forteguerri in particular) for their defeat.[56] And the Tolomei tactic shows that while these magnates at times supported or made use of other dissidents, there was no great mutual confidence or tradition of close cooperation between them, and that the social gulf separating the prominent nobles from the lesser folk was, indeed, far wider than any common political grievances that tended to unite them.

It is all too easy to exaggerate the importance of vividly chronicled battles. Only some four or five hundred troops are specifically said to have fought the rebels, and the loss of life and the expenditures on the government side occasioned by the uprising of October 26 were light. It is tempting, therefore, to agree with the late Robert Langton Douglas or with Dr. Giulio Prunai that this uprising was easily quelled and of little consequence.[57]

But this is not the whole story. Extremely severe penalties were enacted against the rebels and unusually high rewards offered for their capture. Provisions of November 21, 1318, established a reward of £200 for merely pointing out the location of a sentenced rebel and was payable if he was subsequently captured. Anyone who personally seized a rebel and

[55] For the events of Oct. 26, 1318, see Bowsky, "Police Power" [cited above, n. 6], p. 6, and the sources there cited; *C.S.*, 114 (anon. chronicle); and the following pages of the present study.

[56] See, e.g., Agnolo, p. 374.

[57] Robert Langton Douglas, *A History of Siena* (London and New York, 1902), p. 145; Giulio Prunai, "Lo studio senese dalla 'migratio' bolognese alla fondazione della 'Domus Sapientiae' (1321–1408)," *Bullettino senese di storia patria*, LVII (1950), 3–54, at p. 4.

delivered him to the governmental authorities was to receive the munificent sum of three hundred gold florins.[58] Several rebels were captured, tried, and executed, and the urban properties of leading Tolomei were razed.[59] In 1321, when most of the outstanding death sentences were reduced to exile (at a distance of eighty miles from the city of Siena) twelve ringleaders remained subject to the death sentence.[60]

The city of Siena itself was closely guarded for some days after the rebellion, by *contado* contingents among others. (The

[58] Statuti, Siena, 18, fols. 418r-424v, fol. 421r. If the captor himself was under sentence for anything other than "pro pace rupta, pro robbaria, pro incendio, pro prodictione alicuius terre, pro falsa moneta vel falso instrumento" (fol. 422r), and renounced the reward and "pacem habuerit cum principali offenso cuius occasione fuerit condempnatus si viveret vel si non viveret dictus principalis offensus cum eius proximiore sive proximioribus consanguineis ex paterna linea discendentibus" then that captor's own sentences and fines were to be canceled (fol. 421v). For this public recognition by the commune of its inability to control the vendetta completely, see Bowsky, "Police Power," pp. 12–13.

[59] See, e.g., Agnolo, pp. 372, 373; C.S., 114, 115, 171–172 (anon. chronicles). B, 135, fol. 109v (Dec. 31, 1318), records the payment of £116 to a resident of popolo Santo Stefano in the Terzo of Camollia, "Vive Guelfo eo quia cepit Gheruccium carnificem." The lower sum than that stipulated in the legislation of November 21, 1318, probably reflects deductions made for unpaid taxes or fines outstanding against Viva di Guelfo. See also *ibid.*, fol. 108r (Dec. 31, 1318), for £371 paid by the Biccherna to a communal official for payments to "the masters and manual laborers who devastated the goods and property of the traitors of the Sienese commune who disturbed the pacific state of the commune of Siena . . . [and] who uprooted the houses and palaces and vineyards of the said traitors. . . ."

[60] Agnolo, p. 389, who notes that among the twelve were Deo Tolomei, ser Pino and ser Feo Gratia, the brothers of the butcher Cione di Vitaluccio, and Gabriello di Speranza Forteguerri. In 1339 Deo Tolomei paid 1,000 gold florins to obtain the cancellation of this and four other death sentences that had been passed against him, including those for his capture and temporary seizure of the *contado* castle of Menzano in 1320 and his leadership of a large mixed company of mercenaries that had ravaged the Sienese Valdichiana and Valdorcia in 1322 and 1323 (Bowsky, "Police Power," p. 14).

contado commune of Monticiano in the Merse valley alone provided forty-one infantry for this service.[61]) Throughout the entire month of November 1318 "few merchants came to the city because they could not conduct a market because of the infantry and cavalry stationed in the [principal] marketplace [the Campo] for the custody of the city." [62] And despite their victory the Nine hired additional crossbowmen and other mercenaries (numbering about fifty-five in all) who served as a special palace guard throughout the last two months of 1318.[63]

The provisions of November 21, 1318, specifically enjoined each new Podestà to recall the rebellion to a meeting of the City Council within a month after he took office, read those provisions, and inquire whether any new action should be taken against those sentenced for their complicity, save that the Council could not weaken or cancel those provisions. Should he neglect this obligation, the Podestà was subject to a substantial five hundred lire fine.[64] Nor was this one of the many rubrics that the Council ignored or set aside. Even from the inadequate extant records of that council's deliberations we can be certain that it was implemented faithfully for several decades, at least until the fateful outbreak of the Black Death in 1348.[65]

Equally interesting is a measure passed on October 30, 1318, for the protection of the Nine who were in office at the time of the uprising: they received permission to have two bodyguards each, paid at communal expense, and to carry both offensive and defensive weapons in the city throughout their

61 CG, 92, fol. 137v (Oct. 29, 1319).
62 Bowsky, *Finance*, pp. 135–136.
63 B, 135, fol. 105r; B, 136, fols. 99r, 99v.
64 Statuti, Siena, 18, fol. 423r.
65 See, e.g., CG, 94, fols. 195r-199v (Dec. 15, 1320); 103, fols. 23v-25r (July 28, 1326); 106, fols. 13r-14r (July 14, 1328); 140, fols. 3v, 4v, 5r (Jan. 12, 1347); 142, fols. 1r-2v (Jan. 4, 1348).

lifetimes—rare privileges.[66] And this, together with other re-
minders of the rebellion, was carefully enshrined in the body of
the major constitutional redaction completed two decades
later.[67]

Documentation in the Communal Archive at Volterra, some
thirty miles west of Siena, also reveals that the Nine apparently
took pains to conceal from the outside world, and from their
Tuscan neighbors in particular, the seriousness of the rebellion
of October 26.

On October 28, only two days after the uprising, the Nine
wrote to the commune and officials of Volterra:

> that certain Sienese notaries and butchers, enemies of God and
> men, together with their accomplices, wishing to subvert the
> pacific state of the city, late on the twenty-sixth day of the
> present month of October entered into battle in the Campo
> against us and the men of the Sienese commune, and as traitors,
> crying "death to the Nine!" began to fire arrows against the
> men of the Sienese commune and against the palace. Finally,
> though, the aforesaid brave men of the commune acting man-
> fully and powerfully against the said traitors placed them in
> flight; which traitors struck and seriously wounded, fleeing
> ran out of the city of Siena, and some of them remained [be-
> hind] dead. . . .

This was reported to the Volterrans so that they might know
what had occurred, and learn that the Sienese government
again was in control of the situation and that "the city, by the
grace of God, remains in peace and tranquility. . . ." [68]

---

[66] CG, 91, fols. 127v-130v; see also, Statuti, Siena, 18, fol. 417r-417v.
[67] Statuti, Siena, 26, Dist. III, r. 183, fol. 155v; cf. ibid., Dist. III, r.
305, fol. 176r-176v.
[68] Archivio Storico del Comune, Volterra. Archivio Comunale. Deliberazioni, N. 5, Filza A Nera 5, quad. 5, fol. 50r-50v. (This is a copy
of the original Sienese correspondence.) See esp. "quod quidam notarii
et carnifices Senenses dei et hominum inimici cum sui complicibus die

A separate letter of the same day named rebels who had fled and requested the government of Volterra not to receive them, but to capture them and turn them over to the Nine.[69] And, in fact, two days later, on October 30 a council of the "Twelve Defenders and Governors of the Commune and People of the City of Volterra" duly forbade those named Sienese rebels to come to or remain within Volterra and its district "*ad penam averis et persone.*" [70]

Interestingly, the only magnate included on the list sent to Volterra was Gabriello di Speranza, a Forteguerri, and his surname was not included. Ordinarily one might think that this was because he would have been sufficiently well known not to require further identification; though the government might have been expected to provide the Volterran's with every lead possible so that so dangerous a criminal might be the more easily apprehended.

This seemingly trivial point assumes greater importance, however, when we examine the official list of outlawed rebels included by the City Council in its legislation of November 21, 1318, which stated "that ser Antonio di messer Ricovero, his brother Lazzarus, ser Pino di Benincasa, his brother Vannuccio, ser Feo di Grazia, ser Colletto di Chele, his brother Cenghino, ser Tura di Forte, Cione di Vitaluccio, his brothers Ciano, Benedetto, and Galgano, Bandino da Fabbrica and Gualtiere di Penico of Pieve San Giovanni . . . were the principals in

---

XXVI° presentis mensis Octubris de sero volentes statum pacificum Civitatis subvertere contra Nos et gentem comunis Sen. bellum inierunt in Campo Fori, et tamquam prodictores clamantes moriantur Novem contra dictam gentem comunis Sen. et contra palatium sagietare ceperunt. . . ."

[69] *Ibid.*, fol. 50v (a copy). The letter listed "Gabriellus Speranze, Ser Antonius domini Recuperi, Ser Feus magistri Gratie, Ser Collectus Chelis, Ser Feci Benvenuti, Ser Tura Fortis, Ser Pinus Benincasse [*sic*], Cione, Bendictus [*sic*] et Chiantis Canus Vtalucci [*sic*]."

[70] *Ibid.*, quad. 6, fol. 3v.

creating a riot and in waging a battle. . . ." [71] Where are the noble conspirators? The Tolomei, Forteguerri, or Incontri named by Agnolo di Tura or our other chronicle sources? One could, of course, argue that most of these had held back from the actual battle, but their complicity had been discovered at once, they immediately fled the city, and some of their properties were, in fact, destroyed at the government's orders. It is possible that their role was played down in correspondence sent abroad to neighboring governments in order to minimize the seriousness of the threat of October 26, and, hence, the precarious condition in which the commune found itself during the following weeks or even months.

What, however, of the documents prepared for home consumption? When the City Council considered the provisions of November 21, 1318, no one spoke against them and many councillors shouted their approval. Yet the necessity of considering these provisions was only passed by a secret vote of 176 to 49, and final passage by 178 to 47.[72] There was, then, serious opposition even within a major political organ that was largely controlled by the ruling oligarchy.

I suspect that the official lists of the conspirators omitted the great magnates, and in particular played down the role of the powerful Tolomei, in order not to overemphasize the rebels' strength, as a result of the efforts of their numerous and influential clansmen to protect the implicated magnates, and, at least as important, so as to leave room for accommodation with the rebellious nobles and to reconcile them with a regime in whose governance they had long participated and assisted in many ways. And while such an effort may have been unsuccessful in the short run, as witnessed by the activities that messer Deo di messer Guccio Guelfo pursued until at least 1323, eventually even that leading Tolomei seemed reconciled to the govern-

[71] Statuti, Siena, 18, fol. 418v.
[72] CG, 91, fols. 134v-138r.

ment and played a renewed role in the functioning of the commune.[73]

There is, moreover, some evidence that might appear to support Schevill's contention that the Sienese rebellions essentially were class-inspired efforts of economic groups excluded from the government to overthrow the regime and replace it with one of their own. The chronicle of Agnolo di Tura reports that during the trial of four conspirators (all *carnaioli*), who were decapitated in July of 1319, it was discovered that the rebels of October 26 had planned for Sozzo di Deo Tolomei to become the new Podestà.[74] He was the same magnate who had counseled in favor of the judges and notaries on September 13, 1318. (Had the rebels succeeded it would have marked the first return to a native Podestà in Siena since a brief experiment in the early thirteenth century). Success would have given the Tolomei a marked advantage over their fellow magnates, and a base from which to attempt to establish a personal or family signiorial regime similar to those of the Visconti in Milan or the Scaligers at Verona.

While this may have been an ultimate Tolomei goal, the rebels of October 26 had planned a mixed regime according to our chronicled account. Ser Antonio di messer Ricovero, a judge whose family at least came from the *contado* town of Asciano, west of Siena in the Val d'Ombrone, was to become Captain of the People.[75] No mere cipher, ser Antonio was a

[73] See e.g., Bowsky, *Finance*, p. 175.

[74] Agnolo, p. 373. Deo Tolomei had played an important role in Sienese government. Only a year before the rebellion, for example, he had been sent to the Maremma at the express orders of the Nine to serve as communal ambassador and negotiate a needed peace with the powerful Aldobrandeschi count, Jacomo of Santa Fiora, probably because of the numerous Tolomei ties with the Aldobrandeschi: B, 133, fol. 119r (March 26, 1317).

[75] That the judge was called ser Antonio d'Asciano does not tell us when he or his forebears left that *contado* town. For Asciano, see

man of experience in government and well versed in Sienese politics and diplomacy. During the decades preceding the rebellion he had often participated in the debates of the City Council. He had been one of two Sienese ambassadors stationed at Naples for at least four months in 1315, and responsible for sensitive financial operations related to the support of Angevin soldiery destined for major Tuscan Guelf campaigns against Uguccione della Faggiuola and a force of Milanese, Mantuan, and Aretine soldiery.[76] Also of Asciano derivation was ser Pino di Benincasa, a notary destined to hold the new office of Proconsul in the projected government.

And what of the butcher–animal dealers and their share in the new dispensation? The same confessions of the rebels executed in July 1319 revealed that the prospective Bargello, a collector of fines, was to have been a leading butcher, one Cione di Vitaluccio of the *popolo* of San Quirico in Castelvecchio in the Terzo of Città. Several times he had headed companies that farmed the gabelle on meats and animals slaughtered in the city and its immediate environs.[77] Nor was this a run-of-the-mill guildsman. A hitherto unnoticed provision of October 31, 1311,

---

Emanuele Repetti, *Dizionario geografico, fisico, storico della Toscana*, 6 vols. (Florence, 1833–1845), I, 151–156.

[76] Biccherna records show that Cione di Bartolomeo and ser Antonio had paid 9,600 gold florins in Naples to maintain the knights and barons of Duke Charles of Calabria who were proceeding to the war in Tuscany during the summer of 1315 (B, 129, fol. 99v, May 23, 1315); and the disbursement of £9,887/10/- on September 1, 1315, which was to enable those two ambassadors to pay King Robert of Naples for the barons and knights who were to follow Prince Phillip of Tarento to Tuscany that autumn (B, 130, fol. 62r). Cf. B, 129, fol. 113v, for £250 paid as salary to those two ambassadors for 90 days' service at Naples, to July 1, 1315. For some of ser Antonio's interventions at City Council meetings, see, e.g., CG, 81, fol. 144v (Dec. 27, 1312), or CG, 82, fol. 102r (March 13, 1313).

[77] See Bowsky, *Finance*, pp. 142, 320.

shows us that seven years before the rebellion of 1318 the Nine and other Orders had deliberated the actions to be taken against six butchers who had "sold meat falsely" and remained "obstinate in their malice because of the mild penalties imposed for these things by the ordinances of the Sienese commune." They therefore provided that those six and anyone else who sold one meat for another or sold prohibited types of meat should not only be punished according to existing provisions but, further, prohibited from practicing the butchers' trade (*artem carnificum*) for three years. And among the six men specifically named were Cione's brothers Gano and Benedetto.[78] It is, then, no coincidence that the Vitalucci were among the ringleaders of the 1318 rebellion.[79]

The chronicle of Agnolo di Tura can also be interpreted to support another aspect of Schevill's interpretation of the uprising: for the chronicler reports that the battle cry of the rebels in the Campo was "Death to the Nine and *Viva il Popolo!*" [80] The same chronicle relates of the last noteworthy conspiracy to occur before the fall of the Nine, that in 1346:

> There arose a disturbance in Siena on Sunday the 13th of August at the third hour, by reason of a plot and conspiracy arranged by certain of the *popolo minuto* of Siena. And their chief was Spinelloccio, son of messer Jacomo di messer Tavena dei Tolomei.[81] And some of the conspirators raised the dis-

[78] Statuti, Siena, 15, fol. 463r–463v. In addition to the Vitalucci (of the Terzo of Città), the other condemned butchers were Jacomo di Viva and Meo di Maffeo (Città), Puccio di Salvo (Terzo of San Martino), and Baldovino di Paolo (Terzo of Camollio).

[79] Cione di Vitaluccio, incidentally, was the only ringleader of the rebellion specifically reported to have been captured and executed (together with three or four other *carnaioli* seized in the Val di Strove): Agnolo, p. 373; C.S., 114, 171–172 (anon. chronicles).

[80] Agnolo, p. 372. The two anonymous accounts of the October 26 rebellion record the cry only as "Death to the Nine!" or "Death to the lords Nine!" omitting any reference to the Popolo: C.S., 114, 171.

[81] For Spinelloccio Tolomei, see Bowsky, *Finance*, p. 51 n. 13.

turbance and ran to the house of Berto Lotti (whose home is close by the gate of the Franciscans), who was giving a banquet to certain foreigners and Sienese citizens, among whom was Giovanni di Ghezzo Foscherani [one of the Noveschi[82]]. And some of those conspirators, namely Simone of Volterra and two other companions, went there armed and leapt upon the said Giovanni, wounding him many times. They ran out shouting through the arms depot of Ovile, "*Viva il popolo* and death to those who starve us!" for it was a time of great shortage. The son of the said Giovanni, whose name was Meo, seeing his father so wounded, ran home for a sword and shield, and went toward the said Simone to wage vendetta for his father. And the said Simone killed the said Meo, and fleeing through the street was pursued by the shouting Minuccio Scotti and Benedetto Ventura. And the said Simone turned back upon them and wounded them both, and then he fled, shouting "*Viva il popolo* and the Guilds, and death to those who starve us!" And thus he left Siena again safely.[83]

The report of cries of "*Viva il Popolo* and the Guilds!" strikes our attention immediately, even though it does not appear in other accounts of the same events. But before leaping to the conclusion that the alleged rebel battle cry proves a deep-seated and clearly defined split between the ruling oligarchy and other classes of society, we might note that at least one man sentenced to death for "knowingly, falsely and with forethought . . . [conspiring] with some others (*pluribus*) of the city and with foreigners to disturb, shout, and create a disturbance in the aforesaid city [of Siena], and to rush armed to the city, and also to wound, strike, and kill Giovanni di Ghezzo [Foscherani], a *popolano* of the said city, and some other *popolani* of the said city, with the means and intention of disturbing, subverting, and devastating the pacific state of the

---

[82] See, e.g., Bowsky, *Finance*, p. 67 n. 75.

[83] Agnolo, p. 549. This differs from Schevill, *Siena*, pp. 206–207, as he utilized the old Muratori edition of the chronicle, and translated somewhat loosely.

said city . . ." was one of the Noveschi, Francesco di Chele Barocci.[84]

Gene Brucker provides illuminating information. He noted that in the very "summer of 1346, the city [of Florence] was engulfed by rumors that an uprising was planned by rich merchants, magnates, and bankrupts." And what did they intend to shout and use as a rallying cry? "Death to the Ghibellines and *Viva il Popolo* and the Guilds!" [85] For although this was no plot of the *minuti* or less fortunate, the battle cry would be a shout for the *popolo* and the guilds, intended to arouse support among masses sufficiently displeased with the regime, and sufficiently hungry, to participate in its overthrow.

The use of such cries, if they were indeed used, does not in itself prove general support for rebellion and does not automatically reveal to us those behind it. Nor should we forget the suggestion of the contemporary Guelf chronicler, Ferreto de' Ferreti of Vicenza, that throughout Italy the masses always showed a fickle readiness to receive new rulers.[86]

The cry of "Death to the Ghibellines!" was absent in Siena. There the issue of Ghibellinism was not so alive, and did not prove nearly so popular as in Florence.[87]

[84] CG, 153, fols. 22v–23v (Aug. 30, 1353); quotation on fol. 23r. At this session Francesco Barocci's conviction was annulled on the grounds that he had been innocent. Cione di Baroccio served on the Nine Sept.–Oct. 1324 (DR, Oct. 23, 1324), Nov.–Dec. 1329 (DR, Dec. 30, 1329), Sept.–Oct. 1331 (DR, Oct. 6, 1331; cf. Tommasi [cited above, n. 30], II, 250, "Cione di Baroccio Barocci"), Jan.–Feb. 1338 (Capitoli, 3, fol. 59r). Cione and his brother Meo were men of means. According to the Table of Possessions of 1318 they held real property worth £3,782/4/4, including a house in Siena evaluated at £600 and other properties at Monteliscaio, Catignano, Misciano, Pieve Asciata, Selvoli, and Toiano (Estimo, 127, fols. 13r–17v). Together they paid five gold florins in a mezza presta of 1315 in the Terzo of Camollia (Lira, 274, fol. 26r).

[85] Brucker, *Florentine Politics* [cited above, n. 5], p. 113.

[86] Ferreto de' Ferreti, *Historia rerum in Italia gestarum*, ed. Carlo Cipolla, 3 vols., Fonti per la storia d'Italia, XLII–XLIII (Rome, 1908–1920), I, 279.

[87] See, for the present, Bowsky, *Finance*, p. 3.

Even to call upon the Popolo in Siena was to invent an artificial issue. The organization of the Popolo had lost its vigor before the accession of the Nine. It was, in fact, that regime which had reconstituted the office of Captain of the People in 1289 after about two decades of temporary abandonment.[88] We are extremely fortunate in having extant complete membership lists of the Council of the Popolo, Terzo by Terzo, for five years from 1308 to 1313, and a list of the councillors appointed (by the Nine and the other Orders of the city) on October 26, 1351, to serve a six-month term beginning the following November 1.[89] From these it becomes absolutely clear that the leadership of the renewed *popolo* in no way represented a revolutionary class that threatened the regime of the Nine. In each of the first ten lists I can identify a minimum of forty men (out of 150) as Noveschi, and the representation of the ruling oligarchy in the council of the Popolo may well have been considerably larger for thus far I have been able to identify with certainty less than one-fifth of the men who served on the Nine throughout its history.[90] Nor does the picture change when we examine the list of ninety-nine councillors selected in 1351. And the Captain's council did not include only great Noveschi merchants, bankers, and industrialists, some of them nobles; it also numbered in its membership men from the powerful magnate *casati* who should have been excluded both from

[88] For the reconstitution of the office of the Captain of the People, voted by the City Council on March 14, 1289 at the advice of the Nine, see CG, 37, fol. 59r–59v. See also *ibid.*, fol. 60r–60v. (March 16, 1289): a decision that the commune provide a salary for the Captain of the People. For the temporary abandonment of the office, see Ugo Guido Mondolfo, *Il Populus a Siena nella vita della città e nel governo del comune fino alla riforma antimagnatizia del 1277* (Genoa, 1911), p. 53.

[89] See CG, 73, fols. 21r–24r; 74, fols. 13v–14v; 75, fols. 13r–14v; 76, fols. 20r–22v; 77, fols. 25r–28r; 78, fols. 13v–16v; 79, fols. 14r–17r; 80, fols. 13v–15v; 81, fols. 13v–15v; 82, fols. 35r–38r; Concistoro, 3, fols. 90r–91v.

[90] For membership on the Nine, see Bowsky, *"Buon Governo"* and *Finance*.

the Popolo and the Nine.[91] And although the occupations of very few councillors are given in the lists, these include wool manufacturers and silk merchants, as well as notaries and a few butchers. With such leadership, then, the organization of the Popolo was far from being the political organ of an excluded class, and many alive in 1318 could not have remembered a time when the Popolo had not been an unimportant organization, dominated by Noveschi bourgeoisie and nobles.

If, nonetheless, the cry of "Popolo" was used in Sienese rebellions in the first half of the fourteenth century, the question still remains: why would the rebel leaders have thought this to have been an effective rallying cry? Did they believe that those who heard it thought, if ever so generally or vaguely, in terms, for example, of a desire for broader participation in government or of fairer treatment of groups other than oligarchs or magnates in such communal policies as taxation? My own suspicion is that if any such feelings were aroused in the Siena of the Nine, they were for the most part specific and *ad hominem* rather than corporate or class structured, desires for particular personal gain or for something so specific as a particular piece of property.

The entire topic, moreover, of the Popolo in Italian history has yet to be studied from a unified or general viewpoint. The few recent studies that treat the Popolo deal for the most part with one or another individual town, with larger generalizations then drawn or overdrawn. But Siena was not isolated from her Tuscan neighbors. I suspect that the term "Popolo" and other political slogans as well had some very general implications common to most towns, yet, perhaps specifically pertinent to the political, social, and economic conditions in but few of them at any one time. In some ways the utilization of such slo-

---

[91] E.g., among those selected to serve as councillors beginning on May 1, 1309, were Foccio Salimbeni and Andrea Tolomei; councillors of 1351 included Andrea di Vanni Incontri, Bindo di Tura Tolomei, and Pietro di Guido Cacciaconti.

gans may have been as little relevant to actual conditions as some contemporary appeals for a return to or maintenance of "the American way of life" or claims that a political program fosters "private enterprise" or slows down the impetus toward "welfare statism."

As for the guilds, with the exception of two completely controlled by the Nine and the excluded nobles, the Mercanzia (Merchant Guild) and the Wool Guild, they too played an insignificant role in Sienese politics. The government had accommodated the guildsmen by giving them a considerable voice in councils and commissions, but as individuals and not in a corporate capacity. This, also, is not surprising in a city whose industrial base was less than adequate and whose economic strength rested primarily upon its functioning as the marketing center for a rich agricultural region and upon its banking and commercial activities. Nor, in this context, should we fail to recall how few guilds or occupations were involved directly in the uprising of 1318. Even the smiths, though thrown together in the campaign against Massa Marittima, seem to have played no significant role in that rebellion.

If the guilds and the Popolo were not united against the oligarchical regime of the Nine, what was the nature of that opposition and what were its grievances and objectives? Was the principal grievance, indeed, exclusion from government, and was it so interpreted by the incumbent regime?

We have seen that the chief complaints of the judges and notaries and, *mutatis mutandis*, of the butcher–animal dealers, focused upon governmental restrictions and controls of their economic activities and their desires for unrestricted profits.

We should not, however, rule out the possibility that the butchers at least conspired against the regime in a corporate fashion through the instrument of their guild organization, for that organization was outlawed after the 1318 rebellion. The measure of November 21, 1318, specifically ordered "that the butchers of the Sienese city or boroughs cannot, in perpetuity, have any *breve*, statute or orders or any consuls, lords, or rectors or any office." Contravention would subject them to a fine of £500 to be imposed by the Podestà. Other clauses prohibited them from working regularly in or near the Campo, and commanded that there be no more than four butcher shops in any *contrada* of the city or its boroughs under penalty of a one hundred lire fine for each contravention.[92] This last injunction, I believe, was not intended to insure an equality of economic opportunity among the butchers, but to prevent their concentration in a few places, and hence deny them some opportunity of uniting for further mischief. The lengthy measure of November 21 contained no analogous strictures concerning the judges and notaries and did not mention their guild by name, even though it did command individual judges and notaries to report to the Podestà all knowledge they had relating to the possessions, rights, and contracts of persons sentenced for rebellion under penalty of a one hundred lire fine for omission.[93] The guild of judges and notaries was, indeed, outlawed in May of the following year, but this probably was decided only after serious reflection and as a preventive measure and perhaps not because of any direct involvement of the guild itself in the events of October 26, 1318.[94]

As to the magnates, more noteworthy than the involvement of some of the Tolomei and of members of one or two other *consorterie* (one, the Incontri, closely related to the Tolomei),

[92] Statuti, Siena, 18, fol. 422v, esp. "Quod carnaioli de civitate vel burgis sen. non possint in perpetuum aliquod breve, statutum sive ordines vel aliquos consules, dominos vel rectores aut offitium habere."
[93] *Ibid.*, fol. 419v.
[94] See esp. Statuti, Siena, 8, fol. 185r (May 1319): "Capitulum sub rubrica de concedendis berovariis consulibus judicum et notariorum pro eorum suppositis capiendis est cassum in totum"; fol. 187r (May 1319): "De capitulo sub rubrica quod breviature notariorum decedentium deponantur per unum ex iudicibus potestatis sunt cassa illa verba silicet et consules iudicum et notariorum et loco illorum verborum sunt addita hec verba videlicet et consules mercantie vel duo ex eis"; fol. 190v

is the relative absence of magnate participation in the Sienese rebellions. The overwhelming majority of magnate families did not participate in the revolutionary movements. The Salimbeni, perhaps the wealthiest Sienese clan, were not involved, nor were the Malavolti, who had secured a near monopoly over the Sienese episcopate, nor the Sansedoni, whose splendid palace still borders the Campo. Absent, too, were the Saracini (today best known for their sponsorship of the famous Sienese musical academy, the Chigiana), the famous Bonsignori family of the Company of the Gran Tavola, and the Piccolomini, wealthy and strong long before Pius II gained the papal throne in 1458. All, including the Tolomei, had powerful representation at every level of government other than that of the Nine itself, including membership in the other Orders of the city, without whom the Nine took almost no important actions.

The Sienese conspiracies, then, were not very broadly based, and the conspirators themselves not closely united. Some rebels did seek to overthrow the government, but not because of inadequate representation; rather, they sought to replace one oligarchy with another, to control the commune completely, and allow free rein to their own ambitions, economic or signorial.

The government's own appraisal of the situation immediately after the October 1318 uprising, and of the changes needed to insure its continued existence, may more closely approximate the truth than do some modern historical interpretations.

By September 1318 the City Council had begun to consider the advisability of increasing the numbers of those eligible to

---

(May 1319): "Capitulum sub rubrica quod consules notariorum precipiant eorum suppositis per sacramentum et Capitulum sub rubrica quod aliquis non possit opponere dicere vel allegare quod consules notariorum non sint consules sunt cassa in totum cum aliud super ipsa materia sit provisum." Cf. also Agnolo, p. 372, and Massimo Fabio, "Notai" [cited above, n. 48], pp. 85, 86, 89.

serve on the Nine, and perhaps broadening the base from which they were selected.[95] In December it enacted the only significant changes made in the regulations and procedures for election to the Nine until the regime's demise in 1355.[96] Yet the essence of those changes was to try to diminish the advantages that any one family or business company might gain from having too many of its members on the signory at the same time or immediately succeeding one another, to enable more of those men who were eligible for service on the Nine actually to hold that office, and to insure a greater continuity of policy while retaining the Nine as a bimonthly magistracy. If the basis of eligibility for membership on the Nine actually was increased, that increase was minimal and carefully circumscribed. All told, the modifications of December 1318 were minor, but they sufficed for the government to remain in power for nearly four more decades.

That such minor adjustments did suffice and that dissidents rallied relatively little broad support suggests that there was general acquiescence, if not positive satisfaction, with the oligarchical regime and its style of rule, acquiescence or satisfaction that cut across the many social and economic divisions of Sienese society.

The Noveschi allowed themselves a large measure of power and were among those who profited most from the state's economic and diplomatic resources. But even this favoritism they did not carry to excess. Similar advantages were available to other strata of society. The Nine tried to rule in a generally

[95] Statuti, Siena, 18, fols. 404r–406v (Sept. 13, 1318).

[96] CG, 90, fols. 139v–141v (Dec. 6, 1318), and for Dec. 22, 1318: *ibid.*, fols. 151v–154r; Statuti, Siena, 11, fols. 357r–364v (with holes in the middle of several folii); Statuti, Siena, 18, fols. 398r–403r (missing several of the first folii of this action). Cf. also Statuti, Siena, 26, Dist. IV, r. 21–26, fols. 203r–204v, on the election of the Nine as prescribed in this major constitutional redaction of the late 1330s. Cf. also Agnolo, p. 373.

equitable fashion and to support a program of public works and betterment that redounded to the good of all the city's inhabitants. Despite the heavy utilization of indirect gabelle taxes, common to most Italian towns at that time, the Sienese government particularly desired to create as broad and fair a base of taxation as possible. Unlike Florence, Siena continued to impose sizable direct taxes within the city itself, even though they fell quite heavily upon members of the ruling oligarchy. The Nine were vigilant to enforce a policy that would provide abundant and inexpensive food for the great masses of the urban populace, even when this meant curtailing profits that they and the magnates would have gained from the sale of grain at whatever inflated prices the market would bear and at the risk of antagonizing the *carnaioli*.[97]

Other groups of the same or nearly the same affluence as the *carnaioli*, judges and notaries, found sufficient expression for their own interests in the political structure and functioning of government and enjoyed important roles in key councils, legislative, tax, and administrative commissions, sufficient for them not to be tempted to hazard joining the rebels, and, I suspect, also sufficient for them to be suspicious of the selfish motivation of the would-be rebels.

Nor were the salaried masses of laborers so dissatisfied as not to retain a suspicion of the revolutionaries' selfishness. That characteristic would have been most evident to men who had frequent contact with them and ample opportunities to be outraged by the greed of men such as the *carnaioli*, upon whom they depended for a basic staple or the notaries to whom they had to turn for a variety of transactions. And what common bonds of mutual respect and confidence united those humble masses with the haughty and bellicose magnates, so that they might hope for far better conditions under a magnate or sig-

[97] For the material in this paragraph, see for the present Bowsky, *Finance*, esp. chap. x, "The Balance."

niorial regime than those that they experienced under the Nine? Would a magnate's contempt or disdain for his social inferiors have encouraged the great majority of the *minuti* to throw in their lot with him in a desperate venture, feckless of the consequences? The poor may have rioted spontaneously when hungry, but I suspect that in most conspiracies magnates or ambitious *popolani grossi* utilized them for their own purposes. And, as we have seen, it was the *minuti* who suffered most grievously when rebellion failed, a lesson that most did not forget quickly after 1318.

The numerous magnate clans, too, had legal and constitutional outlets for asserting their positions. The commune itself provided them with opportunities for profit and for self-satisfying public display. No class unity bound one *consorteria* to another or separated them inexorably from the ruling oligarchy. (A number of Noveschi families were no less "noble" than houses excluded from the Nine, and several were as wealthy as all but a few of the magnate clans.)

And if the *casati* had a special proclivity for violence (rivaled perhaps by only one Noveschi family, the Petroni), that violence was directed against fellow magnates at least as often as against burger merchant, *contado* peasant, or villager. Sienese peace often was threatened by bloody battles of Salimbeni against Tolomei, or Malavolti against Piccolomini. Yet those very rivalries made impossible a united front against the government. The very strength and prestige of the Tolomei probably led other families to fear the establishment of a Tolomei signory, and of a regime in which their own ambitions might be less favored than under the Nine.[98] (And, indeed, it is unlikely that the Tolomei failure to commit themselves to battle on October 26, 1318 endeared them to the more militant of the

---

[98] Still very useful is Giovanni Cecchini, *La pacificazione fra Tolomei e Salimbeni*, Quaderni dell' accademia chigiana, II (Siena, 1942).

popolani. That caution, or treachery, probably cost them dearly in later years.)

It was, interestingly, only when an external factor existed that most major conspiracies approached the stage of open violence: they occurred either during or immediately after a period of serious food shortage, when fear of starvation made some *popolani* willing to throw caution to the winds and to take a chance that any change would be for the better.[99] (Even after the tremendous upheaval of the Black Death and the frightening incursions of the military companies only the visit to Siena of an imperial candidate made possible the final overthrow of the Nine.)

From a completely different vantage point, it is legitimate to inquire at this point whether our examination of "The Anatomy of Rebellion" suggests a model, or, more likely, at least a group of questions that can advantageously be posed when considering late medieval and renaissance urban conspiracies and uprisings.

At the most immediate level, in order for a rebellion to be launched did there have to exist, for example, an assembly of groups that accepted a common ideology, shared common grievances, rallied to common political slogans or at the least shouted the same battle cries? We should, when possible, take into account class relationships, structures, and values, including psychological as well as institutional patterns of association. What, for instance, was the role of each group in society and what were its special proclivities for or against violent action against the state, and what balance, however precarious, existed among those various groups? In this context it is still useful to

---

[99] The principal periods of shortage in Siena during the regime of the Nine were 1296–1297, 1303, 1306–1307, 1308–1310, 1318–1319, 1323–1324, 1328–1330, 1340, 1346–1347, 1352. See esp. Bowsky, *Finance*, pp. 31–42.

test each town and epoch against the thesis set forth by Giovanni Botero in 1589:

> In every state there are three sorts of people, the wealthy, the poor, and the middle class which lies between these extremes. The middle sort is usually the quietest and the easiest to govern, the two extremes are the hardest to govern, because the rich are drawn towards wrong-doing by the power that goes with wealth, while the poor are equally drawn to it by necessity. . . . Moreover those who have great riches and are distinguished by their noble birth and influential position are too proud and highly bred to suffer subordination, while the needy are as ready to obey an evil command as an honest one. . . . The middle rank are sufficiently wealthy to have no lack of what is required by their station, and yet their affluence is not such as to tempt them into ambitious schemes. They are usually friends of peace, contented with their station and neither exalted by ambition nor prostrated by despair. . . . We may suppose, then, that these middle folk will be peaceful, and proceed to deal with the extremes and the problem of how they should be prevented from causing riots and rebellions.[100]

We should further consider the extent to which existing institutions and modes of thought and association were conducive to the expression of civil violence. The problem is not so simple as might first appear: the vendetta, for example, accustomed men to take the law into their own hands and to resort to arms in defense of their self-understood interests, but the same vendetta worked to create and foster long-standing and deep-seated rivalries that could impede any unity of action among the magnates.

We might similarly inquire to what degree and in what ways

[100] Giovanni Botero, *The Reason of State*, trans. P. J. Waley and D. P. Waley (New Haven, 1956), pp. 82–83 (Book IV, chap. 2). I am grateful to Professor David Herlihy for bringing this passage to my attention in the course of the stimulating paper, "Some Psychological and Social Roots of Violence in Tuscan Cities," elsewhere in this volume.

communal society had developed and perfected instruments to control violence. Were there viable institutionalized means whereby men could effect desired changes without risking the dangers inherent in violence, and that enabled them to believe that they could obtain redress of grievances without having to place in jeopardy their properties and lives and the futures of their families by turning to conspiracy and open rebellion? How effective in this regard were communal constitutions and political organizations? What roles were played by councils and appellate proceedings, by a system of courts and justice, by armed forces, and communal police? How systematically or successfully could a state discover plots and crush them before they attained serious proportions? (We should here analyze the role of *paciarii* within the urban companies or wards,[101] and the utilization of spies and secret accusers.) Germane, too, are certain functions assumed by welfare organizations—religious confraternities, for example, or such a quasi-religious charitable entity as the Hospital of Santa Maria della Scala of Siena—institutions, admittedly, that have been little examined as yet by modern historians. And, lastly, in the present day and age need one emphasize the need to relate to our topic such factors as population and demographic changes, food supply, job availability, rental structures and prices, and other economic considerations?

In each case study the number of these questions that can be answered satisfactorily and the themes that can be pursued fruitfully will depend, of course, upon the nature and quantity of the extant documentation. And I would not be surprised if even in the long run we will have to be content to obtain "anatomies" of individual revolutions or of conspiracies within a single town, rather than arrive at a single pattern that will neatly fit them all. Only, however, when all the pertinent issues

---

[101] For the Sienese *paciarii*, and the differing usage of this term in Florence, see Bowsky, "Police Power," p. 12.

are explored in depth will we be able to attain a more nuanced and accurate knowledge of the role and nature of conspiracy and rebellion in Italian society. Hopefully, however, even the present brief analysis of the anatomy of rebellion in fourteenth-century Siena may help us better to understand the success and the strength of republican regimes in Tuscany (as well as their deficiencies) and to pinpoint some reasons why they did not hasten to follow their northern and eastern neighbors along the pathway from commune to signory.

X

CONTEMPORARY VIEWS ON FACTION AND CIVIL STRIFE IN THIRTEENTH- AND FOURTEENTH-CENTURY ITALY

J. K. Hyde

*C*ONSIDERING the superabundance of violence with which their lives were surrounded, it is at first sight surprising how rarely medieval Italians committed to writing their reflections on the causes, nature, and cure of faction and civil strife. Poets and philosophers could, if they chose, ignore the problems of violence, and even political philosophy could be discussed without any detailed consideration of the forms and extent of civil dissent, but the chroniclers and historians could hardly avoid filling their pages with the whole spectrum of strife, from petty murders and vendettas, through riots, revolutions and battles within and between cities, to the distant clashes of far-off kings, which seem to have been imagined as the more sanguinary and earth shaking the further they were removed from the homeland and knowledge of the writer. One may search in vain through many such writings, from the most rudimentary to some of the most sophisticated, for any conscious reflection on strife, whether civil or of any other kind; it would appear that to many violence seemed such an inseparable part of fallen human nature that to question it was as superfluous as to query the existence of sin itself. For the relatively few who did ask, there existed a standard explanation which was simple in its essence and yet capable of considerable elaboration, so that it could appeal to men of all levels of intelligence, and it seems to have proved so satisfying that very few were prompted to look beyond it.[1]

The fourteenth-century theory of civil discord started from an observation, convincing because it was almost self-substantiating, that periods of disaster follow, or seem to follow, periods of peace and prosperity. In its simplest form, as in Guglielmo Cortusi's description of the prosperity of Padua before the coming of Henry of Luxemburg, it need be little more than a literary device with no causal connection suggested; no more than a profound sense of the instability of things seems to lie behind Giovanni Villani's comment on the popular festivities of 1333, "E parve segno per contrario della futura avversità, siccome più volte avviene delle false e fallaci felicità temporali, che dopo la soperchia allegrezza segua soperchio amarone."[2] The conviction of the mutability of fortune, expressed most graphically in the image of Fortune's Wheel, applied not only to individuals but to cities, kingdoms and, on an even larger scale, to the great world empires, of which that of Rome was to be last. The final cause of such changes was, of course, God, who might be imagined as bringing them about more or less directly, but in the scholastic-scientific intellectual climate of the first half of the fourteenth century, it was possible to link them to the machinery of the universe in many ways. In the forty-first chapter of his twelfth book, Giovanni Villani at-

[1] For what follows, I am particularly indebted to N. Rubinstein, "Some Ideas on Municipal Progress and Decline in the Italy of the Communes," *Fritz Saxl Memorial Essays*, ed. D. J. Gordon (London, 1957), pp. 165–183.

[2] G. Cortusi, *Chronica de Novitatibus Padue et Lombardie*, ed. B. Pagnin, *Rerum Italicarum Scriptores* (cited hereafter as RIS), XII, v (Bologna, 1941), p. 12. G. Villani, *Cronica*, I. Moutier, ed. (Florence, 1823), X, chap. 219. ("And it seems to have been a sign by contraries of coming adversity, as often happens in the false and deceptive happiness of this world, that excessive happiness is followed by excessive grief.")

tempted an interpretation of history based on twenty- and sixty-year periods and multiples of them, marked by the conjunctions of the planets Saturn and Jupiter, and in several places he tries to explain specific events by the current theories of astrology. Somewhat earlier, the Paduan Albertino Mussato had postulated that his city was subject to alternating periods of prosperity and decline of forty or fifty years duration; while not ruling out astral influences, Mussato seems to have favored terrestrial ones such as the site itself or the "flux of the elements," presumably air and water, both of which were regarded as of the highest importance in determining the character of a city.[3]

These "scientific" theories of history, while they are evidence of a healthy search for explanations, were in the last resort sterile, because they placed the causes of historical events entirely outside the field of history, and reduced the historian to making purely mechanical adjustments to make events conform to a predetermined pattern. But there was an alternative line of thought which sought to link periods of prosperity and calamity through moral dispositions of men and societies; it was more historical and therefore more profitable, since it did not simply lay down when changes could be expected to take place but opened the way to insights into the nature of strife itself. This view started from the belief that God frequently manifested his judgments in history through an assortment of scourges: in the case of plague, fire, flood, and earthquake He was regarded as acting more or less directly; but with civil strife the Devil, "the enemy who never sleeps but always sows and reaps," was often envisaged as pulling the strings.[4] But though opinions might differ as to the precise way in which

[3] A. Mussato, *De Traditione Patavii ad Canem Grandem*, *RIS*, X (Milan, 1727), col. 715; Rubinstein, "Ideas," pp. 176 ff.

[4] E.g., G. Villani, *Cronica*, XI, chap. 2 (on the flood of 1333); Dino Compagni, *Cronica*, ed. I. Del Lungo, *RIS*, IX, ii (1913), p. 232.

these judgments were executed, there was remarkable agreement as to the particular social sins associated with this specific scourge. When Dante asked in the third circle of the *Inferno* what were the reasons for Florentine discord, he was given the standard answer:

"Superbia, invidia e avarizia sono
le tre faville c'hanno i cuori accesi." [5]

Dino Compagni attributes the division among the Blacks in 1308 to *invidia* and *avarizia*, while *superbia* appears with *malizia* and a factor of a different order, *gara d'ufici*, as the root causes of all Florence's misfortunes.[6] Giovanni da Cermenate traces the schism within the Della Torre family of Milan to pride and envy. Albertino Mussato fastened on *avaritia* as the prime corrosive force in Paduan society.[7] Behind these views lay a long tradition of classical and Christian thought in which Saint Augustine's highlighting of pride as the driving force of the City of this World occupied a pivotal position. Mussato was certainly influenced by Sallust's analysis of Roman corruption, but in most cases particular sources are hardly to be looked for. Both the ancient and the medieval world had a deep distrust of prosperity.

It is illuminating to see how the social vices were associated with particular groups and categories in society. Pride was the special sin of youth and in this, as Compagni explains, the Devil finds it easier to deceive the young than the old.[8] Envy would attack the great families of the ancient nobility, especially when their position was threatened by upstarts; Giovanni Villani develops this theme with regard to the rivalry of Corso of the

[5] *Inferno*, VI, 74–75.
[6] *Cronica*, pp. 8, 207.
[7] Johannis de Cermenate, *Historia*, ed. L. A. Ferrai, Fonti per la la Storia d'Italia (Rome, 1889), p. 26; Mussato, *op. cit.*, col. 716; Rubinstein, "Ideas," pp. 172–176.
[8] *Cronica*, pp. 66–67.

house of Donati, "gentili uomini e guerrieri e di non soperchia ricchezza," and the Cerchi, "di grande affare . . . e ricchissimi mercatanti . . . morbidi e innocenti, salvatichi e ingrati, siccome genti venuti di piccolo tempo in grande stato e podere." [9] The defects attributed to the Cerchi are mild indeed, probably reflecting Villani's political sympathies and also the relative tolerance accorded to new-made wealth in Florence in his generation; in the more provincial atmosphere of Padua the main animus of the commentators, both simple and sophisticated, was turned on the upstarts who had made their way by avarice and above all usury.[10] While the theologians defined all gain exacted by reason of a loan as usury, the lay world was inclined to condone it when practiced by wealthy bankers and established merchants, reserving their censure for "la gente nuova e' subiti guadagni" which challenged their sense of social stability.[11] While the Paduan charges are leveled against particular individuals and families, Dante and Compagni inveigh mainly against the whole class of evil citizens who have corrupted and depraved the whole world with evil customs and false gains.

These are the main outlines of what may be called the standard theory of civil strife which could be adapted and developed in various ways according to the situation and erudition of the wrter. Did no one consider that revolution might come about through hardship and oppression, and perversion of justice as Aristotle taught? To take two examples almost at random—in 1250 the annals of Piacenza record that the *popolo* of the city led a coup d'etat against the *podestà*, whose policy of

[9] G. Villani, *Cronica*, VIII, chap. 39. ("Noblemen and warriors, but not of outstanding wealth. . . . Great businessmen and very rich merchants but soft and unsuspecting, boorish and ungrateful, being people who had come in a short time to great wealth and power.")

[10] J. K. Hyde, *Padua in the Age of Dante* (Manchester, 1966), pp. 189–190, 260–261.

[11] B. N. Nelson, "The Usurer and the Merchant Prince: Italian Businessmen and the Ecclesiastical Law of Restitution," *Journal of Economic History*, VII, Suppl. (1947) 104–122; Dante, *Inferno*, XVI, 73.

diverting supplies of grain to Parma and allowing the free export of grain from the Piacentine *contado* was causing hardship.[12] In 1343 Giovanni Villani enlarges on the grievances created by Walter of Brienne's financial exactions, sanguinary justice, and moral depravity (all traditional attributes of the tyrant) to account for the rising that led to the duke's expulsion and the violent death of a number of his ministers.[13] In practice, therefore, divisions and revolutions could arise from other bases than pride, envy and avarice, but such cases being, by definition, ones in which the writer was convinced that the grievances were justified, were not looked at as instances of the evil of civil discord at all. Although it was recognized that tyranny could be practiced by classes and groups as well as individuals, the question of resistance to injustice tended to be discussed in the academic framework of the legitimacy or otherwise of tyrannicide, on which opinions tended to be unrealistically cautious.[14] It appears that it was not until the middle of the fourteenth century that the legal problems arising from illegitimate governments in Italian cities—whether, for example, contracts made with or under such governments were binding—were fully and realistically discussed, though cases raising these questions must have been coming before the courts for at least a century.[15] The balance of opinion in the literature tells us no more than that the majority of writers were in favor of the status quo.

Direct comments on the causes of civil faction and strife do

[12] *Annales Placentini Gibellini*, G. H. Pertz, ed., *Monumenta Germaniae Historica Scriptores* (cited hereafter as *MGHS*), Vol. XVIII (Hanover, 1863), pp. 501–502.

[13] *Cronica*, XII, chaps. 1–4, 8, 16–17.

[14] E.g., Thomas Aquinas and Ptolemy of Lucca, *De Regimine Principum*, ed. J. Mathis (Turin, 1948), pp. 6–8, 45–47.

[15] Bartolo da Sassoferrato, "De Tyrannia," in *Opera* (Venice, 1603), IX, fols. 117–119. For a case in Treviso in 1314, see below, p. 297 n. 60.

not exhaust what contemporaries have to say on this subject: indeed, on this as on some other topics, some saw more clearly out of the corners of their eyes than when their gaze was concentrated directly on the object. The real nature of a civil conflict often emerges incidentally in the course of a narrative, while the attitude of the writer may be revealed in a passing remark. The possible field where such information may be found is very wide, and no more has been attempted here than to suggest some of the points of interest to be found in some of the more obvious sources, mainly chronicles and treatises of the thirteenth and fourteenth centuries.

It is necessary first to look at the political context in which intracity strife took place, since it was this which gave it a specific character, although it was often brushed over by contemporaries, who could pass from civil wars to intercity wars or wars involving Pope and Emperor without clearly distinguishing between them. The political setting in this period was the commune, as yet only modified in certain technical points by knowledge of the classical *respublica* and not yet transformed by the Renaissance concept of the *stato*. Although the term "commune" had been used in classical times to denote the municipality and its property in distinction to that of the state, and during the Dark Ages there are occasional references where it seems to signify some kind of provincial assembly, the medieval commune was to all intents and purposes a new concept of the late eleventh century.[16] In some early instances it seems to mean a place and a time at which decisions were reached rather than an institution. The remarkable thing is that the term was so universally accepted; the Genoese equivalent, *compagna*, ceased to be applied to the political organization during the twelfth century, though *communanza*, a word with similar con-

---

[16] P. S. Leicht, " 'Comunitas' e 'comune' nell'alto medioevo," *Scritti vari di storia del diritto* (Milan, 1943), p. 337.

notations, continued in use in the Veneto into the fourteenth century, where it came to signify the political organization of the *popolo*. Early on, the word commune came to be closely associated with the notion of the "common" property of citizenry; in commercial usage, *comune* denoted the common funds of a partnership.[17] In the thirteenth century, chroniclers would refer to a city as being *in commune* when it was ruled by its own *anziani* or priors and was not under the *dominium* of a *signore*. By the fourteenth century, the notion that the commune should afford some kind of representation to all the politically significant classes and interests within the city becomes explicit. According to Marchionne di Coppo Stefani, the duke of Athens justified his strengthening of the artisan representation among the priors with the argument that the offices should be "comuni d'ogni ragione, perchè si chiamava Comune."[18] Walter of Brienne was, of course, a foreigner, and may have had his tongue in his cheek, but Giovanni Villani expresses the representative ideal of the commune even more clearly in his criticism of the oligarchy of 1340, who ruled "non dando parte a' grand nè a' mezzani nè a' minori, come si convenia a buono reggimento di comune."[19] This representation, which in the words of Marsiglio of Padua, should be according to both the numbers and the quality of persons in the community, did not need to be more than approximate because it was only a means to securing what was the most important aim of communal government, impartiality.[20] The idea of attaining impartiality

[17] Florence Edler, *Glossary of Medieval Terms of Business: Italian Series* (Cambridge, Mass., 1934), p. 81.

[18] Marchionne di Coppo Stefani, *Cronica Fiorentina*, ed. N. Rodolico, *RIS*, XXX, i, 1903–1955, p. 199.

[19] *Cronica*, XI, chap. 118.

[20] "considerata quantitate personarum et qualitate in communitate illa super quam lex fertur...." Marsiglio Mainardini, *Defensor Pacis*, ed. R. Scholz, *Fontes Iuris Germanici Antiqui in usum scholarum* (Hanover, 1932), p. 63.

through wider representation is clearly present in Villani's treatment of various constitutional changes in Florence which he describes as intended to "raccomunare la città" or "recare la città più a comune." [21]

There was, in fact, a persisting ambiguity attached to the word *comune*. As a noun, it indicated a form of government, while as an adjective it meant shared, impartial or neutral. When, for example, Compagni says that on the arrival of Charles of Valois in Florence "la gente comune" began to lose strength, he clearly means the neutral and impartial citizens who were not possessed by the *malizia* of either party.[22] But some adverbial forms defy classification; when the eleventh-century chronicler Arnulf says that the citizens of Lodi "in commune deliberant" or the Milanese "communiter igitur statuunt," it is impossible to say whether he imagined them as deliberating and legislating in common or in the commune.[23] It was possible to play on these two meanings, as when Villani says of the two *frati gaudenti* brought into Florence as arbitrators in 1266, "credendo che per l'onestà dell'abito fossono comuni, e guardassono il comune da soperchie spese." [24] The pun must have been irresistible to many moralists and preachers; it recurs, for example, in the sermon given by the Dominican Remigio Girolami before the Florentine Priors during the tense period following the enactment of the Ordinances of Justice in the first half of the year 1293. The notes for this sermon sum up the ideals of communal government so well that they are worth quoting at length.

[21] *Cronica*, IX, chaps. 79, 271; XII, chap. 18.

[22] *Cronica*, p. 101 and n. 2. For the meanings of *comune* see N. Rubinstein, "Marsilius of Padua and Italian Political Thought of His Time," *Europe in the Late Middle Ages*, ed. J. R. Hale, J. R. L. Highfield, B. Smalley (London, 1965), p. 54.

[23] Arnulf, *Gesta Archiepiscoporum Mediolanensium*, MGHS, VIII (Hanover, 1848) pp. 14, 23.

[24] *Cronica*, VII, chap. 13.

"Pass judgment and discern *in comune* what should be done" (Judges 20:7). This text exhorts you to do four things which are very necessary for your office. Firstly, it urges you to make a thorough deliberation about what is to be done, because to discern means really to perceive so that you do not act hastily; as it is in the book of Proverbs, "Discern what is just," and in Job, "The cause of which I was ignorant I have sought out most diligently." Secondly, it urges you to harmonious unanimity, because *in comune*, that is in a common and harmonious will, not pulling hither and thither, as it says in Hosea, "Their heart is divided, now they shall be destroyed," but rather as in Maccabees, "They all decreed *comuni consilio*." Thirdly, you should promote the good of the commune because that which is done *in comune* should be for the common good (*pro bono communis*), that is, useful, pleasant and honorable; not for the good of this or that individual or family, nor for the good of this or that group, but as you were made and put in office by the commune, so you should work for the common good, as it says in Maccabees "Considering the common good of the multitude in general." Therefore you should beware of doing anything contrary to this, either for Giano or for any other reason. Fourthly, it teaches you to be diligent in carrying out the business of your office, because it says "Pass judgment," for you should not leave things in suspense; as in Job, "My lips shall speak a pure judgment." [25]

Over against the commune and the common good stood the *pars* or *parte* and the spirit of faction. The antithesis commune–*pars* was probably a commonplace by the second half of the thirteenth century; it occurs, for example, in the *Chronicon Parmense* under the year 1282 and several times in Rolandino's chronicle, where the moral connotation is made explicit when he says of Ezzelino da Romano's government, "Facta hec tractabantur non per iustitiam set per partem." [26] Villani prefers the

---

[25] G. Salvadori and U. Federici, "I sermoni d'occasione, le sequenze e i ritmi di Remigio Girolami fiorentino," *Scritti vari di filologia a Ernesto Monaci* (Rome, 1901), p. 482.

[26] *Chronicon Parmense*, ed. G. Bonazzi, *RIS*, IX, ix (1902), p. 40;

word *sette* to *parte* but its significance appears to be exactly the same. He retails a curious letter said to have been sent by Robert of Naples to Walter of Brienne soon after he took over the government of Florence, in which the king is made to write "and as they [the Florentines] have governed themselves *per sette*, be sure that you govern yourself *per dieci*, which is the *numero comune* that contains within itself all the individual numbers; that is to say, do not rule them *per sette* nor divided, but *a comune*." [27] But despite all the preaching and moralizing about the common good, it was in fact the parties and factions which dominated the political life of the communes. Just as the persistency with which men adhered to their party or faction, acting not *communaliter* but *per partem*, puzzled and exasperated contemporary moralists and would-be mediators, so the nature of the parties and the interests which underlay their formation remains one of the unavoidable but often insoluble problems confronting the historian of communal Italy.

In a passage which is interesting because of the rarity with which such a thing was attempted, Remigio Girolami sums up the divisions in Florentine society:

One rift is because the Guelphs speak ill of the Ghibellines because they do not surrender, and the Ghibellines of the Guelphs because they wish to drive them out. Another is because the artisans speak ill of the great men because they are devoured by them, because they commit treasons, because they hold on to the goods of their enemies and so on; and on the other hand the great men speak ill of the artisans because they want to dominate and are ignorant, they denigrate the city and so on. The third rift is between the clergy and religious and the laity, because they say of the laymen that they are traitors, perjurers, adulterers and thieves, and this is true

---

Rolandino Patavino, *Cronica Marchie Trivixane*, ed. A. Bonardi, *RIS*, VIII, i (1906), pp. 57, 59, 99.

[27] *Cronica*, XII, chap. 4.

of many. The laity, on the other hand, say the clergy are fornicators, gluttons and slothful, and that the religious are grasping and over-proud, and this is true of some.[28]

It may be instructive to follow up this perceptive contemporary analysis, looking at each of Remigio's lines of division in turn, but in the reverse order from that in which he states them, so as to approach step by step the core of the problem of civil strife in Italian cities.

It is easy to understand why Remigio included the rift between clergy and laity among the divisions that split Florentine society, for it was one that must have concerned him closely. He sprang from the governing class, being the son of one of the leaders of the Primo Popolo; his brother was active in politics and his nephew was exiled for political reasons in 1302.[29] Remigio's writings prove his deep interest in politics, and the frequency with which he was called to preach on political occasions and themes shows that he was esteemed for his opinions on political matters. Remigio therefore lived on the delicate frontier between the ecclesiastical and political spheres, and any tension between them, however slight, must have raised immediate personal problems for him. Almost any chronicle will show that collisions between clergy and the commune took place from time to time, over the perennial issues of ecclesiastical contributions to communal taxation, the punishment of criminous clerks, and—from the later thirteenth century at least —the jurisdiction over laymen claimed by church courts and particularly by the inquisitors in matters of heresy and usury. These conflicts could give rise to bizarre and scandalous happenings, as when a sexually delinquent priest was hung up in a cage in Padua or another, accused of murder, was boiled alive

---

[28] Cit. C. T. Davis, "An Early Florentine Political Theorist, Fra Remigio de Girolami," *Proceedings of the American Philosophical Society*, CIV (1960), 667 n. 40.

[29] *Ibid.*, p. 662.

in Parma; the resultant interdicts could drag on for years, causing no small anguish to the devout.[30] In a critical situation, where a government was insecure for other reasons, a clash with the clergy could prove a serious embarrassment, but there seems to be no evidence that, by themselves, these issues could seriously disturb the stability of a firmly based government and still less could they form the basis for a serious and durable schism in the body politic. To find anything approaching such a situation, it is necessary to go back to the earliest days of the communes in Lombardy at the end of the eleventh century, when the reformist clergy formed an alliance with the *patarini* against the established order. Clearly the clergy alone could not provide the basis for a viable political party; they needed to carry with them a substantial body of the laity, and this they proved on the whole less and less able to do. Indeed, the clerical estate was itself divided; bishops and priests might be Guelph or Ghibelline, many prelates were magnates whose political activities were typical of their class, and the middle and lower clergy no doubt tended to align themselves with the social classes from which they were recruited and among whom they worked.

It is true that an attack on ecclesiastical jurisdictions, including those at the local level, is included in the most profound analysis of Italian political problems, Marsiglio of Padua's *Defensor Pacis*. Some have seen this as an important element in his doctrine, springing from his knowledge of the political experience of the Paduan commune. However, the Paduan government's relations with the local clergy were not particularly bad and conform to the typical pattern.[31] The most serious clash ended in agreement in 1290, when Marsiglio can hardly have

---

[30] *Annales Patavini*, RIS, VIII, i, (1906), Appendix I, p. 189; *Chronicon Parmense*, p. 11.

[31] The only modern study of this subject is L. A. Botteghi, "Clero e comune in Padova nel secolo XIII," *Nuovo archivio veneto*, n.s., IX, part ii, (1905), pp. 215–272. Further research could be very rewarding.

been much more than fifteen years old; and during the years when Marsiglio may be presumed to have taken an active interest in politics, the Paduan commune seems to have got its way without too much trouble, as when the Inquisition was transferred from the Franciscans to the Dominicans in 1303.[32] Indeed, the leading prelates of the city in the first two decades of the fourteenth century, the bishop Pagano della Torre and abbot Gualpertino Mussato of Santa Giustina, were staunch supporters of the existing regime, identifying themselves with it to the extent that they personally organized the Paduan reserves for the defense of the city against the Veronese in a moment of crisis in 1314.[33] It is quite clear, in fact, that Marsiglio's main target in the first part of the *Defensor* was the temporal power of the Papacy and its claim to *plenitudo potestatis* over secular princes and governments.[34] Local church courts are condemned, more or less in passing, because they violate two of Marsiglio's basic tenets—the incapacity of the clergy to possess coercive jurisdiction, and the unity of the Legislator in each city or kingdom.[35] In this latter case, they are a symptom of a wider defect, to which we shall return in due course; the point to be made in the present context is that it cannot be argued from the *Defensor* that Marsiglio regarded the privileges of the clergy as an outstanding cause of the political instability in the communes of his day.

Remigio's observations on the antagonism between the artisans and the great men in Florence raised the whole question of class conflict in medieval Italian cities. The subject is a vast one and will continue to be debated for many years yet, for although the class interpretation is less fashionable than it used to

[32] *Les Régistres de Boniface VIII*, ed. G. Digard, M. Faucon, A. Thomas and R. Fawtier (Paris, 1907–1935), IV, doc. no. 4953.

[33] A. Mussato, *De Gestis Italicorum post mortem Henrici VII, RIS*, X (Milan, 1727), col. 653.

[34] *Defensor Pacis*, pp. 127–137.

[35] *Ibid.*, p. 135.

be, few would deny that class issues were of considerable importance at certain times and places, though why and with what limitations are questions which may always remain open. Contemporaries certainly believed that class conflict was important, and this belief, whether it was true or not, is a fact to be taken into consideration like any other.

The chronicle known as the Guelph annals of Piacenza contains an account of what appears at first reading to be a straightforward class conflict, placed unexpectedly under the year 1090. A brawl between individuals developed into a major struggle between the *milites* and the *populares* of Piacenza. The *populares* succeeded in driving the *milites* out of the city but these held out in the *contado*, cutting off food supplies so as to drive their opponents into making a sortie. While this was going on, the *milites* seized the unguarded city, placing the *populares* in a desperate situation when, we are told, a wave of feeling swept over both sides and the quarrel was made up with mutual kisses of peace and many tears.[36] The story is suspect, even without its unlikely denouement, for the situation and especially the terminology smack of the thirteenth century more than the eleventh. The chronicle, in fact, appears to be the work of a Piacentine who was deeply involved in the conflicts of the first decades of the thirteenth century who, building perhaps on a brief note in an earlier chronicle, placed this story with its obvious moral for his contemporaries right at the beginning of his narrative. When he comes to describe the divisions of his own times, the chronicler reveals that the pattern of class conflict was subject to serious modifications in practice. The party that formed against the ruling consuls in February 1219 consisted of the *popolo* together with certain nobles of the city; these created a *societas* by means of a mutual oath and forced the consuls to reverse their policy and make war on Cre-

---

[36] *Annales Placentini Guelfi*, ed. G. H. Pertz, *MGHS*, XVIII, 411–412.

mona and Pavia. It was only later in the year, when the *popolo* insisted on adding some unspecified clauses to the *breve communis* against the objections of the *milites*, that the division hardened on class lines, and even then it is quite clear that the conflict was not between the classes as such, but between two organizations, the *societas militum* and the *societas populi*, which was a very different thing. In 1222 when the *podestá* of Cremona was brought in to mediate between the parties, he divided the civic offices between the *milites* and those of the *popolo* who adhered to them, and the *popolo* and those of the *milites* who had sided with them, making it clear that each faction drew some support from both classes.[37] Another chronicle of the same period, Gerardo Maurisio's account of the deeds of Ezzelino and Alberico da Romano, shows how a Vicentine citizen and lawyer could be bound to a noble family by ties of patronage and apparently affection; no doubt these existed in many other cases of which we are ignorant.[38] Many class struggles may in fact appear as such because of lack of detailed information and the tendency of the sources to use simple comprehensive terms where their knowledge was deficient.

Chronicles specifically concerned with faction were not unknown in the thirteenth century, but among those of the early fourteenth century, that of Dino Compagni occupies a special position as the most accomplished example of the genre. Although there is a deterioration suggesting haste of composition in the third book, the first two books of this chronicle are very finely organized both in style and content, so that one is justified in looking to Compagni for an interpretation of events which one would not expect to find in a less skillful and ac-

[37] *Ibid.*, pp. 435 ff. G. Levi, *Registri dei Cardinali Ugolino d'Ostia e Ottaviano degli Ubaldini* (Rome 1890), p. 55 n.

[38] Gerardo Maurisio, *Cronica dominorum Ecelini et Alberici fratrum de Romano*, ed. G. Soranzo, RIS VIII, 4 (1914). The point is made by G. Arnaldi, *Studi sui cronisti della Marca Trevigiana nell'età di Ezzelino da Romano* (Rome, 1963), p. 35.

complished writer. Characteristically, Compagni sets the scene in his first chapter by describing the city and *contado* and their inhabitants; of the first he notes that the citizens are proud and quarrelsome and rich with illicit gains, while the *contado* has many noblemen, counts and *cattanei*, who love the city more in discord than in peace and obey more from fear than love.[39] One would expect this theme, introduced at such a significant point, to be developed, and in a sense it is. The superb description of the battle of Campaldino is included in the chronicle because after it the noble and great citizens grew proud and began to commit crimes against the *popolani*.[40] The reaction of the *popolo* to this provocation is the passing of the Ordinances of Justice, which completed the creation of a special category of citizen, the *magnati*, who were placed under certain legal disabilities. Compagni makes it clear that these *potenti cittadini* were not all of noble blood but were classified as *grandi* for a variety of other reasons.[41] However, as they now suffered common disabilities, they could be expected to make a common front against Giano della Bella and the party which had deprived them of their rights. The way in which they went about this is extremely instructive. At a meeting held in San Giacomo d'Oltrarno, Berto Frescobaldi proposed direct action with the words "Gentlemen, I advise that we break out of this slavery. Let us take up arms and go outside and kill as many of the *popolo* as we can, friends and enemies alike, so that we and our sons may never more be subjugated by them." But all those present agreed instead with Baldo della Tosa, who said that this advice was too risky; it would be better to conquer the *popolani* first by craft and then destroy their unity by playing on fear of the Ghibellines; so it was agreed to send out agents to corrupt

[39] *Cronica*, pp. 6–8.
[40] *Ibid.*, p. 31; G. Villani, VII, chap. 132 makes the same point, but stresses the suspicions of the *popolo* rather than the crimes of the nobles.
[41] *Cronica*, p. 38.

and disunite the *popolo* and to slander Giano so that he would be isolated.[42] Whether Compagni's account is fully accurate or not, it is clear that the Grandi in fact held their hand until Giano had aroused the antagonism of important vested interests like those of the guild of judges and notaries, the butchers and the Parte Guelfa, and could be condemned with a semblance of justice for his supposed part in the riots of February 1295. It was not until the following July when, Villani says, the magnates were sure of the support of the Priors, that they took up arms for their rights and even then, had it come to a fight, Villani's view is that they would have been defeated by the *popolo* had they not agreed to make terms with their opponents through mediators, of whom Remigio Girolami was probably one.[43]

The conclusion to be drawn from the events of 1293–1295 is that while Compagni was disposed to see the issues in terms of a class struggle, and although he records strong feelings of class tension, when it came to decisive action the effective political groupings were those that cut across class lines. The leadership of the *popolo* came from great families which were economically hardly distinguishable from the magnates; the magnates on the other hand, did not dare to act until they had substantial support among the *popolo*, and not only among the *popolani grassi* like the judges, but also among the *arti medie* such as the butchers. In the rest of his chronicle, Compagni goes on, albeit unconsciously, to hammer home this lesson. The new rift between the Blacks and Whites divided all classes of citizen, the great, the middle, and the small, although in different proportions.[44] Modern research has confirmed and extended

[42] *Ibid.*, pp. 43–44.

[43] *Cronica*, VIII, chap. 12. Strangely, this event is not mentioned by Compagni.

[44] "Divisesi di nuovo la città negli uomini grandi, mezani e piccolini; e i religiosi non si poterono difendere che con l'animo non si dessono alle dette parti, chi a una, chi a una altra" Compagni, *Cronica*, p. 69.

the significance of Compagni's analysis.[45] It was precisely their interclass structure that gave the new parties their strength and staying power, so that stability could be restored only by the total eradication of one of them from the body politic. Class tension did not disappear, and according to Compagni class feeling was deliberately played on by the Black magnates so as to weaken the resolve of the leading families among the Whites. During the crisis of autumn 1301, the Spini beguiled the Scali with the words "We are indeed friends and kinsmen, and all Guelphs, and we have no other desire than to get rid of the chain that the *popolo* holds from off the necks of you and us alike. *Per Dio*, let us stand together as we ought to do." [46] But this was only a maneuver, for when it came to the test, party loyalty overrode class loyalty, and the way to power lay through binding classes together, particularly the warlike magnates with their personal prestige and the *popolo grasso* with their financial resources and indispensable administrative experience. Such an alliance, formed by Rosso della Tosa after the expulsion of the Whites, is strikingly described by Compagni: "He adhered to the *popolo grasso* because they were his tongs and held the hot iron." [47] It was his rival Corso Donati who failed to win the support of this class, who in the end went to the wall.

It is not hard to see why contemporaries were so conscious of class differences. Classes could be visibly distinguished by their dress and style of life, and it was felt to be right that they should be. The sumptuary laws were in part framed to prevent the lower classes from imitating their superiors in dress; [48]

[45] Notably G. Masi "La struttura sociale delle fazioni politiche fiorentine ai tempi di Dante," *Giornale Dantesco* XXXI, i (1930), 1–28.

[46] *Cronica, Compagni*, p. 117.

[47] *Ibid.*, p. 168.

[48] E.G., "Quia plerumque Florentini cives et artifices non ad rationem sed ad similitudinem magnatum vivere volunt," *Statuto del Capitano del Popolo 1322–25*, ed. R. Caggese (Florence, 1910), p. 226.

though no law forbade enriched citizens to adopt the imposing *palazzo* filled with a numerous retinue of men and horses, or even the coats of arms associated with the nobility, such things were closely watched by fellow citizens and public opinion would react strongly against anyone stepping beyond what was regarded as his proper station. Although the most important status group, the nobility, often had no legal or corporate existence, the guild system made possible very many distinctions between merchants, artisans, and workmen of all kinds. The temptation to simplify by talking in general terms like *arti medie* or *popolo minuto*, when the actual situation was more complex, has always to be reckoned with.

It must be remembered that practically all the writers of the thirteenth and fourteenth centuries express the point of view of the middle or upper *popolani*. Their views of the nobility varied significantly, with the majority probably favorable, for radicalism such as Compagni's was rarely expressed even in Florence. Opinions concerning the lower classes were almost unanimously unfavorable, often violently so. Among the general denunciations of plebian stupidity and violence, Stefani's explanation that the masses and even the middle guildsmen were liable to be deceived by propaganda because they were too numerous to meet together to form a common policy stands out for its reasonableness.[49] The reading of classical authors tended to confirm existing prejudices; Villani did not need Aristotle to tell him of the dangers of democracy, but we need to remember that the government of Florence in 1345, which he denounced as made up of artisans, manual workers and *idioti*, was in fact dominated by the *novi cives* who included a high proportion of the more wealthy *popolani* in the city.[50]

[49] *Cronica Fiorentina*, p. 194.
[50] *Cronica*, XII, chap. 43; G. A. Brucker, *Florentine Politics and Society* (Princeton, 1962), pp. 21 ff. 135.

Turning to Remigio's other division in civic society, the antagonism of the Guelphs and the Ghibellines, the problem ceases to be how far these were viable political parties, for their long survival proves this point beyond doubt, and becomes centered instead on the meaning of the terms themselves and the nature of the factors that gave the parties their identity. These puzzles go back to the thirteenth and fourteenth centuries. Although the Florentine legend of the Buondelmonte murder, dated 1216, pointed in the right direction, no contemporary seems to have linked the origin of the parties with the rivalry of Philip of Swabia and Otto of Brunswick. But the ignorance of the early sources should not be exaggerated. The life of Urban IV, written in 1279, clearly indicates Florence as the place of origin, and the Florentine or at least central Italian provenance of the terms can easily be deduced from, for example, the so-called Ghibelline annals of Piacenza.[51] It was not until the last decade or so of Frederick II's reign that the terms were really established in Tuscany and began to spread into Lombardy, so that Salimbene's pinning of the whole responsibility onto the heretic emperor was not entirely wide of the mark. Paduan tradition also linked the factions with Frederick.[52] It is only with Giovanni Villani and his tale of the feud between two German barons whose castles were called Guelfo and Ghibellino respectively, that the legendary element begins to get out of hand; after him, Bartolo da Sassoferrato took the

[51] Anon., *Vita Urbani IV*, *RIS*, III, 2 (Milan, 1734), col. 413; *Annales Placentini Gibellini*, pp. 498, 511. For a comprehensive introduction to questions relating to the parties, see R. Davidsohn, *Forschungen zur Geschichte von Florenz* (Berlin, 1896–1908), IV, 29–67.

[52] Salimbene di Adam, *Cronica*, ed. G. Scalia (Bari, 1966), I, 550; A. Mussato, *Lodovicus Bavarus*, *RIS*, X, col. 775. Mussato presumably knew the lost verses on the Guelphs and the Ghibellines by Lovato Lovati (d. 1309) noted by Gianfrancesco Capodilista in 1434; see V. Lazzarini, "Un antico elenco di fonti storiche padovane," *Archivio Muratoriano* (Rome, 1908), I, 332.

formation of the parties back to Frederick Barbarossa, and Lapo da Castiglionchio back to the Investiture Contest.[53]

A stereotype of the character of the parties emerged early. Thus the *Vita Urbani:*

> Ecclesiam Guelfa nutrit pars, Imperiumque
> Gibellinorum pars scelerata nimis.

And the stock picture of the wicked Ghibelline, violent, an oppressor of the Church and at least suspected of heresy, is a commonplace with Guelph writers for more than a century. The Guelph portrayal of their own party is more complex; thirteenth-century sources, while they mention faith and loyalty to the Church stress warlike qualities: the good Guelph is like a lion in war.[54] In the fourteenth century, when the position of the Guelphs had become virtually unassailable in Florence, the picture softens; Remigio Girolami likens the Ghibellines to a lion and the Guelphs to a calf, because it is a sacrificial animal, and the artisans and *popolo* are like sheep, innocent and useful.[55] Matteo Villani, in a well-known passage, expresses the idea of the Guelph party as the defenders of the liberty of Italy, opposed to all tyranny, and Lapo da Castiglionchio collects up most of these ideas into a composite picture of the Guelphs as "compassionate, merciful, mercantile and desirous of living in liberty and *a comune*." [56] The foundations of an interpretation that was to dominate the field until almost the beginning of the present century were already laid.

[53] Villani, V, chap. 38; Bartolo, "De Guelphis et Gebellinis," in *Opera,* X, fol. 151; Lapo da Castiglionchio, *Epistola o sia ragionamento,* ed. L. Mehus (Bologna, 1753), pp. 77 ff.

[54] E.g., Andreas Ungari, *Descriptio Victoriae a Karolo Comite, MGHS,* Vol. XXVI (Hanover, 1882), p. 562; F. Pellegrini, "Il serventese dei Lambertazzi e dei Geremei," *Atti e Memorie della Deputazione di Storia Patria per le Provincie di Romagna,* ser. 3, X (1892), 101.

[55] Davis, "An Early Florentine Political Theorist," p. 667.

[56] M. Villani, *Cronica,* VIII, chap. 24 (cf. IV, chaps. 77–78); Castiglionchio, *Epistola o sia ragionamento,* p. 79.

Yet at the same time as the process of idealization of the parties was going on in some quarters, in others the whole viewpoint which they implied was being questioned and rejected under the pressure of events that failed to conform to the traditional pattern. The Guelph-Ghibelline interpretation postulated that the pope and the emperor were the opposite poles of Italian political life by reference to which the party conflicts could be oriented. This was reasonably true during the formative period, from say 1227 to 1268, when the papacy and the Hohenstaufen were fairly continuously opposed to each other, but for the next forty years thereafter the normal situation was for the pope and the imperial claimant to be in uneasy and ineffective alliance, to the confusion of those who continued to think along traditional lines. In fact, the overwhelming successes of the Angevin-Guelph alliance in 1266–1269 caused a reaction in papal circles, so that while some popes continued to back the Guelph party in Italian affairs, others adopted a conciliatory policy aimed at balancing the parties through a return of the exiles, which in effect favored the Ghibellines. The new situation produced different results in various parts of Italy. In central Lombardy, for example, where neither the papacy nor the Angevins had any weighty influence, straightforward power conflicts emerged which cut across the traditional alignments, particularly after 1289 when Obizzo d' Este, the head of one of the leading Guelph dynasties, married the daughter of Alberto della Scala, the leading Ghibelline, and began to swallow up or quarrel with all his Guelph neighbours. Even before this date, the terms Guelph and Ghibelline had dropped out of use in Milanese affairs; contemporaries described the battle of Desio in 1277 as a victory over the Della Torre party by the party of the *cattanei* and the *vavassores*.[57] By 1305, the Church party in Parma, formed under Angevin patronage in 1266–

---

[57] E.G., *Annales Placentini Ghibellini*, p. 565; *Chronicon Parmense*, p. 32.

1268, could be described by the chronicler as the *pars antiqua*, when it was driven from power by a new combination, later known as the *pars nova*, under the leadership of Ghiberto da Correggio.[58] In the Romagna and central Italy, the influence of the papacy and the Angevins kept the old divisions alive in many places; another factor must have been the persistence of the Parte Guelfa in Florence as a corporate, property-owning body exercising a strong practical and ideological influence over the Florentine commonwealth and its neighbors. In these circumstances, the new divisions which arose tended to be seen in terms of the old, and there spread from Florence to Bologna and into the sphere of influence of these two communes, the parties known as the Blacks and the Whites, both claiming with a good deal of justification to represent the true Guelph party.

The paradox of Henry of Luxemburg was that although his avowed aim was to bring factional strife to an end, his intervention served to bring back ideas that had been on the brink of oblivion. Cermenate attests that the parties in Milan were not known as Guelph and Ghibelline before the arrival of the Luxemburger, and many of the *signori* of Lombardy with a checkered past, like Ghiberto da Correggio, must have been in doubt as to what line to take.[59] Guelph opinion was divided between those who took Henry's papal backing seriously and those who ignored it on the grounds that an emperor would be bound to favor the Ghibellines and bring no good to the Guelphs. The first point of view is represented by the Paduan commune and its spokesman, Albertino Mussato, and the second by the Florentine *signoria* from which the Whites, who might well have swung the decision the other way, were excluded. The combined result of Henry's actions and of the

[58] *Ibid.*, p. 91.
[59] Cermenate, *Historia*, p. 30; *Chronicon Parmense*, pp. 85 ff. W. M. Bowsky (*Henry VII in Italy* [Lincoln, Nebr., 1960], p. 30), in describing Ghiberto as a nominal Guelph, fails to convey the full ambiguity of his position.

reactions of his friends and enemies was to revive the Guelph-Ghibelline struggle for a generation, for hardly had the effects of his expedition begun to die away before the Ghibellines found a new protagonist in Lewis of Bavaria, the only imperial claimant to put on the whole antipapal mantle of the Hohen-staufen.

It is therefore generally not until the second half of the four-teenth century that comments appear showing that Italians were ceasing to think in traditional papal-imperialist terms and were beginning to see the parties as local groups in competition for power. An interesting straw in the wind is provided by a lawsuit in Treviso in 1314. A question in the interrogation was "Quid est pars?" and while some witnesses replied in traditional terms, one master Manfredino the tailor, defined "party" with complete realism as "when some of the *popolani* or other persons look to and hold with one magnate, and some with another." [60] By the early 1360s the truth had also dawned on Pietro Azarii, a mordant Lombard notary; early in his chronicle, after giving the time-honored definitions of Guelph and Ghibelline, he adds "but I have seen worse things done by Guelphs among themselves than against Ghibellines and vice versa. And if these two parties were not there, two worse ones would come into being, as will be clear from what follows." [61]

In Florence, the bitter struggles against Pisa and Arezzo seem to have kept the old ideas alive in some quarters; Matteo Villani continually repeats Guelph views, sometimes with a vehemence and a lack of logic suggesting that he felt that they were being challenged. The establishment of the regime of the *nuova gente* in 1343 was probably an important milestone; in 1354 the Florentines, who had refused to recognize John of Bohemia because he was Henry of Luxemburg's son, decided to submit to his

[60] G. B. Picotti, *I Caminesi e la loro signoria in Treviso* (Leghorn, 1905), Appendix, p. 311.

[61] Pietro Azarii, *Liber Gestorum in Lombardia,* ed. F. Cognasso *RIS*, XVI, iv (1926), p. 8.

grandson, Charles IV, much to Villani's disgust.[62] Somewhat
later, Boccaccio's life of Dante, in which he expresses his distaste for Dante's political *animosità*, seems to show that for him
the passions of the early fourteenth century were no longer
alive.[63] Bartolo da Sassoferrato's *De Guelphis et Ghibellinis*
marks a radical break with the past. In this treatise, the jurist,
after giving a traditional account of the origin of the parties,
proceeds to eliminate every premise on which the party view
was based. For Bartolo the parties of his day have no connection
with the empire and the papacy, nor have parties that have the
same name in different cities anything necessarily in common;
a just man under a Ghibelline tyrant will be Guelph, but under
a Guelph tyranny he may be Ghibelline, and the same man may
be regarded as a Ghibelline in one place and as a Guelph in
another. The significance of these views must be modified by
the consideration that they were made in a specialized legal
treatise in the context not of Tuscany but of Umbria, where it
is clear that the ossification of the parties as rigid legal categories
for the purpose of office holding was far advanced. The main
question of the treatise, whether it is legal for a man to change
his party allegiance, which is eventually answered in the affirm-
ative, drives this point home.[64]

For a thoroughgoing historical reassessment of the meaning
of party, it is necessary to turn to Marchionne Stefani who,
equipped with good sources and more intelligence than his immediate predecessors, reworked the salient events of Florentine
history which they had recorded, and brought the story down
to 1385. From his own experience as an officeholder under the
Florentine commune, Stefani concluded that all faction and
party strife could be attributed to a single cause, competition for
office. He applies this concept with great consistency, modify-

---

[62] *Cronica*, IV, chaps. 72–78.
[63] *Opere minori*, ed. E. Bianchi (Florence, 1964), pp. 723–725, 741.
[64] *Opera*, ff. 151–152.

ing his chief authority, Giovanni Villani, whenever necessary. Thus, for Stefani, factions begin in Florence at the time of Barbarossa over competition of the Uberti and other families for the consulship; the Buondelmonte murder and the introduction of the party names only define a preexisting division. Rivalry over the priorate lies behind the movement which created the Ordinances of Justice and the division between Blacks and Whites.[65] These views were not entirely new. Giovanni Villani gives *gara d'ufici* as the cause of division in Florence at least once, and Compagni had even given a certain prominence to this factor, but in both cases it appeared in company with the older moral concepts of *superbia, invidia,* and so on.[66] Stefani's achievement was uneven, for in the early part of his chronicle he retailed many old legends, sometimes in a distinctly worse form than he found them in Villani. But as compared with both Villanis, his view of the empire and papacy, of the Angevins and the whole Guelph political outlook is remarkably realistic and free of sentiment. It is entirely consistent with his attitude that he should firmly defend Florentine politics during the war of the Eight Saints.[67] Modern interpretations tend to give a unique importance to this conflict as a solvent of the Florentine Guelph ideal, yet although a war on this scale with the papacy was something new, Guelph Florence had frequently incurred papal censures in the past and had joined an alliance against a papal legate as far back as 1332. But by 1376 the Florentines were disillusioned with every other member of the old alliance which had been formed over a century before on the eve of Benevento. With the Angevins of Naples, once the sheet anchor of Guelphism, Florentine relations were already so strained by 1341 that even a conservative like Giovanni Villani remarked on the change; his brother Matteo underlines

[65] *Cronica Fiorentina, RIS,* XXX, i, pp. 25, 29, 70, 86, 413.
[66] Villani, XII, chap. 79; Compagni, *Cronica,* pp. 8, 55, 110.
[67] Stefani, *Cronica Fiorentina,* p. 293 ff.

the rapid decline in the power of the kingdom in the decade following the death of King Robert in 1343.[68] The behavior of Walter of Brienne and his followers, enshrined in Florentine political mythology, must have done no good to the prestige of the French. Finally, Matteo Villani reflects the disgust that the abuse of the *ammonizione* procedure by the Florentine Parte Guelfa created in the mind of a traditionally minded member of the governing class.[69] All these elements are found in the cooler, more logical, and more detached mind of Marchionne Stefani in a chronicle that stands on the threshold of Renaissance historiography which was to begin with Leonardo Bruni.

In conclusion, some contemporary solutions to the problems of disunity and civil strife may be considered. There was no question that, in theory, unity was desirable, the greater the better, for history and philosophy taught that in this way cities grew strong so that they were able to subdue their neighbors, while disunity led to weakness and tyranny. Those trained in the current Aristotelian philosophy knew that concord was the result of unity of will among the citizens, which meant that they must place the common good, or the good of the commune, above sectional or individual interests. The less sophisticated chroniclers of the thirteenth century expressed the same kind of thinking when they said or implied that communes should be ruled and men should act *communaliter* and not *per partem*. The most common means advocated for bringing about this concord of wills was rhetoric. This art, which had held a place of high esteem in antiquity, had recovered much of its old prominence with the revival of urban life in Italy. For example, about a quarter of Brunetto Latini's popular encyclopedia is devoted to rhetoric, and about a third of this is, in effect, a treatise on the government of cities.[70] This belongs to

[68] G. Villani, XI, chap. 138; M. Villani, IV, chap. 2.

[69] *Ibid.*, VIII, chap. 24.

[70] *Li Livres dou Tresor*, ed. F. J. Carmody (Berkeley, 1948), pp. 317, 422.

the genre of *podestà* literature, designed to give thirteenth- and fourteenth-century officials a comprehensive guide to their duties.[71] The earliest example, the *Oculus Pastoralis*, belonging to the first half of the thirteenth century, is overwhelmingly rhetorical in content, giving specimen speeches for all kinds of occasion, and this rhetorical basis is still evident in the later treatises of this type. The power of rhetoric can be seen in action in the various peace movements, generally led by friars, which swept Italy from the time of Frederick II onward. Despite their failure to produce lasting results, faith in rhetoric does not seem to have abated during the fourteenth century; indeed, the most accomplished picture of a politician whose strength rested mainly on the power of his oratory is to be found in the contemporary life of Cola di Rienzo, the ill-fated tribune of Rome.[72] Writers, whose professional pride was at stake, were naturally reluctant to admit that the evidence was against rhetoric as the moving power in human affairs; thus Matteo Villani argues from ancient and biblical history that a leader with eloquence and a moderate force will be superior to one with a stronger military force but without eloquence.[73]

Although most of the arguments in favor of civic unity were extremely simple and obvious, there are some which are sufficiently interesting to mention. The deepening interest in Roman history at this period was roused not only by the great power of the Romans but also by the heroic examples of subordination of self-interest to that of the commonwealth which were held to be the foundation of the Empire and its moral justification.[74] More recent history, too, could be used to teach the lessons of unity. As we have seen, a thirteenth-century

[71] See A. Sorbelli, "I teorici del reggimento comunale," *Bollettino dell'Istituto Storico Italiano*, Vol. LIX (1944) pp. 31–136.

[72] Most recently edited by A. Frugoni (Florence, 1957).

[73] *Cronica*, VIII, chap. 1.

[74] E.g., Ptolemy of Lucca, *De Regimine Principum*, pp. 41–44; Dante, *De Monarchia*, II, 5–6.

Piacentine seems to have elaborated on an event of the earliest days of the commune in order to preach peace between classes to his contemporaries.[75] Rolandino, the Paduan chronicler, suppressed the conflicts between the nobility and the *popolo* and stressed the common sufferings of all classes under Ezzelino da Romano for much the same reason.[76] Marchionne Stefani improves on Villani's idealization of the Primo Popolo, stressing that it was a time when public good was placed before private, when the nobles shared in public offices and were loyal to the commune and the *parte*, and when justice was severe but unbiased.[77] Social solidarity is also one of the lessons of Giacomo da Cessolis's allegory on the game of chess which belongs to the early fourteenth century; the nobility, represented by the pieces, and the *popolani*, represented by the pawns, belong to different castes, but are bound together by common interests and must support each other.[78] But perhaps the most extreme arguments possible in favor of peace and the common good were put forward by Remigio Girolami. Deeply imbued with the new Aristotelianism which he had learned at Paris, Remigio applied the doctrine of the relationship between the whole and the part to the commune and the individual citizen virtually without qualification. Thus the citizen detached from his city is like an amputated hand, lacking *virtus* and *operatio*, for the good of a part, insofar as it is a part, is stronger and more natural than the good of the part as a thing in itself. The citizen must therefore sacrifice his time, property and, if need be, his life to the *civitas*, and love it second only to God, because of the

[75] Above, p. 000.

[76] *Cronica, RIS, VIII*, i, pp. 33–34, 118; the assumption of feudal jurisdictions by the Paduan commune which occurred during the period covered by his chonicle is not mentioned by Rolandino.

[77] Stefani, *Cronica Fiorentina*, pp. 42–45; cf. G. Villani, VI, chap. 69.

[78] *Liber de Moribus Hominum et Officiis Nobilium*, ed. E. Köpke, Mittheilungen aus den Handschriften der Ritter-Akademie zu Brandenburg II (Brandenburg, 1879).

similarity that it bears to God; the friar does not even hold back from the treacherous argument that the citizen must love his city more than his own salvation.[79]

These arguments of Remigio's have been described as extremely dangerous,[80] and so they would have been if there had been any danger that anyone's actions would be influenced by them. But in the context of his time, they must be regarded as entirely ineffective. By their origins, associations, and daily practice the communes proclaimed themselves to be not given, godlike, absolute entities to be served and accepted unconditionally, but human contrivances subject to ceaseless change, formed to promote the good of the individual citizens. True, it seems that the first formation of the communes at the time of the Investiture Contest had been forgotten by the thirteenth century, but the re-forming of city government and the absorption of the communes by the various *societates populi* was well recorded, and revolutions resulting in new institutions and regimes continued to occur from time to time, though they became less frequent after about 1340. The commune was a kind of *societas*, imposing important but not unique claims on its members. Though it could be argued that loyalty to family, neighborhood, guild and social group should have been subordinate to the commune that embraced them all, it was hard to deny that parties, intercity leagues, the church and the empire were superior to the commune because they were greater still. The Aristotelian belief in the absolute value of the polis, though sometimes repeated, was not really believed; even Remigio admitted that the Christian's highest allegiance was to the universal church. In practice, it is clear that party loyalty often overrode civic patriotism, as can be seen in the behavior of innumerable groups of exiles. The strength of family ties

---

[79] "De bono communi," partially published by R. Egenter in *Scholastik*, IX (1934) 79–92; see Davis, "An Early Florentine Political Theorist," pp. 668–670.

[80] *Ibid.*, p. 671.

emerges from the Tuscan *ricordi* and *ricordanze;* Donato Velluti's attitude to the commune, for example, seems strictly utilitarian; he values it for what it can give to him and his family in terms of security, employment and honor.[81] Hence a widespread ambivalence toward measures intended to strengthen the coercive powers of the government which showed itself not only in Giovanni Villani's unjustified suspicions of the Florentine police officials,[82] but also in much legislation that tried to make the execution of the law impartial by making it automatic, removing the *arbitrium* of the officials. Compagni records what must have been a common dilemma, when he describes how as *gonfaloniere* he was compelled to act, although his better judgment told him his action would encourage further violence.[83]

The communes do not seem to have evolved adequate symbols to focus the loyalty of the less educated and the masses. It is true that there were various civic ceremonies, commemorative races and the like, and that in the thirteenth century the *carroccio* round which the communal militia rallied in battle seems to have attracted genuine veneration. From the mid-thirteenth century there was a growing mass of civic buildings and some works of art designed to inspire civic patriotism. Yet, as the Lorenzetti frescoes in the Sala dei Nove in Siena prove, it was hard to convey republican ideals without recourse to elaborate personifications which could easily be misunderstood; ignorant observers must often have regarded the figure of the Common Good simply as a prince.[84] In a world where loyalties were mainly personal, the communes offered only the figures of the

[81] *Cronica Domestica*, ed. I. del Lungo and G. Volpi (Florence, 1914), p. 190.

[82] *Cronica*, XI, chaps. 16, 118; M. B. Becker, *Florence in Transition* (Baltimore and London, 1967), I, 135–138.

[83] *Cronica*, pp. 36–37.

[84] N. Rubinstein, "Political Ideas in Siennese Art; the Frescoes by Ambrogio Lorenzetti and Taddeo di Bartolo in the Palazzo Pubblico." *Journal of the Warburg and Courtauld Institutes*, XXI (1958), 179–207.

podestà and the *capitano,* and these were increasingly subject to the surveillance of the law whose guardians were committees whose membership was ever changing. The continued attraction exercised by imperialist ideas and imperial claimants, despite their obvious failure to provide any lasting solution to political problems, and the lasting popularity of heroic literature suggest a desire for a political superman which the republican communes could not even begin to satisfy. Given this mental climate, it is easy to understand the rapid spread of the *signoria.* The advantages offered by the concentration of power on a single family or individual were obvious and immediate; the arguments against despotism or tyranny were moral and rhetorical and tend to be voiced just after an effective signoria had been set up. The cities which generated a strong and deep-rooted antipathy to tyranny seem to have been those which had lost their liberty for a time and then regained it. For example, the experience of Ezzelino da Romano in Padua and Walter of Brienne in Florence appears to have acted as a kind of innoculation against tyranny, creating a strong antibody of opinion which seems to have been largely lacking elsewhere.

Even the greatest minds of the early fourteenth century failed to face up squarely to the question of the *signoria.* Of course Dante denounced tyrants in general terms, but he offers no real safeguards to prevent the monarch whom he put forward as the solution of Italy's political ills from acting in a tyrannical manner. His argument that their subordination of the individual to the good of the commonwealth ordained to rule by God gave the Romans the right as well as the means to subject all peoples is just as alarming in its implications as any of Remigio's.[85] And in practice, Dante welcomed the patronage of *signori* whose right to rule was not, to say the least, incontrovertibly based on justice. For Dante was more interested in the use that was made of power than in how it was

[85] *De Monarchia,* II, 3–13.

established; the only real check on his monarch is imposed by his conscience and character. Dante would have his readers believe that the monarch will act well because his personal interests coincide exactly with those of his state, and he will be free from *cupiditas* because he already possesses everything. Marsiglio of Padua's solution to the problem of the self-interest of the sovereign power is radically different. He was more interested in the way in which law was made than in its content; for him, the only source of law is the legislator made up of the whole body of the citizens or the *pars valentior* which effectively represents the whole body.[86] It is true that he insists on the traditional view that the law must be of general application and it must be just, so that he has reservations about barbaric law which allows the payment of compensation for serious crimes.[87] But in the last resort, the will of the legislator is law, whether it is just or not, and the only safeguard is that the legislator will not act against the interests of the *pars valentior* "since no one knowingly hurts himself or wills injustice." [88] It is the representative character of the legislator which ensures that its interests coincide with those of the whole citizen body, or of its weightier part; other checks and balances are therefore unnecessary, and Marsiglio is free to attack the jurisdiction of the church and of the numerous *collegia* of all kinds which in practice so diffused the sovereignity of the communes of his day. Consent and representation are of the essence of the Marsilian state, and the *pars principans* is supposed to be no more than the servant of the law and the legislative assembly. Yet, inconsistently, Marsiglio describes the *principans* as the *prior* and *noblior* part of the state, the equivalent to the heart in the body of an embryonic animal, imbued with the power to institute the other parts,[89] and it is this more exalted view of the civil government which predominates in the second part of his book where its claims are vindicated against those of the church.

[86] *Defensor Pacis*, ed. Scholz, pp. 62 ff.
[87] *Ibid.*, pp. 50–51.
[88] *Ibid.*, pp. 68–69.
[89] *Ibid.*, pp. 88–91.

In his political life, Marsiglio had, for whatever reason, already served the Della Scala and the Visconti who were aligned against his own native city; moreover, in dedicating the *Defensor* to Lewis of Bavaria and in supporting him on his Italian expedition, Marsiglio was promoting a political structure in which consent and representation of the mass of the citizens had never been seriously attempted and indeed would have been totally impracticable. So Marsiglio, who is the strongest and most profound defender of the commune and its ideals, was also driven to choose between just and effective government, and in practice preferred the latter. The price of civil discord was the *signoria*.

XI

VIOLENCE, DISORDER, AND ORDER
IN THIRTEENTH-CENTURY ROME

Robert Brentano

*L*IKE MANY of us, I have recently suffered peculiar changes in my perception of violence. I clearly remember sitting in the Piazza Paganica last summer and reading this fourteenth-century Roman statute: "We order that no man ought to shoot a bow and arrow or throw stones in places where there are glass windows, like Santa Maria Aracoeli on the Capitol or other churches. Violators will be fined one hundred soldi. . . ."[1] I then thought, and later thought again, at the Aracoeli on the Capitol, what a really violent place Rome must have been in the fourteenth century. I indulged myself in the didactic musing in which historians indulge themselves and thought platitudinously of the necessity of remembering the distance of the past—how far from my sort of civilization and how constantly disturbed must have been a place where this sort of thing had to be forbidden.

When I thought of the same statute this spring it seemed to me almost friendly and familiar. It suggested not only little distance, but little real disturbance of the texture of the fourteenth-century Roman community. In this learning year I have also become much more aware than I was previously of three other things: the ease of violence, its quick and simple arrival; its use as a tool; and its petty but terrible and insistent

---

[1] Camillo Re, *Statuti della città di Roma* (Rome, 1880), p. 172.

degradation of the people involved in it. This new awareness has, obviously, a lot to do with my current interpretation of the nature of violence in thirteenth-century Rome. My pattern is pretty clearly connected with my more general attitudes toward violence and society; but the sparsity of my evidence, its fragmentary quality, has itself to do with the very peculiar survival, and lack of survival, of Roman records. Although the evidence is much richer and more complex than a short paper will suggest, it is very poor in comparison with that for cities like Siena and Florence.[2] The available thirteenth-century records do not come from anything resembling official files; they are difficult sources, mostly scattered, or assembled in the collections of suppressed convents. There are also problems, for anyone who uses them, connected with their current custody, and that of their fourteenth-century successors, which it would be unwise for me to describe here.

I approach the problem of violence in thirteenth-century Rome through two texts which should be kept in mind throughout this paper. The first is a passage from Ferdinand Gregorovius, and the second is a 1235 senatorial edict of Senator Angelo Malabranca. Since my point in using Gregorovius is essentially to disagree with him, or his tone, to show that here he is unreal and Malabranca's edict is real, I should like first to recall him to you as an historian. As I have worked on Rome I have, in an

---

[2] I have in mind the sort of evidence available for William M. Bowsky, "The Medieval Commune and Internal Violence: Police Power and Public Safety in Siena, 1287–1335," *American Historical Review*, LXXIII (1967), 1–7. The evidence for my paper actually comes from that collected for my forthcoming book, *Papal Rome (Innocent III to Boniface VIII)*, in which supporting material is much more heavily cited; I have not been particularly fastidious in avoiding the use of the same adjectives and phrases in paper and book. For a general survey of Roman history, beyond that available in the sources specifically cited below, one can turn to the pertinent volumes of the Istituto di studi Romani's *Storia di Roma*: vols. X, XI, and the medieval part of Vol. XXII, by, respectively, Paolo Brezzi, Eugenio Duprè Theseider, and Carlo Cecchelli (Bologna, 1947, 1952, 1958).

unsurprising way, come to respect some of my very eminent, particularly French, predecessors, less and less; and, in general, I cannot pretend to have been much stimulated by the major histories of medieval Rome. The big exception is the, I think, foolishly disregarded Gregorovius. He seems to me an historian of stature, and his history, in its way, a good way, a great history, but one almost calculated to be underestimated by his scholarly contemporaries and immediate successors. Gregorovius is always alive, sensory, passionate, and evocative. He entered Rome (we know because he recorded it) on October 2, 1852, at 4 o'clock in the afternoon, by the Porta del Popolo. He began his history in 1855 and finished it in 1871.[3] (The historian whom he echoes is obvious.) Gregorovius wrote of Rome's fall to papal power, its desolation. "Rome resembled a huge field, encircled with moss-covered walls, . . . from which rose gloomy towers or castles, basilicas and convents crumbling to decay, . . . broken aqueducts . . . while a labyrinth of narrow streets, interrupted by rubbish heaps, led among these dilapidated remains," and all the while, "the yellow Tiber, passing under broken stone bridges, flowed sadly through the ruinous waste." But Gregorovius also saw the "solemn golden splendour" of Santa Maria Maggiore.[4]

The passage of Gregorovius that I should like you to keep in mind is this description of thirteenth-century Rome and its noble families (in Annie Hamilton's translation):

Everywhere that the eye rested might be seen gloomy, defiant, battlemented towers, built out of the monuments of the ancients, with crenelated enceintes of most original form, constructed of pieces of marble, bricks and fragments of peperino. These were the castles and palaces of Guelf and Ghibelline nobles, who sat thirsting for battle in ruins on the classic

[3] *The Roman Journals of Ferdinand Gregorovius, 1852-1874*, ed. Friedrich Althaus, trans. Annie Hamilton (London, 1907), p. 2.

[4] Ferdinand Gregorovius, *History of the City of Rome*, trans. Annie Hamilton (London, 1894-1902), V, 658-659, 655.

hills, as though Rome were not a city but an open territory, the possession of which was to be disputed in daily warfare. There was not a single nobleman in Rome at the time who was not owner of a tower. . . . Families dwelt among ruins, in uncomfortable quarters, barred by heavy iron chains, with their relatives and retainers, and only now and then burst forth with the wild din of arms, to make war on their hereditary enemies.[5]

(It was while looking at towers, Gregorovius at least later said, that he had formed the idea of writing his history, looking at Trastevere from the Ponte Cestio—this man who grew up an historian, he seems to have thought, because he grew up in the romance of a Teutonic castle on the Polish border.) [6]

The second text is from September 15, 1235.[7] Senator Angelo Malabranca, in the course of reestablishing concord with the pope, Gregory IX, and assuring protection to religious corporations and pilgrims, described and forbade certain Roman activities: "We understand that some, in fact quite a few, of the inhabitants of the area around the basilica of Saint Peter's have, with actual violence, forced pilgrims and Rome-seekers to lodge in their houses." Even more detestably, after pilgrims had already lodged themselves in other people's hospices and were quietly settled, the edict continues, these violent keepers of Vatican *pensioni* burst in upon the poor pilgrims and dragged them off, all unwilling, to their own places, and forced them to stay there. Malabranca as senator decreed that in future this should not occur, that all pilgrims and Rome-seekers should in future lodge where they would and buy only what they wanted and what seemed necessary to themselves.

[5] *Ibid.*, pp. 659–660; cf. *Geschichte der Stadt Rom*, ed. Waldemar Kampf (Basel, 1954), II, 574. Kampf's edition of Gregorovius includes a very useful bibliography.

[6] Gregorovius, *History*, V, 660n; VIII, 705.

[7] *Codice diplomatico del Senato Romano*, ed. Franco Bartoloni, Fonti per la storia d'Italia (Rome, 1948), pp. 143–145.

With these two texts kept before us (one on the romantically unregulated nobility, the other on the commercially regulated tourist trade), I should like to describe, very briefly, thirteenth-century Rome. It is not very well known. Thirteenth-century Rome was a walled city built around the bend of the Tiber and the island. The Aurelian and Leonine walls enclosed an area of well over 3,000 acres. This area was very unevenly populated. The major part of it was very lightly populated, divided into small farms and even papal and monastic vineyards, in which there were simple houses, lean-tos, and dugouts. There were also occasional monasteries, towers and fortresses, and, of course, ruins. This rustic Rome is particularly well preserved in the records of the monastery of San Silvestro in Capite which had extensive possessions between the Trivio or Trevi and the Porta del Popolo; but it is also caught in the records of San Cosimato in Trastevere.[8] The heavily populated part of Rome lay on the east side of the river between the bridge to Sant'Angelo and the bridge to the island. It touched parts of Trastevere, perhaps, and the Vatican, and, to the east, the Trivio and the Suburra. But for the most part it lay in the horn between the southwestern side of the Corso (then the Via Lata) and the river. It is recalled in the crusty underhive of that part of Rome and in Ferreto de' Ferreti's description of the loud, mourning news of Boniface VIII's death "rushing through the alleys and down the blind streets and making the whole place echo."[9] Although the populated city did not at all fill the walls, it burst outside them. Suburban populated areas streamed out of all the gates.

[8] Both fonds are in the Archivio di stato at Rome; see, too, V. Federici, "Regesto del Monastero di San Silvestro in Capite," *Archivio della società romana di storia patria*, XXII (1899), 213–300, 498–538; XXIII (1900), 67–128, 411–447.

[9] *Le opere di Ferreto de' Ferreti Vicentini*, ed. Carlo Cipolla, Fonti per la storia d'Italia (Rome, 1908–1920), I, 164.

About the Romans living inside the city there is abundant evidence of certain sorts. Romans lived with their mothers-in-law: that is, extended families of various generations lived together in one house, or half-house, although the family, as a group, might in fact hold various other properties in other parts of Rome or in the suburbs. Romans paid their rents to landlords, or received their rents as landlords, in both money and produce, and particularly in wine. It is clear that their tenements could be sublet with the permission of the landlord and his retention of his right to ground-rent, but that in the actual area of Rome there was seldom a ladder of more than two proprietors and often there was only one. The simplicity of Rome's vertical tenure is in contrast with the complexity of its horizontal tenure, of reversions, usufructs, and particularly joint holdings.

Romans lived in neighborhoods, although the *rioni* are pale things. Some of the neighborhoods were those of specific crafts and arts and trades: the cloth merchants around San Marco, the fishmongers around Sant'Angelo in Pescheria, the butchers in the Forum of Nerva (by Noah's Ark), the tanners and leatherworkers near the bridge to Sant'Angelo (the Scortecchiaria), the chalkers of the Calcarario (at the Argentina), the sailors of the Ripa. Remaining Roman streets tell (not always in the right place) of ropemakers, keymakers, and the rest. But, although trade, and perhaps class, concentrations existed, the evidence generally pushes heavily in the other direction. The holdings and interests of individual, even minor, families spread over the face of Rome. Boundary descriptions show a constant mixture of classes and occupations, as does also the relatively detailed description, from 1331, of a palazzo of the Ponte family —a grand palazzo and house (near the Ponte's name bridge, to Sant'Angelo) colonnaded, with a garden and close, and solars and upper rooms for the Ponte themselves, but also attached

shops and domiciles for a scribe, the widow of a barber, a sad-
dler, a pruner, a goldsmith.[10] The Ponte women and the barber's
widow lived together by the yellow Tiber and clearly predicted
the palazzi of modern Rome, the Borghese or the Costaguti. In
this mixed city a professional caste of clerics, lawyers, notaries,
and physicians formed a clear nucleus or ballast or backbone of
responsibility.

Although thirteenth-century Rome is very visible, it is not
possible to say how many people lived there. (I believe that a
serious estimate would require almost impossible archaeology,
but in any case, insofar as I know, no serious estimate has been
made.) The traditional guess is 35,000 inhabitants for the pon-
tificate of Innocent III. That guess is based on mysterious evidence and has been tolerated because it does not seem obviously,
wildly wrong. Admitting its fragility, and the absurdity of
medieval counting, cast it against the contemporary estimate
that there were 200,000 pilgrims in Rome at one time during
the Jubilee of 1300—200,000 transient pilgrims, crushing one
another, literally, as the dying former prior of Saint Bee's could
testify. Admit all fallacy (and perhaps replace in your mind the
familiar image of the monks of Saint Paul's raking in the coin
of the pilgrims), and the essence of Rome will still be clear to
you.[11] It was a city dependent upon and swamped by transients
(and witness lists make clear the mobile nature even of the permanent population).

Thirteenth-century Rome, oddly enough, has no easily identifiable ruler or clearly observable governmental structure, although it had a militia, walls, and money. Technically it was
ruled by senators, by a senate.[12] But the most glaring aspect of

[10] Rieti, Archivio capitolare, III. D.1 (and less important III.D.2, 3).

[11] Giovanni Villani, *RIS*, XIII (Milan, 1728), col. 367; *The Chronicle
of St. Mary's Abbey, York*, ed. H. H. E. Craster and M. E. Thornton,
Surtees Society (Durham, 1934), pp. 31, 132, 30; Ventura, *RIS.*, XI
(Milan, 1727), col. 192.

[12] The best introduction specifically to the senate is Bartoloni's *Codice*

senatorial history in the thirteenth century (even admitting the significant change to a form of controlling signory in about 1252) is that this principal governmental organ, the senate, was a shapeless, formless, variable thing. It responded to local and foreign popes, to popular uprisings, to Hohenstaufen and Angevin emperors and kings, and, repeatedly, to the tough, propertied noble families of Rome. When the senate is seen as having a classic form, at all, or fixed number (because its actual number varied from one to fifty-six), it is the form of a pair of ruling nobles—for example, an Orsini and an Annibaldi. This is a way of saying that in a weakly guilded, slackly institutionalized city, the senate and local government in general were unobstructive and flexible and responsive. That was their genius.

The clearest evidence about keeping the peace in thirteenth-century Rome comes from a letter written by Charles of Salerno (acting as his father's representative) to the Angevin Roman chamberlain in 1283.[18] Charles wrote that the chamberlain, the vicar, and the marshal (the crucial official in these affairs) should decide if thirty mounted police guards were sufficient in keeping the city, and that if they were not, the officials might raise the number to fifty. This police guard (military-political) was an extension of the central Capitoline force of judges, notaries (six criminal, three civil), guards, mandatories, and locally based justiciars or executors. It was also an extension of the army. Charles's provisions point up the paradoxical Angevin position in Rome. The Angevins supported, for example, a diversified judicial establishment in Rome, but a number of the judges, like their notaries, were from the kingdom of Sicily.

---

diplomatico (see n. 7); it should be supplemented with Bartoloni's *Per la storia del senato romano nei secoli XII e XIII* (Rome, 1946) (extract from *Bullettino dell'Istituto storico italiano per il medio evo*, LX (1946), 1–108; and Pietro Gasparrini, *Senatori romani della prima metà del XIII secolo finora ignorati* (Rome, 1938).

[13] A. de Boüard, *Le régime politique et les institutions de Rome au Moyen Age, 1251–1347* (Paris, 1920), pp. 290–293.

Charles had troops who could keep order in Rome, and he had external sources of revenue which could pay them. Nothing is more helpful in understanding Charles's success in governing the city than this. He need not rely on a scrappy Roman budget —so he could, for instance, more readily repulse bribes. Again this paradoxical order of repression is connected with the political structure of Rome. The repulsive Charles was, in a way, attractive, because he was neither Annibaldi nor Orsini. His domination did not, for the moment on the surface, make faction so nervous; but his was not, in the normal Roman sense, a responsive government.

The community with which this government had to deal was a violent city. There were very various kinds of violence in thirteenth-century Rome—they move around the definition of violence's edge. It is obviously important to maintain the distinction between political physical violence (and perhaps particularly the violence of revolt) and other violence; it is also important to see it as not cleanly separate from other violence.[14] It is seen distortedly if it is not viewed in its nest of various strands of violence. There was, for example, the flaming violence of the family Colonna, their brilliant violence of eccentricity. There was not only Sciarra at Anagni in 1303, Margherita on Monte

---

[14] I have become very much aware of the problems involved in distinguishing between kinds of violence this year. A friend, who is a pacifist but who supported groups who openly used violent methods this year, recently said that for him the raised voice was violent, that beyond that level he could not make nice distinctions in condemning combatants for their techniques. I strongly disagree, although I understand. It seems to me that there is an important difference, for example, between violence that could reasonably be expected to threaten human life and violence that could not, between physical violence that causes personal injury and that which does not, and also between violence inflicted by authorities upon those subject to them and the violence of individuals. It would thus prove particularly distressing to me if this part of my paper were interpreted to mean that I think all violence is the same and equally noxious; I do think that all violence is related and (excepting only spiritual violence and the violence of the arts) noxious.

Preneste, there was also a mid-fourteenth-century Colonna woman (another Margherita) driven to religious enthusiasms at the elevation during Mass at San Trifone, driven to a realization of Christ and to heavy religious bequests.[15] There was (in the fourteenth century) the family's opposition to Cola, its inspiration of Petrarch. There was Cardinal Giacomo Colonna, the brother of the Blessed Margherita and of the (supposedly) hagiography-writing Senator Giovanni—all grandchildren of Matteo Rosso Orsini. Giacomo is the Colonna cardinal who, with the Colonna pet pope, Nicholas IV, is portrayed in Maria Maggiore's brilliant apse mosaic. This man, when he was young and studying law at Bologna, can be watched one July (20) afternoon, after he had eaten lunch with the Franciscans, sitting at siesta time in the garden—in the July Bologna heat.[16] He was reading the *legenda* of Saint Margaret of Antioch, whose feast it *then* was, and had come to the passage: "Come, virgin Margaret, to the peace of your Christ." Things changed, as if Giacomo were at a play. He saw a vision of his sister between angels. He watched it for a while, and then it moved. And Giacomo ran after it, through the house and into the piazza. Colonna violence was the violence of a family of visionaries.

Rome writhed, notoriously, with various spasmodic violences, with fever, with poison. And there was slack, shoddy violence. It is the kind that shows up when one reads the 1306 record of the two senators appointing a doorkeeper for the Capitol—a Roman citizen, Paolo de Negri, appointed for life.[17] The senators explained the conditions that made a new doorkeeper necessary. Even in the lifetime of the recently deceased keeper of the second door, there had been terrible deficiencies in the keeping of it, and the third door, through which one

[15] Rome, Archivio di stato, Santo Spirito in Sassia, B, 131.

[16] Livario Oliger, "B. Margharita Colonna," *Lateranum*, I (2) (1935), 115; Oliger and the lives he edits are the best introduction to this generation of Colonna.

[17] Boüard, *op. cit.*, pp. 298–299.

gained access to the great hall of the Capitoline palace. It was notorious. Everyone who came to the Capitoline courts knew and talked of the shameful, chaotic disorder there. This Capitoline confusion was a sort of high, institutional parallel to the disorder, the negative violence, of the garbage in the streets—of the stinking vacant lot on the pilgrims' path from Rome to Saint Peter's which the Masters of the Buildings investigated in 1306.[18] (They found the stone markers of Santo Spirito in Sassia.) The foulness of the dunged and garbaged air was thought to endanger the inmates of the hospital of Santo Spirito across the street.

There was also, in Rome, the terrible violence of tyranny. The most famous story is that of the "Guelf" tyrant Matteo Rosso Orsini in the vacancy after Gregory IX's death.[19] He locked up the cardinals in the Septizonium, a sordid and horrid imprisonment: the body of the English cardinal, Robert of Somercote, had not been properly disposed of, as other cardinals lay dying; and guards stood over the cardinals' cubicles and showered them with urine. But there is also Brancaleone's "liberal" violence, his hammering of the Roman nobles, his destruction of the (perhaps) one hundred and forty towers, and his hanging the Annibaldi. These, although acts taken against sources of violence, were violent in their repressiveness.

There was, and perhaps necessarily, violence in changing governments. This was violence encouraged if not required by the institutional weakness of Roman government, the frailty of council and electors—as when in 1237 the "people" (*Romani plebei populum*) overthrew Giovanni Poli and replaced him

---

[18] L. Schiaparelli, "Alcuni documenti dei *magistri aedificiorum urbis* (secoli XIII e XIV)," *Archivio della società romana di storia patria,* XXV (1902), 50–53.

[19] K. Hampe, "Ein ungedruckter Bericht über das Konclave von 1241 im römischen Septizonium," *Sitzungsberichte der Heidelberger Akademie der Wissenschaften,* Philosophisch-historische Klasse, IV (1913), 3–34.

with Giovanni Cenci.[20] This is the other face of flexibility; there were no institutions for making proper governmental change.

Of course there was murder. Oddone di Giovanni Benencasa (or Benecasa) killed a man named Bartolomeo di Benedetto di Bartolomeo sometime before November 1232.[21] We know it because of the sale, or resale, of the murderer's confiscated Tivoli properties. The Orsini consul of Tivoli sold his, the consul's, quarter for sixty lire to four men including at least one Benencasa. In October the aristocratic senator Giovanni Poli had sold his quarter. But in December the murderer himself reappeared. A Roman citizen restored to him and his heirs all that Oddone had given him and also the slashed act of donation. Obviously Oddone had not only avoided execution, but he had evaded total confiscation, in a way that we all know to be rather characteristic (even though, as in the fourteenth-century statutes, opposed). In this murder, punishment, and evasion, it is hard (but possible) to isolate the element that is most clearly violent.

Quite apparently, again, thirteenth-century Rome was a violent society. Roman violence is echoed in that difficult source, the earliest collection of statutes for the city of Rome, a collection composed, probably, in the 1360s and 1370s, but incorporating not only customary procedures but earlier datable enactments. Petty violence, as well as grand, is attacked in the Roman statutes—in, I should think, recognizable and repeated patterns, that is, recognizable to students of other cities and repeated from statutes of other cities. For making a fig at someone the

[20] Louis Halphen, *Études sur l'administration de Rome au Moyen Age* (Paris, 1907), p. 173; Boüard, *op. cit.*, p. 70—the phrase is from Riccardo of San Germano.

[21] For the *pergamene* connected with the Benencase, see Rome, Archivio di stato, San Cosimato, 208, 231, 232, 233, 243, 301, 307; for a similar sort of evasion, in a case of heresy, see Rieti, Archivio capitolare, III.D.10.

fine was twenty soldi—the same for insults. For forcing filth or dung or anything shameful into anyone's mouth it was twenty-five lire, for tearing the clothes off a woman's back, one hundred lire (half to the communal *camera*, half to the woman). It was the same amount for throwing anyone in a well. The city of the statutes was one in which pigs were forbidden to roam and rewards were given for catching wolves (that is, in which the four-footed joined the two-footed in confounding public order). It was a city in which ordinances controlling the sale of meat and the closing of taverns at night and of mills on the feasts of the Virgin were accompanied by ordinances against throwing garbage in the streets (an ordinance not yet effective in Rome and in this like another of the statutes, one regulating divorceless concubinage) and against washing filthy things in the Trevi.

Emerging from the opposition to this melange of petty disorder and violence (of permitted chess and forbidden dice) is the opposition to more serious crimes and those more directly connected with civil disorder. These range from pulling hair, breaking teeth, hands on knives, pushing people off animals, to the bootless and torturable crimes of murder, arson, incest, sodomy, rape or kidnapping of a child, on the one hand, and, on the other, to vine cutting, fortress building, throwing stones from towers, keeping private prisons—usurping the rights of government, provoking civil disorder or undermining order through false money, false witness, false notarization, blasphemy, or "abominable to God and man" shedding one's own family's blood. Much is primitive, and sounds to the English historian like Saxon dooms with tariffs and private prosecution —there was even the counting of armed men at night to make twelve or more a more seriously criminal band. Still, the last regulation, like the painful and elaborate definition of homicides and the worrying with age and class, shows a community troubled by disorder and trying to cope with it. It tried to quell

violence through fines, mutilation (cutting off of members—
hands, ears, feet), another kind of violence, and hanging.[22]

For the Romans' need for violence there were various types
of official, innocuous relief, in a way violent themselves. There
were processions, that of the Veronica, for example, or the
elaborate 1215 Martinmas procession to Santa Maria in Trastevere, with songs and lanterns, or the coronation.[23] More obviously there were the games—the test and requirement of office-
holding nobility, but also release—with animal procession and
slaughter (in the pre-Lenten Testaccio games) and the revealing stich:

> They kill a bear. The devil is killed, the tempter of our flesh.
> Bullocks are killed. The pride of our pleasure is killed. A cock
> is killed. The heat of our loins is killed, so that we may live
> chaste and sober in suffering of spirit, that we may be worthy
> to receive the Body of Christ on Easter day.[24]

It is natural (especially for readers of Professors Little,
Herlihy, and Bowsky) to believe that the anonymity of the
Italian city, particularly aggravated by the transient population
and tourist-hungry industry of Rome, encouraged violence,
and so its necessary release—a circular movement—in the intensity of local relic cults and the enthusiasm of the new orders,
in the violence of association, of connection with party, of
action in the piazza.[25] The search for identity, community, and

[22] Re, *Statuti,* particularly, pp. 72, 73, 92, 93, 95, 101, 103–105, 111–115, 117, 121, 124, 125, 140–142, 146–147, 163, 170, 173–174, 179, 183.

[23] For 1215, see Stephan Kuttner and Antonio García y García, "An Eyewitness Account of the Fourth Lateran Council," *Traditio,* XX (1964), 125, 143–146.

[24] Re, *Statuti,* pp. 241–242.

[25] I refer to a very stimulating paper given by Professor Lester Little at the conference of the Medieval Association of the Pacific at River-side, Calif., in 1969; I had in mind particularly Professors Herlihy's and Bowsky's references to poor crowds (*Medieval and Renaissance Pistoia* [New Haven, Conn., 1967], p. 114, and "The Impact of the Black Death upon Sienese Government and Society," *Speculum,* XXXIX [1964], 7).

association may have been particularly intense in Rome, although in some ways particularly superficial—with almost a Las Vegas air. This search for meaning, memory, recognition, in the anonymous city, probably explains in part the delight with which thirteenth-century men talked of the evil of Rome. Evil is in its way warm and recognizable. But although much of Rome's surface agitation had peculiar causes, some causes were universal, connected with property, the kind of property that men held everywhere. As one watches a case, for example, in which a widow painfully attempts to reclaim dower lands, before the judges of succeeding administrations in the 1250s, one understands the provocation to violence—although one also sees continuity of government.[26]

There were in Rome, in this atmosphere of violence, great repeated periods of political violence and riot, violence of the sort most usually approached by historians—even though this was not Arnold's or Cola's century (nor that of the Cenci and Santa Croce). There were various kinds of rebellion and aggression. One could suggest them with a massive pile of "historical" dates: 1202–1205; 1225–1226; 1228; 1231 (the attack on heretics); 1231–1232; 1234–1235 (the Roman effort to control Rome's utilities like the mint and ovens); 1241; 1255–1257; 1261; 1265 (Charles of Anjou in and out of the Lateran); 1267; 1284; 1303—and many more. For these periods of political disorder to be understood at all, one must be looked at in some detail, its texture realized.

In 1201 Innocent III wrote of Rome, "by the grace of God we hold it in our power." [27] He spoke of a commune (the gift of Constantine, as Gregory IX's biographer put it) essentially regulated by the loose and porous truce of 1188, the basis of

[26] Bartoloni, *Codice diplomatico*, pp. 192–199.
[27] Daniel Waley, *The Papal State in the Thirteenth Century* (London, 1961), p. 39.

later papal communal relations.[28] Innocent's papacy began like most papacies, with the favored relatives of the late pope (in Innocent's case the Boboni-Orsini) as its enemies. Again like most papacies it brought with it the new pope's own greedy relatives (in Innocent's case particularly his brother Riccardo Conti). Present to stir up trouble and to oppose Innocent's control of the city were two demagogues, former senators with famous family names, one of a rising and one of a falling family (both dangerous conditions), Giovanni Capocci and Giovanni Pierleoni. They were doubly dangerous men because they could strengthen family faction with a temporarily roused mob. Through these years Rome was agitated and made active by the wars with Viterbo, in which almost any papal action could be used to provoke popular Roman reaction; the popes could be made to seem insufficiently Roman. (Gregorovius wrote, "Viterbo was the Veii of the Middle Ages to the Romans; they hated the town with a hatred bordering on frenzy.")[29]

Rome exploded in 1202. The explosion burst in various directions, with various centers, at various levels.[30] It brought both civil war and constitutional crisis (although both these phrases seem too pompous and pretentious to be applied to thirteenth-century Roman disorders). They brought a tower war. The image of the tower dominates the narrative, most tantalizingly in Pandulfo of the Suburra's tower called the "bean" and most significantly in Riccardo Conti's Tor de' Conti, which was the dominant, hated (ill gotten, it was said, from

[28] "Vita Gregorii IX," *Le Liber censuum de l'église romaine*, ed. Paul Fabre and L. Duchesne (Paris, 1889–1952), II, 25.

[29] Gregorovius, *History*, V, 163.

[30] *Gesta Innocentii Tertii*, J. P. Migne, Patrologiae Cursus Completus, Series Latina, CCXIV (Paris, 1890), cols. clxxxiii–cxc. The story of the Conti disputes has been told many times, but I still find myself confused by the sequence of events in the *Gesta*. One of the values of the *Gesta*, in fact, is the magnificent way in which it captures the confusion of the time in its prose.

papal funds) center, if there was a center, of the whole affair. It stood by the Forum of Nerva and dominated the crossing of the path from the Colosseum to the Capitol with that from the Vatican to the Lateran. Even after its half-destruction by earthquake in the fourteenth century it is massive and imperious.

In the actual absence of Innocent, an Orsini faction attacked the Conti fortifications defended by Pandulfo of the Suburra, Innocent's senator. Pandulfo tried to cool the factions by exiling the troublemakers of the two factions. He sent one set to the area of Saint Peter's and the other to the area of Saint Paul's. An Orsini cousin, visiting the Orsini exiles, was murdered on the road to Saint Paul's. Then the Orsini tried to rouse the city, in the words of the "*Gesta* of Innocent III," "to excite the furor of the people" against Innocent III and Riccardo.[31] They did this particularly by conducting, or trying to conduct, an elaborate funeral for the victim, with ostentatious public mourning, before Riccardo's house. Public disorder followed.

Parallel to the fight between Conti and Orsini was that between Conti and Poli. It, too, centered on falling and rising family fortunes and the use of the *populus* (and the parody of religious and formal ceremony). The family of the Poli, who held large tenements of the papacy in the Campagna and whose fortunes had fallen disastrously, had borrowed money from Riccardo Conti to sustain themselves. They could not repay. Riccardo planned to regain his losses through a family marriage which would bring him the Poli inheritance. The Poli agreed and then retreated from their agreement. Innocent and Riccardo moved toward the confiscation of Poli properties. The Poli reacted with dramatic violence. They made naked processions through the streets after the model of flagellant penitents. They made a raid on Saint Peter's at Easter time and interrupted divine services. They insulted Innocent III as he went crowned through the city streets. They said that they handed their prop-

[31] *Gesta*, col. clxxxvi.

erties over to the senate and people of Rome. The Poli failed to topple the Conti; but, ironically, in the next generation the Conti of the Poli estates had become Poli in name and, seemingly, in interest.

These Orsini and Poli wars were accompanied and followed by temporary adjustments in the senatorial constitution. Innocent's opponents were disturbed by the existence of only one senator. They sought a return to the fifty-six. Innocent attempted to placate the opposition through the use of medians. But the opposing parties failed to agree and broke, physically, into two defined groups around Pandulfo on the Capitol and around Giovanni Capocci in the neighborhood of Santa Maria domne Rose (on the approximate site of what is now Santa Caterina dei Funari). Medians were captured, favorable senators demanded. In the spring of 1204, Innocent, who had been ill and out of Rome, returned and named a Pierleoni median, who named a Pierleoni senator; but late in the spring war broke out, particularly in struggles around and for major family towers, and most particularly around the Suburra towers on the Magnanapoli and the Capocci towers near San Pietro in Vincoli and San Martino ai Monti. Giovanni Capocci's own unpopularity, as he grew more to be an autocrat, supposedly turned his party to mediation. There was a suggested return to the fifty-six senators, which Innocent thought unwise and unworkable but theoretically accepted. By the following spring Innocent was able to choose a single senator. He chose Pandulfo.

If one turns from this battle to that one hundred years later—as Boniface VIII lay dying in Orsini hands, and (as the scene is recorded in Ferreto de' Ferreti) with Boniface held prisoner near the Vatican and hoping and scheming to escape to the Lateran, from the control of the Orsini to that part of Rome dominated by their enemy the Annibaldi—there seems, in some ways, little change.[32] The turbulence of 1303 like that of 1203

32 Ferreto, I, 156.

was a family war. But there are differences; and one is very much to our point. In 1203 there was repeated dramatic appeal to an admittedly poorly defined populace; and there was repeated experimentation with the senate. Although neither populace nor senate was completely ignored in 1303 (the senate being an Orsini place), they were the senate and the populace of a relatively secure, although not securely held, signory. Boniface VIII had helped establish this security; but it had been formed more specifically by Brancaleone (and the forces that brought him to power) who had in a way handed over the people, by Charles of Anjou who had had money and troops, and by Nicholas III who had made the whole thing Roman and familial again.

On Brancaleone, the central figure in this development, Gregorovius is his most peculiar. He wrote: "Were definite information concerning his government forthcoming, we should find that under him the democracy rose to greater power, and that the guilds attained a more secure constitution." [33] In fact, Brancaleone took Tivoli, against papal policy; and he destroyed towers, and he hanged nobles. In 1255 Brancaleone summoned the "Roman people" and made them form a parliament "in the accustomed way," at the sound of bell and trumpets and the voice of herald.[34] They were brought to express the will of the Roman people, to say *how* Oddone Colonna should be attacked. But there were those in the meeting, the sealed account of the chancellor says, who wished to disturb the stability and peace of the city, in the parliament, on the Capitol. They made noise. They threw rocks. Brancaleone said that no one could be permitted to act thus. He said that the whole force of the city

[33] Gregorovius, *History*, V, 310–311.

[34] Bartoloni, *Codice diplomatico*, pp. 204–206; there is other corroborating evidence about the manipulation of assemblies and their "interpretation:" see, for example, K. Hampe, "Ungedruckte Briefe zur Geschichte König Richards von Cornwall aus der Sammlung Richards von Pofi," *Neues Archiv*, XXX (1905), 687.

should go against both Oddone and the rock throwers. And the chancellor said that no one, whom he could hear, said no. (This, one should remember, is the weakening Brancaleone of 1255.) Brancaleone's is the converse of the Poli populace, the opposite of scattered men stirred to destruction. These are men, some dissident, collected into a Capitol populace to vote yes.

These are the curious "Roman people," the piazza shouters (perhaps Arnold of Brescia's two thousand),[35] variously used by Clement IV, Nicholas III, even Martin IV, the "people" who may have liked, if they were capable of "liking," the Savelli pope and senator, the "people" who were certainly used as excuses for power, and who probably best defined themselves in the militia. This populace is seen in a mirror in the letter Guy, cardinal bishop of Sabina, about to become Clement IV, wrote to Charles of Anjou, in February 1265.[36] It was a letter about the need for governmental pomposity in ruling the Romans, the need for experienced leaders, of presence and style, and for numbers of men—for pageantry, experience, and pressure to mold the mobile populace into a controlled thing.

In Roman war and violence and government one constantly returns to the major families, that is, to the factions with blood-kin families at their centers. Roman families seem sometimes to mock the pattern of provincial and foreign baronages in their own exotic arena. The Orsini and the Colonna may have thought of themselves as being like Clares or Warennes. The city was a curious, frustrating substance for them to work with —this strange collection of the anonymous and the transient. But, after all, there were a few, and only a few, big families. One of them, the Orsini, particularly, or the Conti, might have created an hereditary signory had the potential signory not been tied to the papacy, an office so theoretically sacred, however

[35] Halphen, L'administration de Rome, p. 69.
[36] E. Martène and U. Durand, Thesaurus novus anecdotorum (Paris, 1717), II, cols. 96–97.

occasionally corrupt, that the election to it could not (in the period after Nicholas II) be scrapped. It was necessary to the world. It was also necessary to the prosperity of Rome. So the family wars, this type of violence, the Annibaldi versus the Orsini, helped keep the papacy free from both of them, helped keep the papacy elective (until, one might say, the French destroyed it).

That the disappearance of the world papacy would have been destructive to Rome (was in fact destructive to Rome) is clear. Avignon does coincide with Roman decline. It would be perverse to deny that it had an important effect on Roman economic life, although it was not the sole cause of Rome's decline. There is obvious evidence of this decline in the decline of landlord income (a crucial factor and a crucial symptom in Roman economies) in the early fourteenth century. In, for example, the records of the Hospitallers from the 1330s, of an expected San Basilio urban rental income of something over one hundred and twenty florins, over thirty-five florins were not being returned. It is a dismal list: "Item, the house where Paulucio the gardener lives returns one and one-half florins; it was accustomed to return four and one-half florins." [37] And thus item after item even for the inhabited places. That thirteenth-century Romans had understood the importance of the papal presence is also clear; one recalls Brancaleone's demanding that Innocent IV come back to Rome.

So, in preserving the papacy, familial violence brought some profit to Rome. This violence of family, moreover, has surely been exaggerated. In front of the Tor de' Conti were the stockyards of Rome. Gregorovius's imagined Conti repeatedly bursting "forth with wild din" would have too much disturbed their future lunches.

[37] Biblioteca Apostolica Vaticana, Cod. Vat. Lat. 10372, fol. lr; Mr. Anthony Luttrell, who is working with this manuscript, kindly called it to my attention.

The violence of family regulated, and the violence of hotel-keepers was regulated, so that Rome did not destroy its income. Violence was less socially disruptive than it, at first glance, would seem. Rome was a surprisingly shrewd city. Remarkably lightly governed, it still inspected and supervised how people built their houses and threw away their garbage. (And there were salt councillors, provisioners, and "good-men" when they were needed.) This indicates the ability of the Roman community to function in matters important to its real well-being. (Rome is somewhat reminiscent of Ira Lapidus's Muslim cities; its organization was not institutional in the normal sense.[38]) Senator Angelo Malabranca's 1235 edict for the benefit of pilgrims and Rome-seekers, but also for the benefit of the inhabitants of this "happy city," as he called it, pointed out community self-interest—the self-interest of a community whose prosperity depended upon direct and indirect income from pilgrims and income from the papal court, directly through its patronage, offices, largesse, rents, and purchases, and indirectly from those it attracted.

Violence threatened property, and that threat in itself made violence undesirable. But Roman violence was involved with property in many more ways than just threatening it. At its grandest level, it itself was supported by *contado* properties; it was their function. It was violence that fought to control office and property-granting power. It created government (as J. M. Wallace–Hadrill has shown the feud in a way did);[39] government was perhaps most importantly the arbiter effected by the potential violence of opposed propertied powers.

Roman endemic violence, then, is a disorder that seems so profound that it is reflected in unformed government—so that

[38] Ira Marvin Lapidus, *Muslim Cities in the Later Middle Ages* (Cambridge, Mass., 1967).

[39] J. M. Wallace-Hadrill, "The Bloodfeud of the Franks," in *The Long-Haired Kings* (London, 1962), reprinted from the *Bulletin of the John Rylands Library*, XLI (1958–59), pp. 459–487.

when Boniface VIII seemed in 1299 to control a papal signory, his *camera* still paid antique pensions to Roman judges, making a sort of papal sandwich of the commune, unbelievably unstructured.[40] Even the diplomatic of senatorial sentences argues a sort of incoherence.[41] But upon reflection one can come to see a kind of order—loose, responding to the real structure, the economic structure, of the city.

There was, I think, reasonable, rational disorder and surface violence in thirteenth-century Rome. But, although the violence may have been superficial and even structurally helpful to society, it was, of course, as it must be, degrading and destructive to individual men. It was brutalizing. Hanged men and broken buildings make men less men. So the violence of thirteenth-century Rome may have been socially functional, or sociologically functional, but it must have been humanly destructive, even for the survivors.

[40] A. Theiner, *Codex diplomaticus dominii temporalis S. Sedis* (Rome, 1861–62), I, 365.

[41] For example, Biblioteca Apostolica Vaticana, Santa Maria in Via Lata, cassetta 302, no. 65.

XII

POLITICAL VIOLENCE IN THE
THIRTEENTH CENTURY

Lauro Martines

*T*HE THIRTEENTH century is decisive for the history of most cities in central and upper Italy.[1] Civil
disorder reaches its summit and political institutions their turning point. At the beginning of the century the old consular
nobility is divided and on trial; a stronger and more impartial
executive, the *podestá*, is emerging as the preeminent figure;
new faces appear in government and there is the promise of
extending political rights to more and more men and groups. By
the end of the century, the opponents of popular government
have learnt to deal with the danger presented by the humbler
classes and many cities lie under one-man rule. Represented
mainly by Venice and the Tuscan cities, the exceptions are
governed by oligarchies and will remain so—but for occasional
interludes—for a long time to come.

Scope

In the space of a hundred years most cities passed from republican commune to despotism, some from one type of

[1] One of the best sketches is in chap. iii of G. De Vergottini, *La
rinascita politica medievale*, IV, ii, of E. Pontieri, ed., *Storia universale*
(Milan, 1960–1961); the major themes, followed down to the fifteenth
century, are summarily treated in L. Martines, "Political Conflict in the
Italian City States," *Government and Opposition: A Quarterly of Comparative Politics*, III, i (Winter, 1968), 69–91.

oligarchy to another. But in the passage nearly all experienced popular insurrectionary movements, civil wars, pitched street battles, and political passions on a scale and of an ardor not seen before. It is then that violence in political affairs was most likely to succeed and that men in large numbers were most willing—they were appropriately organized—to engage in it. When the popular forces (i.e., the *popolo*[2]) resorted to violence at the critical moment, they often gained full admission to the commune by obtaining substantial representation in the councils that governed the city.

In the fourteenth and fifteenth centuries, political violence was to have occasional success, especially when committed by ambitious princes, *condottieri*, or powerful members of the urban elite. But the day was gone when large groups of burghers could suddenly, for the first time, break into government by means of violence, as the *societates populi* had done in the thirteenth century. In most cities, economically and socially, the resources for this sort of corporate action were spent by the 1320s or 1330s.

Such are the reasons for devoting this paper to the thirteenth century. The solutions and tumults of that epoch are echoed in the history of the city-state down to the sixteenth century. Violence and suspicion entered into the texture of political life; and no city, not even Venice, wholly recovered from the legacy.

I propose to do several things here: (1) review the causes of political violence in the thirteenth-century city; (2) examine the dominant features of the urban political context, the better to understand both the starting points and limits of politics; (3) try to gauge the intensity of political passion so as to suggest something about the quality of violence; (4) list the typical modes of violence both by and against government; and (5) indicate why violence was necessary.

[2] Commoners of the more substantial sort, seen in opposition to the nobility and organized politically, militarily, and occupationally.

Causes of Violence

It is not easy to deny the testimony of thirteenth-century chroniclers, though they tend emphatically to be moralists. Forced to rely upon them as witnesses, we shall always see some things through their eyes. They attribute the troubles and violence of the age to defects in the moral makeup of citizens. Adducing evidence, they tell us that the rich and illustrious families, like even lesser men, were driven by pride and ambition to dominate the leading offices of the commune.[3] They allege that the result was a keen and grim rivalry, and this was doubtless true. But it is clear that our analysis cannot proceed along these lines, which are too fixed and final, having been sorted out of the context of circumstance, place, and the flux of change.

In 1200, at Milan as at Florence and Pisa and other cities, the commune's gravest internal problem concerned (*a*) the rising pressure of new guilds and other corporate bodies and (*b*) the effect of these upon the discord within the old consular nobility.[4] Marked privilege and disadvantage, power and impotence

---

[3] As in the Genoese *Otoboni Scribae Annales,* in the *Monumenta Germaniae Historica Scriptores* (cited hereafter as *MGHS*), Vol. XVIII (Hanover, 1863), p. 105, under year 1190, "Noverint ergo tam futuri in posterum quam moderni, quod ob multorum invidiam, qui consulatus comunis officium ultra modum cupiebant habere, nonnulle civiles discordie et odiose conspirationes et divisiones in civitate plurimum inoleverant." Or Dino Compagni, *Cronica,* ed. I. del Lungo (Florence, 1939), p. 7, "per loro superbia e per loro malizia e per gara d'ufici, ànno cosi nobile città [Florence] disfatta." Also Dante, *Inferno,* VI, 60–75.

[4] And now chroniclers began for the first time to use the terms *populus and pedites* with specific reference to the popular forces in conflict with the nobility. Examples: *Annales Ptolemaei Lucensis,* in *Documenti distoria italana,* Vol. VI (Florence, 1876), p. 65, under year 1203; *Iohannis Codagnelli Annales Placentini,* ed. O. Holder-Egger (Hanover and Leipzig, 1901), p. 23, under year 1198; *Annales Cremonenses,* ed. P. Jaffé, in *MGHS,* XVIII, 804, under year 1201; *Annales Brixienses,* ed. L. Bethmann, in *MGHS,* XVIII, 815, under year 1196, where the

were abiding facts of life and had always been so. But a boom-
ing economy, closely linking town and country, elevated large
numbers of men and gave them a stake in society. To find protection, to safeguard their gains and extend their rights, they
bound themselves in sworn associations: guilds and neighborhood societies or companies.[5] Privilege—feudal and political
privilege—came gradually under attack. With each year the
new groups became larger, stronger, more insistent, and there
was a corresponding change or improvement in the nature and
effectiveness of their organizations. Politics came under a field
of new strains. The moral constants of the chroniclers—pride,
envy, and ambition—were thus subject to a swiftly changing environment, where pride, for example, might take one form today and another tomorrow.

The feuds that rent the old ruling class were more serious in
some cities than in others. Verona's intraclass divisions cut more
deeply than Siena's.[6] Apart from jealousies and inherited family
hatreds (psychological factors that could naturally be self-
perpetuating), the rivalries among influential families sprang
also from differences of a more determinate sort: differences
between feudal and mercantile interests, between imperial and
papal policies, or between rural and civic values and hence between an older municipal aristocracy and one more recently
arrived from the country. There is much evidence to show that
these differences often turned on competing claims to lucrative

---

guilds are given the part of the popolo, "Et [fuit] discensio magna inter
paraticos et milites."

[5] See especially F. Valsecchi, Comune e corporazione nel medio evo
italiano (Milan, 1948); and G. de Vergottini, Arti e popolo nella prima
metà del secolo xiii (Milan, 1943). But the field deserves very much
more study of the popular sworn associations that cut across guild lines,
such as the Credenza di Sant' Ambrogio in Milan or the "societas sancti
Faustini" founded at Brescia in 1200 (Annales Brixienses, loc. cit).

[6] Cf. L. Simeoni, "Il comune veronese sino ad Ezzelino e il suo primo
statuto," in Miscellanea di storia veneta, ser. iii, XV (1922), 46–47; and
U. G. Mondolfo, Il populus a Siena (Genoa, 1911).

dignities, offices, rights, or livings, with the result that the hatred between two different branches of a leading feudal family could easily end in violence.

Whatever the cause of the original differences between blocs of consular families, the new men and sworn associations arrived on the scene in such a way as to complicate and intensify the discords.[7] Indeed, by the second or third decade of the thirteenth century, at Milan, Cremona, Piacenza, Brescia, Bologna, Florence, Pisa, Perugia, and other cities, the decisive struggle in the whole context of discord arose from the growing tensions between privilege and institutionalized disadvantage: that is to say, between the men who had political power and those who could realistically aspire to it, while having little or none at all. The conflict born of this inequality calls for emphasis. For behind the imponderables of psychology and moral failure was the fierce scramble for concrete rights and benefits. These included the distribution of hearth taxes, the collection of tolls and customs, the competence of courts, guild privileges (such as control of particular trades), and profitable claims to communal rights and properties.

In short, one of the principal causes of political conflict derived from the determination of the powerful to remain so and the growing desire of the new men to have a voice in the decisions that affected the entire community. Between about 1210 and 1260, in city after city, the *popolo* demanded and got the right (though at times the victory was temporary) to control one-half or a majority of the seats in the major councils and offices of the commune.[8]

[7] So much so at Verona, for example, that even the merchant class split. The comital party, like the faction around the Monticoli, included many merchants as well as *milites*. The city's leading historian denies that Verona saw a clear division between *popolo* and *nobiltà* (Simeoni, *op. cit.*, p. 47).

[8] Examples: *Annales Mediolanenses Breves*, in *MGHS*, XVIII, 391, in 1212; *Annales Placentini Guelfi*, in *MGHS*, XVIII, 454n, in 1233;

Chronicle literature suffers from no shortage of references to the arrogance and violence of noblemen. Bred to the profession of arms, reared partly in castles or fortified urban dwellings, accustomed to giving commands and receiving deference, they were not the sort who countenanced insults or who took easily to new regulations, nor were they patient with threats to their rights and privileges. Their bearing and self-assurance were contagious: being at the head of the commune, they tended to serve as examples to others. From the earliest times, accordingly, we find rich merchants—for example, the Monticoli and Crescenzi of Verona—closely imitating the ways (and, one must assume, the outlook) of the nobility. Here again, therefore, the influence of class was paramount.

Historians have not been tempted to discuss the impact of rapid economic and social change on the behavior and values of feudal noblemen in and around the Italian cities. Lately or long since removed, by choice or coercion, from their country seats to the aggressive, fast-growing cities, where they now lived for much of the year, noblemen long retained an intimate contact with the country, its people, and customs. The effect of swift change upon men of this type cannot be determined with any certainty; records, even in ideal circumstances, rarely provide conclusive answers to a question like this. Yet the question demands a response, for the period from about 900 to 1250 saw an economic transformation on a vast scale. "By feudal grant or usurpation, by deeds of sale or exchange, but most of

---

Annales Parmenses Maiores, in *MGHS*, XVIII, 670, in 1244; U. Gualazzini, "Il Populus Cremonae e l'autonomia del comune," in *Rivista di storia del diritto italiano*, XI (May–Dec., 1938), pp. 317–366, 512–555, especially pp. 519–522; Mondolfo, *op. cit.*, pp. 35–36; E. P. Vicini, ed., *Republica Mutinensis*, 2 vols. (Milan, 1929–1932), I, xix, in 1250 and following; N. Kamp, *Istituzioni comunali in Viterbo nel medioevo* (Viterbo, 1963), chap. 3; and A. Hessel, *Geschichte der Stadt Bologna von 1116 bis 1280*, in *Historische Studien*, Vol. LXXVI, (Berlin, 1910), pp. 334 ff.

all, it seems, by perpetual leases, the great estates of crown, Church and nobility were being broken up and redistributed among a new middle-class of landholders, *gente nuova* of obscure origin, who found in the renting of land a convenient means of building up property and exploiting the opportunities of agricultural development."[9] In the process, many noble families died out or were destroyed, but the many who survived (as at Milan, Florence, and Pisa) had to suffer the rise of men of no social account, new men who amassed properties in town and country.

The velocity of such change, involving nothing less than "a revolution in property," could not fail to affect noblemen in and outside cities. It rendered them more tenacious and irrational about their claims, prerogatives, and expectations, just as it encouraged the new men to be more hopeful and more insistent. The rights and political powers exercised by noblemen within the commune thus became all the more prized. Trained to bear arms, noblemen were ready for combat. But the critical rate of historical change intensified this readiness. War as a mode of business, of acquisition or economic pursuit, became a daily affair. And this also, in addition to commercial rivalry and party conflict, belongs to the immediate background of the intercity wars that scar the twelfth and thirteenth centuries.

I am suggesting that there were grinding economic strains on the nobility of central and upper Italy, owing to which many noblemen took to trade and piracy (especially at Pisa and Genoa), while many others took to war (as at Milan, Florence, Perugia, and Rome).[10] Of all the events that interest thirteenth-

[9] P. J. Jones, in "The Agrarian Life of the Middle Ages," in *The Cambridge Economic History of Europe*, Vol. I (Cambridge, 1966), p. 400.

[10] Thus at Genoa, not surprisingly, from the middle years of the twelfth century, certain noblemen already depended upon the returns from the buying up of government debts (T. O. De Negri, *Storia di Genoa* [Milan, 1968], pp. 265–267; and the *Otoboni Scribae Annales*, in *MGHS*, XVIII [Hanover, 1863], p. 101, years 1185–1186).

century chroniclers, war is foremost: the activity most willingly
and lengthily described.[11] The capture of arms and prisoners,
the collection of ransom, and the seizure of goods and livestock
made up the immediate prizes of successful warfare.[12] A good
conscience was not hard to come by. If it was absurdly easy to
justify piracy and naval wars against the Saracens, it was not
difficult to find other forms of self-righteousness to vindicate
the bloody commercial and maritime wars between Genoa and
Pisa. Once a state of war existed, no annalist, Genoese or Pisan,
seems to have had any trouble shedding his scruples, even when
he was at pains to itemize the monetary value of ships and
cargoes taken in battle by his compatriots.[13] The haul was considered booty and made, or furbished, many a private fortune.
Not surprisingly, leading Pisan and Ligurian naval commanders
and merchant adventurers were usually noblemen who claimed
—or whose forebears had exercised—feudal jurisdictions.

When the Milanese nobility, in its struggle against the *popolo*, fought tenaciously to retain its monopoly over cathedral
canonries and other profitable church posts (a traditional privilege), it seems clear that the tenacity derived in part from economic necessity.[14] And when, at Florence and elsewhere, many

[11] Good examples of this are provided in the *Annales Pisani*, ed. M. L.
Gentile (Bologna, 1930), VI, ii, of the *Rerum Italicarum Scriptores*
(cited hereafter as *RIS*); and the *Annales Placentini Gibellini*, in *MGHS*,
XVIII, 457 ff.

[12] E.g., the Guelf *Codagnelli Annales Placentini, loc. cit.*, p. 19, under
year 1189. In these circumstances corruption and bribery among leading figures could not have been uncommon. For a striking case at
Verona in 1217, see Simeoni, "Il comune veronese," pp. 41–43; or the
Corpus Chronicorum Bononensium, ed. A. Sorbelli, in *RIS* (Citta di
Castello, 1911), XVIII, 1, ii, p. 90, where we find that in 1225 "Molti
nobili della parte di Rizardo conte de Sancto Bonifatio corupti per
dinari lassarono el dito conte et andarono alla parte de Saglinguera."

[13] Gentile, *Annales Pisani*, pp. 27, 39; *Annales Ianuenses*, ed. L. T.
Belgrano, in *Fonti per la storia d'Italia*, II (Rome, 1901), pp. 91, 99, 103.

[14] G. Franceschini in his part of vol. IV of the *Storia di Milano*
(Milan, 1955–1956), pp. 289, 291; I. Ghiron, "La Credenza di Sant' Am-

of the commune's rights and properties found their way into the private hands of the old consular nobility, it seems clear that here too were the signs of economic necessity, as well as of dishonesty and greed.[15] Yet the driving need for better sources of income persisted. From the second half of the thirteenth century, we find the first *signori*—the coming race of autocrats —exploiting this want by conferring lands, rights, and fiefs on those whose loyalty they needed.

I have called attention to three sets of causes that interacted to produce political violence in the thirteenth-century urban situation. (1) Set against the background of a dynamic economy, the differences between privilege and disadvantage gradually issued in dangerous tensions, for the class of commoners —mostly excluded from the major political decisions—became larger every day and came to rely more and more upon men of substance and experience. (2) Owing to their traditions and to their military and political place in society, noblemen offered their allegiance to pride of family, rank, and prowess. To the dangers posed by the velocity of social change they reacted by intensifying the qualities for which they were known; but the result was violence in streets and political councils. (3) The breakup of the big estates, the price revolution, and the resulting strain of economic need pushed noblemen (i.e., the political class par excellence) into war, piracy, and adventurous trade; to stubbornness in their confrontations with the political demands of the new men; and to internecine rivalries over the material benefits that went with public office.

These were the primary causes of political violence. There were other causes as well, causes or contributory factors, but

---

brogio, o la lotta dei nobili e del popolo in Milano, 1192–1292," *Archivio storico lombardo*, III–IV (Dec., 1876), 602.

[15] P. Santini, "Studi sull' antica costituzione del comune di Firenze," part vi, *Archivio storico italiano*, ser. 5, XXXII (1903), 32–35; *Annales Civitatis Vincentiae*, ed. G. Soranzo, in *RIS*, VIII, v, p. 11, under year 1263.

they were more indirect, more subtle, and so are better treated in connection with the context of politics. The resources or exigencies of any particular scene evidently affect the actors.

The Context of Politics

Urban political life had two different but related levels: local politics, which included internal affairs as well as matters pertaining to the countryside and surrounding cities; and international politics, which put the city into the broad spectrum of relations between Church and Empire. In principle, nearly all central and north Italian cities [16] were under the sovereign but distant rule of the Empire; in spiritual matters, all were under the imperium of the Church with the pope as head. Empire and Church were the supreme authorities. When they clashed, the cities and their diocesan administrations were inevitably drawn into the fray.

Bishops and antibishops sided with Rome or the Empire, but because of their substantial temporal powers, they wagered more than individual lives and careers: the administration of the rising urban centers was in the balance. Whence the question, who will rule locally? Between about 1080 and 1130, in town after town, the budding commune reached out for more and more self-government, using one power against the other, pope against emperor, bishop against antibishop, or papists against imperialists. The commune triumphed.[17]

Troubled and weakened by violent controversy, the tandem of supreme authority set a disturbing example to the nobility and burghers. Church and state contested de facto their mutual jurisdictions, whatever the admissions in principle. The cities

---

[16] Venice was the outstanding exception.

[17] See A. Solmi, *Il comune nella storia del diritto* (Milan, 1922); W. Goetz, *Le origini dei comuni italiani*, Ital. trans., I. Zapperi and R. Zapperi (Milan, 1965); and P. Brezzi, *I comuni cittadini italiani* (Varese and Milano, 1940).

flourished and developed under the shadow of a continuing crisis of authority and in the process profited. Wherever local power, comital or episcopal, was supremely contested (and undermined), it was not long before the commune moved in and took over. I assume that such pointed institutional change —involuntary abdication and usurpation—went at times to confuse and disorient the urban ruling class. Duplicity, violence, and doubt, as seen on the international level and between contenders of the highest authority, easily passed down to the level of local politics. It became possible and even practical to challenge local communal authority, the preeminent *cives* and families having already disputed the authority of bishop, pope, and emperor.

A profound crisis of authority racked the age: it was the psychological context of politics, the very atmosphere of the mushrooming cities. The state was critically deficient. There was no effective centralizing power. The communes ignored, tricked, assaulted, or simply rejected the sovereign authority. The victories of Barbarossa and Frederick II were no sooner won than the cities plunged back into their arrogant separatism, sustained by their vigorous economic and social energies.

From the first years of the twelfth century and in fact earlier, noblemen—*cives* and others—had reacted to the authority crisis by forming communes: noblemen and notables bound in sworn associations which gradually assumed ever more public functions and powers. In the major urban centers, the commune rapidly took on the features of a small state, making war and peace, collecting taxes, and seeking generally to regulate the public life of the fast-growing city. At the same time, the city brought forth new social groups, new men who also in their turn sensed danger. Despite the commune, and partly because of it, something was wanting—a sovereign or higher authority potent enough to sanction and safeguard the gains and benefits won by the new groups. Between about 1190 and 1230, in one city after another, there was a pullulation of organized merchant groups, guilds, and secret associations, swiftly followed by the formation of armed companies of commoners and societies of noblemen.[18] Neither sovereign state (Empire) nor commune could offer security to the city's different groups, with the result that these reacted (apparently spontaneously) by congealing into tightly knit, at times secret, organizations. Moved by a powerful esprit de corps, the members were bound by religious and fraternal oaths. In the situation, the recourse to arms was only a step away. Authority inside the city was shattered yet once more. The new men and groups defied the commune in a number of different ways, depending upon the city and moment. They challenged its jurisdictions, ignored its claims, demanded more participation in its proceedings, assaulted its officials and public buildings, or took up arms against the staunchest of its supporters—the powerful nobility, the *milites* (or a part thereof), or even against the rich merchants and bankers.[19] In practical terms these gentlemen were the commune.

Civil discord became most critical during the middle decades of the thirteenth century [20] and persisted, in some instances, into the fourteenth century. The legal foci of authority were exceedingly uncertain. Respecting all the major issues in local politics, fear, doubt, intimidation, malaise, and disorder were in the air. And the commune was powerless to restore trust, being

[18] Valsecchi, *op. cit.*; De Vergottini, *Arti e popolo*; and F. Niccolai, "I consorzi nobiliari ed il comune nell' alta e media Italia," *Rivista di storia del diritto italiano*, XIII (1940), 116–147, 292–342, on the sworn associations of noblemen.

[19] At Milan, for example, in the early thirteenth century, the rich old merchant group already had sharp differences with the lesser tradesmen (Franceschini, *op. cit.*, IV, 135); at Lucca there was a similar conflict in 1258: "discordiam in civitate Lucana inter populum macrum et grassum" (*Annales Ptolemaei Lucensis*, p. 79).

[20] At Bergamo, Piacenza, Milan, Bologna, Genoa, Florence, Siena, Perugia, and other cities.

dominated by an oligarchy of noblemen and rich merchants who did not themselves draw back from violence: on the contrary.

The general mood and movement to band together, to incorporate, to arm, to grab public rights, or at any rate to seek a more solid position in or outside the commune, expressed the determination of the new men not only to defend recent gains but also to preserve personal identities through the power and force of a collective identity.[21]

The question of personal and group identity merits attention. For politics is the play of groups playing for power and its rewards; and in times of compelling stress, when identities are put on trial, it seems evident that the identity of groups becomes a matter of major importance and the commitment of individuals all the more urgent. Here again we touch upon a commanding feature in the context of politics. And if we may know identities through a pinning down or recognition of loyalties, then it makes sense to ask, what was the "condition" of loyalty in the thirteenth-century city?

Meaningful political loyalties were often confused or in conflict, save at the most immediate ranges.[22] The latter included the family, the family consort (*consorteria*), the guild, and the guild consort (i.e., the order or association of guilds). For noblemen and for certain of the great merchants and bankers, the first political devotion was due to the family or family consort. For artisan, shopkeeper, and most merchants the first such devotion went to the guild or guild consort. Following fast on these were the loyalties to a neighborhood society of peers, to a faction or political grouping, to a social order, and finally to

[21] On the fraternal-like bonds between guild members see L. Martines, *Lawyers and Statecraft in Renaissance Florence* (Princeton, 1968), pp. 26–27.

[22] The observations in this paragraph draw upon and relate very disparate sources but also contain a frankly speculative note.

the commune itself, or even, for many a nobleman, to the emperor.[23] This hierarchy of loyalties was not so orderly as I have made it seem. For when there was a conflict among the different groupings or levels, as frequently there was, loyalty fell short somewhere along the line. Should men obey *consorteria* or commune, commune or emperor, guild or *societas populi*, *societas* or commune?

In sum, owing to the uncertain status of authority and to the corporate assaults on public rights, loyalty—and so identity— was no easy or clear condition. Thus the reason for the fervent commitments of *cittadini* at the immediate ranges, that is, to family or guild; and thus also the loyalty, at a more distant range, to whatever seemed to favor these. But it was the second, more distant range that citizens found shifting and uncertain: there decisions became trickier and the ground more treacherous.[24]

With authority itself on trial, the practice of politics went on in a context in which rules were insufficiently binding or always breaking down. Authority had no established lines. The government often proved less potent than the great families or armed companies of commoners. The welter of organized groups was too strong for the commune; but whenever the commune was strong enough, it was rarely impartial enough, being run by a fraction of the community—noblemen, rich

[23] The last of these could make for dramatic situations, as in the chain of events involving Ansaldo and Andreolo de Mari, who in 1240–1241 captained a series of imperial naval attacks against their native Genoa, Ansaldo repeatedly taking a fleet into the very port. The De Mari were dedicated imperialists. Yet ten years later they were called back to Genoa and all was forgiven (De Negri, *Storia di Genova*, pp. 343–344, 354).

[24] Hence the fascinating picture in Dino Compagni's *Cronica*, which is centered on Florentine political and factional strife. The main problem among rival political leaders in Florence was in the constant temptation to make political decisions on the basis of the most immediate interests and calculations: for to wander out beyond these limits meant going out into a world of uncertainty.

merchant bankers, or a partisan coalition thereof. Often, therefore, as an interested participant or citizen, you made your point not by cleaving to a procedure, which most likely got you nowhere, but by assaulting the government palace and bloodying the face of the *podestà*. Then, I suspect, men found out who they were.

It remains to point out that the context of politics also included the physical city itself: the circumvallation and narrow streets, the more open spaces of marketplace and parish church, and the massive family dwellings (first of wood and later, in the thirteenth century, of stone). City walls gave a sharp demarcation to the urban space as a whole. The contained area was closely cut up or partitioned, certainly by the early thirteenth century, when many cities, because of their crowded conditions and dramatic increases in population, were facing the need to build a third circle of walls. Specific trades were concentrated in certain streets and quarters: the artisans, shopkeepers, or merchants associated with a given craft or product tended to cluster in one street or area. Kindred concentrations occurred at the level of neighborhood or district, where a particular clan or cluster of families was apt to enjoy social and political preeminence. Therefore, when political controversy resulted in violence and broke out into the streets, the neighboring *consorteria*, armed company, or guild was able to assemble its members quickly. Once in battle, noblemen and burghers had recourse to a variety of lethal devices—including powerful crossbows, catapults mounted on rooftops, and the sudden stretching of chains across streets to prevent the passage of horsemen. The use of fire was common. I mention these details so as to convey an image, however rough, of the physical aspects of civil war. I mean to suggest that in a tense political situation the very layout of the city was an invitation to violence.

Political Passion

The ardent Ghibelline cardinal, Ottaviano degli Ubaldini (d. 1273), is reported to have said: "If I have a soul, I have lost it a thousand times over for the Ghibellines." Dante plunged him with other heretics into the burning plain of hell's sixth circle.[25]

Religious sentiment often entered into political commitments, intensifying the tone of feeling in politics. Decrees of political exile, for example, were frequently read out in church as a first formality. Men bound themselves to political factions or parties as they did to other sworn associations—by oath. In moments of extreme tension, leading members of the commune sometimes assembled and swore on the Holy Bible to keep the peace. Conspirators preparing to disrupt the peace or overthrow the government inevitably bound themselves by oath. Indeed, it would appear that no major political move was ever made without a prior appeal to God and the saints. In war the army's supreme trial turned on its defense of the *carroccio*—the cart bearing the banners of the commune and an altar.

Of course these examples also serve to illustrate the general temper of the age; but the constant, insistent mixture of religious appeal and political undertaking was remarkable. The task of realizing important political ends was viewed as a kind of sacred enterprise: a task of such importance as to merit the highest sanctions. Many of Dante's outstanding sinners were men who achieved fame or notoriety by their public actions: contemporaries more readily saw them as men of passion or powerful feeling. Like eschatology, politics also dealt with final things.

The quality of political sentiment may also be gauged by noting certain images in the chronicles of the period. One of the most concrete and striking of all images shows us physical assaults on the *podestà*, the chief official of the commune in the

[25] *Inferno*, X, 120, and notes to any scholarly edition.

first half of the thirteenth century. Scholarly literature gives no idea of the frequency of such violence. Again and again, we come on instances of attacks on his person.[26] Angry noblemen or tradesmen catch him in the streets or force their way into his chambers: they smash his teeth or cut out his tongue, beat, blind, or simply slay him. He is the focus of fury, the object of the raging discontent with government or commune. Not seldom, as a matter of fact, he was no more than the creature of the dominant faction. But this was beside the point. Frustration had triggered the assault. If the assailants were noblemen, the injured or slain official had perhaps been guilty of sentencing one of their kinsmen to death or to payment of a heavy fine; if they were merchants or artisans, most probably he had seemed the incarnation of a regime which had spurned their grievances. In any case, assaults on the *podestà* gave a vent to feelings that had no access to other means of effective protest or change. Not that assault necessarily led to change, but it gave a temporary deliverance.

Still another gauge of political passion was in the penalties imposed for political violence or irresponsibility. Guilt by association was commonly taken for granted and not infrequently punished by exile or denial of political rights. Torture was customary. Governments encouraged secret denunciation. Capital punishment or exile awaited those presumed guilty of insurrection, conspiracy, or secret contact with the enemy. Regular court procedure was denied in the trial of all such crime; generally, magistrates availed themselves of the most expedient methods and justice. When conspirators, rebels, or sworn enemies of the regime escaped, governments were not above employing hired assassins to go after them.[27] One of the most common penalties stipulated the confiscation of property and,

[26] E.g., *Corpus Chronicorum Bononensium*, II, 58 (year 1195), 77 (year 1213); or the slaying of the consul, Angelo de Mari, in Genoa in 1187 (*Otoboni Scribae Annales*, p. 101).

[27] Practiced at Venice by the Ten in the 1320s and after.

in the case of prominent individuals, razing of their imposing family houses (*palazzi*). In the second half of the thirteenth century, the methodical razing of great family *palazzi* or towers was governed by the desire not only to expunge all traces of particular individuals but also to extirpate the memory of their forebears. This accorded very well with the imposition of exile on the masculine descendants of the accused, another common penalty. Prominent social and political standing signified esteemed forebears as well as the promise of lineal descendants. Hence in punishing a political antagonist by taking his life, razing his family seat, and exiling his masculine descendants, governments seemed to find a way of also striking out at his past and future. In politics, death itself was not the supreme penalty.

Violence Illegal and Legitimate

There is no need to dwell on acts of political violence as such. It is important, however, to single out the typical modes, the more effectively to bring out—by contrast—the nature of legitimate or governmental violence. For it is this sort of violence that scholarship tends to ignore.

Effective political violence in the thirteenth century was the work of well-organized groups: associations of noblemen (such as the "societas de Galiardis" at Milan), family *consorterie*, guildsmen, or the armed companies of the parishes or *contrade*. Very often the internal appointment of an organization was so thorough, as in the case of the *popolo*, that it all but replicated the institutional forms of the commune itself: including *arrengo* (general assembly), judicial officials, consulate, advisory bodies, legislative council, voting procedures, forms of election, eligibility norms, and duration of terms in office.[28]

[28] See Martines, *Lawyers and Statecraft*, pp. 51–54, centering on parallels between communal and guild organization.

The typical modes of political violence were limited. I list ten: frank and sustained refusals to heed the laws of the commune; the formation of secret political societies; incitement to riot or insurrection; armed attacks on leading political figures, on their houses, or on members of the enemy faction; armed attacks on public officials or on their houses; armed attacks on government buildings; making war on one's home city, as was frequently done by political exiles (*fuorusciti*); attacks *armata manu* on the buildings of a guild, of a society of noblemen, or of another notable sworn assocation; physical assaults on ecclesiastical dignitaries, on their officials, or on their places of residence; and, finally, we have to allow for a more general category, such as "conspiracy," which might take in anything from illegal movement to consorting with guilty parties. There was always a distinct strain of political violence in attacks on local prelates or in armed assaults on the buildings of sworn associations.

As the catalogue suggests, there was no scarcity of occasions for violent physical contact. Restricted more or less to the sharply delimited space of a walled-in city, men found that explosive acts gave a temporary outlet to feelings of rage and frustration. But in addition to their cathartic value, these acts were also substantive in themselves. Politics made no sense without them; without such acts the political discourse was missing an essential term, for often, as on occasion citizens and subjects clearly perceived, violence was the only vehicle for getting the redress of just and urgent grievances. This being so, we are driven to the surprising conclusion that violence had the potential for being a constructive force in politics.

Confronted with acts of physical violence, governments were no less physical—if one may so say—in hitting back. They were primed for violence. Indeed, in a certain sense their violence was prior.

In the thirteenth century, most Italian communes had a

sound enough legal basis, except, perhaps, during the period of their confrontation with Frederick II; and even then jurists found arguments to support communal claims. Much doubt and confusion, however, attended the legal status of particular communal governments. The autonomy of the commune had a legal basis, due in large measure to the Peace of Constance (1183) and the force of prescriptive right. But what, precisely, gave legality to any particular government? There was hardly a major commune that failed to see a half dozen or more violent changes of government in the course of the thirteenth century. The question of the sufficient legality of these governments had no easy solution in law; today few if any jurists or legal historians would want to entertain it. We may therefore turn to a different and prior solution—the one provided by practice.

When a group or the articulate part of a social class seized political power, instantly drawing all the commune's offices under its control, the victors established a new government and used all its resources to help secure and legalize their position. From that moment on they—yesterday's usurpers—began to make and administer the laws; they drew on the dignity of the city's political institutions; they defined the legal and the illegal; they took control of the courts; they *became* the government. Whereupon yesterday's heads of government became today's outlaws, exiles, or prisoners.

Prescription and the quiddities of lawyers aside, the opponents or enemies of the new government long continued to consider it illegal. In their view, any action directed against it was morally, legally, and politically defensible. Needless to say, the government responded in kind, however ambiguous or shoddy its legality. The situation was, obviously, exceedingly problematic. Thus the necessity to speak of legitimate or governmental violence.

The typical modes of such violence—the work of governments de facto—ran along these lines: suspension of critical parts of the constitution; the apparently legal transfer of power to one man or a small group of men (or, conversely, to a much larger group); a listing and publication of the men proscribed; the normalization of secret denunciation and arbitrary arrest; the use of irregular or summary court poceedings; the changing of procedures regarding elections and voting in council; the enactment of harsh ordinances against the right to associate, to assemble, or to discuss politics; the amassing of armed men in and around the city; finally, the use of an all-pervasive intimidation (generated by the overturning of power) to keep men divided and dissent silent. In addition, there were all the intangibles that cling to the exercise of political authority, whatever its status de jure, and these went to protect or to enhance the condition of the men who exercised it.

It is true that once a decade or two had passed since the last coup d'etat, the immediate tensions faded, the triumphant group lost some combativeness, and the new government was less and less driven to conduct its internal affairs at the edges of violence. Nevertheless, the resentments and grievances inside the city persisted and the many citizens still in exile, noblemen especially, did not forget. They invested their lives and fortunes in the struggle. For them and their secret allies back home, the existing government continued to be an illegal assembly or had, at any rate, no higher claim than the exiles themselves.

The Necessity of Violence

However different from one another, dozens of small cities were subject more or less to a similar pattern of events. In commune after commune, citizens witnessed a complex trend: an expanding commercial economy, rapid expansion of the urban center, and continuous immigration from the rural areas into the city; fragmentation of the large old estates; bickering and violent controversy among noble families; acute discontent with existing governments; the rise of new men in large numbers; the mushrooming of sworn associations; conflict between public and private right (commune *vs.* group organization); confrontations between *popolo* and *nobiltà* or between privilege and disadvantage in one of several other forms; disorientation, passionate commitment, and sudden excesses of political violence (ramifications of the authority crisis).

If this configuration had been limited to a few cities, we could not speak of political violence in terms of necessity or inevitability. But because there was an insistent and widespread repetition of events, it is difficult to see what men could have done, in practical terms, to avoid violence. Historians have no license to posit an easy freedom to be restrained. Too often, in the thirteenth-century Italian city, doing the restrained or "peaceful" thing would have required the renunciation of self-identity.

Part of this analysis relies upon the notion of identity. I assume that at least in European society, when rising or privileged groups and individuals sense a serious danger, they will do what they can to protect themselves and their identities. But necessity, or rather the elements that made for it, derived not only from the struggle for identities but also from other forces and pressures.

Looking back to the thirteenth century and taking into consideration both what came before and what came after, we can be sure of certain things. It is clear, certainly, that no one man, group, or institution had the power *and* will to retard or reverse the dynamic economy of the cities. Hence nothing could arrest the rise or check the aspirations of new men. The enfeeblement of the state and upsurge of the commune, a factious commune, resulted in no adequate guarantees of security for the new and old corporate groupings. These therefore made provision for their own safety, formed intercorporate alliances, and in the process clashed.

The commune was born through a pooling of privilege and by according privilege survived. For noblemen first, and later for merchant oligarchies, privilege, that is, power to the relative few, was the most essential part of political identity; it could not be surrendered without enormous resistance. And so naturally, when the new men and organizations came to constitute a challenge by the very vigor of their existence, the privileged fought. At the critical moment, neither the institutions of the commune nor its ruling groups were flexible enough to admit change swiftly enough to keep the thrust of discontent from turning into insurrection. There was no way for the men at the helm of things to be flexible enough.

A crisis of authority, the rapidity of social change, and the effects of economic need went to stir up passions and bewilder men, particularly those of the class subject to the keenest stresses, the class faced with a fundamental challenge to its authority: the old municipal aristocracy and the urbanized feudal nobility.[29] In this class in crisis, this ruling class which had so much trouble ruling, men experienced the most stultifying disorientation, with all the attendant mysteries of individual and group psychology. They could not focus politically: thus their startling divisions and fratricidal rivalries. In many a city, individual noblemen and noble houses joined forces with the *popolo*, which valued their experience and social weight and very often put them into positions of leadership. The Torriani of Milan and Provenzan Salvani of Siena afford two well-known illustrations of this. But it would be a mistake in method to allow the complexity, both apparent and real, of the political struggle to obscure the decisive play of social and economic forces in the background.[30] The fine details of any complex event can so possess the historian as to cloud his vision and clog his narrative with unrelated or insignificant facts.

[29] Thus the nostalgic melancholy (strikingly apposite) of representations made by Dante's Cacciaguida, spokesman for the old nobility of Florence's innermost circle (*Paradiso*, XV–XVII).

[30] The major weakness of an otherwise outstanding study: E. Cristiani, *Nobiltà e popolo nel comune di Pisa* (Naples, 1962).